EVOLUTIONARY INTERPRETATION AND INTERNATIONAL LAW

This unique book brings together leading experts from diverse areas of public international law to offer a comprehensive overview of the approaches to evolutionary interpretation in different international legal regimes. It begins by asking what interpretation is, offering the views of expert authors on the question, its components and definitions. It then comments on situations that have called for evolutionary interpretation in different international legal regimes, including general international law, environmental law, human rights law, EU law, investment law, international trade law, and how domestic courts have, on occasions, interpreted treaties and other international legal instruments in an evolutionary manner. This timely, authoritative compendium offers an in-depth understanding of the processes at work in evolutionary interpretation as well as a prime selection of the current trends and future challenges.

Evolutionary Interpretation and International Law

Edited by
Georges Abi-Saab
Kenneth Keith
Gabrielle Marceau
and
Clément Marquet

•HART•
OXFORD • LONDON • NEW YORK • NEW DELHI • SYDNEY

HART PUBLISHING

Bloomsbury Publishing Plc

Kemp House, Chawley Park, Cumnor Hill, Oxford, OX2 9PH, UK

HART PUBLISHING, the Hart/Stag logo, BLOOMSBURY and the Diana logo are trademarks of Bloomsbury Publishing Plc

First published in Great Britain 2019

A catalogue record for this book is available from the British Library.

Library of Congress Cataloging-in-Publication data

Names: Evolutionary interpretation in different international legal systems (Conference) (2018 : Faculte de droit de Geneve). | Abi-Saab, Georges, editor. | Keith, Kenneth James, editor. | Marceau, Gabrielle, editor. | Marquet, Clément, editor.

Title: Evolutionary interpretation and international law / edited by Georges Abi-Saab, Kenneth Keith, Gabrielle Marceau and Clément Marquet.

Description: Oxford, UK ; Chicago, Illinois : Hart Publishing, 2019. | Includes bibliographical references and index.

Identifiers: LCCN 2019021090 (print) | LCCN 2019022041 (ebook) | ISBN 9781509929900 (EPub) | ISBN9781509929887 (hardback)

Subjects: LCSH: International law—Interpretation and construction—Congresses.

Classification: LCC KZ1285 (ebook) | LCC KZ1285 .E96 2019 (print) | DDC 341—dc23

LC record available at https://lccn.loc.gov/2019021090

ISBN: HB: 978-1-50992-988-7
ePDF: 978-1-50992-989-4
ePub: 978-1-50992-990-0

Typeset by Compuscript Ltd, Shannon

To find out more about our authors and books visit www.hartpublishing.co.uk. Here you will find extracts, author information, details of forthcoming events and the option to sign up for our newsletters.

PREFACE

GABRIELLE MARCEAU

For several years I have been encouraged to set up a study group or organise a conference at the University of Geneva on a substantive topic that I could explore in depth. I decided the time was ripe for this when, in 2014, Laval University in Québec City, my home town, invited me to preside over a conference on the WTO's 20th anniversary and present a paper on a WTO theme reflecting this milestone. I chose the topic of evolutive or evolutionary interpretation, because when the WTO Appellate Body first referred to this issue in the *US – Shrimp* case, many believed this was unique and even revolutionary. I was soon to understand that it was not. The tension between security and predictability of the law, on the one hand, and the real life situation where changes can take place between the conclusion of a treaty and its eventual interpretation and application, on the other hand, exists in all legal systems and regimes. The WTO context is nonetheless quite unique, because the WTO Agreement contains provisions – the GATT – dating back to 1947, as well as subsequent understandings and agreements – all of which were adopted together in December 1993 to enter into force on 1 January 1995, in parallel with the already existing provisions of the GATT 1947.

When I gave a first overall presentation of the concept of 'evolutionary interpretation' in September 2015 at Laval University, my starting questions were 'what exactly is evolutionary or evolutive interpretation? What does the concept of evolutionary interpretation cover? What does it add to the existing provisions of the Vienna Convention on the Law of Treaties (VCLT)?'. Because WTO case law on evolutionary interpretation was quite limited, I decided to explore the answers to these questions in general international law and in other legal regimes to see what I could learn from them. My pursuit of answers to seemingly simple questions led me to the realization that it is far from clear what evolutionary interpretation is all about, when evolutionary interpretation should be used, and why it was used in some cases but not others. With the help of my assistant, my research continued, and my understanding started to evolve.

I gave a second presentation on the topic in April 2016 at a Harvard Law School conference marking the WTO's 20th anniversary. By then, I was making progress towards mapping out the different types of changes that could occur between the time of the conclusion of a treaty and the time of its interpretation and application: sometimes the 'applicable law' had changed, other times it was the social, political, or technical contexts that had changed: what was reasonable in 1900 or even 1950 may no longer be reasonable in 2000. When generic terms are used in treaties, there may seem to be more interpretive 'space' for taking changes into account – but is it all only about the terms used in the original treaty?

In January 2018, I published an article in French in the *Revue générale de droit international public*, in which I revamped that initial map into a typology of the different categories of evolutionary interpretation. Beyond the catch-all name of evolutionary interpretation, what implications could this typology have on a practical level? The categories suggested in my article could also guide one's reading of this book: thus, evolutionary interpretation can be understood not just as an abstract concept, but as a meaningful practice embodied in the terms used in a treaty, its social and legal context, the continuation of its object and purpose through time, or the evolution of the law surrounding the instrument under interpretation.

A substantially amended English version of my French article was published in December 2018 in the *Journal of International Economic Law*, where I tried to develop how each of those categories of changes – could be taken into account along the stepping stones of a VCLT. From this, I concluded that even if evolutionary interpretation did not add a positive rule of interpretation to those already existing in the VCLT, it bore at the very least a symbolic weight. Evolutionary interpretation embodies not only an interpretative process, but also a message that law can, and sometimes must, adapt to multiple social, legal, technological and political changes. It can serve as an intellectual compass to face upcoming challenges. As Ruth Bader Ginsburg, quoting Paul Freund, has said: 'Judges do read the newspapers and are affected, not by the weather of the day, … but by the climate of the era'.[1]

In spite of having worked on these articles, I had a growing sense that there were other ways of answering the seemingly simple questions about the nature and use of evolutionary interpretation. I became more than ever convinced that we needed to have a broader work, gathering together experts from different fields of international law to discuss what evolutionary interpretation is, when is it used, and how is it applied in different legal systems and international regimes.

The result was a decision to organize conference at UNIGE in October 2018; and I was most honoured when Professor Georges Abi-Saab accepted my invitation to lead the discussions. I cannot think of any other international expert on treaty interpretation better qualified to bring an understanding of fundamental and global considerations of which interpretation is one of the most important and cross-cutting. I am very grateful to the Rectorate of the University of Geneva, its Law Faculty and my Department of Public International Law, as well as the Global Studies Institute, for their financial support for this conference and for the

[1] R Bader Ginsburg, M Hartnett and WW Williams, *My Own Words* (New York, Simon & Schuster, 2016) 161.

publication of this book. This support allowed us to gather academics, practitioners and other experts from all around the word for two days of intense discussion on the topic. The rich exchanges sharpened our awareness of evolutionary interpretation, allowing us to develop a deeper insight into the way evolutionary interpretation covers all forms of internal and external changes that take place during the life of a treaty. When the decision was taken to publish conference papers from interested participants, additional experts were invited to join our project, and their contributions, included in this volume, have enhanced our collective appreciation of the potential and limits of the concept of evolutionary interpretation. While it is true that every regime seems to have some concept of evolutionary interpretation, they each have their own peculiarities, which are brought to the fore throughout this book. The chapters reflect the diversity of approaches that can be found in the practice of international courts and tribunals and in other international institutions. But we also looked at how domestic courts deal with the evolutionary interpretation of treaties they use in their decisions. I believe all these perspectives have contributed to the richness of this publication and to furthering debate on this fundamental topic.

This book could not have reached such an international standard without the professionalism and commitment of our legal editor Siobhan Ackroyd, who was sponsored by the Global Studies Institute. The entire evolving research project that delivered this book benefited hugely from the multifaceted and invaluable contributions from my assistant, Clément Marquet. I am grateful to Laurence Boisson de Chazourne who encouraged me very early on to delve into the substantive labyrinths of international law. Thank you also to Roberta Bassi, who supported this project from its inception, and to Hart Publishing, who published our book in an exceptionally short time. This publication was further enhanced when Kenneth Keith agreed to make use of his exceptional international law expertise to draw together all the different threads offered by the authors, with a view to developing a rich and coherent conclusive assessment of the various manifestations of evolutionary interpretation and identifying where further questions lie.

Overall, it seems that views of international experts on evolutionary Interpretation range from those who believe that a treaty interpreter should apply an evolutionary interpretation to all sorts of situations; to others, who consider that evolutionary interpretation is a useless sophism, as the rules of the VCLT already offer all the tools necessary to deal with changes, if these rules are interpreted and applied properly. This book aims to help readers appreciate the breath of evolutionary interpretation, whose application calls for an appropriate balance to be struck between security, predictability and effectiveness in the interpretation and application of international law. And with this in mind, my understanding of evolutionary interpretation continues to evolve.

TABLE OF CONTENTS

PART II
EVOLUTIONARY INTERPRETATION IN ATYPICAL INSTITUTIONAL SETTINGS

PART III
EVOLUTIONARY INTERPRETATION IN HUMAN RIGHTS AND ENVIRONMENT LAW

PART IV
EVOLUTIONARY INTERPRETATION IN WTO LAW

A. Systemic Approaches to Evolutionary Interpretation

PART VI
EVOLUTIONARY INTERPRETATION IN EU LAW

PART VII
CONCLUSION

LIST OF CONTRIBUTORS

Georges Abi-Saab is Emeritus Professor of International Law at the Graduate Institute of International and Development Studies, where he taught from 1963 to 2000. He also served as Judge ad hoc of the International Court of Justice, a former Judge of the Appeals Chamber of the International Criminal Tribunal for the former Yugoslavia (ICTY) and Rwanda (ICTR), a former Commissioner of the United Nations Compensation Commission, and former Chairman of the Appellate Body of the World Trade Organization. He is Honorary Professor at Cairo University's Faculty of Law and a Member of the Institute of International Law since 1981. abisaab@bluewin.ch

Eirik Bjorge is a professor of law at Bristol University Law School. His research and teaching are within the fields of public international law and domestic public law. He holds a PhD from the University of Oslo and a DPhil from the University of Oxford. eirik.bjorge@bristol.ac.uk

Graham Cook is a Counsellor with the Legal Affairs Division of the WTO Secretariat. In that capacity, he serves as a legal adviser to WTO dispute settlement panels. He has delivered a range of training activities on WTO dispute settlement for government officials, both in Geneva and abroad, and has taught and lectured at the Universities of Geneva and Barcelona, and at the World Trade Institute in Bern. He has authored several publications on WTO dispute settlement. He received both his LLB and LLM from the Faculty of Law at the University of British Columbia. Prior to joining the WTO Secretariat in 2006, he worked as a lawyer with the Government of Canada. graham.cook@wto.org

Luigi Crema is a researcher and adjunct professor of international law at the Università degli Studi of Milan. He holds a joint PhD from the Universities of Geneva and Milan, and has been a visiting fellow at the New York University School of Law and a visiting professor at the University of Notre Dame Law School. luigi.crema@unimi.it

Mariana Clara de Andrade is a PhD researcher at the University of Milano-Bicocca (Italy), MPhil in Law and International Relations (Federal University of Santa Catarina, Brazil). m.deandrade@campus.unimib.it

Mattias Derlén, LLM, LLD, is Professor of Law at the Department of Law, Umeå University, Sweden. His areas of interest include law and language, constitutional EU law and empirical legal research. mattias.derlen@umu.se

Christian Djeffal is associated researcher at Alexander von Humboldt Institute for Internet and Society and the Center for Technology, Society, and Law at University of Zurich. He obtained his PhD from Humboldt University of Berlin, where he worked as researcher for Georg Nolte. christian.djeffal@hiig.de

Oliver Dörr (Professor, University of Osnabrück) received his legal education in Berlin (Dr iur 1995) and London (LLM. 1989) and qualified as professor of law at the Free University of Berlin (2002). Since 2004 he has been holding a chair of Public Law, European Law, International and Comparative Law at Osnabrück university (European Legal Studies Institute). In 2006 he was visiting professor at Andrássy University in Budapest and in 2015 at Cardinal Stefan Wyszyński University in Warsaw. He served as Dean of the law faculty in Osnabrück in 2009–10. oliver.doerr@uni-osnabrueck.de

Malgosia Fitzmaurice holds a chair of public international law at the Department of Law, Queen Mary University of London (QMUL). She specialises in international environmental law; the law of treaties; indigenous people and water law. She publishes widely on these subjects. She has delivered a lecture on the International Protection of the Environment at The Hague Academy of International Law. Professor Fitzmaurice was invited as a Visiting Professor to and lectured at various universities worldwide, such Berkeley Law School; University of Kobe; Panthéon-Sorbonne (Paris I). She is the Editor in Chief of *International Community Law Review* journal and of the book series published by Brill/Nijhoff *Queen Mary Studies in International Law*. m.fitzmaurice@qmul.ac.uk

Aikaterini Florou is a legal and policy officer with the Directorate for Energy of the European Commission. She holds a PhD in international investment law from Sciences Po Law School, an LLM from the Fletcher School of Law and Diplomacy, and a Master's degree from Athens Law School. She has been a scholar and tutor at the Hague Academy of International Law and a visitor at Berkeley Law School, and she has also worked at the OECD and the WTO team of the European Commission's Legal Service. aikaterini.florou@sciencespo.fr

Marina Fortuna is a PhD researcher at the University of Groningen. She obtained her LLB degree from the Babes-Bolyai University and her LLM degree in Public International Law from the University of Groningen. Her PhD research focuses on the interpretation of customary international law in the practice of international courts and tribunals, and is conducted under the supervision of Professor Dr Panos Merkouris within the ERC-funded project TRICI-Law. Marina's area of interest and research includes interpretation, customary international law, the law of state immunity, international dispute settlement and state responsibility. m.fortuna@rug.nl

Gloria Gaggioli is Swiss National Science Foundation (SNSF) Professor at the Law Faculty of the University of Geneva as well as Lecturer at the Geneva Academy of International Humanitarian Law and Human Rights and at the University of Neuchâtel (Switzerland). Prior to joining the University of Geneva, she served as Legal Adviser in the legal division of the International Committee of the Red Cross (ICRC). Gloria.Gaggioli@unige.ch

Sévane Garibian is an SNSF Professor at the Law Faculty of the University of Geneva (UNIGE), an Associate Professor at the Law Faculty of the University of Neuchâtel and a Faculty member of the Geneva Academy of International Humanitarian Law and Human Rights. She is currently leading the SNSF research programme 'Right to Truth, Truth(s) Through Rights: Mass Crimes Impunity and Transitional Justice' at UNIGE. She is the author of many publications in the field of International Criminal Law, Transitional Justice and Human Rights. Sevane.Garibian@unige.ch

Charalampos Giannakopoulos is a Visiting Research Consultant at the Centre for International Law, National University of Singapore. He obtained his PhD from the Graduate Institute of International and Development Studies in 2018. In the past, he has worked as a legal consultant at UNCTAD (Investment Agreements Section). His research interests include international investment law, international adjudication, treaty interpretation, legal theory and philosophy. charalampos.giannakopoulos@graduateinstitute.ch

Jenya Grigorova is an associate at Sidley Austin LLP. Jenya holds a PhD from Paris 1 Sorbonne University and an LLM from NYU. jenya.grigorova@gmail.com

Sondre Torp Helmersen is an Associate Professor at the Inland Norway University of Applied Sciences. He holds a PhD from the University of Oslo and an LLM from the University of Cambridge. He previously worked at the Norwegian Ministry of Foreign Affairs. s.t.helmersen@cantab.net

Kun Hui is a PhD Candidate at the University of Ottawa, Faculty of Law. His research includes China's and Chinese State-Owned Enterprises' sovereign immunity claims under international and national laws. He is a legal research intern at Tereposky & DeRose LLP. His work at the firm touches upon both NAFTA and non-NAFTA investment treaty arbitration proceedings. khui@tradeisds.com

Kenneth Keith is a professor emeritus at the Victoria University of Wellington, New Zealand, where he taught for more than 20 years, and a member of the Institut de Droit International. He was earlier a legal adviser in the New Zealand Department of External Affairs and the United Nations Secretariat, a member of law reform bodies, a judge of appeal in the Pacific and a member of several international arbitral tribunals. From 1995 to 2006 he was a judge of the New Zealand Court of Appeal and Supreme Court, which replaced the Judicial Committee of the Privy Council in London, on which he also sat, as New Zealand's final court of appeal. From 2006 to 2015 he was a judge of the International Court of Justice. Ken.Keith@vuw.ac.nz

Robert Kolb has been Professor of Public International Law at the Law Faculty, University of Geneva since 2007. Prior to 2007, he worked as a legal adviser to the International Committee of the Red Cross (ICRC) and Swiss Federal Department of Foreign Affairs. He was also Secretary of the Institute of International Law, Lecturer in Public International Law at the Graduate Institute of International and Development Studies. Robert.Kolb@unige.ch

Nicolas Levrat has been full Professor at the Law Faculty of the University of Geneva since 2001. He was Director of the European Institute (2007–12) and the founder and first director of the Global Studies institute at the University of Geneva (2012–15). He's currently Director of the International Law Department. He teaches and researches institutional issues in international and European Law. He is also promoting interdisciplinary approaches for global governance as the co-director of the 'Geneva Transformative Governance Lab'. Nicolas.Levrat@unige.ch

Kendra Magraw is a PhD candidate at the Graduate Institute of International and Development Studies in Geneva. Ms Magraw specialises in international investment law and policy, as well as international sports law and international dispute settlement. She has worked in private practice, as well as at, among others, ICSID, the International Investment Agreement Section of UNCTAD and the ICJ.

Gabrielle Marceau, PhD, has been Senior Counsellor in the Legal Affairs Division of the WTO Secretariat since September 1994. Her main function is to advise panellists in WTO disputes, the Director-General's Office, the Secretariat and WTO Members on WTO-related matters. Gabrielle Marceau is also Associate Professor at the Law Faculty of the University of Geneva. She has published different articles and book in WTO related matters. gabrielle.marceau@unige.ch

Clément Marquet is a PhD Candidate at the Law Faculty of the University of Geneva. He specialises in international dispute settlement systems and WTO law. His PhD research revolves around the notion of consent to international jurisdiction. clement@marquet.ch

Donald McRae is Professor Emeritus in the Faculty of Law at the University of Ottawa. He has published widely on the international law of the sea, international trade and investment law and international dispute settlement. He has been a judge ad hoc in the International Court of Justice and was a member of the United Nations International Law Commission from 2007–16. Donald.Mcrae@uottawa.ca

Makane Moïse Mbengue is Professor of International Law at the Faculty of Law of the University of Geneva. He is also an Affiliate Professor at Sciences Po Paris (School of Law). He has acted and acts as expert for the African Union, the United Nations Economic Commission for Africa, the United Nations Environment Programme (UNEP), and the International Institute for Sustainable Development (IISD) among others. He acts as counsel in disputes before international courts and tribunals and as adviser for governments. He is involved in the negotiations of several International Investment Agreements in Africa. makane.Mbengue@unige.ch

Nina Mileva is a PhD researcher at the University of Groningen. She obtained her Bachelor of Liberal Arts and Sciences (Honours) from the Amsterdam University College, and her Master's in Public International Law (LLM) from Utrecht University. Her PhD research is on the interpretation of customary international law under the supervision of Professor Panos Merkouris, within the ERC-funded project TRICI-Law. She was a junior researcher at Utrecht University, and obtained practical experience from the International Criminal Tribunal for the Former Yugoslavia (ICTY) and the International Criminal Court (ICC). Nina's area of research includes legal theory, customary international law, interpretation, and the interplay between domestic and international law. n.mileva@rug.nl

Malvika Monga is a Legal Affairs Officer with the Trade in Services and Investment Division at the World Trade Organization. She obtained her LLM in International Dispute Settlement from the Graduate Institute of International and Development Studies and her LLB from the London School of Economics and Political Science. She has previously worked in the private sector and in other international organisations such as UNCTAD and the World Bank Group. malvika@monga.org

Paolo Palchetti has been a Professor of International Law at the University of Macerata since 2011, where he is also coordinator of the PhD in Legal Sciences, as well as vice-president of the Doctoral School. He holds a PhD from the University of Milan. palchetti@unimc.it

Jennifer Radford is a founding partner of Tereposky & DeRose LLP. She is an experienced litigator who has appeared before Canadian courts, Canadian trade and administrative tribunals and international arbitral tribunals. She represents domestic and foreign clients in trade and investment matters, including investor–State disputes and trade remedies. She also represents foreign States and embassies carrying out diplomatic missions in Canada. In this capacity, she acted as counsel in precedent-setting court cases involving complex State and diplomatic immunity issues. jradford@tradeisds.com

Gregory Tereposky is a founding partner of Tereposky & DeRose LLP. He regularly acts as counsel in WTO disputes and NAFTA trade and investor–State disputes. He also frequently appears before Canadian courts and trade tribunals. He was appointed as a panellist in the WTO dispute *European Union – Anti-Dumping Measures on Imports of Certain Fatty Alcohols from Indonesia*. He has advised in international trade negotiations, such as NAFTA and Uruguay and Doha Rounds of WTO negotiations. He is the founder and Editor-in-Chief of *TradeLawGuide* (www.tradelawguide.com) and a co-founder of Investor-State *LawGuide* (www.investorstatelawguide.com). gtereposky@tradeisds.com

Isabelle Van Damme, PhD, is Counsel at Van Bael & Bellis and a Member of the Brussels Bar. Her practice focuses on WTO law, EU law and public international law. She previously worked as a référendaire in the chambers of Advocate General Sharpston, at the Court of Justice of the European Union and was a lecturer and the Turpin-Lipstein Fellow at the University of Cambridge, Clare College. ivandamme@vbb.com

Peter Van den Bossche is Director of Studies of the World Trade Institute and Professor of International Economic Law at the Faculty of Law of the University of Bern, Switzerland. Since 2018, he serves as President of the Society of International Economic Law. From 2009 to 2017, he was a Member of the Appellate Body of the World Trade Organization and served as its chairman in 2015. peter.vandenbossche@wti.org

Julian Wyatt built his expertise in international law as an academic and practitioner in Geneva, Switzerland. An Australian barrister and solicitor, he currently works at Proxenia Legal in Melbourne, Australia while continuing to pursue his research interests as a Visiting Fellow at the Centre of International & Public Law at the Australian National University. Dr Wyatt has published (in English, French and German) on a number of different topics of international law and international dispute settlement. He has also acted as counsel for States in several international disputes. mail@julianwyatt.com

The opinions expressed are only those of the authors and do not bind their respective organisations. The chapters should not be construed as constituting legal advice.

ABBREVIATIONS

ACHR	American Convention on Human Rights
BIT	Bilateral Investment Treaty
CARU	Administrative Commission of the River Uruguay (Comisión Administradora del Río Uruguay)
CETA	Canada–European Union Comprehensive Economic and Trade Agreement
CIL	Customary international law
CJEU	Court of Justice of the European Union
CSFP	Common security and foreign policy
DSB	Dispute Settlement Body
DSU	Dispute Settlement Understanding
DVI	Digital Visual Interface
EEA	European Economic Area
EEC	European Economic Community
ECHR	European Convention on Human Rights
ECSR	European Committee on Social Rights
ECtHR	European Court of Human Rights
EFTA	European Free Trade Association
EHRR	European Human Rights Reports
EIA	Environmental Impact Assessment
EP	European Parliament
ESC	European Social Charter
ETS	Emission Trading System
EU	European Union
FET	Fair and equitable treatment standard

FPD	Flat-panel display device
FTA	Free trade agreement
FTC	NAFTA Free Trade Commission
GA	General Assembly
GATS	General Agreement on Trade in Services
GATT	General Agreement on Tariffs and Trade
GC	Grand Chamber
HRC	UN Human Rights Committee
IACtHR	Inter-American Court of Human Rights
ICC	International Criminal Court
ICCPR	International Covenant on Civil and Political Rights
ICJ	International Court of Justice
ICSID	International Centre for Settlement of Investment Disputes
ICT	International Criminal Tribunal
ICTR	International Criminal Tribunals for Rwanda
ICTY	International Criminal Tribunals for the former Yugoslavia
IDI	Institut de droit international
IIA	International investment agreement
ILC	International Law Commission
ILR	International Law Reports
IPPA	Investment Promotion and Protection Agreement
ISDS	Investor–State dispute settlement
ITA	Information Technology Agreement
IVF	In-vitro fertilisation
JHA	Justice and Home Affairs
MEP	Member of the European Parliament
MFN	Most Favoured Nation
MST	Minimum standard of treatment

NAFTA	North American Free Trade Agreement
OHIM	Office for the Harmonisation of the Internal Market
PCA	Permanent Court of Arbitration
PCIJ	Permanent Court of International Justice
SADC	South African Development Community
SCC	Stockholm Chamber of Commerce
SPP	State party pleading
TBT	Technical Barriers to Trade
TEC	Treaty establishing the European Community
TEEC	Treaty establishing the European Economic Community
TEN-E	Trans-European Networks for Energy
TEU	Treaty of the European Union
TFEU	Treaty on the Functioning of the European Union
TRIPS	Trade-Related Aspects of Intellectual Property Rights
UN	United Nations
UNCITRAL	United Nations Commission on International Trade Law
UNCTAD	United Nations Conference on Trade and Development
UNHCR	United Nations High Commissioner for Refugees
USMCA	United States–Mexico–Canada Agreement
VCLT	Vienna Convention on the Law of Treaties
WTO	World Trade Organization

1

About the Book

GABRIELLE MARCEAU AND CLÉMENT MARQUET

> There is no part of the law of treaties which the text-writer approaches with more trepidation than the question of interpretation.[1]

More than half a century ago, Lord McNair had already highlighted the undeniable appeal of discussing the multifaceted notion of 'interpretation'. The question of interpretation through time figures prominently as part of the appeal or lure of this subject. In this regard, one could note that the Southeast Portico of the Thomas Jefferson Memorial in Washington DC reads as follows:

> I am not an advocate for frequent changes in laws and constitutions, but laws and institutions must go hand in hand with the progress of the human mind. As that becomes more developed, more enlightened, as new discoveries are made, new truths discovered and manners and opinions change, with the change of circumstances, institutions must advance also to keep pace with the times. We might as well require a man to wear still the coat which fitted him when a boy as a civilized society to remain ever under the regimen of their barbarous ancestors.

In a few lines, the third President of the United States eloquently expressed an issue that is still at the heart of debates in the field of law, even more so in international law: how does law withstand the test of time? The interconnectedness between law and society makes it necessary for the former to remain in touch with the latter. Indeed, the social purpose of law would be rendered pointless without a mechanism allowing it to change and adapt to the emerging needs and habits of new generations. This is the role evolutionary interpretation plays.

By nature, international law – in particular international treaties – is a slow-moving body of rules. Long consensus-building, shifting political alliances and complicated amendment procedures all make for difficult law-making. In turn, the material contents of law can lose touch with a changing reality that does not wait for the rules to catch up. Can those rules, sometimes drafted centuries ago, still be relevant in today's world? How do moral, technological or legal changes that

[1] AD McNair, *The Law of Treaties* (Oxford, Oxford University Press, 1961) 364.

have taken place since the conclusion of the treaty affect the interpretation of an old provision? Evolutionary interpretation can be found in this nook of international law. It allows judges – and other interpreters – to take into account all these changes, and to adapt the understanding of law to changing times.

This book, which offers discussions from experts on so-called evolutive or evolutionary interpretation, aims at examining the notion of evolutionary interpretation in both its underpinnings and its application. What is the basis for evolutionary interpretation and when is it a legitimate tool for interpretation? Is there any semblance of unity in its use by judges across various legal regimes? What types of changes does it encompass? Through this analysis, the coherence of the international legal system is questioned.

In this regard, and because diversity begets richness, leading experts from diverse areas of international law were brought together for a conference in October 2018 at the University of Geneva. We asked Professor Georges Abi-Saab for his advice and guidance on the topic, not only because of his tremendous experience in international law, but also because of his transversal approach. Having been an adjudicator in some of the main fora of the international sphere, his understanding of the international law system is second to none.

After the conference some of the participants agreed to continue to work on the same theme with additional experts for the publication of the present book. The authors have diverse backgrounds and expertise. Some are already well established and respected authors, others are younger academics or practitioners, and some young voices were chosen through a call for papers. All authors have already researched the topic of evolutionary interpretation, so as to provide an informed and innovative contribution.

The book starts with Professor Abi-Saab recalling what 'interpretation' is about, followed by discussions of the basic assumptions about evolutionary interpretation in the international legal system generally. It then turns to more regime-specific discussions, with in-depth analyses of the approaches adopted in human rights and environmental law, in the law of the World Trade Organization (WTO), international investment law and the law of the European Union (EU).

One of the notable features of this book is its wide array of contributors. It provides multiple points of view on evolutionary interpretation, because one single voice would not do justice to the level of intricacy and controversy surrounding the subject. From one regime to the other, even the very definition of evolutionary interpretation can change completely, let alone its operation. For all these reasons, contributions by multiple authors, each a specialist in her or his field, is not only preferable, but also necessary.

As mentioned, this book is divided into distinct parts. The first two deal with questions relating to the international legal system in general, while the next four closely examine specific regimes.

The first part proposes different approaches to the theoretical justification of evolutionary interpretation itself. First, Robert Kolb argues that evolutionary interpretation amounts to '*rebus sic stantibus* writ small', before Christian Djeffal further discusses the possible added value of the concept and the underlying purpose of using evolutionary interpretation. Following up on his doctoral research, Eirik Bjorge then underlines the crucial role the intention of the parties plays when adapting a treaty's reading through time. Julian Wyatt turns to linguistics to determine which circumstances warrant an evolutionary interpretation. Finally, Donald McRae emphasises the importance of context – broadly defined – in the whole process. In sum, this first section aims at offering a broad overview of the possible understandings of evolutionary interpretation. Rather than being regime specific, it lays the groundwork for the rest of the book by providing a solid footing for the broader theoretical debate about interpretation. Going beyond a given set of rules, it suggests a rethinking of the very purpose and foundations of the interpretative process, through the lens of societal evolution.

The second part considers evolutionary interpretation in some unusual contexts. Evolutionary interpretation is not limited to treaty interpretation by international adjudicators. Indeed, national courts, treaty bodies, international organisations or States themselves may also interpret international law, and acts other than treaties can be the object of evolutionary interpretation. International judges are not the only interpreters of international law, and domestic judges also participate in the shaping of international rules. Here, Kenneth Keith first delves into evolutionary interpretation as used by national courts. This change of focus also appears in Luigi Crema's contribution, in which the interpretative role of treaty bodies is explored. Closing this part on evolutionary interpretation in atypical settings, Paolo Palchetti discusses the notion of evolutionary interpretation outside the framework of treaties. Since other acts, such as unilateral ones or resolutions of international organisations are also subject to interpretation, their adaptation through time is no less important. This part aims at offering a refreshing broader picture of evolutionary interpretation, outside the well-trodden paths of treaty law.

The third part turns to a regime-specific approach, by looking at human rights and environmental law. Gloria Gaggioli starts by assessing the status of evolutionary interpretation in human rights law generally, before Oliver Dörr debates the European Court of Human Right's approach to evolutionary interpretation. Turning to environmental law, Nina Mileva and Marina Fortuna analyse how evolutionary interpretation contributed to the development of the field of environmental law and, reversely, how this field is one of the main contributors to the case law dealing with evolutionary interpretation. Malgosia Fitzmaurice then discusses the impact of evolutionary interpretation on the right to a clean environment. Finally, Sévane Garibian examines the issue from the point of view of international criminal law, and its interaction with human rights law. In particular, the issues of legitimacy plaguing the existence of the tribunals in this field is closely related to their use of evolutionary interpretation. Overall, a picture emerges from these contributions, in which a teleological interpretation takes a front-row seat: human rights courts and tribunals tend to adopt a purpose-heavy reading of the law, which is reflected in this section.

The fourth part's focus is on international trade law, and more specifically WTO law. Some have argued that WTO law is quite progressive in its treatment of evolutionary interpretation, in particular through the landmark case *US – Shrimp*. To discuss this, the section is split into two sections, the first looking at systemic questions, where the second delves into the more specific recourse to evolutionary interpretation at the hands of WTO adjudicators. Thus, in the first section, Isabelle Van Damme looks into the reasoning underlying the recourse of this interpretative tool and argues that several factors affect whether and how references to evolutionary interpretation are made. Next, Graham Cook unties the conceptual knot presented by the distinction between evolutionary interpretation and application. As a side issue, he questions where the changes of meaning really lie. Clément Marquet then offers a glimpse into the future, through his analysis of possible uses for evolutionary interpretation as early as the treaty negotiations stage. While remaining regime specific, this section nevertheless discusses more general elements of the notion of evolutionary interpretation.

In the second section of this part, Sondre Torp Helmersen identifies patterns in the Appellate Body's jurisprudence, and questions whether true evolutionary interpretation is really an important part of it. Peter Van den Bossche further discusses the use of evolutionary interpretation in the WTO, and in particular whether so-called evolutionary interpretation is, indeed, evolutionary. Mariana Clara de Andrade then draws links between the Appellate Body's use of evolutionary interpretation and the Dispute Settlement Body's ongoing discussion with the Appellate Body. Finally, Jenya Grigorova focuses on a distinct part of international trade law, through the shifting sands of trade in energy. Here, evolutionary interpretation can serve as a tool to include newer concerns about the environment into already existing sets of rules.

While staying in the field of international economic law, the fifth part nevertheless changes gears, with a look at investment law. Makane Mbengue and Aikaterini Florou begin with an assessment of the state of play of evolutionary interpretation in a world of fragmented tribunals and little *stare decisis*. Kendra Magraw then looks at the recourse that States make to evolutionary interpretation in their submissions during dispute settlement proceedings. In a similar vein, Jennifer Radford, Gregory Tereposky and Kun Hui offer a distinct take on evolutionary interpretation in NAFTA (North American Free Trade Agreement). In particular, they look at the Free Trade Commission's statements and their use as interpretative tools in disputes. Finally, Charalampos Giannakopoulos and Malvika Monga delve deeper into the field, by examining the evolution of the Fair and Equitable Treatment standard through time and interpretation. Ultimately, this part demonstrates how fragmented the world of international investment law is. It remains to be seen whether evolutionary interpretation (whether or not it is subject to agreed additional principles) can serve as a tool for coherence. However, arbitrators' reluctance to explicitly use evolutionary interpretation is a significant hurdle.

Finally, a brief part on EU law underlines two specificities of this union. First, Nicolas Levrat analyses the gap-filling role held by the Court of Justice of the European Union and in particular how its use of evolutionary interpretation defines the homogeneity (or lack thereof) of the EU's legal system. Mattias Derlén then discusses the consequences of interpreting EU law in all of its official languages, and the dynamism an evolutionary interpretation can inject into EU-wide interpretation.

These parts do not aim at creating a 'clinical isolation' between the regimes. Rather, the emphasis on the diversity of approaches in the first two parts of the book help understand why different regimes might go separate ways, for dealing with similar and related concerns: the fact that several elements of the interpretation process may change and evolve between the conclusion of a treaty and the moment of its interpretation and application. Indisputably, depending on the regime under scrutiny, different weights are given to each part of the holistic interpretative process. Whether through a teleological interpretation, an intention-heavy one, an insistence on the plain meaning of the terms or a reference to the importance of the context, some sort of evolutionary interpretation still finds a way. It remains to be seen if all these elements are, in one way or another, different sides of the same coin. They also reflect the long-standing debate, also present in this book, regarding the very purpose of interpretation. Is the interpreter attempting to find the true intention of the parties, at the time of conclusion of the treaty? Or is it simply the result of the interpretative process, through the proper application of the formal rules of the VCLT to the text of the treaty? The eternal battle between objectivists and subjectivists plays the first role when discussing evolutionary interpretation.

Another element stands out in these chapters: the difficulty of even defining evolutionary interpretation. Indeed, is it sufficient for an adjudicator to say that his or her interpretation is evolutionary? Or are there more objective criteria? Is it possible to presume a situation of evolutionary interpretation where no mention is made of it? Since the reader is unable to know what the outcome of a case would have been but for the choice the adjudicator made, the situation is unclear. There is no 'control group' to provide an objective distinction between a case where evolutionary interpretation is used and one where it is not. This makes it difficult to define more clearly the situations calling for evolutionary interpretation and those where such recourse is not warranted. Had the tribunal decided not to mention evolutionary interpretation, would the results have been different? These questions further shape the role of evolutionary interpretation and provide a glimpse into its symbolism. The question of the definition of evolutionary interpretation is intimately linked to its perceived purpose. As the famous saying goes, 'Not only must Justice be done; it must also be seen to be done'.[2] It is possible that evolutionary interpretation plays such a role, having not only a legal, but also a moral function. It displays the sort of 'progress' that is required by the ever-moving fabric on

[2] *R v Sussex Justices, ex p McCarthy* [1924] 1 KB 256.

which law is written. Ultimately, societal evolution drives necessary changes in law, one way or another. As Giovanni Distefano put it: 'l'ordre juridique constitue un système "inscindible" en "perpétuel devenir" étant donné que ses normes tendent naturellement à s'adapter aux exigences sociales' ('the legal order constitutes an indivisible system, in perpetual progress, given that its norms naturally tend to adapt to social needs').[3]

[3] G Distefano, 'L'interprétation évolutive de la norme internationale' (2011) 115 *Revue générale de droit international public* 373, 384.

2

Introduction: A Meta-Question

GEORGES ABI-SAAB

A dilemma that frequently faces someone introducing a colloquium or a collective book on a given subject is how to say something relevant without treading on what might be said by subsequent interveners.

One way of circumventing this dilemma is to address a question that transcends the subject, while remaining relevant, a meta-question, such as clarifying the premises of the subject to situate it in its larger context.

The subject of 'evolutionary interpretation' assumes that it is a species of interpretation. But what do we mean by interpretation in the first place? And in what sense and from what angle can it be qualified as 'evolutionary' (or evolutive)? In other words, 'interpretation' needs interpretation.

Indeed, the term interpretation is used in current, and particularly legal, language to designate at least three different objects or referents, two of which refer to the stages of a mental or intellectual operation and the third to the output or outcome of this operation.

1. Interpretation as a 'process of cognition'. This is the wider etymological meaning of interpretation, as the very process of grasping or apprehending the sense of a word, a sentence, or a normative proposition, of identifying and delimiting its substance. It is a purely intellectual activity, studied by different disciplines under different denominations: the theory of knowledge in philosophy, cognitive theories in psychology, the theories of communication in linguistics, as well as by modern theories of literary criticism, etc. Each of these theories endeavours to explain in its own way how the mind grasps external reality, takes hold and deciphers it for itself, particularly when this reality is not material or sensuous, but social or conceptual, even if it is expressed in words like law. In their diverse approaches, these theories provide a variety of tools to seize the meaning of a word, a sentence or a logical or normative proposition.

But is this intellectual process of identifying meaning sufficient by itself to produce a final interpretation of a legal text?[1] I turn for an answer to a great master,

[1] I leave aside for the moment the question of interpretation of non-written law.

Hans Kelsen, who responds in the negative. This is because words, not to speak of words in the context of a sentence or a general normative proposition, are very rarely, if ever, 100 per cent 'univocal', in the sense of 'having only one proper meaning; capable of one single interpretation; unambiguous'.[2] Thus, even when we have a written normative proposition with an absolutely clear hard core, this hard core is always surrounded by a penumbra or a margin of indeterminacy, however narrow it may be.

This means that the purely intellectual process – which Kelsen defines as 'cognitive ascertainment of the meaning of the object that is to be interpreted'[3] – can only be an intermediate stage towards a final interpretation, since it cannot go beyond tracing the outer-limit around possible meanings that can be accommodated within the normative proposition, that which in turn implies the recognition of the existence of several such possibilities within these limits.

2. Interpretation as an 'act of volition'. If every normative proposition comprises a penumbra or margin of indeterminacy, and can thus accommodate more than one meaning, a second step or stage of the interpretative operation becomes necessary: choosing between alternative possible meanings. But choice is an exercise of free will, an act of 'volition', and a conscious 'decision'.

Saying that the final interpretation is the result of the wilful choice of the interpreter does not mean, however, that this choice is totally free. This is contrary to what some schools of thought profess. For instance the New Haven School considers that rules and normative propositions in general are 'open-ended', 'open textures' that can be stood on their head, and made to say the thing and its opposite, according to the subjective views and values of the interpreter. Likewise, some post-modern writers view rules as mere shopping lists from which the interpreter-judge chooses, as well as from the factual matrix of a case, those elements that, when combined, produce his or her preferred outcome.

Yet, the choice of the interpreter is not and cannot be totally free. It is limited primarily by the constraining effect of normativity. For normative propositions cannot by definition be totally open-ended and reversible, *pace* the pundits of New Haven, without losing all their directive power, ie, being emptied of all their normative substance and quality. And saying that they comprise a penumbra of indeterminacy (corresponding to the interpreter's margin of free choice) posits the existence of a clearly determinable (or rather determined) hard core of meaning, surrounded by this penumbra that prolongs and completes it, thus projecting different shades of the total meaning of the text. These shades are variations on (and of), a common theme (the hard core), however radically different they may

[2] *Shorter Oxford English Dictionary on Historical Principles*, 6th edn, vol 2 (Oxford, Oxford University Press, 2007) 3445.

[3] H Kelsen, *The Pure Theory of Law*, 2nd edn (trans Max Knight) (Berkeley, CA, University of California Press, 1970) 351.

be from each other, and have to echo it, albeit with a distinctive touch, to remain within its orbit, and thus within the circle of possible interpretations. In other words, it is the hard core that sets the outer-limit of logically possible interpretations of the rule or normative proposition.

How large or narrow the penumbra or margin of indeterminacy is, depends on the linguistic and normative consistency of the text. The more tightly woven and thickly textured it is, the more the 'decision-map' is covered, or to use a more familiar analogy, the more the picture is detailed and finely grained (ie, the more pixels it has), the less 'degrees of freedom' the interpreter will have in terms of probability theory.

Are there other constraints on the interpreter's freedom of choice within the penumbra of indeterminacy? One may think in this respect of the principles or 'rules of interpretation' of Articles 31 and 32 of the Vienna Convention on the Law of Treaties (VCLT), on the legal nature and import of which – whether they are real legal norms or mere logical axioms – the doctrinal debate continues.

As far as their formal legal status, these rules are clearly legal norms. They feature in a general open convention to which an overwhelming majority of the international community of States are parties, and which are recognised, even by the few States that remain outside the Convention, as well as by major international judicial and adjudicative bodies (eg, the International Court of Justice (ICJ) and the World Trade Organization Apellate Body) as a codification of general customary rules.

By contrast, it is more difficult to gauge their exact legal import. They play a useful role by introducing a modicum of order in the intellectual operation of interpretation, earmarking the main elements to be taken into consideration during this operation, and proposing a logical way of proceeding (*une démarche*) going from the text to be interpreted, to its internal context (within the same instrument), to the external context (relevant elements outside the instrument).

But these 'rules', as codified in VCLT Articles 31 and 32, present a serious danger of being taken for what they are not, namely an iron framework and railroad that rigidly encase and direct the intellectual operation of interpretation, automatically and inexorably, to the proper final interpretation. This image is a grossly distorting caricature, as neither the list of elements is necessarily exhaustive, nor the proposed sequence a rigid series of watertight exclusivist stages, in the sense that if one provides an answer, the interpreter is precluded from going further into any of the following, hierarchically ordered ones.

Interpretation is a holistic operation; it is a purposive conscious activity that cannot be reduced to a clock-like mechanical movement or a mathematical equation that automatically provides the right answer. There will always be an essential spring or parameter missing, indispensable for such a mechanism or equation to function, namely human judgement, which is a constitutive part of any decision or other purposive action.

The rules of interpretation, as codified in VCLT Articles 31 and 32, play a positive, persuasively directive, moderate role, by providing a logical, though standard, road map, with signposts flagging out major stations. But they are far from being determinative of the final interpretation: that which led some authors to question their legal nature.

If the principles of interpretation are moderately directive and non-determinative of the final outcome, ie, that the interpreter's freedom of choice within the penumbra of indeterminacy is quite large as long as he or she does not overstep its outer limit, the question arises: what other factors or considerations may bear on the interpreter's choice, and more particularly those that may favour and/or motivate his choice of an 'evolutionary interpretation'? A question better tackled in the conclusions, after we have examined in some detail the meaning and significance of 'evolutionary interpretation' in diverse contexts.

3. Interpretation as an 'authoritative rendition'. The interpretative operation yields a final product, also referred to as 'interpretation', consisting of a rendering of the meaning of the interpreted text. In evaluating the 'authority' of this final product, ie, the weight it carries in the eyes of the community, particularly the legal community, one has to keep in mind the interpreter's status and position: interpretation by whom and for what purpose? Is it the interpretation by an author of a scientific book? Of a legal adviser to a foreign ministry during the negotiations of a bilateral treaty or of a general codification convention? Of a legal counsel of a State party to an actual or probable dispute? Of a judge in deciding a case before him or her? Of a collective organ, to clarify the meaning of a norm of its own creation, or of its constitution, or with a view to its application to a particular situation?

The 'authoritativeness' (its degree or lack of it) of each of these interpretations, is a function of the above-mentioned factors: the status of the interpreter and the objective of the interpretative operation that determines its orientation. Thus, for gauging this quality in the above-mentioned types of interpretation, we must start by excluding all those put forward *pro domo*, ie, in the course of the interpreter's defence of his own interests or position, or of those he represents. These interpretations may have indirect legal effects (recognition, admission, estoppel, etc). But they do not, and cannot carry an iota of 'authoritativeness', because they are indelibly tainted by a suspicion of subjective bias that annihilates the possibility of them being seen as an unimpeachable reference.

This means that 'authoritativeness' is different from legal effect (though it can subsume it). Some of the above interpretations have a direct legal effect, attached to the formal position of the interpreter within the legal system, such as interpretation by the legislature, which enjoys the *erga omnes* binding force of law, or interpretations in judicial decisions, which are *res judicata* (in French they are significantly described as having *l'autorité de la chose jugée*), ie, a relative legally binding force, limited to the parties (but an indirect *erga omnes* binding force, in the form of an injunction of non-obstruction vis-a-vis third parties). And this, whether or not one considers that the interpretation in question is correct.

The legal effect is attached to the formal status of the interpreter and the legal nature of the instrument carrying the interpretation. In other words, it is the instrument as such, given its source and nature within the legal system, that imparts to the substantive interpretation it carries (regardless of the soundness or unsoundness of this interpretation) the quality of direct and final pronouncement of the law on its subject matter, thus deploying all the legal effects that law attaches to such a pronouncement. In a way, one can describe such a pronouncement as enjoying or having the 'authority' of law. But 'authority' would then be in the general and formal sense of 'due respect to law', owing to its mandatory and enforceable character, ie, to its binding and ultimately coercive power. This is obviously very different from the intrinsic 'authority' or 'authoritativeness' and persuasive power of the substantive interpretation itself.

What makes for this intrinsic quality that begets recognition, respect and deference, even beyond the logical persuasiveness of the reasoning; so that even if one disagrees with some of it, one feels, with awe, the discomfort of having to challenge a well-nigh impregnable presumption of verity?

My short answer, after long reflection, is borrowed from the Ancient Greek philosophy concept of 'place' (*topos*, *locus* in latin). The answer can be found in two such places: the first is the site of an 'oracle', the second of a 'temple'. Neither of them is seen by the community as the lawgiver, but both are considered the conduits and voices that express the law: in one via a person (be it mythified), because of its foreknowledge and foresight; the other via an institution, because of its collective wisdom and sacralised function.

When I delivered the General Course at The Hague Academy in 1987, just after stepping down from the bench of the ICJ as judge ad hoc, I gave the following example, passing from Greek antiquity to present-day actuality:

> What I say here on the podium of the Academy (which is situated in the park of the Peace Palace, the seat of the ICJ) is the opinion of a professor, a doctrinal opinion. At best, and exceptionally, if the professor is very well known and generally considered as an 'authority' in the field, like Anzilotti in his time, his lectures would correspond to the description of the third phrase of article 38(1)(d), of the Statute of the ICJ, as part of 'the teachings of the most highly qualified publicists of the various nations'. If the same lecturer crosses the alley in the park to get to the Great Hall of Justice, 20 meters afar, and sits on the bench of the ICJ, his pronouncements, whether as part of collective decisions, or even as separate or dissenting opinions, correspond to the description of the first two phrases of article 38(1)(d): 'Subject to the provisions of Article 59, judicial decisions'.[4]

The text of Article 38(1)(d) makes a clear distinction between its two components, pointing out the direct legal effects of judicial decisions, owing to their institutional character, ie, their formal position within the legal system: legal effects having

[4] This is a free translation with slight elaboration of the original French text. See G Abi-Saab, 'Cours général de droit international public' (1987) 207 *Recueil des cours de l'académie de droit international* 9.

precedence over their secondary clarificatory effect at one remove, as general interpretations of the law. By contrast, the writings of publicists are deprived of any direct legal effect, because of their personal character; and their mention in second place suggests, consciously or unconsciously a certain hierarchy, perhaps because people in general tend to give greater credence to institutions than to persons, however wise and learned they may be. But both diffuse this intangible quality of intrinsic authority.

******

Where does 'evolutionary interpretation' fit in this spectrum of meanings of 'interpretation', and how does the adjective 'evolutionary' qualify or modify these meanings in the different branches and regimes of international law?

That is largely the subject of this book.

PART I

Evolutionary Interpretation in International Law Generally

3

Evolutionary Interpretation in International Law: Some Short and Less than Trail-Blazing Reflections

ROBERT KOLB

I. Introduction

Much has been written on the topic of evolutionary interpretation in international law, mainly in the context of treaty law.[1] The concept is however wider and can be used for the interpretation of every type of legal act embodying a normative message. What are the main constitutive elements of evolutionary interpretation? As we know, for the formation of customary international law, the International Court of Justice requires two elements: practice and legal opinion.[2] In evolutionary interpretation, there are also two constituent elements: time and change. It is because human existence is stretched in time that things change. And when things change, the understanding of them can attach either to the past or to the present. A choice must be made if there is a conflict of meaning at these two ends of the equation. If the choice goes to the past, the interpretation is historical; if it goes to the present, it is evolutionary. Neither method is absolute. It depends on the circumstances which one of these methods and ends prevails. Moreover, it is possible to combine both and to have part historical and part evolutionary elements. Viewed from this perspective, evolutionary interpretation is a sort of doctrine *rebus sic stantibus* writ small, and therefore much more acceptable than the potentially destabilising old-styled *clausula*. It allows the treaty interpreter to channel less significant changes and to smoothly adapt the law; and thereby to avoid calling its big and threatening brother, codified and somewhat tamed now under Article 62 of the Vienna Convention on the Law of Treaties, onto the scene

[1] See the monograph of E Bjorge, *The Evolutionary Interpretation of Treaties* (Oxford, Oxford University Press, 2014).

[2] *North Sea Continental Shelf (Federal Republic of Germany v Denmark; Federal Republic of Germany v Netherlands) (Judgment)* [1969] ICJ Rep 3, 41 ff.

to undo legal regimes leaning too much to forms of historical petrification or ossification.[3] In summary, evolutionary interpretation concerns all shades of casting away or reducing the original or historical meaning attached to a norm in favour of a contemporary reading, ie, a reading and understanding at the time the interpretation is undertaken.

If evolutionary interpretation concerns time and change, some more precision can be given to the elements that can change in time. Indeed, there is no limit to possible changes. All elements of a norm, its normative text and its normative surroundings, can change. Let us look more closely into that issue.

II. Endogenous Changes

Some changes are of an *endogenous nature*: they concern the text of a norm (when there is one), ie, the sense to be given to its terms.[4] These changes can touch upon three types of circumstances. First, the change can be factual: thus, the term 'telegraph' can be interpreted in an evolutionary way and under teleological considerations to encompass the formerly unknown 'telephone',[5] because the *ratio legis* of a provision can and should be equally applied to both devices. By the same token, the term 'aerial engines' does not mean the same thing in the age of the zeppelin as it does in modern times, with airplanes and also space shuttles able to fly in the atmosphere. Second, the change can be legal: for example, in ancient parlance, ie, in the eighteenth century, the term 'embargo' often meant requisition,[6] while, among other things, it now means the severance of commerce or the deliveries of goods to a territory. A correct interpretation of the term in an old treaty may result in preference being given to the original meaning. But only an evolutionary understanding of the term allows us to spot the problem of time and change. Third, there can be mixed evolutions of fact and law, ie, situations where the two elements are so closely intertwined that they cannot be reasonably disentangled. Thus, 'maritime areas under national jurisdiction' formerly meant the territorial waters. Under the current law of the sea, these areas would probably have to be extended to all areas where the coastal State has sovereign rights, in particular to the 200-mile exclusive economic zone.[7] Similarly, the 'parties to a

[3] Vienna Convention on the Law of Treaties (adopted 23 May 1969) 1155 *United Nations Treaty Series* 331.

[4] Editors' note: It should be noted that the terms 'endogenous' and 'exogenous' are used somewhat differently from those in G Distefano, 'L'interprétation évolutive de la norme internationale' (2011) 115 *Revue générale de droit international public* 373.

[5] See *Netherlands v Nedlloyd*, District Court of Rotterdam (1977) 74 *International Law Reports* 212, 215–16.

[6] S Neff, *War and the Law of Nations, A General History* (Cambridge, Cambridge University Press, 2005) 110.

[7] On the exclusive economic zone, see Arts 55 ff in the United Nations Convention on the Law of the Sea (adopted 10 December 1982) 1833 *United Nations Treaty Series* 3.

dispute' under Chapter VI of the United Nations Charter were in the past mainly, if not solely, States. In its newer practice, the United Nations Security Council gives a much broader and thus evolutionary interpretation to the relevant provisions, encompassing non-State entities and addressing recommendations of all types to them.[8] As a last example under this category, the term 'war munition' has possibly to be read differently in the context of an 1899 treaty and in the Second World War, due to technological advance, so that even 'fuel' could now perhaps be included in that category.[9]

III. Exogenous Changes

The other type of change is of an *exogenous* nature: it concerns the environmental surroundings of the normative proposition.[10] Here again, the change can bear on three circumstances. First, it can concern social circumstances, ie, evolutions in society, in its values and perspectives. Thus, the social understanding of 'family' or the acceptance of 'sexual orientation' have changed radically in recent decades, at least in mainstream occidental societies. Under human rights law, rights of homosexuals have undergone a significant shift;[11] and the notion of family is not any more limited to the traditional nuclear family. This evolutionary interpretation is not due to the change of the sense of words contained in the treaties. Rather, it is concerned with the change of the underlying social conceptions. Second, change can concern legal circumstances. Thus, in the law relating to the maintenance of peace, the term 'war' was abandoned in favour of the legally broader term 'force' in the *jus contra bellum* and 'armed conflict' in the *jus in bello*.[12] This means that the older treaties on the law of war, in particular The Hague Regulations of 1899 and 1907, containing the term 'war', are today interpreted as referring to an 'armed conflict'. Thus, the issue is turned to a pure question of fact as to the existence of hostilities or other hostile relationships, and not to the existence of a state of war triggered by some declaration of war as an act of will. Third, there are mixed changes of circumstances, where once more the factual and legal elements are hard to disaggregate. Thus, the concept of 'continental shelf' in the law of the sea has evolved over time. Initially, it referred to a physical and geological reality; at the

[8] See L Borlini, *Il Consiglio di sicurezza e gli indivudui* (Milan, Giuffrè, 2018) 75 ff.

[9] This was one holding in *NV Bataafsche Petroleum Maatschappij* (1956) Court of Appeal of Singapore, 23 *International Law Reports* 810, 846–47 (Whitton J).

[10] In legal theory, some authors consider that these normative surroundings (the social environment to which the norms refer) are part of the norm, calling that part of it the 'Normbereich': *cf* F Müller and R Christensen, *Juristische Methodik*, 8th edn, I (Berlin, Duncker & Humblot, 2002) 34 ff.

[11] eg, under Art 12 of the European Convention on Human Rights, 'right to marry' *cf* W Schabas, *The European Convention on Human Rights, A Commentary* (Oxford, Oxford University Press, 2015) 528 ff.

[12] See for the *jus in bello* R Kolb and R Hyde, *An Introduction to the International Law of Armed Conflicts* (Oxford, Hart Publishing, 2008) 75–76; and for the *jus ad bellum*, R Kolb, *International Law on the Maintenance of Peace* (Cheltenham, Edward Elgar Publishing, 2018) 62, 329–30.

time of the adoption of the United Nations Convention on the Law of the Sea[13] it had become, legally speaking, merely a space measured on the basis of its distance from a baseline (usually 200 nautical miles).[14]

IV. Conclusion

All elements of the norm and its environment can change and thus trigger changes in the point of reference of interpretation. Whether one wants to extend the concept of evolutionary interpretation to all these situations or rather coin different terms for the different hypotheses advanced here is a matter of discussion. There are arguments in favour of a single term, which avoids over-complicating the subject matter without a corresponding legal gain. It stands to reason that the situations giving rise to evolutionary interpretation are often linked with teleological or purpose-oriented interpretation, in particular in the shade of the doctrine of 'emergent purpose', ie, a purpose which unfold in time, adapts and evolves.[15] There is also a link to extensive interpretation; hence there are critics of evolutionary interpretation in some circles, for example, in Switzerland concerning the European Court of Human Rights. It must however be stressed that there is no intrinsic link between an evolutionary interpretation and an expansive interpretation. Thus, if the now creeping sovereignism and nationalism, if not blunt unilateralism, continue to develop, eventually a restrictive form of evolutionary interpretation will emerge. In the same way, in the Middle Ages, the evolving statute law of the towns led to a progressively restrictive interpretation of the common law of the day, ie, the Roman-Canon law.[16] No shift in understanding of anything carries with it the end of history. The evolution catches the evolutionary itself. Sometimes the interpreter can credibly attach the evolutionary interpretation to the intent or presumed intent of the lawgiver. The lawgiver can indeed have contemplated that the law ought to evolve and the terms used to be interpreted in an evolutionary matrix. In other situations that reference to some original intention for instilling evolution may become fictional. Then, the judge (if there is one) may devise a change in the meaning, since in international law the parties have given to that judge the mandate to settle their dispute. This includes the implied authority to interpret the law, and hence also to interpret it sensibly.

At the close of these very brief reflections, it is useful to emphasise that evolutionary interpretation is inevitable. Certainly, the question of its reasonable balance

[13] Above n 7.

[14] See Art 76, para 1, United Nations Convention on the Law of the Sea, above n 7. Compare the 'natural prolongation' approach in the *North Sea Continental Shelf* cases, above n 2, 29 ff.

[15] G Fitzmaurice, 'The Law and Procedure of the International Court of Justice 1951–4: Treaty Interpretation and Other Treaty Points' (1957) 33 *British Year Book of International Law* 203, 208.

[16] See M Sbriccoli, *L'interpretazione dello Statuto* (Milan, Giuffrè, 1969).

and use remains eternally with us. But its necessity as a tool to keep the law at the height of contemporary expectations, *tenir le droit à la hauteur du temps*, cannot be doubted. This is after all what the legislator and even the people demand: not some outdated, formal and inapplicable interpretation attached to the eternal past, but a working interpretation for the conditions of our times. Law is a practical instrument for our life together. Purely 'originalist' meanings[17] are beside the point. They must be at least completed and blended with the eternal return of the 'now'. The end of history is an illusion – since the end itself constantly ends.

[17] The debate on this issue in the US Supreme Court is known. An originalist approach is advocated in A Scalia, *A Matter of Interpretation, Federal Courts and the Law* (Princeton, NJ, Princeton University Press, 1997). An evolutionary approach is advocated in S Bryer, *Making Our Democracy Work, A Judge's View* (New York, Vintage Books, 2010). On this question, see G Huscroft and B Miller, *The Challenge of Originalism: Theories of Constitutional Interpretation* (Cambridge, Cambridge University Press, 2011); C Wolfe, *How to Read the Constitution: Originalism, Constitutional Interpretation, and Judicial Power* (Lanham, MD, Rowman & Littlefield Publishers, 1996); DL Hudson, *The Handy Supreme Court Answer Book* (Detroit, MI, Visible Ink Press, 2008).

4

An Interpreter's Guide to Static and Evolutive Interpretations: Solving Intertemporal Problems According to the VCLT

CHRISTIAN DJEFFAL

I. Introduction: Untying the Gordian Knot

The oldest questions never really get old. Take the intertemporal question of treaty interpretation as an example. Is an evolutive interpretation of international treaties possible and if so, how are interpreters to choose between static and dynamic interpretations? The earliest modern writers of international law like Hugo Grotius or Alberico Gentile already addressed the question whether and how treaties can be updated.[1] And they used examples stemming mostly from antiquity but also from their own times. The very same questions are still being discussed by coevals while the stream of publications, conferences and lectures never seems to dry up. On the contrary, scholars always disagree on how to answer these questions. What's more, the disagreement between scholars is almost perfectly symmetrical. Hugo Grotius, for example was generally in favour of an evolutive meaning of terms,[2] while Emer de Vattel found that international law generally had to be interpreted statically as it was construed at the time of the conclusion of the treaty.[3] To illustrate the problem, both authors used the very same example from antiquity between Rome and Carthage, in which the term 'allies' was under question. Was this term to be

[1] For an overview over the treatment of this question see C Djeffal, *Static and Evolutive Treaty Interpretation: A Functional Reconstruction* (Cambridge, Cambridge University Press, 2016) 48–54.

[2] H Grotius, *On the Law of War and Peace: Translation of the Edition of 1646 by Francis Kelsey, [De jure belli ac pacis libri tres]*, vol 2 (Oxford, Clarendon Press; Humphrey Milford 1925) 409 (original 276, Book II, chapter XVI, II).

[3] E de Vattel, *The Law of Nations or the Principles of Natural Law: Translation of the Edition of 1758 [Droit des gens ou principes de la loi naturelle, appliqués à la conduite et aux affaires des Nations et des Souverains]* (Fenwick trans) vol 3 (Buffalo, NY, WS Hein 1995; [1916]) 212 (Book 2, chapter 17, mn 297).

understood as referring to alliances at the time of the conclusion of the treaty or as dynamic reference to contemporaneous alliances? It is very telling that Grotius interpreted this statically and gave preference to the time of the conclusion of the treaty,[4] even though he generally favoured evolutive interpretations. The opposite is true for Vattel.[5] He found that the term ought to be interpreted dynamically, although his residual position was to interpret treaties statically. International legal scholarship has disagreed on this question ever since. One aspect that sets today's international legal scholarship apart from the times of Grotius and Vattel is the rule of interpretation contained in Articles 31 and 32 of the Vienna Convention on the Law of Treaties (VCLT). The early modern writers and their heirs had to 'find' the rules of interpretation and what they found varied greatly over the course of history.[6] In contrast, the VCLT provides for a rule of interpretation that is agreed among the majority of States and that is considered to have the status of customary international law. This rule was designed to solve all interpretative issues including the intertemporal question of treaty interpretation. Is it really capable of doing that?

This chapter aims to show how the intertemporal question can be solved according to the VCLT rule of interpretation. In order to show this, the chapter will not limit itself to looking at the wording and the apparent elements of the rule of interpretation. To assist the interpreter to solve questions of interpretation, the chapter will explain what process lies behind the rule of treaty interpretation, ie, how the process of treaty interpretation as envisaged by the VCLT actually works. The chapter will then address how this process works in practice in different international legal regimes. It will conclude by assessing the pros and cons of the VCLT rule of treaty interpretation in order to deepen the understanding and the awareness of interpreters.[7]

The first step is, however, to arrive at a clear definition of the intertemporal question. It is assumed here that an intertemporal question occurs if there are or can be competing views on whether the meaning of the text of a treaty has changed over time. If the meaning of the text has changed, this is called an evolutive interpretation.[8] If the meaning of the text has not changed, this is called static interpretation. The necessary element to identify an evolutive interpretation is the

[4] Grotius, above n 2, 415 (original 278, Book II, chapter XVII, XIII).

[5] Vattel, above n 3, 217–18 (Book 2, chapter 17, mn 309).

[6] DJ Bederman, *Classical Canons: Rhetoric, Classicism and Treaty Interpretation* (Aldershot, Ashgate, 2001).

[7] This chapter denotes Arts 31 and 32 VCLT as rule of interpretation since Art 31 is called 'general rule of interpretation'. As will be shown, Arts 31 and 32 form an integrated system of interpretation which is best denoted as rule and not as rules of interpretation.

[8] The term 'evolutive' is synonymously used with other terms like 'evolutionary' or 'dynamic interpretation'. There is no apparent difference between those terms. See also the reflection by E Bjorge, *The Evolutionary Interpretation of Treaties* (Oxford, Oxford University Press, 2014). While the International Court of Justice (ICJ) uses the term 'evolutionary' when talking about the nature of a specific text, the European Court of Human Rights (ECtHR) calls changes of interpretation 'evolutive interpretation'.

change in its meaning. It is true that changes in interpretation are by far not the only interesting aspects of treaty interpretation in international law. They entail, however, specific problems and questions and are to be dealt with separately from broader categories such as activist interpretation.[9]

The question of how to deal with intertemporal problems of treaty interpretation was addressed on several occasions in the process of preparing the VCLT.[10] Despite several attempts to solve the problem directly or indirectly, the result of the discussions at the International Law Commission (ILC), the Sixth Committee of the General Assembly of the United Nations and Vienna Conference was always the same: to leave intertemporal questions to the ordinary process of treaty interpretation. After the conclusion of the VCLT, the prestigious Institut de droit international took another shot at the question and discussed it at length. The result, however, was again to leave the question open.[11] But how can interpreters deal with such questions using the VCLT rule of interpretation? This chapter argues that interpreters can use the VCLT more effectively if they have a deeper knowledge about how the VCLT actually works. Therefore, the chapter will first describe how the VCLT rule of interpretation can be applied to intertemporal questions irrespective of the context (II. 'A Pure VCLT Solution'). In a second step, the chapter will explain, how the VCLT rule of interpretation is to be used in different contexts such as before different courts and tribunals (III. 'Solutions in Practice'). The last part will highlight the upside and downside of such a system of interpretation in order to inform interpreters how to use it most effectively (IV. 'Conclusion and Theoretical Underpinnings'). This chapter aims to show that the VCLT rule of interpretation is a special method working well if applied to complex problems. The complexity of intertemporal problems might make it very complicated to solve them. They might look at a complex multitude of threads and knots. But cutting right through the issues, like cutting through the Gordian knot, it is important to reflect on how to use this tool.

II. A Pure VCLT Solution

Behind the words of Articles 31 and 32 VCLT lies a certain understanding of the process of interpretation. This part of the chapter will show how this process works and how it helps interpreters to solve issues of interpretation. To understand the VCLT rule of interpretation, one must take note of the difference between means and results of interpretation. Interpreters can use certain means to arrive at certain

[9] P Mahoney, 'Judicial Activism and Judicial Self-Restraint in the European Court of Human Rights: Two Sides of the Same Coin' (1990) 11 *Human Rights Law Journal* 57.

[10] Djeffal, *Static and Evolutive Treaty Interpretation*, above n 1, 158–62.

[11] M Sørensen, 'Le problème dit du droit intertemporel dans l'ordre international' (1973) 55 *Annuaire de l'Institut du droit international* 1.

results of interpretation. The ultimate obligation in Article 31 paragraph 1 is to take certain interpretative techniques into account. This points more to the means of interpretation and the process of using them than to any particular interpretative result.

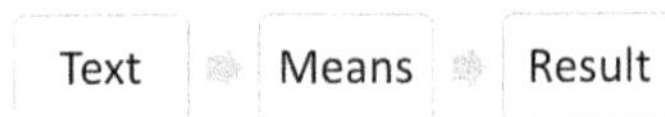

According to this way of thinking, an evolutive interpretation is an interpretative result in which the meaning of a treaty has changed over time. In contrast, a static interpretation is an interpretation that has remained stable over time. Neither static nor evolutive interpretation is a means in the sense that it influences the process of interpretation. While it might be possible to invent and contend that there are means of interpretation like principles and presumptions pointing in one or the other direction, they have not found their way into the VCLT. This is of the utmost importance since it means that the VCLT is more focused on the process than on the actual result. The importance of this distinction also flows from the legally binding nature of the rule of interpretation. As the rule of interpretation is enshrined in a treaty, it is mandatory for interpreters. If the rule of interpretation directly impacts upon interpretative results, its legal nature would have grave consequences. Yet, the distinction between means and results also entails the possibility that interpreters are forced to use certain means of interpretation while having discretion regarding the interpretative result.[12]

A. Collecting Arguments

The VCLT rule of interpretation obliges the interpreter to 'take into account' certain means of interpretation. Article 31 VCLT refers to several means that are best described as interpretative techniques of interpretation. Techniques are categories of arguments that are typically used in legal interpretation. Article 31 paragraph 1 contains three techniques: the text of the treaty; its context and its object; and purpose. While Article 31 paragraph 2 describes what is to be understood by context, paragraph 3 mentions three more categories, namely: subsequent agreements; subsequent practice; and the relevant rules of international law. The interpreter is obliged to check for all arguments falling under the techniques mentioned. But what does it mean to look for arguments that fall under the techniques mentioned in Article 31 of the VCLT? It means checking each category to see whether there are arguments pointing towards a solution. What does the text of the treaty exactly say? Are there hints or arguments to be taken from

[12] For the fact that the VCLT leaves discretion to the interpreter see G Nolte, 'Introduction' in G Nolte (ed), *Treaties and Subsequent Practice* (Oxford, Oxford University Press, 2013) 2.

the context? Is there any subsequent practice in the application of the treaty? This approach is very different from other approaches the VCLT could have employed, such as the use of maxims, principles or presumptions.

Techniques are abstract in nature and not necessarily tied to any static or dynamic result. Interpretative techniques are open when it comes to intertemporal questions. So, the object and purpose can be used in favour of a dynamic solution and the parties' subsequent practice could reinforce an unchanging meaning of the treaty. On the contrary, the text and context can point towards a changing meaning. If an interpreter checks for possible arguments that fall under certain interpretative techniques, she or he must be open to the possibility that those arguments go either way. It is important to enquire into each of the techniques to have an overview of all arguments relevant for the resolution of the dispute. It is possible that more than one argument will fall under a certain category. Take, for example, the context of the treaty. One part of the treaty might indicate the static nature of the treaty while another clause indicates an evolutive reading.

B. Argumentative Weight and Balancing

If an argument falls under one of the categories in Article 31, it has to be taken into consideration. The interpreter must qualify the argument and assess its argumentative weight. This means that there is no natural hierarchy between arguments falling under Article 31. The interpreter must assess the argumentative weight in view of how they apply to the interpretative question. Is the ordinary meaning of the text clearly pointing in one direction or is it rather open and vague? Is there a subsequent agreement clearly addressing the issue? In answering such questions, the interpreter will assess whether she or he is dealing with strong or weak arguments. The techniques in Article 31 are not the only means of treaty interpretation within the scope of the VCLT rule of interpretation. They carry, however, more argumentative weight than the supplementary means of interpretation in Article 32. Those supplementary means, including the preparatory works of the treaty and the circumstances of its conclusion, can be resorted to according to Article 32 when certain requirements are met. This is the case when the interpretation according to Article 31 of the VCLT left the meaning obscure and ambiguous or leads to a result which is manifestly absurd or unreasonable. Considering that this test is itself subject to interpretation, the hierarchy inserted between Article 31 and Article 32 effectively results in more argumentative weight for arguments falling under the techniques mentioned in Article 31.[13]

[13] This goes in line with the ILC commentary which stresses that supplementary means should not be 'alternative autonomous means' but mere aids to the interpretation: ILC, 'Final Draft Articles on the Law of Treaties, Report of the International Law Commission on the Work of its 18th Session' (4 May to 19 July 1966) UN Doc A/CN.4/191 223. A difference in argumentative weight is also assumed in a slightly different terminology by W Karl, *Vertrag und spaetere Praxis im Voelkerrecht: zum Einfluß der Praxis auf Inhalt und Bestand völkerrechtlicher Verträge* (Berlin, Springer, 1983) 187.

The arguments based on techniques mentioned in Article 31 count more. They have more weight. If they point in one direction, they cannot be dethroned by supplementary means of interpretation. As a result, the *travaux préparatoires* carry by definition less argumentative weight. This result was very controversial at the Vienna Conference, especially when the US delegation introduced a different proposal.[14] This proposal failed. Therefore, interpreters will have to primarily resort to arguments derived from Article 31 VCLT. If they all point in one direction, supplementary means of interpretation do not need to be mentioned. This also applies to the *travaux préparatoires*.

When arguments deriving from the interpretative techniques are collected and weighed, they have to be balanced against each other. The fourth ILC Special Rapporteur on the Law of Treaties described the process of balancing as follows: there was no

> intention of creating an order in which a series of rules should be successively applied; the Commission's idea was rather that of a crucible in which all the elements of interpretation would be mixed: The result of that mixing would be the correct interpretation.[15]

This crucible metaphor is still popular today. The quote suggests that Waldock understood the process of interpretation as an integrated argumentative process rather than a mechanical application of specific rules. All arguments are to be seen together, when they point in different directions; they are to be weighed and balanced against each other. In particular in contentious cases, not only arguments will be balanced. There will be choice between solutions. There could be a contended meaning A and an alternative meaning B and the interpretative techniques could either point towards one or the other meaning. Intertemporal questions deal by definition with alternatives that relate to different points in time. The interpreter will finally have to decide among the different alternatives.

C. Summary

Sir Humphrey Waldock, the fourth Special Rapporteur on treaty interpretation, has famously described process as a 'single combined operation'.[16] All the techniques laid out in Article 31 are to be assessed. Arguments derived from the techniques take precedence over other supplementary means of interpretation. All arguments are to be put in a crucible. That means they are to be weighed and balanced against each other. Mostly, arguments will be made regarding two or more possible meanings of the treaty. Ultimately, the interpreter will have to decide the issue. The result

[14] See C Djeffal, 'Establishing the Argumentative DNA of International Law: A Cubistic View on the Rule of Treaty Interpretation and its Underlying Legal Culture(s)' (2014) 5 *Transnational Legal Theory* 128, 131–37.

[15] Comment by Special Rapporteur Waldock, ILC, above n 13, 267 para 96.

[16] ibid, 219.

of the argumentative exercise also functions as justification of that decision. This single combined operation also works in the case of intertemporal questions. First all techniques have to be considered, arguments for a static or dynamic solution have to be collected. The interpreter has to weigh the arguments against each other and balance them. In this process, neither the *travaux préparatoires* nor the circumstances at the conclusions of the treaty nor any other supplementary means carry as much weight as compared to the other rules of interpretation. Finally, the interpreter will have to decide between a static and dynamic meaning. It goes beyond the confines of this chapter to prove that the means of interpretation will have an effective impact on decision-making, but there are indications that this is the case.[17] Either way, it has long been recognised that the function of rules of interpretation also extend to ex post facto justifications. This means that an interpretation in accordance with the VCLT rule of interpretation also serves as effective justification for the answers to intertemporal questions.

III. Solutions in Practice

The VCLT rule of interpretation not only prescribes a certain process of interpretation, it also offers flexibility to interpreters on several levels. The whole set-up as a single combined operation leaves discretion to the interpreter considering interpretative results. Yet, an analysis of the practice of international courts and tribunals has shown that this flexibility also extends to other levels. Considering that the rules of interpretation have to operate in very different situations, such as different treaties, different categories of parties to the dispute and different dispute resolution mechanisms, this flexibility is crucial if the rule of interpretation is aimed to operate as a rule of general international law. This flexibility has allowed the coining of specific approaches in specific fora. Courts and tribunals for example have taken particular stances on how to interpret the VCLT when describing the goal of interpretation. It is of the utmost importance for interpreters dealing with intertemporal questions to be aware of these differences.

A. General Approach

While the VCLT rule of interpretation is characterised by openness towards the goals of interpretation and the intertemporal question, this is not necessarily the case for all interpreters using the VCLT. Interpreters often take a certain stance towards the intertemporal question favouring static or dynamic results.

[17] Y Shereshevsky and T Noah, 'Does Exposure to Preparatory Work Affect Treaty Interpretation? An Experimental Study on International Law Students and Experts' (2017) 28 *European Journal of International Law* 1287.

The European Court for example first established its general approach in *Tyrer*, in which it stated that the 'Court must also recall that the Convention is a living instrument which, as the Commission rightly stressed, must be interpreted in the light of present-day conditions'.[18] The Court continued to use this phrase whenever intertemporal questions were at issue.[19] This general approach signals that evolutive interpretations are possible and the treaty is to be viewed as developing over time. The International Court of Justice (ICJ) also allows for evolutive interpretations if they can be traced back to the 'presumed intentions' of the parties to the treaty.[20] The International Law Commission has re-emphasised this solution. Whereas the European Court of Human Rights (ECtHR) approach allows for arguments in a more objective manner, the ICJ's approach requires the interpreter to – at least rhetorically – put her- or himself in the shoes of the parties at the time of the conclusion of the treaty. When addressing an actor or speaking on behalf of an institution, the interpreter will have to pay homage to the general approach. This is even though both courts apply the VCLT rule of interpretation. The jurisprudence of the ICJ also shows how the general approach towards evolutive interpretation can shift significantly over time.[21] In a first phase, the ICJ openly found that evolutive interpretations were not possible but in effect interpreted in an evolutive manner on several occasions. In the course of the Namibia cases, the Court changed its general intertemporal stance and generally focused on the intentions of the parties as the focal point. In later case law, the Court broadened its approach even more, now looking into the presumed intentions. This process of opening up in relation to evolutive interpretation shows that the general stance on evolutive interpretation can differ substantially and arguments as well as justifications have to be mindful of that.

B. Interpretative Techniques

Another aspect that can differ depending on the forum is the exact interpretation of the interpretative techniques. The VCLT rule is enshrined in a treaty, and like any treaty it is open to interpretation. But how to interpret a rule of interpretation. Attempts to interpret a rule of interpretation run the risk of ending up in endless argumentative circles. In the absence of a general authority dealing with these issues, there is no choice but to allow authoritative decision-makers to choose one interpretation. These choices can put wider or narrower limits on interpretative techniques and at least indirectly impact the solution of intertemporal questions.

[18] *Tyrer v United Kingdom* Series A no 26 (1978) 2 EHRR 1, para 31.

[19] *Bayatyan v Armenia* [GC] (2012) 54 EHRR 15, para 102; *Christine Goodwin v the United Kingdom* [GC], (2002) 35 EHRR 18 and 35 EHRR 447, para 75.

[20] *Dispute Regarding Navigational and Related Rights (Costa Rica v Nicaragua) (Judgment)* [2009] ICJ Rep 213, 242, para 64.

[21] For a full discussion of the respective case law see Djeffal, *Static and Evolutive Treaty Interpretation*, above n 1, 234–51.

One question is how the object and purpose ought to be ascertained.[22] One could contend that the object and purpose of a treaty is to be derived from the preparatory works as a reflection of the intentions of the parties. Yet, one could also analyse the text of the treaty using the ordinary means of treaty interpretation excluding the object and purpose. One could also look at all possible evidence, even if it is not linked to the treaty. Differing opinions might have an impact on the answer to intertemporal questions.

Take, for example, the use of subsequent practice as established in different fora.[23] The WTO Appellate Body has famously required a practice that is concordant, common and consistent.[24] In contrast other courts such as the ICJ and the ECtHR have accepted subsequent practice even in the absence of universal practice. The ICJ, for example, referred to several resolutions of the UN General Assembly none of which was accepted unanimously.[25] The ECtHR also found that the practice of the 'great majority'[26] would be sufficient to count as subsequent practice and held in one case that practice not shared by four States out of 47 could amount to subsequent practice.[27]

C. Examples

There are multiple examples of courts and tribunals dealing with intertemporal questions.[28] In *Rantsev* the ECtHR, for example, had to deal with the question of whether human trafficking of persons would fall under Article 4 of the European Convention on Human Rights (ECHR) and amounted to slavery or forced and compulsory labour.[29] In these situations, humans are forced to go abroad and then find themselves in vulnerable situations and open to exploitation. The Court found that trafficking was a new phenomenon that did not fall under the meaning of the text of the treaty. Nevertheless, the Court found that new treaties in international law called for a change of interpretation. While the technique of looking at the

[22] R Bernhardt, 'Evolutive Treaty Interpretation, Especially of the European Convention on Human Rights' (1999) 42 *German Yearbook of International Law* 11, 24 ff; I Buffard and K Zemanek, 'The "Object and Purpose" of a Treaty: An Enigma?' (1998) 3 *Austrian Review of International and European Law* 311.

[23] See also Part II of this book.

[24] For an in-depth inquiry, see G Nolte, 'Subsequent Practice as a Means of Interpretation in the Jurisprudence of the WTO Appellate Body' in E Cannizzaro (ed), *The Law of Treaties Beyond the Vienna Convention* (Oxford, Oxford University Press, 2011).

[25] *Legal Consequences of the Construction of a Wall in the Occupied Palestinian Territory* (Advisory Opinion) [2004] ICJ Rep 136, 149, para 27.

[26] *Sigidur A Sigurjónsson v Iceland* Series A no 264 (1993) 16 EHRR 462, para 35.

[27] *Bayatyan v Armenia*, above n 19, para 103.

[28] M Fitzmaurice, 'Dynamic (Evolutive) Interpretation of Treaties, Part I' (2008) 21 *Hague Yearbook of International Law* 101; M Fitzmaurice, 'Dynamic (Evolutive) Interpretation of Treaties, Part II' (2010) 22 *Hague Yearbook of International Law* 3.

[29] *Rantsev v Cyprus and Russia* (2010) 51 EHRR 1, paras 272–82.

ordinary meaning of the text of a treaty favoured a static reading, the relevant rules as provided for in Article 31(3)(c) called for an evolutive interpretation. After weighing and balancing the arguments, the Court found that the law had changed. In *Stummer*, the Court had to decide whether the fact that detainees were excluded from a national pension scheme would amount to a violation and whether the exception in Article 4(3)(a) of the ECHR should be interpreted more restrictively.[30] The Court acknowledged the evolution in international law and the fact that the meaning of the text had not changed. It also found that subsequent practice of the parties to the treaty was not conclusive. In essence, it ruled that the treaty was to be interpreted statically in this instance. The ICJ had to deal with an intertemporal question in *Navigational and Related Rights*. The question was whether the term '*commercio*' in a treaty between Costa Rica and Nicaragua, which was concluded in 1858 would include the phenomenon of tourism. The Court relied on the ordinary meaning of the terms of the treaty, which it found to be generic and open to change, with the context and the object and purpose of the treaty all pointing towards an evolutive interpretation. Therefore, the Court decided in favour of an evolutive solution.[31] These examples show how collecting, assessing and balancing arguments in order to solve intertemporal issues works in practice.

IV. Conclusion and Theoretical Underpinnings

This chapter will conclude by highlighting reasons that lie behind the use of the VCLT rule of interpretation. When relying on the VCLT rule of interpretation, interpreters must also know and understand the implications, whether positive or negative, of using such an instrument.

A. Organising International Legal Argumentation

One consequence of using the VCLT rule is that it provokes interpreters to express legal arguments clearly and openly. Interpreters are forced to enquire into different legal aspects of the problem and to explain how they weigh and balance those arguments against each other. In contrast, the VCLT has no specific preference whether to interpret statically or evolutively. The consequence of this is that intertemporal disputes are looked at from a legal point of view in an all-encompassing manner. This cuts off any easy solution relying on presumptions or principles.

[30] *Stummer v Austria* [GC] (2012) 54 EHRR 11, paras 112–34.

[31] *Navigational and Related Rights*, above n 20, 240 ff, para 56 ff. See analysis by M Dawidowicz, 'The Effect of the Passage of Time on the Interpretation of Treaties: Some Reflections on *Costa Rica v Nicaragua*' (2011) 24 *Leiden Journal of International Law* 201.

Nonetheless, the rule of interpretation helps to gather a more complete picture of all available arguments. And it puts more pressure on the interpreter to justify her or his decision. The ability to organise international legal argument may be one of the major reasons for the success of the VCLT rule of interpretation. Today, the VCLT rule of interpretation is generally applied by courts and tribunals.[32] It has attained something of the status of an international grammar or language of treaty interpretation in international law. It helps in the exchange of arguments irrespective of ideological or professional assumptions. It can effectively bridge the gap between what some international lawyers conceive to be interpretative communities.[33]

B. Providing Flexibility to Interpreters

The fact that the VCLT provides flexibility for interpreters on different levels is another advantage. As was shown above, the interpreter has discretion concerning the interpretative result. Since the VCLT leaves the goal of interpretation as well as some interpretative issues regarding its interpretation open, authoritative bodies can agree on how to use this flexibility to coin an approach that fits the circumstances in which they operate. This can be done in the context of an overall framework that applies to all actors in international law. Important dispute resolution mechanisms have the authority to establish their own approaches to the interpretation of Articles 31 and 32 VCLT and even to define a fitting goal of interpretation. The ICJ recently adopted its own approach of looking into the assumed intentions of the parties. Extensive comparisons have shown the differences regarding certain techniques or aspects of the VCLT. These differences provide evidence of the adaptability of the VCLT rule of interpretation. Despite the great attention on theories of fragmentation and self-contained regimes it is hardly appreciated that the VCLT rule of interpretation provides for a general framework while staying adaptable and changeable in order to account for the specificity of certain treaties or dispute resolution mechanisms. Interpreters have to be aware of this flexibility. A successful communication requires them to frame their arguments in accordance with the context in which they are operating.

C. Cutting Off Unnecessary Doctrinal Debates

The fact that the VCLT works very well is also grounded in the absence of any unnecessary content that is doctrinal in nature and does not add anything to the

[32] R Gardiner, 'The Vienna Convention Rules on Treaty Interpretation' in DB Hollis (ed), *The Oxford Guide to Treaties* (Oxford, Oxford University Press, 2012).

[33] M Waibel, 'Interpretive Communities in International Law' in A Bianchi, D Peat and M Windsor (eds), *Interpretation in International Law* (Oxford, Oxford University Press, 2015).

process of treaty interpretation. This might be considered as one of the advantages of collective efforts in multi-stakeholder groups like the ILC, uniting practitioners in different functions, and academics having a rich body of experience, which is also complemented by its exchanges with the Sixth Committee of the UN General Assembly. If collective efforts work, they produce lean and workable solutions like the VCLT rule of interpretation and cut off everything that is not vital and necessary. The final result of the ILC is a lot leaner than the first proposals. It sets forth a single combined operation relying on interpretative techniques. It did not engage in the collection of maxims of interpretation, nor did it have a difficult system of presumptions or material principles. It even left the goal of interpretation open and did not take a stance in the discussion between the subjective and objective nature of interpretation. The fact that the VCLT came up with a well-defined process on how to solve interpretative issues with interpretative techniques and a process of balancing and weighing makes the old debate about the subjective or objective nature of interpretation practically superfluous. While it is possible for decision-makers to communicate a stance in that regard, the process of interpretation can well work without mentioning the objective or subjective nature of the process of treaty interpretation. It is therefore possible to avoid the difficult questions and intricacies in the debate between objective and subjective interpretation that have existed for a long time.[34] While this does not exclude any theoretical criticism of the VCLT rule of interpretation as a method, it ensures that the rule works in practice. It makes life easier for interpreters and has the potential to improve argumentative processes.

D. No Direct Normative Guidance

The absence of any normative guidance makes it easier and not harder to solve intertemporal questions. Intertemporal questions necessarily involve change. This can call into question the original interpretation of the text in issue, but it can also call into question the normative preference expressed in the rule of interpretation. In such cases, the rule of interpretation would become part of the problem instead of being part of the solution. The fact that the VCLT rule of interpretation contains so little direct normative preferences is most probably no coincidence. There is a very good historical explanation for applying this to the rule of interpretation as a whole as well as to its specific stance on intertemporal openness. During the time leading up to the conclusion of the VCLT in 1969, international relations were characterised by several divides in the international community. There was a divide between the Western and the Eastern blocs. The ideological differences between liberalism and communism were significant and the normative ideas

[34] M Koskenniemi, *From Apology to Utopia: The Structure of International Legal Argument* (Cambridge, Cambridge University Press, 2005) 344–45.

regarding many topics of international law were very different. There was also a growing community of decolonised and non-aligned States that were confronted with a corpus of international law they had never negotiated and to which they could only accede. To even try to come up with a set of material norms guiding the content of all international legal treaties could only have been considered an impossible endeavour. In a time of uncertainty about how the world order would develop, it must have been even harder to agree on a clear-cut rule for solving future disputes arising out of intertemporal questions.

The history of treaty interpretation has shown that it is hard to predict and solve all interpretative issues using one set of interpretative means. It is even harder to come up with one set of interpretative means that can deal with all possible future intertemporal issues. This might also be the reason why collective bodies never came up with a clear-cut solution and left the intertemporal question for the ordinary process of treaty interpretation, while scholars have been trying to come up with solutions for some 400 years now. If a group contains enough experiences and perspectives, the normative preferences cancel each other out and they cannot agree on a solution. This does not mean that the VCLT is simply an agreement to disagree or to put it more elegantly a 'disagreement reduced to writing'.[35] On the contrary, there might be a lot of wisdom in leaving the intertemporal question open if there is a general way on how to deal with interpretative questions. The VCLT rule of interpretation provides for such a process. It is a general agreement on how to deal with questions of interpretation that works very well with intertemporal questions. It is a framework for exchanging legal arguments that sparks conversation and discourse. It is a flexible tool allowing for adoption in very different circumstances without losing its overall function. And it might be one of the best shots at fulfilling the promises of general international law. One day, there might be another and better system of interpretation. But until this day comes, it is crucial for interpreters to know how to deal with the VCLT rule of interpretation and to understand how and why it works. The practice of international courts and tribunals has shown that interpreters using the rule can solve intertemporal disputes successfully. This proves that the VCLT rule of interpretation is a tool that effectively aids the peaceful settlement of disputes on the international plane.

[35] P Allott, 'The Concept of International Law' (1999) 10 *European Journal of International Law* 31, 34.

5

Time Present and Time Past: The Intention of the Parties and the Evolutionary Interpretation of Treaties

EIRIK BJORGE

I. The Vienna Rules and the Intention of the Parties

This chapter concerns the marrying of past and present in treaty interpretation. The main argument is that the evolutionary interpretation of treaties in the present is to be considered to be closely connected with the intention of the parties, which by definition will lie in the past. This first, and most important, part sets out the general background to treaty interpretation in international law, and shows that this general background is as pertinent to the evolutionary interpretation of treaties as to any other type of interpretation. The second part asks whether the evolutionary interpretation of treaties has retrospective effect. The third part analyses the importance of subsequent agreements and subsequent practice. The fourth part concludes this chapter.

Treaty interpretation in accordance with the rules codified in Articles 31–32 of the Vienna Convention on the Law of Treaties (VCLT)[1] aims to establish the parties' consent in relation to a set of facts. Put another way, the object of treaty interpretation is establishing the common intention of the parties. It is hardly surprising that Articles 31–32 of the VCLT make no mention of the common intention of the parties.[2] After all, the common intention of the parties is the very thing to be to be discerned in interpreting a treaty.[3] This is the approach taken

[1] Vienna Convention on the Law of Treaties (adopted 23 May 1969) 1155 *United Nations Treaty Series* 331.

[2] The only mention of intention, or any variation thereof, is in Art 31(4): 'A special meaning shall be given to a term if it is established that the parties so intended'.

[3] C de Visscher, *Problèmes d'interprétation judiciaire en droit international public* (Paris, Pedone, 1963) 50.

by international courts and tribunals. Two recent examples bear this out. First, in *Delimitation of the Border between the State of Eritrea and the Federal Democratic Republic of Ethiopia* the Ethiopia–Eritrea Boundary Commission observed that, in interpreting the treaties before it:

> The Commission will apply the general rule that a treaty is to be interpreted in good faith in accordance with the ordinary meaning to be given to the terms of the treaty in their context and in the light of its object and purpose. Each of these elements guides the interpreter in establishing what the Parties actually intended, or their 'common will'.[4]

Second, in *Rhine Chlorides* the tribunal observed that the general rule of interpretation codified in Article 31 of the VCLT:

> Should be viewed as forming an integral whole, the constituent elements of which cannot be separated. Moreover, this is the approach that is now taken by the International Court of Justice and by certain international arbitral bodies. All the elements of the general rule of interpretation provide the basis for establishing the common will and intention of the parties by objective and rational means.[5]

Four important principles can be drawn from the arbitral determinations in *Ethiopia–Eritrea Border* and *Rhine Chlorides*. First, the principle referred to above, that the parties' intention is what has to be to be established, and, as that is the outcome of the interpretative process, it would have been nonsensical for intention to have been listed as one of the means of interpretation that provides the basis for its own establishment.[6] Second, the intention to be established is the *common* intention of the parties, not the intention of only one or some of them.[7] Third, and following logically from the second, the means of interpretation to be relied on for the establishment of the parties' intention are 'objective and rational'[8] means. They are not meant to provide glimpses of the subjective will or inner minds of the treaty parties or the treaty makers but rather to be objective and rational externalisations and allow an interpreter to deduce intention.[9] Fourth, the intention of the parties is necessarily a presumed or objectivised intention of the parties.[10]

Plainly, interpretation, even of seemingly clear words in the treaty, on the basis of an objective means of interpretation, and in pursuit of an objectivised intention of the parties, will be a subjective undertaking because rational minds can and will disagree on the correct interpretation.[11] To give one example, the clearly drafted

[4] 'Delimitation of the Border between Eritrea and Ethiopia' (2002) 130 *International Law Reports* 1, 34, para 3.4, citing the tribunal chaired by Lord McNair in *Argentina/Chile Frontier Case ('Palena')* (1966) 38 *International Law Reports* 10, 89.

[5] *Rhine Chlorides (Netherlands/France)* (2004) 144 *International Law Reports* 259, 293, para 62.

[6] See de Visscher, above n 3, 50.

[7] Sir Humphrey Waldock, *International Law Commission Yearbook* (1964/II) 58, para 21.

[8] *Rhine Chlorides*, above n 5, 293, para 62.

[9] F Capotorti, *Convenzione di Vienna sul diritto dei trattati* (Milan, CEDAM, 1969) 36.

[10] G Gaja, 'Trattati internazionali' (1999) 15 *Digesto delle discipline pubblicistiche* 344, 355–56.

[11] See, eg, RE Fife, 'Les techniques interprétatives non juridictionnelles de la norme internationale' (2011) 115 *Revue générale de droit international public* 367; C Miles, 'Indeterminacy' in J d'Aspremont

provision in Article 77(4) of the United Nations Convention on the Law of the Sea,[12] provides that the coastal State exercises over the continental shelf sovereign rights for the purpose of exploring it and exploiting its natural resources and where

> [t]he natural resources referred to in this Part consist of the mineral and other non-living resources of the seabed and subsoil together with living organisms belonging to sedentary species, that is to say, organisms which, at the harvestable stage, either are immobile on or under the seabed or are unable to move except in constant physical contact with the seabed or the subsoil.

The aspect of this provision on sedentary species has been interpreted very differently by writers and States.[13] (What of crabs that can move long distances and climb over rocks and into tubs and in other ways lift themselves up from the seabed or subsoil? What of lobsters? What of shells that can jump by clapping?) These interpretations have been subjective in that, for example, that they have taken colour from the broader interests of the State at issue, and the broader views of the interpreter. Nevertheless, all of those who have put these varying interpretations forward have argued their interpretation was the correct one on the basis of the same means of interpretation. There is, in other words, agreement on what are the means of interpretation on which the interpretation will be based.

This approach, where the means of interpretation set out in Articles 31–32 of the VCLT are relied upon with a view to establishing an objectivised intention, is the correct approach to take to understand the concept of the evolutionary interpretation of treaties.[14]

The International Law Commission (ILC) took this approach in its draft conclusions on subsequent agreements and subsequent practice on the interpretation of treaties. Conclusion 8, entitled 'Interpretation of treaty terms as capable of evolving over time', states:

> Subsequent agreements and subsequent practice under articles 31 and 32 may assist in determining whether or not the presumed intention of the parties upon the conclusion of the treaty was to give a term used a meaning which is capable of evolving over time.

and S Singh (eds), *Fundamental Concepts for International Law: The Construction of a Discipline* (Cheltenham, Edward Elgar Publishing, 2019).

[12] United Nations Convention on the Law of the Sea (adopted 10 December 1982) 1833 *United Nations Treaty Series* 3; the provision is based on Art 2(4) of the 1958 Geneva Convention on the Continental Shelf (adopted 29 April 1958) 499 *United Nations Treaty Series* 311.

[13] See, eg, FV Garcia Amador, *The Exploitation and Conservation of the Resources of the Sea: A Study of Contemporary International Law*, 2nd edn (Leiden, Sijthoff, 1959) 128; MM Whiteman, 'Conference on the Law of the Sea: Convention on the Continental Shelf' (1958) 52 *American Journal of International Law* 629, 639; O de Ferron, *Le droit international de la mer II* (Geneva, Droz, 1960) 210; C Rousseau (1963) 67 *Revue générale de droit international public* 133, 134; F de Hartingh, 'La position française à l'égard de la Convention de Genève sur le plateau continental' (1965) 11 *Annuaire français de droit international* 725, 731.

[14] This is the argument made in E Bjorge, *The Evolutionary Interpretation of Treaties* (Oxford, Oxford University Press, 2014); and E Bjorge, 'The Convention as a Living Instrument: Rooted in the Past, Looking to the Future' (2016) 36 *Human Rights Law Journal* (Colloquy in Honour of Judge Paul Mahoney) 243.

In its Commentary the ILC observes that:

> Draft conclusion 8, by using the phrase 'presumed intention', refers to the intention of the parties as determined through the application of the various means of interpretation that are recognized in articles 31 and 32 … [A]lthough interpretation must seek to identify the intention of the parties, this must be done by the interpreter on the basis of the means of interpretation that are available at the time of the act of interpretation and that include subsequent agreements and subsequent practice of parties to the treaty. The interpreter thus has to answer the question of whether parties can be presumed to have intended, upon the conclusion of the treaty, to give a term used a meaning that is capable of evolving over time.[15]

It follows from this approach to treaty interpretation that evolutionary interpretation, in Marceau's words, 'fait partie intégrante de chacune des règles d'interprétation de la [convention de Vienne] et s'avère plutôt une expression imprécise qui viserait plusieurs règles traditionnelles'.[16] That means that the evolutionary interpretation of treaties, being based on the rules of interpretation codified in the VCLT, operates like other types of interpretation to establish the intention of the parties.[17] But it also means, as Nolte has observed, that the draft conclusion aims to instil in those who interpret treaties a measure of caution when they decide whether in a specific case to adopt an evolutionary interpretation or not.[18]

International courts and tribunals also take this approach. The case law of the International Court of Justice (ICJ), in judgments such as *Namibia*,[19] *Aegean Sea*,[20] and *Navigational Rights*,[21] is well known, and will not be repeated here.[22] The ICJ's approach to treaty interpretation is to establish the 'intention of its authors as reflected by the text of the treaty and the other relevant factors in terms of interpretation'.[23] That approach, the ICJ explained in relation to generic treaty terms in *Navigational Rights*

> is founded on the idea that, where the parties have used generic terms in a treaty, the parties necessarily having been aware that the meaning of the terms was likely to evolve over time, and where the treaty has been entered into for a very long period or is 'of continuing duration', the parties must be presumed, as a general rule, to have intended those terms to have an evolving meaning.[24]

[15] ILC Report 2018, A/73/10, 67, para 9.

[16] G Marceau, 'L'interprétation évolutive par le juge OMC: sophisme ou nécessité?' (2018) 122 *Revue générale de droit international public* 23, 50.

[17] ibid, 48–49.

[18] G Nolte, 'Treaties and their Practice' (2018) 392 *Collected Courses of the Hague Academy of International Law* 206, 360.

[19] *Legal Consequences for States of the Continued Presence of South Africa in Namibia (South West Africa) notwithstanding Security Council Resolution 276 (1970)* (Advisory Opinion) [1971] ICJ Rep 16, 35.

[20] *Aegean Sea Continental Shelf (Greece v Turkey)* (Judgment) [1978] ICJ Rep 3.

[21] *Dispute Regarding Navigational and Related Rights (Costa Rica v Nicaragua)* (Judgment) [2009] ICJ Rep 213.

[22] Bjorge, *The Evolutionary Interpretation of Treaties*, above n 14, 76–83.

[23] *Navigational and Related Rights*, above n 21, 237, para 48.

[24] ibid, 243, para 66.

The Grand Chamber of the European Court of Human Rights (European Court) exemplified this approach in *Magyar Helsinki Bizottság v Hungary*.[25] The case fleshes out the well-known approach of the European Court, set out in *Tyrer v United Kingdom*, according to which the European Convention on Human Rights (ECHR) is a 'living instrument' to be 'interpreted in the light of present-day conditions'.[26] That case concerned the interpretation of Article 10(1) of the ECHR: 'Everyone has the right to freedom of expression. This right shall include freedom to hold opinions and to receive and impart information and ideas without interference by public authority and regardless of frontiers'.[27]

A non-governmental organisation, Magyar Helsinki Bizottság (the Hungarian Helsinki Committee), had sought information concerning the work of an ex officio defence counsel, which the Hungarian authorities had classified as personal data that was not subject to disclosure under Hungarian law. The Grand Chamber concluded that, in the circumstances of the case, Article 10(1) of the ECHR included a right to access to information.

The Grand Chamber began by noting that Article 10(1) provides that 'the right to freedom of expression … shall include the freedom to hold opinions and to receive and impart information and ideas without interference by a public authority'.[28] As a matter of broad contextual interpretation, it noted that compared with other international instruments, such as Article 19 of the International Covenant on Civil and Political Rights (ICCPR),[29] the provision does not in terms encompass a freedom to *seek* information.[30] But the question of whether the provision embodied a right to access to the requested information would, held the Court, necessitate 'a more general analysis of this provision in order to establish whether and to what extent it embodies a right of access to State-held information'.[31]

[25] *Magyar Helsinki Bizottság v Hungary* [GC] App no 18030/11 (ECtHR, 8 November 2016).

[26] *Tyrer v United Kingdom* (1978) 58 *International Law Reports* 339, 353. See Sir Nigel Rodley, '*Tyrer v United Kingdom*' in E Bjorge and C Miles (eds), *Landmark Cases in Public International Law* (Oxford, Hart Publishing, 2017) 325.

[27] Convention for the Protection of Human Rights and Fundamental Freedoms (European Convention on Human Rights) (adopted 4 November 1950) 213 *United Nations Treaty Series* 221.

[28] *Magyar Helsinki Bizottság v Hungary*, above n 25, para 117.

[29] International Covenant on Civil and Political Rights (adopted 16 December 1966) 999 *United Nations Treaty Series* 171.

[30] Such broad contextual interpretation is often adverted to by international courts and tribunals: *Air Services Agreement of 27 March 1946 (United States v France)* (1978) 54 *International Law Reports* 304, 334, paras 66–67; *Maffezini v Kingdom of Spain* (2000) 124 *International Law Reports* 1, 24, para 58; *Acquisition of Polish Nationality* (Advisory Opinion) [1923] Series B no 7, 14–15; *Interpretation of the Convention of 1919 concerning Employment of Women during the Night* (Advisory Opinion) [1932] Series A/B no 50, 381; *Affaire relative à l'or de la Banque nationale d'Albanie (Etats-Unis d'Amérique, France, Italie, Royaume-Uni)* (1953) 12 *Reports of International Arbitral Awards* 13, 48; *Ambatielos Claim (Greece, United Kingdom)* (1956) 12 *Reports of International Arbitral Awards* 83, 109; R Kolb, *Interprétation et création du droit international* (Brussels, Bruylant, 2006) 463.

[31] *Magyar Helsinki Bizottság v Hungary*, above n 25, para 117.

Referring to its previous jurisprudence, the Court emphasised that it would interpret the provision in accordance with Articles 31–33 of the VCLT,[32] adding that

> [r]egard must also be had to the fact that the context of the provision is a treaty for the effective protection of individual human rights and that the Convention must also be read as a whole, and interpreted in such a way as to promote internal consistency and harmony between its various provisions.[33]

The Court stressed that the question whether, in the absence of express reference to access to information in Article 10, an applicant's complaint that he or she was denied access 'can nevertheless be regarded as falling within the scope of this provision is a matter which has been the subject of gradual clarification in the Convention case-law over many years'.[34] Given the opportunity the Grand Chamber was afforded in *Magyar Helsinki Bizottság* to take stock of its case law, the Court found it 'useful to take a broader look at the question of the extent to which the right of access to information can be gleaned from Article 10'.[35]

It appeared from the *travaux préparatoires* that a previous version of what was to become Article 10 had contained the right to seek information: but there was no record of any discussions that led to this being omitted or any debate on the elements that constituted freedom of expression.[36] Against that background, the Court was not persuaded that any conclusive relevance could be attributed to the *travaux préparatoires*.[37] However, the drafting history of one of the later additional protocols to the Convention revealed 'a common understanding between the bodies and institutions of the Council of Europe that Article 10, paragraph 1 of the Convention, in its wording as originally drafted, could reasonably be considered as already comprising the "freedom to seek information"'.[38] The Court observed furthermore that

> in the great majority of the Contracting States, in fact in all the thirty-one States surveyed with one exception, the national legislation recognises a statutory right of access to information and/or official documents held by public authorities, as a self-standing right aimed at reinforcing transparency in the conduct of public affairs generally.[39]

[32] ibid, para 119.

[33] ibid, para 120. This is in line with *Mamatkulov and Askarov v Turkey* [GC] (2005) 41 EHRR 25 and 41 EHRR 494, para 111; and *Golder v United Kingdom (Pl)* Series A no 18 (1979) 1 EHRR 524, para 29 where the Court stated in relation to the VCLT that 'its Articles 31 to 33 enunciate in essence generally accepted principles of international law to which the Court has already referred on occasion. In this respect, for the interpretation of the European Convention account is to be taken of those Articles subject, where appropriate, to "any relevant rules of the organization" – the Council of Europe – within which it has been adopted (Article 5 of the Vienna Convention)'. See P Palchetti, 'Halfway between Fragmentation and Convergence: The Role of the Rules of the Organization in the Interpretation of Constituent Treaties' in M Andenas and E Bjorge (eds), *A Farewell to Fragmentation* (Cambridge, Cambridge University Press, 2015) 488.

[34] *Magyar Helsinki Bizottság v Hungary*, above n 25, para 127.

[35] ibid, para 133.

[36] ibid, para 135.

[37] ibid.

[38] ibid, para 136.

[39] ibid, para 139.

This is an exemplification of the European Court relying on the parties' subsequent practice so that it 'may assist in determining whether or not the presumed intention of the parties upon the conclusion of the treaty was to give a term used a meaning which is capable of evolving over time'.[40]

The Court was satisfied that a broad consensus existed among the Contracting States on the need to recognise the individual right at issue. This was confirmed, in the view of the Court, by recourse to other rules of international law, under Article 31(3)(c) of the VCLT, as a similar right was granted in Article 19 of the ICCPR and Article 19 of the United Nations Universal Declaration.[41] In relation to the former, United Nations bodies such as the Human Rights Committee had determined that the right of access to public interest data and documents was 'inherent in freedom of expression'.[42]

The Court referred to an 'evolving convergence as to the standards to be achieved' within the Contracting States,[43] and 'a perceptible evolution in favour of the recognition, under certain conditions, of a right to freedom of information as an inherent element of the freedom to receive and impart information enshrined in Article 10'.[44] In conclusion, there was, inherent in Article 10, a right or obligation which may arise, first, where disclosure of the information has been imposed by a judicial order which has gained legal force and, secondly, in circumstances where access to the information is instrumental for the individual's exercise of his or her right to freedom of expression, in particular 'the freedom to receive and impart information' and where its denial constitutes an interference with that right.[45]

The interpretative approach of the European Court in *Magyar Helsinki Bizottság* was put into context and explicated in more detail by Judge Sicilianos in his Concurring Opinion, which was joined by President Raimondi, and where it was pointed out that what the Concurring Opinion called

> the evolutive method of interpretation has been used by other international and national judicial bodies, including the International Court of Justice, the arbitral tribunals, the supreme courts of France, the United Kingdom, Germany, etc (see E Bjorge, *The Evolutionary Interpretation of Treaties*, Oxford, Oxford University Press, 2014, and *id*,

[40] Draft Conclusion 8 on subsequent agreements and subsequent practice; ILC Report 2018, A/73/10, 67.

[41] GA Res 217(III), 10 December 1948.

[42] *Magyar Helsinki Bizottság v Hungary*, above n 25, para 143. See *Ahmadou Sadio Diallo (Republic of Guinea v Democratic Republic of the Congo)* (Judgment) [2010] ICJ Rep 639, 664, para 66, where the ICJ held that 'it should ascribe great weight to the interpretation by this independent body that was established specifically to supervise the application of that treaty. The point here is to achieve the necessary clarity and the essential consistency of international law, as well as legal security, to which the individuals with guaranteed rights and the States obliged to comply with treaty obligations are entitled'. See also P Couvreur, *The International Court of Justice and the Effectiveness of International Law* (Leiden, Brill, 2017) 6–7.

[43] *Magyar Helsinki Bizottság v Hungary*, above n 25, para 150.

[44] ibid, para 151.

[45] ibid, para 156.

> 'The Convention as a Living Instrument Rooted in the Past, Looking to the Future', to appear in *Human Rights Law Journal*, 'Colloquy in Honour of Judge Paul Mahoney'). In other words, although the 'living instrument' doctrine has been emphasised by the Court, the resulting interpretative approach is not exclusively tied to the Convention (or to the other conventions and treaties for human-rights protection). It extends far beyond this context and is part of national and international judicial practice in respect of many other areas of international law, and even of law in general.[46]

Judge Sicilianos and President Raimondi made the point, secondly, that although the 'living instrument' doctrine and the underlying evolutionary method of interpretation may appear innovative, they are in reality 'in line with the presumed intention of the Contracting States'.[47] In conclusion Judge Sicilianos and President Raimondi cited the words of a former President of the Court on the relationship between the intention of the parties and evolution:

> To borrow the phrasing of a former President of the Court, Sir Humphrey Waldock … 'The meaning and content of the provisions of the Convention will be understood as intended to evolve in response to changes in legal or social concepts'.[48]

The approach taken by the European Court in *Magyar Helsinki Bizottság*, where the Court took the occasion to engage in what it termed a 'a general analysis'[49] of the interpretation of Article 10(1) of the ECHR, is well aligned with the approach taken by other international courts and tribunals, including the ICJ, and by the ILC.

II. Do Evolutionary Interpretations have Retrospective Effect?

This leads to the question whether, on the correct understanding, Article 10 always had that meaning or whether it received it only when the Court made its evolutionary interpretation in 2016. In other words, does the interpretation have

[46] Concurring Opinion Judge Sicilianos, joined by President Raimondi, para 4.

[47] ibid, para 5.

[48] ibid, para 5; H Waldock, 'The Evolution of Human Rights Concepts and the Application of the European Convention on Human Rights' in *Mélanges offerts à Paul Reuter – Le droit international: unité et diversité* (Paris, Pedone, 1981) 547; Bjorge, *The Evolutionary Interpretation of Treaties*, above n 14, 11–12. In his dissenting opinion, joined by Judge Kjølbro, Judge Spano took the view in para 16 that the Court had laid too much stress on the object and purpose of the ECHR: 'The principle requiring a practical and effective interpretation of the Convention, by reference to its object and purpose, is not an open invitation for the judges of this Court to elevate any positive development in the member States to the level of a binding international norm, thus limiting the States' sovereign and democratic rights. In other words, even though the Convention is a human-rights treaty it "must surely be wrong … to say that because of the importance of the object and purpose of human rights treaties this particular element of interpretation should take on greater importance when one is interpreting [such] treaties than when one is interpreting other types of treaty"' (see Bjorge, *The Evolutionary Interpretation of Treaties*, above n 14, 36).

[49] *Magyar Helsinki Bizottság v Hungary*, above n 25, para 117.

retrospective effect? The answer suggested in the ICJ jurisprudence and its predecessor's seems to be in the affirmative. The Permanent Court of International Justice in *German Minority Schools* emphasised that when it interpreted a treaty provision, then

> in accordance with the rules of law, the interpretation given by the Court to the terms of the Convention has retrospective effect – in the sense that the terms of the Convention must be held to have always borne the meaning placed upon them by this interpretation.[50]

The principle is, in the words of President Basdevant's *Dictionnaire de la terminologie du droit international*, that, in the interpretation of a convention, the convention 'doit être réputée avoir eu toujours le sens déterminé par cette interprétation'.[51]

The ICJ followed this approach in its *LaGrand* jurisprudence.[52] The ICJ in *LaGrand*[53] interpreted Article 41 of its statute[54] on the basis that 'the object and purpose of the Statute is to enable the Court to fulfil the functions provided for therein'.[55] A few years later in *Bosnian Genocide*, the Court observed that its determination in *LaGrand* as to the binding effect of orders regarding provisional measures was not to be read so as to suggest that provisional measures indicated before *LaGrand* were not binding, 'since in the [Judgment in *La Grand*] the Court did no more than give the provisions of the Statute the meaning and scope that they had possessed from the outset'.[56]

There is a connection here with the approach taken by the European Court in *Magyar Helsinki Bizottság*, which, in making its evolutionary interpretation, pointed out that it was no more than engaging in the 'gradual clarification in the Convention case-law over many years'.[57] In relation to that interpretation, the point is perhaps a fortiori as leading publicists had since the 1990s taken the view that a right to access to information did indeed inhere in Article 10(1).[58] The European Court was no more than catching up. If one views evolutionary interpretation as

[50] *Access to German Minority Schools in Upper Silesia* (Advisory Opinion) [1931] PCIJ Series A/B no 40, 19.

[51] J Basdevant, *Dictionnaire de la terminologie du droit international* (Paris, Sirey, 1960) 545. See also P Daillier, M Forteau and A Pellet, *Droit international public*, 8th edn (Paris, LGDJ, 2009) 276.

[52] *LaGrand (Germany v United States of America)* (Merits) [2001] ICJ Rep 466.

[53] ibid, 506, para 109. See C Miles, '*LaGrand*' in E Bjorge and C Miles (eds), *Landmark Cases in Public International Law* (Oxford, Hart Publishing, 2017).

[54] Statute of the International Court of Justice (adopted 26 June 1945) 892 *United Nations Treaty Series* 119.

[55] Couvreur, above n 42, 82. See also G Guillaume, 'Methods and Practice of Treaty Interpretation by the International Court of Justice' in G Sacerdoti, A Yanovich and J Bohanes (eds), *The WTO at Ten: The Contribution of the Dispute Settlement System* (Cambridge, Cambridge University Press, 2006) 469; Bjorge, *The Evolutionary Interpretation of Treaties*, above n 14, 116–17.

[56] *Application of the Convention on the Prevention and Punishment of the Crime of Genocide (Bosnia-Herzegovina v Serbia and Montenegro)* (Judgment) [2007] ICJ Rep 230, para 452.

[57] *Magyar Helsinki Bizottság v Hungary*, above n 25, para 127.

[58] See G Nolte, 'Die Herausforderung für das deutsche Recht der Akteneinsicht durch europäisches Verwaltungsrecht' (1999) 52 *Die öffentliche Verwaltung* 363, 369.

no more than the latest stage in a clarification which comes about by degrees and over time, and it is based on an intention of the parties 'which is, by definition, contemporaneous with the treaty's conclusion',[59] then it makes eminent sense to say that evolutionary interpretations must have retrospective effect.

III. Subsequent Agreements and Subsequent Practice of the Parties

Nolte has laid particularly strong emphasis on the importance of the subsequent agreements and subsequent practice of the parties in relation to treaty interpretation and to the evolutionary interpretation of treaties.[60] In his view,

> and contrary to widespread assumptions, the text of a treaty – in the sense of the 'ordinary' or a 'special' 'meaning of its terms' – is not, under Article 31, paragraph 1, a more important means of interpretation than its context or the object and purpose of a treaty.[61]

He points to the statement by the ILC in 1964, where it stated that:

> [T]he Commission's approach to treaty interpretation was on the basis that the text of the treaty must be presumed to be the authentic expression of the intention of the parties, … making the ordinary meaning of the terms, the context of the treaty, its objects and purposes, and the general rules of international law, together with authentic interpretations by the parties, the primary criteria for interpreting a treaty.[62]

Therefore, subsequent agreements between the parties and subsequent practice in the application of the treaty which establish the agreement of the parties possess, in his view, 'the same importance for the process of interpretation as the ordinary meaning of the terms of the treaty, the context of these terms, and the object and purpose of the treaty'.[63] He recognises, however, that there are limits to the importance of subsequent practice and agreements in the interpretative process. For example, he points out that 'international courts mostly begin their reasoning in a given case by analysing the ordinary meaning of the terms of the treaty', leaving the examination of State practice until later in the interpretative process.[64] I make two points in that regard.

First, the text of the treaty does enjoy primacy vis-à-vis the subsequent agreements and subsequent practice of the parties. This is because, in the words of the Special Rapporteur Sir Humphrey Waldock, 'the signed text is, with very few

[59] *Navigational and Related Rights*, above n 21, 242, para 63.
[60] Nolte, 'Treaties and their Practice', above n 18, 336–361.
[61] ibid, 336. *cf* I Sinclair, *The Vienna Convention on the Law of Treaties* (2nd edn, Manchester, MUP, 1984) 130.
[62] *ILC Yearbook* 1964 II, 204–5, para 15.
[63] Nolte, 'Treaties and their Practice', above n 18, 336.
[64] ibid, 337.

exceptions, the only and the most recent expression of the common will of the parties'.[65] Similarly, as the International Court has held in numerous judgments: 'Interpretation must be based above all upon the text of the treaty'.[66] Now the 'text of the treaty' is distinct from and broader than the notion of the 'terms' of the treaty. It must be correct, as the tribunal in *Rhine Chlorides* observed, that '[r]elying on the text does not mean relying solely, or mainly, on the ordinary meaning of the terms. Such a notion would effectively ignore the references to good faith, the context, and the object and purpose of the treaty'.[67] But it remains that the text of the treaty, and the means of interpretation which can be drawn from the text, are given pride of place as compared with the subsequent agreements and subsequent practice of the parties.

Second, and following from the first point, another limit on the importance of subsequent practice and agreements is set by the object and purpose of the treaty. Reuter summarised the most prominent means of interpretation when he observed that the purpose of treaty interpretation is 'to ascertain the intention of the parties by reference to the form, the final clauses and especially the object and purpose of the treaty'.[68] The importance of the object and purpose of the treaty as compared with subsequent practice and agreements was pointed out by the ICJ in *Whaling*.[69] There the Court held that the functions conferred by the International Convention for the Regulation of Whaling[70] on the International Whaling Commission 'have made the Convention an evolving instrument'.[71] But, at the same time, the Court stressed that while subsequent agreements, in the shape of amendments to the Schedule of the Convention, and subsequent practice, in the shape of recommendations by the Whaling Commission, might 'put an emphasis on one or the other objective pursued by the Convention', such subsequent practice or agreements 'cannot alter its object and purpose'.[72]

This means that, although they may well bleed into one another in the sense that the one may be drawn on in order to establish the other, the object and purpose of a treaty in some sense enjoys primacy vis-à-vis subsequent practice and agreements of the parties. It is inaccurate, therefore, to say that subsequent practice and agreements of the parties enjoy 'the same importance for the process

[65] *ILC Yearbook* 1964 II, 56; *ILC Yearbook* 1966 II, 220, citing (1950) 43 *Ann de l'Inst* 199.

[66] *Territorial Dispute (Libyan Arab Jamahiriya v Chad)* (Judgment) [1994] ICJ Rep 6, 22, para 41; *Maritime Delimitation and Territorial Questions between Qatar and Bahrain (Qatar v Bahrain)* (Jurisdiction and Admissibility) [1995] ICJ Rep 6, 18, para 33; *Legality of Use of Force (Serbia and Montenegro v Belgium)* (Preliminary Objections) [2004] ICJ Rep 279 318, para 100.

[67] *Rhine Chlorides*, above n 5, 293, para 63.

[68] P Reuter, *Introduction to the Law of Treaties* (J Mico and P Haggenmacher trans) London, Paul Kegan International, 1995) 24.

[69] *Whaling in the Antarctic (Australia v Japan: New Zealand intervening)* (Merits) [2014] ICJ Rep 226.

[70] International Convention for the Regulation of Whaling (adopted 2 December 1946) 161 *United Nations Treaty Series* 72.

[71] *Whaling in the Antarctic*, above n 69, 247, para 45.

[72] ibid, 251, para 56.

of interpretation as the ordinary meaning of the terms of the treaty, the context of these terms, and the object and purpose of the treaty'.[73]

IV. Conclusion

Kolb has observed in connection with evolutionary interpretation in international law that 'when things change, the understanding of them can attach either to the past or to the present'.[74] If, as has been argued in this chapter, the evolutionary interpretation of treaties in the present is considered to be closely connected with the intention of the parties, which by definition will lie in the past, then the only remaining tense is the future. TS Eliot was no doubt correct to observe, in *Burnt Norton*, that time future, too, will remain closely connected with the past:

> Time present and time past,
> Are both perhaps present in time future,
> And time future contained in time past.

[73] Nolte, 'Treaties and their Practice', above n 18, 336.
[74] R Kolb, 'Evolutionary Interpretation in International Law: Some Short and Less than Trail-Blazing Reflections', ch 3 in this book.

6

Using Intertemporal Linguistics to Resolve the Problem at the Origin and Core of the Evolutionary Interpretation Debate

JULIAN WYATT

While the topic of this chapter may appear out of place in an edited volume on 'evolutionary interpretation', intertemporal linguistics in fact drills down directly into the epicentre of the evolutionary interpretation debate. In this chapter, I will explain why we need to move beyond what has become a fragmented and confused discussion of evolutionary interpretation to the more refined problem of intertemporal linguistics (section I). I will then demonstrate that teachings from fields outside international law, principally linguistics, are required to resolve the entirely legal problem of how international adjudicators should interpret treaties through time (section II).

I. Why We Need to Move Beyond 'Evolutionary Interpretation' to 'Intertemporal Linguistics'

It is widely accepted that international law's evolutionary interpretation doctrine first came to prominence in paragraph 53 of the International Court of Justice's *Namibia* Advisory Opinion.[1] In that Advisory Opinion, as in the most important

[1] *Legal Consequences for States of the Continued Presence of South Africa in Namibia (South West Africa) notwithstanding Security Council Resolution 276 (1970)* (Advisory Opinion) [1971] ICJ Rep 16, 31–32, para 53. See, eg, B Stern, 'Interpretation in International Trade Law' in M Fitzmaurice, O Elias and P Merkouris (eds), *Treaty Interpretation and the Vienna Convention on the Law of Treaties: 30 Years On* (Leiden, Martinus Nijhoff Publishers, 2010) 120 ('This notion of concepts that are, by definition, evolutionary was first introduced, as we know, by the International Court of Justice (ICJ) in the *Namibia* case, decided in 1971').

previous instances in which a proto-evolutionary approach appears to have been advanced,[2] it was the interpretation of a treaty – the Covenant of the League of Nations[3] – that was at issue.[4] At its origin and at its core, the doctrine of evolutionary interpretation is – and always has been – a doctrine of evolutionary *treaty* interpretation.

That the doctrine of evolutionary treaty interpretation emerged as a counterpoint to the so-called principle of contemporaneity is a lesser known, but equally incontestable historical fact. The expression 'principle of contemporaneity' was first coined by Sir Gerald Fitzmaurice in 1957,[5] but the approach to the interpretation of treaties through time that it consecrated had already been strongly favoured in key international law texts ranging from the works of Wolff[6] and Vattel[7] to the main textbooks of the post-Second World War era.[8] This principle stood for, in the concise language used by Judge Spender in 1962 advisory proceedings of the Court, 'a general rule […] that words used in a treaty should be read as having the meaning they bore therein when it came into existence'.[9]

As is often the case, it was only after this accepted approach had been stated as a 'principle' and 'general rule', that attention turned to whether it should permit exceptions and ultimately whether there was any merit in the approach in the first place. Indeed, one should not lose sight of the fact that the famous paragraph 53 *Namibia* dictum itself introduced the 'by definition evolutionary' notion critical to the development of the doctrine as a qualification to the then dominant

[2] See, eg, '*The North Atlantic Coast Fisheries Case (Great Britain, United States)*, Grounds for the Dissent to the Award on Question V by Dr Luis M Drago' (1910) 9 *Reports of International Arbitral Awards* 203 (Permanent Court of Arbitration Arbitral Tribunal); DW Bowett, *United Nations Forces a Legal Study of United Nations Practice* (London, Stevens, 1964) 307–08.

[3] Treaty of Peace at Versailles 1919, Part I: Covenant of the League of Nations.

[4] *Legal Consequences for States of the Continued Presence of South Africa in Namibia (South West Africa)*, above n 1, 31, para 53.

[5] G Fitzmaurice, 'The Law and Procedure of the International Court of Justice 1951–4: Treaty Interpretation and Other Treaty Points' (1957) 33 *The British Yearbook of International Law* 203, 212 ('VI. Principle of Contemporaneity. The terms of a treaty must be interpreted according to the meaning which they possessed, or which would have been attributed to them, and in the light of current linguistic usage, at the time when the treaty was originally concluded.')

[6] C Wolff, *Jus naturae: Methodo scientifica pertractatum*, vol 6 (1746) 328 (Book VI, ch III, para 471: 'pacta interpretanda sunt secundum usum loquendi ejus temporis, quo condita fuerunt').

[7] E de Vattel, *Le droit des gens, ou Principes de la loi naturelle appliqués à la conduite et aux affaires des nations et des souverains*, vol I (J-P Aillaud, 1835) 464 (livre II, ch XVII, para 268: 'L'interprétation de tout Acte & de tout Traité doit donc se faire suivant des Règles certaines, propres à en déterminer le sens, tel qu'ont dû naturellement l'entendre les intéressés, lorsque l'Acte a été dressé & accepté').

[8] See, eg, C Rousseau, *Droit International Public* (Paris, Sirey, 1970) 282 ('It goes without saying that the interpreter must take into account the meaning of the words at the time of the conclusion of the treaty, because there is a presumption that this meaning has been adopted by its authors' (present author's translation)).

[9] *Certain Expenses of the United Nations (Article 17, paragraph 2, of the Charter)* (Advisory Opinion) Separate Opinion of Judge Sir Percy Spender [1962] ICJ Rep 182, 186–87.

static approach,[10] Judge Bedjaoui noting in his *Gabčíkovo–Nagymaros* Separate Opinion that *Namibia* was simply a 'special situation' in which the evolutionary approach was taken as an exception to the 'primary necessity of interpreting an instrument in accordance with the intentions of the parties at the time of its conclusion'.[11] Numerous modern-day scholarly texts addressing evolutionary interpretation directly contrast it with the principle of contemporaneity.[12]

Clearly, the evolutionary treaty interpretation doctrine began its life as an exception to the principle of contemporaneity and ultimately ended up as a counterpoint to it. Whereas the principle of contemporaneity requires interpreters to use the meaning of a treaty term it had when the treaty was concluded, the evolutionary treaty interpretation doctrine prefers the different meaning that a treaty term may end up having at the later time when the treaty falls to be interpreted or applied. At its core and essence, the evolutionary treaty interpretation doctrine constitutes a position on the issue of whether to use the original or later-emerging meaning of treaty terms subject to diachronic semantic change.[13]

However, evolutionary interpretation is rarely defined so narrowly, largely because it has come to be used so frequently in ways that go beyond this relatively confined question. Since the *Namibia* Advisory Opinion of 1971, the evolutionary interpretation doctrine has found expression as a justification for adjudicatory acts outside the scope of interpretation, including departing from existing case

[10] *Legal Consequences for States of the Continued Presence of South Africa in Namibia (South West Africa)*, above n 1, 31–32, para 53. ('Mindful as it is of the primary necessity of interpreting an instrument in accordance with the intentions of the parties at the time of its conclusion, the Court is bound to take into account the fact that the concepts embodied in Article 22 of the Covenant – "the strenuous conditions of the modern world" and "the well-being and development" of the peoples concerned – were not static, but were by definition evolutionary, as also, therefore, was the concept of the "sacred trust".')

[11] *Gabčíkovo-Nagymaros Project (Hungary v Slovakia)* (Judgment) Separate Opinion of Judge Bedjaoui [1997] ICJ Rep 120, 122–23, paras 9–10.

[12] See, eg, N Kontou, *The Termination and Revision of Treaties in the Light of New Customary International Law* (Oxford, Clarendon Press; Oxford University Press, 1994) 17; R Bernhardt, 'Evolutive Treaty Interpretation, Especially of the European Convention on Human Rights' (1999) 42 *German Yearbook of International Law* 11, 17; J Pauwelyn, *Conflict of Norms in Public International Law: How WTO Law Relates to Other Rules of International Law* (Cambridge, Cambridge University Press, 2003) 266; J Pauwelyn, 'The Nature of WTO Obligations' (2002) Jean Monnet Working Papers 30; H Van Gellecum, 'Environmental Law in the Context of Article 31(3)(C) of the Vienna Convention on the Law of Treaties: Reconciling Treaty Interpretation and Progressive Environmental Norms: The Pulp Mills Case and Beyond' [2012] SSRN eLibrary 14, papers.ssrn.com/sol3/papers.cfm?abstract_id=1989468; ST Helmersen, 'Evolutive Treaty Interpretation: Legality, Semantics and Distinctions' (2013) 6 *European Journal of Legal Studies* 127, 146; United Nations, 'Report of the International Law Commission, Fifty-Seventh Session' (2005) Supplement No 10 (A/60/10) 219–20, available at: untreaty.un.org/ilc/reports/2005/2005report.htm, paras 473, 479.

[13] See also: J Wyatt, 'An Original or Modern-Day Meaning for Treaty Terms? The Problem of Intertemporal Linguistics in the Case Law of International Courts and Tribunals' (University of Geneva, 2017) 259–399, available at: archive-ouverte.unige.ch/unige:102376; J Wyatt, *Intertemporal Linguistics in International Law* (Oxford, Hart Publishing, 2019), ch 3.

law,[14] introducing external norms as applicable law,[15] and even finding that States have impliedly modified the terms of their treaty.[16] Moreover, evolutionary interpretation has come to mean different things to international lawyers in different sub-fields of international law. Indeed, this volume bringing together international lawyers with specialised knowledge of different sub-fields of the discipline itself provides proof of how the rarely defined doctrine of evolutionary interpretation has come to take on so many different meanings.

Most significantly, a schism has developed between those who still see evolutionary interpretation as a principle of treaty interpretation, and others who see it as a jurisprudential philosophy favouring outcomes more in keeping with modern-day laws and values. Careful study of how the doctrine of evolutionary treaty interpretation has been invoked by international courts and tribunals reveals that there is a form of the doctrine – particularly prevalent in international case law relating to human rights and the environment – that is less worried about whether a treaty should be given its original or modern-day meaning, and more worried about what outcome the interpretation given will achieve.[17] While these two main forms of the doctrine may both be referred to as 'evolutionary (treaty) interpretation', they are fundamentally very different.

As comparative lawyers know very well, it is extremely difficult to meaningfully discuss the merits of a doctrine if that doctrine means different things to different people. Without any clarity about what the doctrine means or which form of it should be analysed, discussion is likely to go no further than mentions of how the doctrine has been invoked and where it might find its basis or justification. The competing notions of what evolutionary interpretation entails are so different that an investigation of the merits of the doctrine will require posing very distinct questions for each form of the doctrine. The merits of evolutionary treaty interpretation as a doctrine favouring the meaning of a treaty term at the time of its application (form A) can only be evaluated in contradistinction to the merits of a principle of interpretation favouring the meaning of a treaty term at the time of its conclusion. By contrast, the merits of evolutionary treaty interpretation as a doctrine justifying progressive adjudication (form B) can only be evaluated in the context of an assessment of the proper role of international adjudicators, especially when they are faced with the interpretation and application of a treaty that appears to be out of step with modern-day values.

No study – and certainly no paper – can purport to offer meaningful observations on two questions of such breadth and depth, so this chapter leaves the second question to other chapters in this volume and does not even purport to

[14] See, eg, *Stafford v The United Kingdom* [GC] (2002) 35 EHRR 1121, paras 68–69.

[15] See, eg, *Award in the Arbitration regarding the Iron Rhine ('Ijzeren Rijn') (Belgium v Netherlands)* (2005) 27 *Reports of International Arbitral Awards* 35, 72–75, paras 78–84.

[16] See, eg, *Öcalan v Turkey* [GC] (2003) 37 EHRR 238, para 198.

[17] See, Wyatt, 'An Original or Modern-Day Meaning for Treaty Terms?', above n 13, 213–57, ch 6; Wyatt, *Intertemporal Linguistics in International Law*, above n 13, ch 3.

address it. Instead, this chapter returns to the sense of the evolutionary treaty interpretation doctrine that dominated when the doctrine first emerged and deals uniquely with the first-mentioned task: the question of original or modern-day meaning.

Yet, with so much of the case law and literature dealing with a doctrine of evolutionary interpretation that purports to do much more than simply take a position on this question, the author cannot, in good conscience, speak of 'evolutionary interpretation' and instead must, in the finest Heideggerian tradition, adopt other, less-loaded language. Fortunately, there is no need to resort to neologisms in this instance because there is already a notion that raises the original and core question of evolutionary treaty interpretation without the extra baggage that the doctrine has acquired since the *Namibia* Opinion. The so-called 'problem of intertemporal linguistics' – introduced by the esteemed international jurist and expert on international dispute resolution, Shabtai Rosenne, in some regrettably too often ignored contributions to International Law Commission and Institut de droit international debates occurring at the time of the emergence of the evolutionary interpretation doctrine – specifically raises the narrower yet undeniably important question of how an interpreter should respond to the problem caused by changes in the meaning of treaty terms through time.[18]

The benefits of focusing on the problem of intertemporal linguistics instead of the doctrine of evolutionary interpretation are manifold. First, we avoid the confusion potentially generated by examining a *doctrine* understood in different ways and used for different purposes by focusing instead on a precise practical legal *problem* that can be defined independent of subjective value judgements. Second, we can also avoid the main difficulty inherent in an exploration of evolutionary interpretation *qua* progressive adjudication, namely of generally evaluating whether it is appropriate to give the international adjudicator an enhanced, law-updating role across structurally and practically very different sub-systems of international law. Third, with Rosenne's notion of intertemporal linguistics we can go beyond the unduly narrow question regarding the temporal aspect of Article 31(3)(c) of the Vienna Convention on the Law of Treaties (VCLT) to investigate whether international adjudicators should acknowledge all changes that have repercussions for the interpretation of treaty terms, whether those changes arise from the development of international law or from other developments such as those of a social, moral, economic or mere linguistic nature. And, fourth, because of how it is expressed, the notion of intertemporal linguistics gives us the added benefit of pointing to the link between interpretation and language and onwards to the field of linguistics, a field which is largely neglected by the international law community, but which the

[18] M Sørensen and Institut de droit international, 'Le problème dit du droit intertemporel dans l'ordre international, première partie' (1973) 80–81 (Observations of Shabtai Rosenne dated 10 July 1969, para 9). See also United Nations International Law Commission, *Yearbook of the International Law Commission*, vol 2 (United Nations, 1966) 95–96, para 7.

present author has found to be particularly fertile ground for developing a solution to the problem of how to interpret treaties through time.

II. Why International Adjudicators Should Use an Approach Inspired by the Field of Linguistics When Interpreting Treaties Through Time

In the somewhat traditional field of public international law, there will always be some unease about a foray into the external field of linguistics to resolve what is clearly a legal problem. Indeed, one might object that the issues posed by the consideration of the question of original or modern-day meaning of treaty terms is already complex enough without adding the somewhat abstruse concepts of linguistics into the mix.

The tools offered by the field of international law itself are, however, clearly inadequate to adequately resolve this problem. On matters of treaty interpretation, modern-day international lawyers still lean heavily on the interpretative rules in Articles 31–33 of the now 50-year-old VCLT,[19] rules which themselves openly neglected to take a position on the problem of intertemporal linguistics.[20]

Moreover, the intensification and diversification of international dispute settlement since the adoption of the VCLT has revealed its interpretative rules to be simply too flexible to offer any firm guidance to international adjudicators faced with a choice between the original or modern-day meaning of treaty terms. Because Articles 31–32 of the VCLT contain, as the result of a well-known compromise between different interpretative schools, a broad range of different and often competing interpretative considerations with scant hierarchy between them, interpreters 'applying' these rules can readily justify the outcome that they wish to reach, but are not told where they should start their enquiry or in which direction they should proceed.[21]

Back when third-party international dispute settlement remained a rarity and the corpus of international law was highly incomplete, international adjudicators needed rules and principles capable of justifying their 'greenfield' decisions. In today's more evolved system of international dispute settlement, sources of

[19] Vienna Convention on the Law of Treaties (adopted 23 May 1969) 1155 *United Nations Treaty Series* 331.

[20] See especially, United Nations Conference on the Law of Treaties, 'United Nations Conference on the Law of Treaties, First Session, Vienna, 26 March–24 May 1968 Official Records' (United Nations, 1968) 184 (Sir Humphrey Waldock [Expert Consultant], Thirty-third meeting – 22 April 1968, para 74); Wyatt, 'An Original or Modern-Day Meaning for Treaty Terms?', above n 13, 149–52, s 4.3; see also: Wyatt, *Intertemporal Linguistics in International Law*, above n 13, ch 5.

[21] I Sinclair, *The Vienna Convention on the Law of Treaties*, 2nd edn (Manchester, Manchester University Press, 1984) 1 ('The Convention is the product of many conflicting interests and viewpoints and has the customary vices of compromise. Among these is a tendency to overcome points of difficulty by expressing rules at a level of generality and abstraction sufficient to hide the underlying divergences'); Wyatt, *Intertemporal Linguistics in International Law*, above n 13, ch 5.

justification (for judicial flexibility) have become much less important, whereas sources of guidance regarding the most complex issues – and therefore greater predictability – are becoming increasingly critical.

At the same time that international law has begun crying out for more refined rules of interpretation, the field of linguistics has blossomed, bringing great conceptual clarity to our understanding of how language is processed and therefore to the scientific essence of the act of interpretation. In particular, linguistics analyses the different types of uncertainty (or inconclusiveness) that call for judicial interpretation and draws an important distinction between ambiguity and vagueness.[22] In legal practice, no such distinction is made and these two terms are often used interchangeably, but in linguistics and in some areas of legal theory a contest between two senses of a (polysemous) word is ambiguity, whereas clarifying the precise meaning of one of those senses is the distinct notion of vagueness.[23]

Some terms are only ambiguous and some only vague, but many are both ambiguous and vague. In such situations, linguistics – and particularly the recently burgeoning field of computational linguistics – tells us that it is more logical, efficient and accurate to carry out word sense disambiguation before we tackle problems caused by vagueness.[24] To take a classic example, the English word 'bank' is both polysemous and vague. Modern-day search software will first determine whether the speaker means 'bank' in the sense of financial institution or in the sense of a river bank. Only once it is clear that the speaker is speaking of bank in the financial institution sense, will the algorithms dealing with the vagueness in that sense of the word come into play, determining whether, for that speaker, a bank extends to, for example, a credit union or an insurance company that sells financial products.

Treaty terms that pose the problem of intertemporal linguistics are always ambiguous as between their original sense (*acception*) and the different sense that they had at the time of the treaty's application: the problem inherently arises as a result of *semantic* change.[25] Irrespective of whether any of the senses of the treaty term to be interpreted is also vague, there is no reason not to conduct the simpler and more constrained process of disambiguating between the two competing senses first and separately from the more complex task of delineating the precise scope of a particular sense of a treaty term.

Once we have understood that it is usual – where the difference is semantic – to disambiguate before de-vaguefying, we need not stay on the terrain of linguistics for long. Indeed, it appears to us that international law has itself already impliedly accepted this same approach, with Article 31(4) of the VCLT requiring an interpreter to disambiguate between the ordinary and special meaning of a

[22] See, eg, M Pinkal (ed), *Logic and Lexicon*, vol 56 (Dordrecht, Springer Netherlands, 1995) 73.

[23] See, eg, R Dickenson, *The Interpretation and Application of Statutes* (Boston, MA, Little, Brown, 1975) 49 ('Whereas "ambiguity" in its classical sense refers to equivocation, "vagueness" refers to the degree to which, independently of equivocation, language is uncertain in its respective application to a number of particulars').

[24] See, eg, N Ide and J Véronis, 'Introduction to the Special Issue on Word Sense Disambiguation: The State of the Art' (1998) 24 *Computational Linguistics* 2.

[25] Wyatt, *Intertemporal Linguistics in International Law*, above n 13, chs 4 and 7.

treaty term before considering the precise scope of whichever sense the term was intended to be used in.[26] While reference to an external field such as linguistics might still be unusual in the traditional domain of international law, the method that modern-day linguistics suggests for resolving complex interpretative problems is in fact not completely foreign to international law, or even to the specific area of treaty interpretation.

The disambiguation required by the problem of intertemporal linguistics is obviously a more difficult disambiguation than that required by Article 31(4) of the VCLT, because the drafters of a treaty were not confronted with the modern-day meaning, but only the prospect that the meaning of a term used may change through time. The relevant enquiry is therefore not into whether the original or modern-day meaning of a treaty term was intended, but whether a fixed or mobile sense-intention was assigned to that term – what my work calls the 'temporal sense-intention'.[27]

At this point, one might assert that we have moved too far from the international legal problem and introduced too much complexity. However, while the notion of temporal sense-intention may initially seem complex, it is in fact but an application of linguistic facts to the particular problem of whether to give a treaty term its original or later-emerging meaning. Communicative intention defines the meaning of an utterance and the sense-intention is nothing more than the element of the drafter's communicative intention that is capable of disambiguating between competing senses of a polysemous word. In the context of intertemporal linguistics and the diachronic semantic change that it necessarily entails, that sense-intention is itself temporal.

Equally, while the notion of temporal sense-intention may seem completely foreign to international law, several of the more sophisticated judicial and scholarly attempts to resolve the problem of intertemporal linguistics have already highlighted considerations that can easily be understood as part of identifying it. Judge Guillaume (as judge ad hoc) and Professor Pellet (as counsel) in the *Related Rights* case along with Judge Bedjaoui in the *Gabčíkovo-Nagymaros* case have even spoken briefly about the umbrella notions of '*renvoi fixe*' and '*renvoi mobile*' which, while used in relation to specific meanings rather than simply openness to diachronic semantic change, come close to the approach suggested by my linguistics-inspired analysis.[28] Several illustrious scholars on the topic of evolutionary treaty interpretation – including some contributors to this

[26] Vienna Convention on the Law of Treaties ('Article 31 … 1. A treaty shall be interpreted in good faith in accordance with the ordinary meaning … 4. A special meaning shall be given to a term if it is established that the parties so intended').

[27] Wyatt, 'An Original or Modern-Day Meaning for Treaty Terms?', above n 13, 717–69, ch 16; Wyatt, *Intertemporal Linguistics in International Law*, above n 13, ch 8.

[28] *Dispute Regarding Navigational and Related Rights (Costa Rica v Nicaragua)* (Judgment) Declaration of Judge ad hoc Guillaume [2009] ICJ Rep 290, 294, para 9; *Dispute Regarding Navigational and Related Rights (Costa Rica v Nicaragua)*, Verbatim record of public sitting held 5 March 2009 at 10am, 49–50 (Pellet [for Nicaragua]); *Gabčíkovo-Nagymaros Project (Hungary v Slovakia)* (Judgment) Separate Opinion of Judge Bedjaoui, above n 11, 121–22.

volume – have highlighted the importance of many of the key factors that should be used for determining which temporal sense-intention was held by the parties concluding the treaty, principally context[29] and intention.[30]

What my linguistics-inspired analysis emphasises and hopes to guarantee is that we should at first be looking at the context and intention not in relation to the precise meaning of the treaty term at issue, but instead only insofar as they are relevant to revealing the temporal sense-intention. This means that we should only enquire into the aspects of context and the types of intention that can reveal the assignment of a fixed or mobile sense-intention to the treaty term at issue. For example, a specific intention to commit States to a particular evolving standard of conduct – such as not subjecting a resident to 'inhuman or degrading treatment or punishment'[31] – is a relevant indicium of a mobile sense-intention for those words and implies a dynamic interpretation. By contrast, a general and purely teleological type of intention – for example, the intention of liberalising international trade[32] – will not reveal either a fixed or mobile sense-intention capable of appropriately resolving a problem of original or modern-day meaning. This is because the directionality of the semantic change might, depending on how language evolves and the context in which the treaty term appears and falls to be applied, end up advancing or impeding the achievement of that intended goal. Trade lawyers will appreciate this point. After all, a broadening of the notion of 'sound recording distribution services' included in a schedule in which a State liberalises its trade in services will advance the achievement of a teleological intention aimed at the liberalisation of international trade, whereas a broadening of the meaning of 'exhaustible natural resources' to include not just oil and minerals but also dolphins will, because the relevant term defines the scope of an exception to commitments aimed at freer trade,[33] actually impede the achievement of that same teleological intention.[34] In order to conclude whether semantic changes to the meaning of treaty terms such as broadening should be followed or ignored, we must therefore identify the more general and more abstract form of intention that asks whether the drafters intended the relevant treaty terms to follow changes in language and the social, legal, political and moral developments that such language change reflects.

[29] See the chapter by D McRae, 'Evolutionary Interpretation: The Relevance of Context', ch 7 in this book.

[30] See the chapter by E Bjorge, 'Time Present and Time Past: The Intention of the Parties and the Evolutionary Interpretation of Treaties', ch 5 in this book.

[31] European Convention for the Protection of Human Rights and Fundamental Freedoms, as amended by Protocols Nos 11 and 14 1950 (adopted 4 November 1950) 213 *United Nations Treaty Series* 221, Art 3.

[32] General Agreement on Tariffs and Trade (1947) (adopted 30 October 1947) 55 *United Nations Treaty Series* 187, preamble.

[33] ibid, Art XX(g).

[34] See generally: Appellate Body Report, *China – Measures Affecting Trading Rights and Distribution Services for Certain Publications and Audiovisual Entertainment Products*, adopted 19 January 2010, WT/DS363/AB/R; GATT Panel Report, *United States – Restrictions on Imports of Tuna*, circulated 16 June 1994, DS29/R.

The difference between this aspect of the drafters' communicative intention – a linguistic phenomenon – and the outcome-oriented intentions with which we usually associate the often controversial notion of 'intention' in the law of treaty interpretation could not be starker or more important. It is submitted that international adjudicators can only respond consistently and appropriately to the original problem at the core of the evolutionary treaty debate by accepting the linguistic facts of how language is processed. They should identify a temporal sense-intention to disambiguate between the original and later-emerging senses of a treaty term before they seek to delineate the term's precise semanto-pragmatic scope. As I have written elsewhere, this approach is consistent with the vast majority of the existing case law actually tackling problems of intertemporal linguistics and can work in practice if one is cognisant of the differences between different types of treaties, clauses and terms and prepared to adopt rules of thumb and presumptions for the sake of greater consistency and predictability.[35]

Indeed, one of the principal benefits of following this somewhat formalist approach is that it takes uncertainty out of decision-making in the increasingly used and maturing international dispute settlement system. It provides greater conceptual clarity in a complex area characterised by great confusion and unpredictability. It also gives clear signals to treaty makers around which they can structure the drafting of their treaties, should they wish to remove the risk that an international court and tribunal will denature the terms of their bargain.

Attacks levelled against such an approach are most likely to come from quarters that understand evolutionary treaty interpretation as a doctrine supporting progressive adjudication. However, as noted above, the issue of whether international adjudicators should be afforded scope to update the law – or to apply technically inapplicable law – in order to achieve justice or positive outcomes for society, while often argued under the banner of evolutionary interpretation, is in fact a separate and often non-interpretative question. This chapter considers solely the original question at the core of the notion of evolutionary interpretation and therefore presumes that the adjudicator intends to respect the terms of the treaty directly applicable to the dispute between the parties. Discussion of this question should accordingly not be contaminated by jurisprudential policies largely developed in a distinct context which asks whether the adjudicator should be bound to apply the terms of the applicable treaty at all. Indeed, as this brief overview of how we might respond to the problem of intertemporal linguistics has hopefully shown, once the separate questions arising under each of the competing notions of 'evolutionary interpretation' are disentangled, there is scope for considerable refinement of the still quite young international dispute resolution system in relation to interpretation – a topic of the utmost importance not only to third-party international dispute settlement, but to contemporary international law as a whole.

[35] Wyatt, 'An Original or Modern-Day Meaning for Treaty Terms?', above n 13; Wyatt, *Intertemporal Linguistics in International Law*, above n 13.

7

Evolutionary Interpretation: The Relevance of Context

DONALD McRAE

I. Introduction

Is there such a thing as 'evolutionary' interpretation? The idea of evolutionary or evolutive interpretation assumes that there is an interpretation that is evolving or that has to be evolved by the interpreter. But, arguably the term evolutionary adds nothing to the word interpretation – there is just interpretation and there is no need to qualify it as evolutionary. Interpretation may involve looking at considerations from the past and it may involve taking account of present considerations or circumstances. The question becomes, what are the relevant factors when interpreting the terms in a treaty?

'Evolutionary interpretation' certainly has a place as a descriptive term. If a provision of a treaty is interpreted differently today from the way it was interpreted 20 years ago, then it would be correct to say that the interpretation has evolved. But, something more than that is meant by the term 'evolutionary interpretation'. It involves giving a term a present meaning, rather than a meaning that it might have had in the past. However, while the term 'evolutionary interpretation' has come into common usage, it is not clear that the interpretative process undertaken when interpretation is said to be evolutionary is different from interpretation in any other circumstance. That is the central point made in Eirik Bjorge's seminal book, *The Evolutionary Interpretation of Treaties*.[1] As he points out, evolutionary interpretation involves simply an application of the normal rules of treaty interpretation, that is Articles 31 and 32 of the Vienna Convention on the Law of Treaties (VCLT).[2]

The key question implicit in the idea of evolutionary interpretation is whether an interpreter should look at meaning at the time when a question of interpretation arises or whether meaning should be established on the basis of what the

[1] E Bjorge, *The Evolutionary Interpretation of Treaties* (Oxford, Oxford University Press, 2014).
[2] ibid, 2–3.

words might have meant at the time the treaty was concluded. The underlying question is whether the words should convey only a contemporaneous meaning (that is meaning at the time of the conclusion of the treaty) or a meaning that takes account of subsequent developments.

II. The Intention Conundrum in Evolutionary Interpretation

The justification often given for evolutionary interpretation is that it reflects the intention of the parties.[3] But, is seeking the intention of the parties a helpful way of thinking about evolutionary interpretation? The intention of the parties is not a factor in the basic rule of interpretation in Article 31(1) of the VCLT. It comes up only in Article 31(4) in reference to terms with a special meaning. The Convention gets away from the intention of the parties as a methodological device and provides a more objective process for interpretation. The Vienna rules provide a mechanism for ascertaining meaning and there is no room left for a self-standing consideration of the intention of the parties. The result can be said to reflect the intention of the parties. But that is only a characterisation of the result of the interpretative process. It is not a description of the method to ascertain interpretation. Thus, while the intention of the parties may be a helpful way to characterise the object of interpretation and its outcome, the intention of the parties has no role to play as a method of interpretation.

Nonetheless, it is hard to eliminate the idea of the intention of the parties from treaty interpretation discourse. The jurisprudence of the International Court of Justice regarding the interpretation of treaties is frequently expressed in the pre-Vienna Convention language of the intention of the parties, even though the Convention is solidly established law.

If the issue is really the meaning at the time of application as opposed to the meaning at the time of the negotiation and conclusion of the treaty, what justifies interpreting provisions of a treaty as at the time of the application of the treaty? The time of application is the time when the question of interpretation arises. After all, the intention of the parties is expressed at the time the treaty is concluded.[4] On the basis of an 'intention of the parties' theory, reliance has to be placed on the fiction that the parties looked ahead and contemplated the situation that would arise at the time of application.

Various rationales have been advanced for interpreting a treaty in the light of the circumstances that exist at the time of application. In the *Namibia*

[3] ibid, 2.

[4] *Dispute Regarding Navigational and Related Rights (Costa Rica v Nicaragua)* (Judgment) [2009] ICJ Rep 213, para 63: 'the terms used in a treaty must be interpreted in light of what is determined to have been the parties' common intention, which is, by definition, contemporaneous with the treaty's conclusion'.

Advisory Opinion[5] the Court relied on the perceived intentions of the parties, but also seemed to intuit evolution from the terms actually used. The Court in the *Navigational Rights* case[6] justified looking at subsequent meaning on the ground that the parties had used a generic term. It has been argued that the subject matter of the treaty will dictate whether the term is to be looked at in light of the present-day meaning. The principle of good faith and the object and purpose of a treaty have also been referred to as justification. Julian Arato has argued that the nature of the obligation is the critical factor.[7]

III. The True Scope of the Context

However, one area where insufficient attention has been given is that of context. Under Article 31(1) of the VCLT, the words of a treaty are to be given their ordinary meaning 'in their context'. Article 31(2) states that the context 'shall comprise in addition to the text, including its preamble and annexes', agreements or other instruments made or accepted by the parties 'in connexion with the conclusion of the treaty'. Article 31(3) provides that subsequent agreements and subsequent practice are 'to be taken into account' together with the context.

It is commonly said that the provisions of Article 31(2) relating to context are exclusive. Writing at the time of the adoption of the VCLT, JG Merrills said: 'It must be noted, however, that "context" is restricted in Article 31(2) to the text, preamble and annexes of the treaty, together with certain agreements and instruments relating to the treaty which are relegated to Article 32'.[8]

But is it right that Article 31(2) restricts the meaning of context to the things actually included there? The word 'comprise' is not necessarily limiting. It is defined as 'being made up of'.[9] But, it can also mean, 'compose', or 'include'. The equivalent in the French text '*comprend*' can also mean '*inclure*'.[10]

Moreover, if you look at what courts do, they seem implicitly to look at a context broader than the express words of Article 31(2). Take the famous example of evolutionary interpretation in *US – Shrimp*.[11] Why did the World Trade Organization

[5] *Legal Consequences for States of the Continued Presence of South Africa in Namibia (South West Africa) notwithstanding Security Council Resolution 276 (1970)* (Advisory Opinion) [1971] ICJ Rep 16, para 53.

[6] *Navigational and Related Rights*, above n 4, para 66.

[7] J Arato, 'Accounting for Difference in Treaty Interpretation over Time' in A Bianchi, D Peat and M Windsor (eds), *Interpretation in International Law* (Oxford, Oxford University Press, 2015) 207–08.

[8] JG Merrills, 'Two Approaches to Treaty Interpretation' (1969) 4 *Australian Yearbook of International Law* 55, 56.

[9] *Merriam Webster Dictionary*, 'Comprise', available at: www.merriam-webster.com/dictionary/comprise.

[10] Le Petit Robert, *Dictionnaire alphabétique et analogique de la langue française: Edition 2019* (Paris, Le Robert, 2018) 491.

[11] WTO Appellate Body Report, *United States – Import Prohibition of Certain Shrimp and Shrimp Products (US – Shrimp)* adopted 6 November 1998, WT/DS58/AB/R.

(WTO) Appellate Body think it was appropriate to interpret 'exhaustible natural resources' to include what had been traditionally understood as renewable marine resources and not limit the application of the term to mineral resources? In fact, the case is not as evolutionary as often supposed since the General Agreement on Tariffs and Trade (GATT) became effective for WTO Members on the entry into force of the WTO, not long before the *Shrimp* case was brought.[12]

But the Appellate Body treated it as a case involving the meaning of terms at the time the issue of interpretation arose and not as of the date when the GATT was drafted. It adopted the language of the *Namibia* Advisory Opinion that the words were 'by definition, evolutionary'.[13] Although it linked this to the preamble to the WTO Agreement, the preamble being an accepted part of the context, the Appellate Body looked much further than the preamble. It looked at the Law of the Sea Convention, at the Convention on Biological Diversity, and the Convention on the Conservation of Migratory Species of Wild Animals. In light of this material, the Appellate Body concluded that it was 'too late in the day' to limit Article XX(g) to non-living resources.[14]

In short, the Appellate Body considered that it was appropriate as part of the interpretative process to consider the context in which the provision was being applied; it did not allow the context in which the provision was drafted to govern. The clear implication from the *Shrimp* case is that the context in which a provision is being applied is a legitimate part of the interpretative material for a tribunal. And that context is not rigidly limited to the text, preamble and annexes, or to contemporaneous agreements and other instruments. It is the broader context of the reality of international relations applicable to the matter in question. In taking this approach, the Appellate Body in the *Shrimp* case was reflecting the Court's statement in the *Namibia* Advisory Opinion that, 'an international instrument has to be interpreted and applied within the framework of the entire legal system prevailing at the time of the interpretation'.[15]

IV. Concluding Thoughts

Two initial conclusions can be drawn from this.

First, the context in which the ordinary meaning of the words are to be assessed in accordance with Article 31(1) of the VCLT is not limited to the specific items listed in Article 31(2). It includes, as the Court said in the *Namibia* Advisory Opinion, 'the framework of the entire legal system prevailing at the time of interpretation'.

[12] The World Trade Organization agreements entered into force on 1 January 1995 and the request for consultations was made on 8 October 1996.

[13] *US – Shrimp*, above n 11, para 130.

[14] ibid, para 131.

[15] ibid, para 130, fn 109.

Second, a court or tribunal must look at the context not just when the treaty was concluded, but also at the time of its interpretation. The *Namibia* Advisory Opinion mandates that, although it uses the term 'evolutionary'.

What about the principle of contemporaneity? Does it mandate looking only at context at the time the treaty was concluded? Here I would refer to the investment cases of *ICS*[16] and *Daimler*.[17] Both are decisions that arguably did not apply an evolutionary interpretation. How should they be viewed?

Both cases involved the vexed issue of the scope of 'Most Favoured Nation' (MFN) clauses. The issue was whether the term 'treatment' in the relevant bilateral investment treaty (BIT), which governed the scope of MFN protection, referred to substantive matters or could cover procedural matters including dispute settlement. The tribunal in both cases took the view that the term treatment had to be interpreted in accordance with the principle of contemporaneity which 'requires that the meaning and scope of this term be ascertained as of the time when [the parties] negotiated their BIT'.[18]

Both tribunals thus looked at events occurring when the parties negotiated the BIT – the 1990s – to ascertain what meaning they must have ascribed to the word treatment at that time. This included the International Law Commission's draft articles on MFN, cases at the time dealing with MFN and the World Bank Guidelines on the Treatment of Direct Foreign Investment. Now, while the stated aim of this enquiry was searching for the intention of the parties, in Vienna Convention terms it was seeking to locate the terms in their 'context', as required by Article 31(1). And that context was broad ranging, not limited to the specific content of Article 31(2).

Do the *ICS* and *Daimler* cases suggest that a treaty interpreter must look at the context at the time of interpretation? Those cases did not involve a clash between meaning at the time of the treaty's conclusion and meaning at the time of its interpretation. There was simply no evidence before those tribunals of a different or contrary meaning at the time of interpretation so the question of choosing one over the other did not arise. What had changed was that some tribunals had given an expansive meaning to the word 'treatment' but this was not because of any perceived change in context. In other words, in *ICS* and *Daimler* there were no contextual factors to show that the meaning of the word 'treatment' had changed from the time the treaty was concluded.

This distinguishes those cases from the *Shrimp* case, where the evidence suggested that the meaning of 'exhaustible natural resources' at the time of drafting the GATT in 1947 could well have been different from the meaning at the time of its interpretation in 1998.

[16] *ICS Inspection and Control Services Limited (United Kingdom) v The Republic of Argentina*, UNCITRAL PCA Case No 2010/09, Award on Jurisdiction,10 February 2012.

[17] *Daimler Financial Services AG v Argentine Republic*, ICSID Case No ARB/05/01, Award, 22 August 2012.

[18] *ICS*, above n 16, para 289. See to the same effect, *Daimler*, above n 17, para 220.

The commonly held assumption of evolutionary interpretation is that meaning changes over time and thus interpretation must adapt or evolve. But this does not seem to be the correct way to view the interpretative process. And, it is not the way in which an issue arises in reality. A court or tribunal is faced with a question of interpretation that it must decide at the time of the request for interpretation. It is a question about how the treaty is to be applied between the parties now – not how it might have been applied at some time in the past. The court must look at the context that exists at the time of interpretation. And that is not because some words in the treaty direct it to do so. And it is not because of the presumed intention of the parties. It looks to the context at the time of the interpretation of the treaty because that is what interpretation in accordance with the VCLT requires.

In that sense all interpretation is evolutionary, in that it seeks to give meaning now to the provisions of a treaty that may have been negotiated many years ago. It is just that in most instances there is no change from the relevant context at the time the treaty was concluded and the relevant context at the time of its interpretation.

But, if the context at the time of interpretation is different from the context at the time of the conclusion of the treaty, as arguably occurred in the *Shrimp* case, the trend in the jurisprudence is clear. Even though it may have misguidedly been expressed as reflecting the intention of the parties, where a choice has to be made between the context at the time of the conclusion of the treaty and the context at the time of its application, the choice is to be made in terms of the context at the time of interpretation. Thus, what the principle of evolutionary interpretation says is that in interpreting treaties, the context at the time of the interpretation is the relevant context to guide an interpreter.

PART II

Evolutionary Interpretation in Atypical Institutional Settings

8

Evolutionary Interpretation of International Law in National Courts

KENNETH KEITH*

I. Resolving Continuity and Change in International Law Concerning …

All legal systems must resolve, in part at least, the tension between continuity and change, heritage and heresy. We refer briefly to examples of this proposition in national law before addressing the more particular matters covered in the title.

Benjamin N Cardozo, a great American judge, memorably declared almost a century ago that 'A *constitution* states … not rules for the passing hour, but principles for an expanding future'. He was there contrasting different legal instruments – one size does not fit all. He called in support a leading French judge who had affirmed that French courts adapted the Napoleonic codes adopted more than a century earlier in an evolutionary sense.[1] He referred as well to US court decisions that required that as circumstances changed so too may the meaning or at least the application of broad texts such as 'public use' or 'public interest'.[2] To take another example, consider national legislation that protects the tenancy of 'members of the family' of a tenant who has died. Would that protect a de facto heterosexual partner? 'No' said a British court in 1949 but 'yes' in 1975. And a same-sex partner? 'Yes' said the top British court in 1999. Referring to the evolution of social attitudes to homosexual behaviour it quoted this passage from an earlier case:

> I regard the progressive development and refinement of a public and professional opinion at home and abroad … as an important feature of this case. A belief which

* Thanks to Anna Singleton for her research help.

[1] BN Cardozo, *The Nature of the Judicial Process* (New Haven, CT, Yale University Press, 1921) 83.

[2] Cardozo quoted from Munroe Smith, professor of Roman Law and Comparative Jurisprudence, Columbia University, M Smith, *Jurisprudence* (New York, Columbia University Press, 1909) 28–30. According to the French judge, 'we do not inquire what the legislator willed a century ago, but what he would have willed if he had known what our present conditions would be', Cardozo, above n 1, 84.

> represented unquestioned orthodoxy in Year X may have become questionable by Year Y and unsustainable by Year Z. Public and professional opinion are a continuum.[3]

The impact of changing circumstances including social attitudes, the character of the legal instrument in issue and the generality of the language used can also be seen in two cases about the political rights of women decided in 1908 and 1929. In the former the top British court held that women graduates of Scottish universities did not qualify as voters in spite of legislation entitling to vote 'every person whose name is … on the register … of the general council of [the] University and not subject to any legal incapacity'. To return to our first sentence, the court declared that inveterate usage, practice since time immemorial and a settled and uniform constitutional practice and principle demanded the rejection of their claim.[4] But a generation later, after women's suffrage had been accorded widely, the senior court in the Commonwealth ruled that women were 'persons' and as such able to be appointed to the Canadian Senate. The British North America Act 1867 'planted in Canada a living tree capable of growth and expansion within its natural limits … "Like all written constitutions it has been subject to development through usage and convention"'. There are, continued the court paralleling Cardozo, statutes and statutes, calling for different approaches to interpretation – just as, we would add, there are treaties and treaties. The judges in 1929 were not concerned with what may have been supposed to have been intended in 1867, but with what had been said.[5] The 'living tree' metaphor might be compared to the restrictive metaphor used by the same court just a few years later about the 'watertight compartments' of the ship of the State of Canada. Although, it was 'now sailing on larger ventures and into foreign waters' the court struck down New Deal legislation designed to implement international treaties which Canada had accepted – an executive action which again would not have been contemplated in 1867.[6] That static view of distributed powers within a federation may be contrasted not only with the 'person' case but also, more relevantly, with a US Supreme Court judgment holding that federal legislation implementing a US–UK treaty dealing with a matter which would, but for the treaty, have fallen within State power prevailed:

> When we are dealing with words that also are a constituent act, like the Constitution of the United States, we must realise that they have called into life a being the development of which could not have been foreseen completely by a most gifted of its begetters.[7]

[3] *Gammans v Eakins* [1950] 2 KB 302; *Dyson Holdings Ltd v Fox* [1976] QB 503; and *Fitzpatrick v Sterling Housing Association Ltd* [2001] 1 AC 27 quoting from *R v Ministry of Defence ex p Smith* [1996] QB 517. See also R Kolb, 'Evolutionary Interpretation in International Law: Some Short and Less than Trail-Blazing Reflections' (ch 3); D McRae, 'Evolutionary Interpretation: The Relevance of Context' (ch 7); and O Dörr, 'The Strasbourg Approach to Evolutionary Interpretation' (ch 12) in this book.

[4] *Nairn v University of St Andrews* [1909] AC 147.

[5] *Edwards v Attorney-General for Canada* [1930] AC 124.

[6] *Attorney-General for Canada v Attorney-General for Ontario* [1937] AC 326.

[7] *Missouri v Holland* 252 US 416, 433 (1920).

II. Foreign State Immunity …

We now turn to instances of national courts considering the evolution (or not) of international law. The first example concerns foreign State immunity from the jurisdiction of national courts, an area of international law in which national courts and legislatures have long been engaged. (The International Court of Justice (ICJ) in a 2012 judgment referred to cases from 18 jurisdictions and legislation from 10, as well as international conventions none of which were directly applicable.)[8]

We limit ourselves to cases in common law jurisdictions. In 1805 Marshall CJ, speaking for the US Supreme Court, held that a French public armed ship was immune from the jurisdiction of US courts. In exploring an unbeaten path with few if any aids, the Court had to rely on general principles. A State's jurisdiction within its own territory was necessarily exclusive and absolute, subject only to consent, express or implied. Implied consent arose from the relaxation of territorial jurisdiction by reason of the perfect equality and absolute independence of sovereigns. The Court did however recognise that when merchant ships enter for the purpose of trade the situation was different.[9] That hint was acted on by Sir Robert Phillimore in holding in 1879 that a packet conveying mails and carrying on commerce and belonging to the King of Belgium did not come within the category of vessels exempt from process of law. He drew that line between the King and the trader on the basis of earlier English and American decisions and quoted a Dutch scholar from the eighteenth century: immunity did not extend to strictly commercial activity.[10] The Court of Appeal, however, reversed the decision: the independence and equality of the foreign State required absolute immunity from jurisdiction, in that case in respect of a claim for damages resulting from a collision.[11]

In 1920 another claim in respect of a foreign-owned ship engaged only in commercial activities – this time for salvage – failed at first instance and on appeal, the Court of Appeal deciding that it was bound by its earlier decision.[12] The first instance judge said he had reached his conclusion with great reluctance.

[8] *Jurisdictional Immunities of the State (Germany v Italy: Greece intervening)* (Judgment) [2012] ICJ Rep 99.

[9] *Schooner Exchange v M'Faddon* 11 US 116 (1812).

[10] *The Parlement Belge* (1879) 4 PD 129.

[11] *The Parlement Belge* (1879) 5 PD 197.

[12] *Porto Alexandre* [1920] P 30. This case illustrates another aspect of our first sentence: the attitude of courts to their earlier rulings on the law. Did they have the power to overturn their earlier decisions or was parliamentary action called for? Late in the Victorian era the final Court in the United Kingdom had decided that it was bound by its earlier decisions. It reached that conclusion after hearing argument only against that proposition and without further deliberation, *London Street Tramways v London County Council* [1898] AC 735. It was only in 1966 by way of a Practice Statement that it declared that it would modify that practice and, while treating its former decisions as normally binding, it would depart from an earlier decision when it appeared right to do so, [1966] 1 WLR 1234. For the Court of Appeal compare the cases in 1950 and 1976 in n 3 above.

And one of the Court of Appeal judges, commenting that State default in meeting its obligations would lead to an unwillingness to salve State-owned ships or to employ them in carriage, in effect suggested that a treaty be negotiated to deal with the matter, as in fact happened in 1926, with the adoption of the International Convention for the Unification of Certain Rules relating to the Immunity of State-Owned Vessels. Such vessels if engaged in commerce were to be subject to the same liabilities and obligations and procedures as privately owned vessels.[13]

Notwithstanding that development, the earlier hints and the great increase in state trading activity, notably in the USSR, in 1938 the senior judge in the House of Lords saw two propositions of international law engrafted into domestic law as well established and beyond dispute: the courts will not implead a foreign sovereign, nor will they seize or detain property which is his or of which he is in possession or control. On the second the judge rejected any limit based on the commercial use of the vessel. That is, he adopted an absolute position, but others on the panel questioned whether the immunity should continue to be accorded to commercial ships owned by foreign countries. One referred to the 'absurdity' of the situation.[14]

That absurdity was also being recognised by scholars and within the executive branches of government. We take one instance from each. In 1951 Professor Hersch Lauterpacht reviewed not only the practice of many courts in recognising limits to the absolute immunity of foreign States in national courts but also changes in national law subjecting the State to the jurisdiction of its own courts. Just as that State was subject to the courts in respect of claims in contract and tort so too should foreign States be.[15] In the following year the Acting Legal Adviser to the US Department of State, in a letter to the Attorney-General, recorded the department's conclusions that immunity of foreign States should no longer be granted in certain cases. Even those States supporting the absolute theory recognised exceptions, for instance in respect of property (other than diplomatic or consular) in the forum State. The decisions of courts in many countries (which he listed) showed a movement towards refusing immunity in respect of private as opposed to public acts of the foreign State; this restrictive theory was also supported by a school of influential writers; and 10 of the 13 countries listed as supporters of the absolute theory had ratified the 1926 Brussels Convention relating to State-owned ships engaged in commerce – an important area of cases on State immunity.[16] It was not until 1976 that British judges 'abandoned their [inflexible adherence] to the rule of absolute immunity and their fervent faith in the rigidity of a formula':

> If a government department goes into the market places of the world and buys boots or cement – as a commercial transaction – the government should be subject to all the

[13] International Convention for the Unification of Certain Rules relating to the Immunity of State-owned Vessels (adopted 10 April 1926) 176 *League of Nations Treaty Series* 199. Excepted were ships of war and others engaged in non-commercial activity, with the qualification that proceedings could be brought in the home state in respect of collisions, salvage and repairs.

[14] *The Christina* [1938] AC 485.

[15] H Lauterpacht, 'The Problem of Jurisdictional Immunities of Foreign States' (1951) 28 *The British Yearbook of International Law* 220.

[16] 26 Dept State Bull 984 (1952).

> rules of the market place. The seller is not concerned with the purpose to which the purchaser intends to put the goods.[17]

Lord Denning, whose words those are, sought support from developing jurisprudence in many jurisdictions: from State practice; from Galileo, speaking of the earth: 'But it does move'; and from the English courts' application in the eighteenth and nineteenth centuries of the then modern rules of international law to condemn slavery. Was England to wait until every other country recognised the change?

> At first a trickle, then a stream, last a flood. England should not be left behind on the bank. 'We must take the current when it serves, or lose our ventures'.
>
> Julius Caesar, Act IV, sc III.[18]

That metaphor, reflecting a particular judge's view of the judicial role and a general relaxation of the rules of precedent in British courts, may be contrasted with the use by another highly regarded English judge of the proposition that one swallow does not make a rule of international law when he rejected another proposed limit on State immunity[19] – a proposal also rejected by the ICJ.

III. The Liability of International Airline Operators …

Among the many treaties which come before national courts we select three: the Convention relating to the Status of Refugees 1951;[20] international human rights instruments, notably the 1950 European Convention and the International Covenant on Civil and Political Rights 1966;[21] and the Warsaw Convention for the Unification of Certain Rules relating to International Carriage by Air adopted in 1929 only two years after Charles Lindberg flew across the Atlantic.[22]

The dates of the first and last highlight the obvious need for updating by one means or another. The refugee challenge in 1951 was seen as being largely limited to Europe (and parties to the Convention could adopt that geographic limit) and

[17] FA Mann, 'The State Immunity Act 1978' (1979) 50 *The British Yearbook of International Law* 43. The International Law Commission was also about to engage on its work that led to the 2004 UN Convention. For a comprehensive discussion see H Fox and P Webb, *The Law of State Immunity*, revised and updated 3rd edn (Oxford, Oxford University Press, 2013).

[18] *Trendtex Trading Corp v Central Bank of Nigeria* [1977] 1 QB 529 (CA); shortly before the Privy Council had rejected a claim of immunity in In Rem proceedings, *Philippine Admiral* [1977] AC 373.

[19] *Jones v Saudi Arabia* [2007] 1 AC 270, 288.

[20] Convention relating to the Status of Refugees (adopted 28 July 1951) 189 *United Nations Treaty Series* 137; see also the 1967 Protocol, Protocol relating to the Status of Refugees (adopted 31 January 1967) 606 *United Nations Treaty Series* 267.

[21] Convention for the Protection of Human Rights and Fundamental Freedoms (adopted 4 November 1950) 213 *United Nations Treaty Series* 221 and International Covenant on Civil and Political Rights (adopted 16 December 1966) 999 *United Nations Treaty Series* 171.

[22] Convention for the Unification of Certain Rules Relating to International Carriage by Air (adopted 12 October 1929) 137 *League of Nations Treaty Series* 11.

it related only to those who were refugees before 1951. A 1967 protocol removed both the territorial and the temporal limits. Those changes to the 1951 Convention have been accompanied by massive increases in the numbers of refugees, but the central definition of a refugee has remained the same.

Over the past 90 years international air transport has been transformed far beyond even the most fevered imagination of those who gathered in Warsaw in 1929. The maximum amounts that can be recovered by passengers and freight operators on a non-fault basis have been increased several times by treaty and by agreements among airlines. But, again, central features of the treaties have remained constant, including the right of a passenger to recover in case of a 'bodily injury' ('*lésion corporelle*' in the sole authoritative French text) caused by an 'accident' in the course of an international flight. Those two terms have also been retained in the Montreal Convention for the Unification of Certain Rules for International Carriage by Air of 1999.[23]

The human rights treaties use broad terms such as 'cruel and unusual' or 'degrading' and 'inhuman … treatment' or 'punishment' and general words such as 'arbitrary' and 'unreasonable' which may well have evolving application or interpretation, reaching back to long before the adoption of the international text.

Further, getting agreed formal change to such treaty texts may be difficult. And there are as well, forces for continuity, for heritage: consider the policies of many governments around the world towards migration; or airline corporations concerned about the financial costs of more extensive obligations towards passengers arising from a broader reading of accident or bodily injury.

We begin with that 1929 Warsaw Convention. Could claims be made for mental injury that did not result from bodily injury? 'No' said the US Supreme Court in 1991.[24] In justifying this limit the Court recorded that the Convention's primary purpose was to limit the liability of air carriers in order to foster the growth of the fledgling commercial aviation companies. The limit was designed to enable air carriers to attract capital that might otherwise be scared away by the fears of a single catastrophic accident.[25] But should that purpose continue to prevail, given the much greater safety of air travel? Modern aircraft are no longer fledglings: the wing span of the Airbus A380, which can carry 800 passengers, is 80 metres compared with 15 metres for the Spirit of St Louis, which carried just Lindberg and took seven times as long to cross the Atlantic.[26]

[23] Convention for the Unification of Certain Rules for International Carriage by Air (adopted 28 May 1999) 2242 *United Nations Treaty Series* 309.

[24] *Eastern Airlines Inc v Floyd* 499 US 530 (1991).

[25] AF Lowenfeld and AI Mendelsohn, 'The United States and the Warsaw Convention' (1967) 90 *Harvard Law Review* 497, 499.

[26] For an update to the article cited in the preceding note see MK Cunningham, 'The Montreal Convention: Can Passengers Finally Recover for Mental Injury?' (2008) 41 *Vanderbilt Journal of Transnational Law* 1043, 1048–50. That article also records the major drop in the fatality rate from 45 fatalities per 100 million passenger miles in 1925 to 0.03 in 2001, a drop of 1500 per cent, 1052, fn 61.

The attempts in 1999 of the US delegation to remove '*corporelle*' ('bodily') from the phrase '*lésion corporelle*' failed. Notwithstanding the retention of the original wording, the US Sixth Circuit Court of Appeals has recently rejected any requirement that mental injury be caused by bodily injury. When a single accident causes *both* bodily injury and mental anguish that mental anguish is sustained 'in case of' the bodily injury.[27] The Court referred in support to an explanatory note supplied to the US Senate when it consented to the ratification of the 1999 Convention and a statement agreed at the Conference which adopted the Convention. The Court considered that by 1999 the aviation industry was anything but fledgling and the purpose of the new Convention was not to protect the aviation industry but rather to provide a modernised uniform liability regime. The Court rejected the contrary ruling of the Second Circuit Court of Appeals, setting up the prospect that the US Supreme Court may soon have to resolve the matter.

National courts have also given conflicting readings to the word 'accident'. The US Supreme Court has read it narrowly as being a fortuitous, unexpected, unusual or unintended event; it was also to be external to the passenger.[28] That position has however been rejected by the High Court of Australia and the UK House of Lords.[29]

IV. Refugee Status …

As noted, the Refugees Convention now has a much wider temporal and geographic scope than it did in 1951 but its definition of 'refugee' and exclusions from that status have remained unchanged. We consider one issue arising from each.

A refugee is a person who 'owing to a well-founded fear of being persecuted for reasons of race, religion, nationality, *membership of a particular social group* or political opinion' is outside their country of nationality, or unwilling to return to it. How is the emphasised ground to be understood now? Of the five grounds, as many have said, this has the least clarity. Answers to the question have been given not just by national courts, but by national and regional law and policymakers, the Office of the UN High Commissioner for Refugees (UNHCR) and associated bodies and the States parties. Also significant is the developing law of international human rights. The preamble to the 1951 Convention invokes the affirmation in the UN Charter and the Universal Declaration of Human Rights of the entitlement of all human beings to fundamental human rights and freedoms without

[27] *Doe v Etihad Airways* 30 August 2017, no 16–1042.

[28] *Air France v Saks* 470 US 392, 400 (1985).

[29] *Povey v QANTAS Airways 2005 HCA 33 and In Re Deep Vein Thrombosis and Air Group Litigation* [2006] I AC 495. See also J Wyatt, 'Using Intertemporal Linguistics to Resolve the Problem at the Origin and Core of the Evolutionary Interpretation Debate' (ch 6); and O Dörr, 'The Strasbourg Approach to Evolutionary Interpretation' (ch 12) in this book.

discrimination. A 2001 UNHCR study demonstrates that several States through legislative policy and court decisions have recognised that refugee status may be available to members of the following groups: women suffering sexual violence, or domestic violence, or trafficking or other social harms.[30] Refugee status may be available even if the persecutor is not the State. So the top British court in 1999 had held that two Pakistani women fleeing from allegations and severe sanctions under the law, with the local authorities being unwilling to help them, were entitled to claim refugee status.[31] The judges emphasised the Convention's preamble. Moreover, the concept of the social group is a general one and cannot be confined to those social groups which the framers of the Convention may have had in mind, particularly when the 1967 changes are taken into account. Further, for one judge, it was important to have regard to the evolutionary approach that must be taken to international agreements of this kind. Account may then be taken of changes in society and of discriminatory circumstances that may not have been obvious to those drafting the Convention.

A later survey (2012) documents the inclusions within the social group ground of individuals fearing persecution on the basis of their homosexuality, cases from seven jurisdictions being cited.[32] In a leading UK case a judge said that at one time there would have been a debate about whether homosexuals constitute a 'particular social group' but in more recent years it has come to be accepted that, at least in societies which discriminate against homosexuals, they are to be so regarded.[33] The survey also considers family, age, disability and women fearing female genital mutilation as falling within the ground, depending on the circumstances. It concludes by referring to the conclusion of an inter-governmental ministerial meeting on the sixtieth anniversary of the 1951 Convention. The representatives of 155 States reaffirmed that the Conventions and Protocol are the foundation of the international refugee protection regime and have enduring value and relevance. They recognised the importance of respecting and upholding the underlying principles and values – perhaps including the readings of the text which go beyond the framers' expectations.[34]

The protection of the Convention does not extend to a number of persons. They include, under Article 1F(c), 'any person with respect to whom there are serious reasons for considering that … he has been guilty of acts contrary to the purposes and principles of the United Nations'. This exclusion, like others, brings into potential conflict two principles: on the one side, given the protective human

[30] See in particular the work done around the fiftieth anniversary of the 1951 Convention, captured in E Feller et al, *Refugee Protection in International Law – UNHCR's Global Consultations on International Protection* (Cambridge, Cambridge University Press, 2003).

[31] *Islam v Home Secretary* [1999] 2 AC 629.

[32] M Foster, UNHCR Legal and Protection Policy Research Series … 'Membership of a Particular Social Group' (August 2012).

[33] *HJ v Home Secretary* [2011] 1 AC 596.

[34] HCR/MINCOMMS/2011/6.

rights character of the Convention, the exclusion had to be restrictively interpreted and cautiously applied – a position supported by the UNHCR and more broadly; but, on the other, the expression 'purposes and principles of the UN' as spelled out by Articles 1 and 2 of the Charter is very broad. What might it be seen as covering 70 years on? The UK Supreme Court for instance has included within the scope of the phrase international terrorist acts, reflecting UN treaties and Security Council resolutions, adopted long after 1951, and an attack on the International Security Assistance Force, which was operating in Afghanistan from late 2001 under a Security Council mandate allowing it to engage in armed combat. International terrorism, although with a very long history, would hardly have been in the minds of the 1945 and 1951 drafters. Further, the Force was not established in the ways contemplated by the Charter; in fact that has never happened.[35] The Court discusses a decision of the Supreme Court of Canada relating to a refugee who was a major drug dealer, actions in breach of UN narcotics conventions. The majority, emphasising the drafting history of the Convention, held that the exclusion did not apply to the refugee. The minority, by contrast, gave much more weight to the major harm, internationally as well as nationally, that drug trafficking was causing. They said this about the wording of the exclusion:

> It cannot be the case that this interpretation of the exclusion must be forever restricted. As international law develops, the content of a phrase such as 'contrary to the purposes and principles of the United Nations' must be capable of development.[36]

V. The Infliction of Cruel and Unusual Punishment …

How is the prohibition on cruel and unusual or inhuman and degrading punishment or treatment, included in English law since 1688, in the US Constitution since 1791 and in international treaties and declarations since 1948 now to be understood? Consider the death penalty or mandatory life sentences for youth offenders or those with mental incapacity.

The way we have put the question takes us back to the first part of the chapter: such issues are essentially the same whether seen as a matter of purely national law or seen more widely including international law. And as with those earlier cases, the US Supreme Court, speaking in 2005, stated that:

> The prohibition against 'cruel and unusual punishments', like other expansive language in the Constitution, must be interpreted according to its text, by considering history, tradition, and precedent, and with due regard for its purpose and function in the constitutional design. To implement this framework, we have established the propriety and

[35] *Al-Sirri v Home Secretary* [2013] 1 AC 745.

[36] *Pushnapathan v Canada Minister of Citizenship and Immigration* [1998] 1 SCR 782; see similarly *Re Piracy lure Gentium* [1934] AC 586, 592–93.

> affirmed the necessity of referring to 'the evolving standards of decency that mark the progress of a maturing society' to determine which punishments are so disproportionate as to be cruel and unusual.

The Court's review led to its striking down the death penalty for offenders under 18.[37] In 2001 it had held that executing mentally retarded prisoners was also now in breach of the prohibition. In 2010 it ruled that juvenile offenders could not be sentenced to life imprisonment without parole for non-homicide offences.[38] And two years later it extended that holding to children who committed murder.[39]

All these decisions were made by a divided Court with the minority claiming that the majority had claimed for itself a legislative power. In 1989 the Court had upheld the death penalty imposed on a juvenile who was 17 at the time he committed a murder. The Court made the point that at the time the Bill of Rights was adopted the common law theoretically permitted capital punishment to be imposed on anyone over seven.[40] Accordingly, the argument had to depend on 'evolving standards of decency', calling for interpretation in a flexible and dynamic manner but the Court in 1989 found no consensus against the death penalty in such cases as that before them in federal and State legislation and the practice of prosecutors and juries.

An evolutionary approach may also be seen in British and Privy Council cases related to the European Convention, which is part of UK law under the Human Rights Act 1989 and of some Commonwealth constitutions. The cases have concerned a wide range of topics. A divided Judicial Committee in an appeal from Trinidad and Tobago upheld a law providing for mandatory death sentence for murder. The dissent begins with these words:

> In recent years the Privy Council has generally shown itself to be an enlightened and forward-looking tribunal. It has of course recognised that the provisions of any constitution must be interpreted with care and respect, paying close attention to the terms of the constitution in question. But it has also brought to its task of constitutional adjudication a broader vision, recognising that a legalistic and over-literal approach to interpretation may be quite inappropriate when seeking to give effect to the rights, values and standards expressed in a constitution as these evolve over time. It is such an approach which Lord Wilberforce stigmatised, in the phrase of Professor de Smith which he made famous, as 'the austerity of tabulated legalism': *de Smith, the New Commonwealth and its Constitutions* (1964), p 194; *Minister of Home Affairs v Fisher* [1980] AC 310, 328.[41]

The dissent cited the 'living tree' metaphor, a practice that has continued in British cases, for instance in relation to self-incrimination, liability in respect of soldiers

[37] *Roper v Simmons* 543 US 551 (2005).
[38] *Graham v Florida* 560 US 48 (2010).
[39] *Miller v Alabama* 567 US 460 (2012).
[40] *Stanford v Kentucky* 492 US 361 (1989).
[41] *Matthew v Trinidad and Tobago* [2005] 1 AC 433, para 34, see also paraS 42–44.

on active duty abroad and removal from the UK.[42] Such references indicate a willingness on the part of those courts to consider the treaty obligations, particularly those cast in broad terms, as having a changing meaning or application over time.

VI. In National Courts

We have selected only four areas of international law in this survey of national court decisions. Many more could be chosen: for instance, extradition and mutual assistance; tax and social benefits; tariff determinations; international child abduction; international adoptions; international criminal law (piracy, slave trading, human trafficking, war crimes, labour rights, narcotics, torture, corruption, terrorism); maritime matters; other aspects of civil aviation; intellectual property. In many, the possible choice of an evolutionary interpretation would not have arisen. The treaty, the law in issue, would have been seen as having retained its initial meaning, whatever that was.

Those areas of law have in common with the four chosen that litigation relating to disputes arising within them is much more likely to be resolved at the national rather than the international level. By their very nature, issues of immunity from the jurisdiction of national courts will arise in the first instance in those courts, although they may, if rarely, proceed to international litigation. Disputes between airlines and passengers and cargo owners have stayed in national courts. Refugee cases arise between the person claiming that status and the State of attempted refuge. It will be for its institutions, including its tribunals and courts, to resolve any dispute; while the ICJ does have jurisdiction under the 1951 Convention over disputes between State parties to it, no such case has ever been brought and it is hard to imagine that happening. Claims drawing on international human rights instruments will have at their core the national constitutional and legal system and will be resolved by national courts, at least in the first instance.

The qualification in that last phrase leads to an important feature of the areas of law we have considered: the possible role of international bodies of various kinds. So, as mentioned, State immunity cases may be taken to international courts such as the ICJ. States and airlines may move to adjust their liability regimes. The Office of the UNHCR and associated bodies provide important commentary on the developing understanding of the 1951 Convention and, in a less formal way, relevant tribunal members and judges exchange information and ideas at conferences. And the European Court of Human Rights and human rights treaty bodies

[42] *Brown v Stott* [2003] 1 AC 681, 703; *Smith v Ministry of Defence* [2014] AC 52 para 43; *N v Secretary of State for the Home Department* [2005] 2 AC 296, paras 21–22; and *GS (India) v Secretary for State for the Home Department* [2015] 1 WLR 3312, para 38. See also the dissenters in *Moohan v Lord Advocate* [2015] AC 901, para 105.

and the UN Human Rights Council enable issues that have been dealt with at the national level to be addressed further.

Another feature of the treaties, other than the first, we have considered is significant: they use language that may be seen as open textured and capable of differing applications over the years: 'particular social group'; 'purposes and principles of the UN'; 'cruel and unusual treatment'. Something of that characteristic may also be seen in the law of State immunity as the Prince becomes a trader, or at least the context in which a 'Sovereign' is to be seen sharply changes. A further element is also relevant – the great difficulty, even impossibility of amending the treaty texts, a matter matched by the fact that the UN Convention on the Jurisdictional Immunity of States and their Property, which was adopted as long ago as 2004 has not yet come into force, having so far attracted only 22 of the necessary 30 State parties.

The pervasive role of national courts in deciding international law issues appears clearly in the 180 volumes of the *International Law Reports*, which now cover 100 years. The first volume for the years 1925 and 1926 (then called the *Annual Digest of Public International Law Cases*) included cases from 34 States as well as some international tribunals. The editors, Arnold Duncan McNair and Hersch Lauterpacht, in the preface to that volume said that the work was prompted by the thought that there is more and more international law already in existence and daily accumulating 'than this world dreams of' and by the conviction that it is more international law that this world wants. That suspicion, they said, ripened into certainty as they prepared the early volumes. They would, we suggest, be astonished to see the product of their initiative with, for instance, 140 volumes covering just the last 50 years.[43]

[43] See further RY Jennings, 'The Judiciary, International and National, and the Development of International Law' (1996) 45 *International & Comparative Law Quarterly* 1, a lecture celebrating the publication of the 100th volume of the *ILR* in 1995.

9

The Interpretive Work of Treaty Bodies: How They Look at Evolutionary Interpretation, and How Other Courts Look at Them

LUIGI CREMA

I. Introduction

'Treaty bodies' is a catch-all expression that refers to the commissions and committees made up of individuals acting in their personal, independent capacities, which, depending on the institution, may be requested to carry out ordinary monitoring activities or quasi-judicial procedures overseeing the correct implementation or violation of the underlying treaties.[1] Today several agreements have set up such committees to perform this activity. This chapter focuses on the pronouncements of the so-called United Nations treaty bodies,[2] which receive and consider complaints from individuals, and the European Committee on Social Rights (ECSR),[3] the 15-member body that hears collective complaints of European Social Charter (ESC) violations, where these have taken an evolutionary approach.

Treaty bodies are not *judicial courts*, characterised by the authority to issue decisions binding upon the parties. At the same time, they are also not *political organs*, such as the Human Rights Council. They envisage an independent role for

[1] A theoretical, full account on the purpose of the activity of these organs, dated, not obsolete, but rather still sharp, can be found in A Cassese, *Il controllo internazionale: contributo alla teoria delle funzioni di organizzazione dell'ordinamento internazionale* (Milan, Giuffrè, 1971); L Borlini, 'Il controllo internazionale tra standardizzazione, coordinamento e contaminazione', in F Salerno (ed), *La codificazione nell'ordinamento internazionale ed Europeo* (Naples, ES, 2019, forthcoming).

[2] NS Rodley, 'UN Treaty Bodies and the Human Rights Council' in S Daws and N Samarasinghe (eds), *The United Nations Vol 6* (Los Angeles, CA, SAGE, 2012).

[3] O De Schutter, *The European Social Charter: A Social Constitution for Europe* (Brussels, Bruylant, 2010). On the functioning of the ECSR, see below, section III.

their members, and have procedures, often adversarial in structure, which provide both complainants and respondent states with the occasion to present their views.[4] Their activities might have an impact on the definition and redefinition of the rights which they monitor.

The purpose of this chapter is not just to mine the instances in which treaty bodies, such as the ECSR or the UN treaty bodies, use an evolutionary approach in interpreting the content of the underlying treaties – there are some, but not many (section III). The aim of this chapter is also to reflect on whether and how the work of these committees of experts contributes to the clarification and evolution of the concepts enshrined in the underlying treaties, and is potentially used by judicial organs, such as national and international courts, to define and develop the contents of their treaties (section IV). In other words, this chapter looks both at how committees view the evolution of the underlying treaties and at how other courts, especially the Italian Constitutional Court in two very recent cases, regard the activities of the committees as they interpret, update and redefine the contents of their treaties.[5]

II. The Many Ways to Understand Evolution

The term 'evolution', a concept international law borrowed from biological theories on the differentiation of species, and then from deterministic sociology, is a broad one, and can be looked at from different angles. In terms of the legal techniques it may encompass, it may be used to refer to several kinds of interpretive reasoning.[6] Giovanni Distefano, in a 2011 article, explains the different interpretive techniques used by international courts and tribunals to adopt a dynamic, not static, interpretation of a treaty.[7] Similarly, Gabrielle Marceau, in analysing the evolutive interpretations adopted by the World Trade Organization (WTO), considers several methods of interpretation (generic terms, contextual, teleological,

[4] Marchesi talks about 'legal control' as opposed to the 'political control' of the Human Rights Council and the 'judicial control' of the regional human rights courts, A Marchesi, *La protezione internazionale dei diritti umani* (Milan, Franco Angeli, 2011) 97.

[5] It is not my intention here to review all such cases. A very recent paper by M Kanetake, 'UN Human Rights Treaty Monitoring Bodies before Domestic Courts' (2018) 67 *International & Comparative Law Quarterly* 201 provides an updated and thorough account of this dynamic in courts. I will focus on two very recent Italian cases that dealt with this issue and brought interesting points to light. See, below, section IV.

[6] In what can also be called 'dynamic interpretation': M Fitzmaurice, 'Dynamic (Evolutive) Interpretation of Treaties and the European Court of Human Rights' in A Orakhelashvili and S Williams (eds), *40 Years of the Vienna Convention on Treaties* (London, British Institute of International and Comparative Law, 2010); L Crema, 'Subsequent Agreements and Subsequent Practice Within and Outside the Vienna Convention' in G Nolte (ed), *Treaties and Subsequent Practice* (Oxford, Oxford University Press, 2013) 22.

[7] G Distefano, 'L'interprétation évolutive de la norme international' (2011) 115 *Revue générale de droit international public* 373.

systemic) that lead to an evolution of the meaning of a term.[8] The International Court of Justice (ICJ) has so far taken a narrower approach, labelling as 'evolutionary' a specific interpretive technique: that is, when the parties originally adopted generic terms capable of changing their meanings over time.[9] In legal scholarship, however, it is more common to see the expression used more broadly.[10]

In terms of its content, lawyers use 'evolution' according to two different meanings. First, it has a pragmatic meaning, as 'adaptation', denoting the natural, determined, neutral operation of fine-tuning a given meaning to adjust to new realities that impose or demand (for systemic, contextual, or linguistic reasons) the evolution of an otherwise static text.[11] Second, it is used, in idealistic terms, to mean 'progress': that is, interpretation of a treaty's content towards the achievement of a certain end.[12] Eirik Bjorge, in 2014, strongly struck out against a political reading of evolutionary interpretation, reaffirming and re-exploring its neutrality and its validity in any legal context.[13] However, particularly when it comes to certain kinds of treaties, such as human rights treaties, any interpretation involving evolution is difficult to describe in purely technical terms, if only to distinguish between new realities that evolve the meaning of a treaty rather than breach it.[14] Therefore, when we talk about 'evolutionary interpretation', the political dimension cannot be entirely removed.[15]

III. Treaties as Living Instruments: A Spotlight on the UN Treaty Bodies and the ECSR

The expressions 'evolutionary' or 'evolutive interpretation' are not often found in the texts of UN bodies. And although the ECSR does not mention evolutionary

[8] G Marceau, 'L'interprétation évolutive par le juge OMC: sophisme ou nécessité ?' (2018) 122 *Revue générale de droit international public* 23, 39–48; the term 'evolutive interpretation' was first used by the WTO in the WTO Appellate Body Report, *United States – Import Prohibition of Certain Shrimp and Shrimp Products* (*US – Shrimp*) adopted 6 November 1998, WT/DS58/AB/R, para 130.

[9] *Dispute Regarding Navigational and Related Rights (Costa Rica v Nicaragua)* (Judgment) [2009] ICJ Rep 213, para 64.

[10] In addition to Distefano, above n 7, and Marceau, above n 8, see R Bernhardt, 'Evolutive Treaty Interpretation, Especially of the ECHR' (1999) 42 *German Yearbook International Law* 11, 15.

[11] This is the approach taken, eg, by the ILC in dealing with Subsequent Agreements and Subsequent Practice, *cf* G Nolte (Special Rapporteur), *Second report on subsequent agreements and subsequent practice in relation to treaty interpretation* (26 March 2014) UN Doc A/CN.4/671, 24–30.

[12] With the risk of incurring criticism about the legitimacy of such an operation. I have already explored the pragmatist and the idealist alternatives in describing evolution in L Crema, 'Subsequent Practice in *Hassan v United Kingdom*: When Things Seem to go Wrong in the Life of a Living Instrument' (2015) 15 *Questions of International Law, Zoom-in* 3, 15–18.

[13] E Bjorge, *The Evolutionary Interpretation of Treaties* (Oxford, Oxford University Press, 2014) 6–9.

[14] Crema, 'Subsequent Practice in *Hassan v United Kingdom*', above n 12, 19–22.

[15] F Zarbiyev, *Le discours interprétatif en droit international contemporain* (Brussels, Bruylant, 2015) 165–69.

interpretation, in many instances, it relied on the living instrument doctrine originally used by the European Court of Human Rights (ECtHR).[16]

In 2003, the UN Committee on the Elimination of Racial Discrimination had to decide whether the Australian court's decision not to remove a sign from the grandstand of a sporting ground in Queensland, named the 'ES "Nigger" Brown Stand' in honour of a sporting and civic personality, Mr ES Brown, violated the Convention's provisions on the elimination of all forms of racial discrimination.[17] The Committee found that there was a violation, and explained:

> The Committee has taken due account of the context within which the sign bearing the offending term was originally erected in 1960, in particular the fact that the offending term, as a nickname probably with reference to a shoeshine brand, was not designed to demean or diminish its bearer, Mr Brown, who was neither black nor of aboriginal descent … Nevertheless, the Committee considers that the use and maintenance of the offending term can at the present time be considered offensive and insulting, even if for an extended period it may not have necessarily been so regarded. The Committee considers, in fact, that the Convention, as a living instrument, must be interpreted and applied taking into the circumstances of contemporary society. In this context, the Committee considers it to be its duty to recall the increased sensitivities in respect of words such as the offending term appertaining today.[18]

In the same year, the United Nations Human Rights Committee was requested, inter alia, to decide whether Canada violated the right to life under Article 6.1 of the International Covenant on Civil and Political Rights (ICCPR) by deporting an individual to the United States, where he was under sentence of death, without ensuring that the death penalty would not be carried out.[19] The Committee had previously decided on a similar question, and in this case decided to refer to

[16] This dynamic approach can be traced back to the case of *Tyrer v United Kingdom* (1978) 58 *International Law Reports* 339, 353. As explained by a former ECtHR president, Luzius Wildhaber, 'The European Court of Human Rights in action' (2004) 21 *Ritsumeikan Law Review* 83, 84: 'The "living instrument" doctrine is one of the best-known principles of Strasbourg case law. It expresses the principle that the Convention is interpreted "in the light of present day conditions", that it evolves through the interpretation of the Court'.

[17] Mr Brown, 'who was also a member of the body overseeing the sports ground, and who died in 1972, was of white Anglo-Saxon extraction and who acquired the offending term as his nickname, either "because of his fair skin and blond hair or because he had a penchant for using 'Nigger Brown' shoe polish". The offending term is also repeated orally in public announcements relating to facilities at the ground and in match commentaries'. CERD, *Stephen Hagan v Australia*, Communication no 26/2002, 20 March 2003 (UN Doc CERD/C/62/D/26/2002, 2003) para 2.1. In 1999, after the request from Stephen Hagan, the trustees of the sports ground and then the mayor decided not to remove the offending term, after considering the views of numerous members of the community who had no objection to its use on the stand, the results of a public meeting chaired by a prominent member of the local indigenous community, and attended by a cross-section of the local Aboriginal community, ibid, para 2.2.

[18] ibid, paras 7.2–7.3.

[19] CCPR, *Roger Judge v Canada*, Communication no 829/1998, 5 August 2002 (UN Doc CCPR/C/78/D/829/1998, 13 August 2003) paras 10.1–10.7.

the living instrument doctrine to justify a departure from its previous case law. It observed:

> While recognizing that the Committee should ensure both consistency and coherence of its jurisprudence, it notes that there may be exceptional situations in which a review of the scope of application of the rights protected in the Covenant is required, such as where an alleged violation involves that most fundamental of rights – the right to life … The Committee is mindful of the fact that the abovementioned jurisprudence was established some 10 years ago, and that since that time there has been a broadening international consensus in favour of abolition of the death penalty … The Committee considers that the Covenant should be interpreted as a living instrument and the rights protected under it should be applied in context and in the light of present-day conditions.[20]

The practice of the ECSR on this is also interesting. The Committee is composed of 15 independent experts elected for six years, renewable for just one additional term, by the Committee of Ministers of the Council of Europe.[21] The Committee carries out two functions: first, a general review of State parties' domestic implementation of the ESC; second, an adversarial procedure to hear collective claims initiated by certain representative entities allowed to participate in the proceedings.[22]

The ECSR has not often commented on the theoretical foundations and detailed operations of the living instrument doctrine. It assumes the existence of the doctrine, in the wake of ECtHR case law. In a series of decisions adopted on 7 December 2004, regarding a claim brought by the World Organisation against Torture, the ECSR looked at both domestic and international sources to determine the evolved meaning of the 'living' ESC: 'The Committee furthermore recalls that the Charter is a living instrument which must be interpreted in light of developments in the national law of member states of the Council of Europe as well as relevant international instruments'.[23]

[20] ibid, para 10.3.

[21] The oversight procedure for the implementation of the Charter is defined in Part IV of the Charter as amended by the Protocol of Turin of 1991, Arts 21 *et seq*, and, in particular, in Art 25, concerning CEDS. These provisions have now been reproduced in Art C of Part IV of the revised Social Charter of 1996. RR Churchill and U Khaliq, 'The Collective Complaints System of the European Social Charter: An Effective Mechanism for Ensuring Compliance with Economic and Social Rights?' (2004) 15 *European Journal of International Law* 417.

[22] H Cullen, 'The Collective Complaints System of the European Social Charter: Interpretative Methods of the European Committee of Social Rights' (2009) 9 *Human Rights Law Review* 61.

[23] *World Organisation against Torture (OMCT) v Italy*, Merits, Complaint No 19/2003, 7 December 2004, para 41. The Committee goes on to explain: 'In its interpretation of Article 17 the Committee refers, in particular to, Article 19 of the United Nations Convention on the Rights of the Child as interpreted by the Committee on the Rights of the Child; Article 3 of the European Convention of Human Rights as interpreted by the European Court of Human Rights … Recommendation No R (93) 2 on the medico-social aspects of child abuse adopted by the Committee of Ministers on 22 March 1993; Recommendation No R (90)2 on social measures concerning violence within the family adopted by the Committee of Ministers on 15 January 1990; Recommendation No R (85)4 on violence within

The ECSR had occasion to stress the importance of the evolutionary interpretive approach again in 2006, in *Marangopoulos Foundation for Human Rights (MFHR) v Greece*, when it made clear that the ESC must be interpreted 'in the light of the current conditions'.[24]

The principle also appears in *Defence for Children International (DCI) v the Netherlands*. This case is significant, because it provides the most complete and detailed account of the interpretive rules and techniques guiding the ECSR's activity, citing previous cases and providing a sort of state-of-the-art explanation for its interpretive method:

> The Committee recalls that the Charter was envisaged as a human rights instrument to complement the European Convention on Human Rights. It is a living instrument dedicated to certain values which inspired it: dignity, autonomy, equality, solidarity … and other generally recognised values. It must be interpreted so as to give life and meaning to fundamental social rights … The Committee interprets the Charter in the light of the rules set out in the [VCLT], among which its Article 31§3(c) … Indeed, the Charter cannot be interpreted in a vacuum. The Charter should so far as possible be interpreted in harmony with other rules of international law of which it forms part … The Committee considers that a teleological approach should be adopted when interpreting the Charter, ie it is necessary to seek the interpretation of the treaty that is the most appropriate in order to realise the aim and achieve the object of the treaty, not that which would restrict to the greatest possible degree the obligations undertaken by the Parties … It follows *inter alia* that restrictions on rights are to be read restrictively, ie understood in such a manner as to preserve intact the essence of the right and to achieve the overall purpose of the Charter.[25]

The ECSR, in conclusion, takes an evolutionary approach to interpreting the ESC, by referring to the living instrument doctrine developed by the ECtHR. In so doing, the just-quoted decision makes clear that the ECSR does not look to the mere passage of time as the primary basis for evolving meanings. Rather, it looks chiefly at the underlying values inspiring the Charter: 'dignity, autonomy, equality, solidarity … and other generally recognised values'. It sees the Charter's evolution as a living doctrine that moves towards the fulfilment of certain ideal values, close to a teleological interpretation, rather than the neutral update of an outdated meaning. This is an example of the 'idealistic' idea of evolution, as opposed to the pragmatic one, mentioned in the introduction.

the family adopted by the Committee of Ministers on 26 March 1985; Recommendation 1666 (2004) "Europe-wide ban on corporal punishment of children" adopted by the Parliamentary Assembly on 24 June 2004'. In identical terms see *World Organisation against Torture (OMCT) v Portugal*, Merits, Complaint No 20/2003, 7 December 2004, para 33; *World Organisation against Torture (OMCT) v Ireland*, Merits, Complaint No 18/2003, 7 December 2004, para 54; *World Organisation against Torture (OMCT) v Greece*, Merits, Complaint No 17/2003, 7 December 2004, para 30; *World Organisation against Torture (OMCT) v Belgium*, Merits, Complaint No 21/2003, 7 December 2004, para 37.

[24] *Marangopoulos Foundation for Human Rights (MFHR) v Greece*, Merits, Complaint No 30/2005, 6 December 2006, para 164.

[25] *Defence for Children International (DCI) v the Netherlands* Merits, Complaint No 47/2008, 20 October 2009, paras 34–36.

IV. The Relevance of the Case Law of Organs of Control in International Law, Between Ordinary Meaning, Subsequent Practice, and Supplementary Means

So far, we have seen how certain treaty bodies use an evolutionary approach (or rather the living instrument doctrine) in the interpretation of their underlying treaties. A second issue, however, concerns the way that States and courts transpose treaty obligations into their own legal systems. In particular, do they consider the treaties to be agreements to which States consented, untouchable by any other authorities (and that only States, through their practice, interpretive declarations, or official protocols may adjust and reshape their contents), accompanied by non-binding commentaries issued by treaty bodies? Or do they consider the text to be living on in the work of these committees, and evolving directly through the interpretations that those bodies give to them? The third option is for States to consider the value of committee interpretations on the merits, and to endorse or reject them, so that they sometimes play a role in the development of a text's interpretation.

On the one hand, these committees are made up of independent experts, whose authority derives from their qualification as specialists in the ongoing work of reading and interpreting the texts in question. This authoritativeness is diminished by the fact that they lack the consent of States, which would give their decisions binding effect. On the other hand, their expertise potentially suffers from insularity: it is possible that their lack of exposure to the general needs of a society limits their perspective, and it is not surprising that they have never received the full consent from States that would make their decisions binding.

This problem came up very clearly with regard to the weight and importance of the General Comments in interpreting the ICCPR. In Draft General Comment number 33, the Human Rights Committee attributed the weight of subsequent practice to a General Comment, under Article 31(3)(b) of the Vienna Convention on the Law of Treaties (VCLT).[26] Some States, in particular the United States, disagreed with this view,[27] rejecting classifying the interpretive legal value of General

[26] 'In relation to the general body of jurisprudence generated by the Committee, it may be considered that it constitutes "subsequent practice in the application of the treaty which establishes the agreement of the parties regarding its interpretation" within the sense of article 31(3)(b) of the Vienna Convention on the Law of Treaties, or, alternatively, the acquiescence of States parties in those determinations constitutes such practice', Draft general comment No 33. 'The obligations of States parties under the Optional Protocol to the International Covenant on Civil and Political Rights' (Second revised version as of 18 August 2008) CCPR/C/GC/33/CRP.3, 25 August 2008, para 17.

[27] Comments of the United States of America on the Human Rights Committee's 'Draft general comment 33: The Obligations of States Parties under the Optional Protocol to the International Covenant Civil and Political Rights', 17 October 2008, para 17, available at: www.state.gov/documents/organization/138851.pdf.

Comments as an authentic, official interpretation of the ICCPR (a power not found in the Covenant). Ultimately, that excerpt was removed from the final version.[28]

The issue also emerged, albeit in different terms, in the case law of the ICJ. If the Draft General Comment just mentioned was using the *subsequent practice* tool to frame the activity of the Human Rights Committee, the ICJ reasoning touched more on the concept of *ordinary meaning*.

In 2004, in the Advisory Opinion on the Wall in Palestine, the ICJ interpreted the ICCPR through the work of the Human Rights Committee, although without explaining the exact relevance of this reference in its reasoning.[29] Then, in 2010, in the judgment on the merits of the *Diallo* case, the ICJ discussed the relevance of the UN bodies overseeing the implementation of the UN Covenant on Civil and Political Rights, and of the UN Convention against Torture and other Inhuman and Cruel Treatments. The Court succinctly observed:

> Although the Court is in no way obliged, in the exercise of its judicial functions, to model its own interpretation of the Covenant on that of the Committee, it believes that it should ascribe great weight to the interpretation adopted by this independent body that was established specifically to supervise the application of that treaty.[30]

Despite the fact that the ICJ took a partial step back from this statement a few years later,[31] it has indicated that these bodies have some weight – in *Diallo* it was 'great weight', while an independent body's interpretation was merely considered in the later case – in interpreting the treaty, but that this interpretation is not binding upon the parties, and cannot be confused with an authentic interpretation of the treaty. In other words, the voice coming from the technical, specialised body of experts studying and dealing with the cases at stake is relevant, but does not have the final say, and the parties to a treaty, and the courts adjudicating over them, remain free to adopt the treaty bodies' interpretation or to reject it.

These decisions do not enter into the merits of whether these decisions provide help in understanding the current, ordinary meaning of a term. If we consider that the meaning underlying a term of international law lives on in the work of these treaty bodies, alongside the work of States, international courts, international organisations, and so on, the importance of the work of these treaty bodies comes into play at the beginning of every interpretive reasoning in understanding

[28] General Comment 33, 620 Report of the Human Rights Committee, Official Records of the General Assembly, Sixty-fourth Session, Supplement No 40 (A/64/40) vol I, annex V.

[29] *Legal Consequences of the Construction of a Wall in the Occupied Palestinian Territory* (Advisory Opinion) [2004] ICJ Rep 136, 179–90, 192.

[30] *Ahmadou Sadio Diallo (Republic of Guinea v Democratic Republic of the Congo)* (Judgment) [2010] ICJ Rep 213, para 66; E Bjorge, 'Case Concerning Ahmadou Sadio Diallo' (2011) 105 *American Journal of International Law* 534; P Palchetti, 'The Authority of the Decisions of International Judicial or Quasi-judicial Bodies in the Case Law of the International Court of Justice: Dialogue or Competition?', Decisions of the ICJ as Sources of International Law? Gaetano Morelli Lectures Series Vol 2 (Rome, International and European Papers Publishing, 2018) 107.

[31] *Obligation to Prosecute or Extradite (Belgium v Senegal)* (Judgment) [2012] ICJ Rep 422, paras 100–02.

what is the current, ordinary meaning of a term. However, this conclusion would give an interpretive power to the treaty bodies that is not provided for in their statutes. Here the distinction between linguistic theories on ordinary meaning, and the institutional framework separating international mechanisms from full political bodies such as States is hard to draw.[32] Concern for the institutional framework would tend to frame the work of treaty bodies as supplementary means under Article 32 of the VCLT, and not as primary sources to assess the current ordinary meaning under Article 31(1) of the VCLT. The treaty bodies themselves speak to their vision of the current ordinary meaning, but States decided not to grant them binding authority in the treaties and reaffirm their ultimate authority over the ordinary meaning by framing treaty bodies' interpretations as supplementary.

This struggle is reflected in Conclusion 13 of the ILC's recent final report on Subsequent Agreements and Subsequent Practice in relation to Treaties:

> 2. The relevance of a pronouncement of an expert treaty body for the interpretation of a treaty is subject to the applicable rules of the treaty.
>
> 3. A pronouncement of an expert treaty body may give rise to, or refer to, a subsequent agreement or subsequent practice by parties under article 31, paragraph 3, or subsequent practice under article 32. Silence by a party shall not be presumed to constitute subsequent practice under article 31, paragraph 3 (b), accepting an interpretation of a treaty as expressed in a pronouncement of an expert treaty body.
>
> 4. This draft conclusion is without prejudice to the contribution that pronouncements of expert treaty bodies make to the interpretation of the treaties under their mandates.

The analysis of international practice carried out by the Special Rapporteur Georg Nolte, did not provide a conclusive determination of the interpretive weight of these decisions, but adopted this equivocal language ('may give rise', 'silence … shall not be presumed to constitute'), leaving room for further contextual analysis to assess their relevance.

V. The Relevance of the Case Law of Organs of Control in Two Recent Italian Decisions

The same troubled relationship also affects domestic courts. In a recent article, Machiko Kanetake commented on several cases of domestic courts dealing with treaty bodies' interpretations. She observed a 'selective and partial accommodation of international findings by domestic courts, which both approve and contest the treaty bodies' opinions and their legitimacy'.[33] More recently, the Italian Constitutional Court was asked about the interpretive role played by

[32] C Marquet, 'Prospective Linguistics and Trade: The Art of the Deal', ch 18 in this book.
[33] Kanetake, above n 5, 204.

ECSR pronouncements, particularly those coming from the collective system of complaints, in determining the content of the ESC.[34] In its judgment, the Italian Constitutional Court stresses that the ESC 'features distinctive aspects that are highly specific compared to ordinary international agreements, which aspects it shares with the ECHR', and that the ESC is an 'international source,' therefore falling under Article 117(1), of the Italian Constitution, which states that Italy shall comply with international obligations.[35] However it establishes that the pronouncements of the European Committee on Social Rights, although authoritative, *do not bind* domestic judges in the interpretation of the ESC, 'especially if … the expansive interpretation proposed is not confirmed by our principles of constitutional law'.[36]

Such a conclusion is very different from what the same Constitutional Court has said about the ECtHR regarding the interpretation of the ECHR, and the independent life of the notions enshrined therein: 'Since … the provisions of the ECHR live through the interpretation given to them by the ECtHR, the examination of constitutionality must give consideration to the norm as a product of interpretation, and not the provision considered in itself'.[37]

The Italian Constitutional Court then grounded this direct link between the national and international realms, which connects the evolution of the rights enshrined in the ECHR through ECtHR case law to the Italian Constitution, in Article 32.1 of the ECHR, recognising the exclusive competence of the Court on all the issues concerning the interpretation and application of the ECHR and its protocols. Ten years later, the Italian Constitutional Court returned to Article 32, using it to find that the system of protection of human rights established with the ECHR is unique, and distinguishing it from the ESC.

> In contrast to the ECHR, the European Social Charter does not contain any provision the effect of which is equivalent to Article 32(1), which provides that '[t]he jurisdiction of the Court shall extend to all matters concerning the interpretation and application of the Convention and the Protocols thereto …' In turn, the Additional Protocol to the European Social Charter Providing for a System of Collective Complaints does not contain any provision analogous to Article 46 ECHR, which asserts that '[t]he High Contracting Parties undertake to abide by the final judgment of the Court in any case to which they are parties', a provision which establishes the status as *res iudicata* of the judgments given by the ECtHR in relation to the state(s) that are parties to the case as

[34] On the ESC see above nn 21 and 22.

[35] Italian Constitutional Court, Judgment 120/2018, para 10.1 of the Conclusions on points of law. Art 117 states: 'Legislative powers shall be vested in the State and the Regions in compliance with the Constitution and with the constraints deriving from EU legislation and international obligations'. The Italian Constitutional Court offers a translation of the most relevant Judgments and Orders; Judgment 120/2018 is available at: www.cortecostituzionale.it/documenti/download/doc/recent_judgments/S_2018_120_EN.pdf.

[36] ibid, para 13.4 of the Conclusions on points of law.

[37] Italian Constitutional Court, Judgment 348/2007, para 4.7 of the Conclusions on points of law.

> well as the actual dispute ruled upon by the Court … Within the context of the relations thereby framed between the European Social Charter and the signatory states, the decisions of the Committee, whilst being authoritative, are not binding on the national courts when interpreting the Charter, especially if – as in the case at issue here – the expansive interpretation proposed is not confirmed by our principles of constitutional law.[38]

In some places the wording is reminiscent of the *Diallo* case, and reiterates that the Committee's decisions can be authoritative, although they are not binding per se.[39] Unlike *Diallo*, however, the Italian Constitutional Court then enters into the merits of the question of whether the ECSR's interpretation is authoritative, and concludes by introducing an element of suspicion on its interpretive methodology. In holding that the ECSR's work is not authoritative in this case, and explaining why it does not adopt it, the Italian high court called it an 'expansive interpretation' that would not be in line with the principles of the Italian Constitution. In light of what the Court considered to be a stretched interpretation, it found it more reasonable to stay within constitutional parameters.

A few months later, the Italian Constitutional Court had the occasion to go back to the same issue. This time the Court did not make any reference to the different legal frameworks of the ECHR and the ESC. To the contrary, by noticing that there was an overlap between constitutional and international sources, the Italian Constitutional Court took a less dismissive attitude towards the ECSR's case law.[40] In the case, the Court had to decide on the constitutionality of a law establishing fixed compensation in termination of employment cases. In order to reply to the question, the Court considered Article 24(1)(b) of the ESC,[41] and the interpretation given by the ECSR to it:

> In the decision given in relation to collective complaint no 106/2014, filed by the *Finnish Society of Social Rights against Finland*, the European Committee of Social Rights clarified that compensation is adequate if it is capable of ensuring adequate redress for the actual harm suffered by the worker dismissed without a valid reason and of dissuading the employer from the unjustified termination of contracts. The line of argumentation followed by the Committee thus involves an assessment of the system of compensation in terms of its dissuasive effect, and at the same time of its giving due consideration to the loss suffered (paragraph 45).[42]

Importantly, the Court then concluded that 'the decisions of the Committee have authoritative status, although are not binding on national courts'.[43]

[38] Italian Constitutional Court, Judgment 120/2018, para 13.4 of the Conclusions on points of law.
[39] Above n 25.
[40] Italian Constitutional Court, Judgment 194/2018.
[41] Which recognises 'the right of workers whose employment is terminated without a valid reason to *adequate* compensation or other *appropriate* relief' (emphasis added).
[42] ibid, para 14 of the Conclusions on points of law.
[43] ibid.

VI. Law versus Non-Law; My Values versus Your Values. Is there Room for Common Ground to Assess Evolution?

This chapter began with an inward-looking approach, focusing on the activities of the independent treaty bodies, and how they look at the evolution of the underlying treaty (section III). Then it looked outwards, to see how international law considers treaty bodies' decisions in interpreting a treaty (section IV) and if the Italian Constitutional Court, in applying the ESC, considers it to be clarified and evolved by the interpretation of the treaty body overseeing its application (section V).

It found that, while the term 'evolutionary interpretation' does not appear in treaty body decisions, some refer to the 'living instrument doctrine'. This theory is very rarely explained, but is rather borrowed wholesale from the ECtHR. In the pivotal *Defence for Children International (DCI) v the Netherlands*, the ECSR clearly linked the doctrine to the values underlying the ECS, explicitly taking an evolutionary interpretation grounded on a teleological approach, showing an idealistic, rather than pragmatic approach to the evolution of treaties (above, sections II and III).

The second part of the chapter looked at the interpretive power of these decisions in the eyes of international and domestic courts (sections IV and V). International law has struggled over the past 20 years to frame, once and for all, the interpretive weight of these decisions. The notion that a General Comment could amount to subsequent practice under the VCLT has been explicitly rejected. The difficulty, in terms of the institutional framework, to consider non-binding decisions as capable of building the evolved-and-now-ordinary meaning of a term has not been explicitly addressed by the ICJ, and lurks in the background of its case law and of the ILC work on subsequent agreements and subsequent practice. While treaty bodies claim that their living instrument interpretations define a meaning that is (now) ordinary (and are, therefore, a primary means of interpretation under Article 31.1 of the VCLT), a reading attentive to the institutional framework, to the interpretive powers attributed in treaties to treaty bodies, and to the theory of the sources of law, would tend to put them under Article 32 of the VCLT as supplementary means (above, section IV). This distinction drawn by the ILC can be misleading: supplementary means of interpretation come into play when a term is obscure or when there is a need to confirm it; Article 32 does not address the question of whether an instrument, a decision, is binding or not binding. The difference here is not between having a clear term, and an obscure one in need of some help to clarify it, but rather it is the one between law (term in a treaty and its customary ordinary meaning, under Article 38(1)(b) of the ICJ statute), and non-law in the form of subsidiary help (under Article 38(1)(d) of the ICJ statute). The issue is not about what is clear or unclear, but rather about who has power to say what the law is (that is, to define its evolved meaning).

Two recent decisions by the Italian Constitutional Court bolstered the ICJ's conclusions in the *Diallo* case that the work of treaty bodies cannot be considered binding for the interpretation of the underlying treaties, but that they have 'an authoritative status'. However, while *Diallo* generally attributed 'great weight' to treaty body interpretations, the Italian Constitutional Court entered into the merits of analysing whether to follow a specific iteration of the ECSR's work. Thus, in one case, it found that the ECSR 'extensive' interpretation of the rights enshrined in the Charter was not convincing, and preferred to look at Italian constitutional principles to interpret the ESC. In the second case, the Court observed that the constitutional and international sources were overlapping and considered a previous ECSR decision to clarify the meaning of the ESC. What is striking about the two decisions is the different weight that the Italian Constitutional Court gave to ECSR decisions in the space of a few months (although the Court explained this in one decision by referring to the relative proximity of the given ESC right to a corresponding Italian constitutional value). In the first case, the Court took a minimalist approach, grounded in the text of the ESC: in the second case, it did not hesitate to consider an ECSR case that shed light on an ambiguous provision.

There is also another relevant point that emerges from these cases. The first Italian decision, the 'sovereignist' (as we would say today) or 'dualist' (taking the more traditional term) one, in order to ground its interpretation, decided to look at other Italian constitutional values:

> [T]he decisions of the Committee, whilst being authoritative, are not binding on the national courts when interpreting the Charter, especially if – as in the case at issue here – the expansive interpretation proposed is not confirmed by our principles of constitutional law.[44]

The ECSR, too, in interpreting its articles, looked at the values underlying the treaty:

> [The ESC] is a living instrument dedicated to certain values which inspired it: dignity, autonomy, equality, solidarity … and other generally recognised values. It must be interpreted so as to give life and meaning to fundamental social rights.[45]

Neither decision is unorthodox. In particular, the ECSR approach can easily be framed under the reference to the object and purpose of Article 31(1) of the VCLT. However, what is striking is that the decisions are equally insular, relying only on their own systems. It seems that any broader reflection on shared values is not possible. The context – the immediate legal context – prevails. This makes it easy for a supreme court to label the work of a treaty body as expansionist, or for an international entity to label state activities as parochial. However, this results in an interpretive stand-off that shows few signs of forward progress, and increasing reciprocal mistrust.

[44] Italian Constitutional Court, Judgment 120/2018, para 13.4 of the Conclusions on points of law.

[45] *Defence for Children International (DCI) v the Netherlands*, Merits, Complaint No 47/2008, 20 October 2009, para 34.

10

Evolutionary Interpretation of Unilateral Acts of States and International Organisations

PAOLO PALCHETTI

I. Introduction

The general rules of interpretation set out in Articles 31 and 32 of the Vienna Convention on the Law of Treaties (VCLT) do not directly deal with the possibility of having recourse to evolutionary interpretation. However, as is frequently observed, correctly applying the method of treaty interpretation envisaged by these general rules provides an adequate answer to the question of whether evolutionary interpretation is permitted in a given case.[1] Thus, by giving weight to elements such as the ordinary meaning of the terms employed, the context or the object and purpose of the treaty, the general rule set out in Article 31(1) may justify the view that,

> where the parties have used generic terms in a treaty, the parties necessarily having been aware that the meaning of the terms was likely to evolve over time, and where the treaty has been entered into for a very long period or is 'of continuing duration', the parties must be presumed, as a general rule, to have intended those terms to have an evolving meaning.[2]

[1] See especially E Bjorge, *The Evolutionary Interpretation of Treaties* (Oxford, Oxford University Press, 2014). See also D McRae, 'Evolutionary Interpretation: The Relevance of Context', ch 7; and E Bjorge, 'Time Present and Time Past: The Intention of the Parties and the Evolutionary Interpretation of Treaties', ch 5 in this book. However, for the view that Arts 31–33 are 'too flexible to offer any firm guidance to international adjudicators faced with a choice between the original or modern-day meaning of treaty terms', see J Wyatt, 'Using Intertemporal Linguistics to Resolve the Problem at the Origin and Core of the Evolutionary Interpretation Debate', ch 6 in this book.

[2] *Dispute Regarding Navigational and Related Rights (Costa Rica v Nicaragua)* (Judgment) [2009] ICJ Rep 213, 243, para 66.

The role assigned by Article 31(3) to subsequent agreements and subsequent practice, as well as to the relevant rules of international law, provides further grounds supporting recourse to evolutionary interpretation.[3]

If the general rules set out in the VCLT provide adequate guidance on the conditions for the evolutionary interpretation of treaties, it is less clear whether one can rely on these rules for addressing the evolutionary interpretation of acts other than treaties, particularly unilateral acts of States, or acts and resolutions of international organisations. How far the general rules of treaty interpretation can be used, by analogy, for interpreting acts other than treaties remains surrounded by a certain ambivalence. As we will see, international courts are generally inclined to use the rules of treaty interpretation as a starting point to define the method to be followed when interpreting unilateral acts. Yet, they also emphasise the need to consider the special nature of the acts to be interpreted and, for that purpose, appear to accord to certain elements an importance that is different from that accorded to the same elements in the context of treaty interpretation. When assessing the conditions for an evolutionary interpretation of unilateral acts of States or international organisations, this difference in the nature of the act to be interpreted and in the elements that are relevant for the purposes of interpretation must necessarily be taken into consideration. In particular, the fact of giving weight to elements that are not the same as in the context of treaty interpretation may imply that the conditions required for the evolutionary interpretation of unilateral acts of States or international organisations may also be different.

In practice, the need for evolutionary interpretation is less likely to arise in the case of unilateral acts than in the case of treaties. Indeed, State practice or the case law of international courts has little to offer on this issue. This is not surprising. As noted by the International Court of Justice (ICJ), unilateral acts creating legal obligations for a State 'often are very specific',[4] including as to the duration of their legal effects, thereby reducing the scope for a possible evolutionary interpretation. A need for evolutionary interpretation is less likely to arise in the case of resolutions of international organisations, as a resolution can be easily replaced, and frequently are replaced, by new resolutions. Although less relevant in practice, the evolutionary interpretation of unilateral acts by States and international organisations remains an issue that is worth exploring, particularly because it allows us to shed light on the differences, if any, between the method of interpretation applicable to such acts and that applicable to treaties.

The next paragraphs, which provide some initial thoughts on a largely unexplored issue, will focus on three categories of unilateral acts, namely treaty

[3] See, eg, G Distefano, 'L'interprétation évolutive de la norme internationale' (2011) 115 *Revue générale de droit international public* 373; L Crema, *La prassi successiva e l'interpretazione del diritto internazionale scritto* (Milano, Giuffré, 2017) 325–30. On the importance of 'context', within the meaning of Art 31(2), for the purposes of evolutionary interpretation see especially G Marceau, 'L'interprétation évolutive par le juge OMC: sophisme ou nécessité?' (2018) 122 *Revue générale de droit international public* 23, 37–38.

[4] *Nuclear Tests (Australia v France)* (Judgment) [1974] ICJ Rep 253, 268–69, para 48.

reservations, unilateral declarations by States capable of creating legal obligations, and Security Council resolutions. These three categories have been chosen because the case law of international courts and the work of the International Law Commission (ILC) have provided some interesting elements for discussion.

II. Reservations to Treaties

Reservations to treaties are acts having a somewhat hybrid nature. As the definition of reservation contained in Article 2(1)(d) of the VCLT makes clear, they are 'unilateral statements' which, however, are strictly associated with a treaty, as they purport 'to exclude or to modify the legal effect of certain provisions of the treaty' in their application to the reserving State.

Being a unilateral act, the identification of the 'true intention' of the reserving State, as opposed to its 'declared intention', tends to acquire a role that goes beyond the role of the intention for treaties. This implies that the circumstances of the preparation and formulation of the reservation are to be given a particular weight when interpreting such reservation. I will revert to this point later when dealing more broadly with the interpretation of unilateral declarations of States capable of creating legal obligations. It suffices here to note that this element is now reflected in the *Guide to Practice on Reservations to Treaties* adopted by the ILC.[5] For the purposes of determining the intention of the author of the reservation, Guideline 4.2.6 requires that, in addition to the text of the reservation and the object and purpose of the treaty, 'the circumstances in which the reservation was formulated' be given adequate consideration.[6]

When compared with other unilateral acts, the distinctive feature of reservations is that, as the ILC put it, 'reservations are acts attached to a treaty' and that, '[c]onsequently, the treaty is the context that should be taken into account for the purposes of interpreting the reservation'.[7] The relevance of the treaty for the interpretation of the reservation is an element that deserves attention when assessing the

[5] *Guide to Practice on Reservations to Treaties*, *Yearbook of the International Law Commission* 2011, vol II, Part Two, 26–38.

[6] Guideline 4.2.6 provides that '[a] reservation is to be interpreted in good faith, taking into account the intention of its author as reflected primarily in the text of the reservation, as well as the object and purpose of the treaty and the circumstances in which the reservation was formulated'.

[7] See the commentaries to Guideline 4.2.6, in *Report of the International Law Commission on the Work of its Sixty-Third Session* UN Doc A/66/10/Add.1, 468. For the observation that 'a reservation must be interpreted by examining its text in accordance with the ordinary meaning which must be attributed to the terms in which it has been formulated within the general context of the treaty of which the reservation forms an integral part', see Inter-American Court of Human Rights, *Restrictions to the Death Penalty (Arts 4(2) and 4(4) American Convention on Human Rights)* Advisory Opinion OC-3/83 Series A no 3, para 65. For another example of a unilateral act that forms part of a treaty framework, one can refer to the WTO schedules of commitments. On the interpretation of schedules of commitments in WTO law, see A Orakhelashvili, *The Interpretation of Acts and Rules in Public International Law* (Oxford, Oxford University Press, 2008) 477–80.

possibility for an evolutionary interpretation. Two points are particularly significant in this respect. The first concerns the role of the object and purpose of the treaty for the purposes of interpreting the reservation. In its Advisory Opinion on the *Reservations to the Genocide Convention*, the ICJ established a link between the interpretation of a reservation and the object and purpose of the treaty in question by noting that '[i]t must clearly be assumed that the contracting States are desirous of preserving intact at least what is essential to the object of the Convention'.[8] The ILC relied on this statement for including the object and purpose of the treaty among the main elements to consider in interpreting a reservation.[9] The importance attached in this context to the treaty's object and purpose could justify the evolutionary interpretation of the reservation. In fact, the preservation of the treaty's object and purpose is frequently regarded as a ground supporting resort to this type of interpretation. One may refer, in this respect, to the arbitral tribunal's position in the *Iron Rhine* case, which referred to evolutionary interpretation as ensuring 'an application of the treaty that would be effective in terms of its object and purpose'.[10] The evolutionary interpretation of the reservation may find an additional ground in the fact that the 'object and purpose of the treaty' is itself an evolving concept. Indeed, as noted by the ILC, 'the object and purpose of a treaty was likely to evolve over time'.[11]

The strict interdependence between the reservation and the treaty may also be relevant in determining the meaning to be attributed to the terms employed in the reservation. This is the case, in particular, when the same, or similar, terms are used both in the reservation and in the treaty. In the *Aegean Sea Continental Shelf* case, the ICJ observed that 'there is clearly a high probability, if not an actual presumption, that reservations made in terms used in the treaty are intended to relate to the corresponding categories in the treaty'.[12] In particular, the Court made the point that 'it is reasonable to presume that there is a close link between the concepts of territorial status in the General Act and in Greece's instrument of accession to it'.[13] The Court's approach in this case is of particular interest, since the Court clearly interpreted in an evolutionary manner the expression 'territorial status' contained in Greece's reservation as well as in the General Act. In doing so, the Court relied on the fact that the expression 'territorial status' was a generic term 'denoting any matters comprised within the concept of territorial status under general international law' and that the treaty to which the reservation related was 'a convention for the pacific settlement of disputes designed to be of the most general kind and of

[8] *Reservations to the Convention on Genocide* (Advisory Opinion) [1951] ICJ Rep 15, 26–27.

[9] See Guideline 4.2.6, above n 6.

[10] *Award in the Arbitration regarding the Iron Rhine ('Ijzeren Rijn') (Belgium v Netherlands)* (2005) 27 *Reports of International Arbitral Awards* 35, 73, para 80.

[11] See *Report of the International Law Commission*, above n 7, 362. See also, on this point, G Fitzmaurice, 'The Law and Procedure of the International Court of Justice 1951–4: Treaty Interpretation and Other Treaty Points' (1957) 33 *The British Year Book of International Law* 203, 208.

[12] *Aegean Sea Continental Shelf (Greece v Turkey)* (Judgment) [1978] ICJ Rep 3, 23.

[13] ibid, 29.

continuing duration'.[14] The link between the treaty and the reservation establishes a presumption to the effect that, if the meaning to be attached to the treaty terms has evolved, the same or similar terms employed in the reservation should also be interpreted in an evolutionary manner.[15]

III. Unilateral Declarations of States Capable of Creating Legal Obligations

The importance of the *Nuclear Tests* cases for the identification of the principles applicable to unilateral declarations of States capable of creating legal obligations needs hardly to be stressed. While the 1974 judgments of the Court did not deal with the possibility for an evolutionary interpretation of this category of unilateral acts, the long-standing dispute over nuclear testing in the South Pacific region provides an illustration of the potential relevance of such a question. In 1974, the ICJ recognised that, as a consequence of its unilateral statements, France had an obligation not to conduct any further atmospheric nuclear tests and that, in the event of a resumption of nuclear tests in the atmosphere, the basis of the Court's judgment would have been affected.[16] When, in 1995, France announced its intention to conduct a series of underground nuclear weapons tests, New Zealand asked the Court to establish that the resumption by France of such tests would affect the basis of the 1974 judgment. To support its claim that underground nuclear testing was also covered by the Court's judgment, New Zealand heavily relied on the need to take account of developments that had occurred after 1974. It first contended that contemporary scientific evidence, which was not available in 1974, showed that underground nuclear testing might lead to some of the same environmental consequences as atmospheric testing.[17] It also pointed to 'changes in the law' concerning nuclear testing that 'were capable of affecting the basis of the 1974 Judgment'.[18] Admittedly, New Zealand did not ask the Court to interpret in an evolutionary manner France's declarations.[19] Indeed, there was substantially no room for an interpretation to the effect that France's binding commitment not to carry out further atmospheric nuclear tests included underground testing.

[14] ibid, 31.

[15] See also the commentaries to Guideline 4.2.6 of the International Law Commission, *Report of the International Law Commission*, above n 7, 471–72, which however specifies that this presumption applies 'provided that the change does not turn out to be contrary to the intention of the author of the reservation, as manifested at the time the reservation was formulated'.

[16] *Nuclear Tests (New Zealand v France)* (Judgment) [1974] ICJ Rep 457, 477, para 63.

[17] *Request for an Examination of the Situation in Accordance with Paragraph 63 of the Court's Judgment of 20 December 1974 in the Nuclear Tests (New Zealand v France) Case* (Order) [1995] ICJ Rep 288, 297–98, para 32.

[18] ibid, para 34.

[19] A vague allusion to a possible interpretation to that effect of French declaration is made by Judge Weeramantry in his Dissenting Opinion, ibid, 336.

French statements were clear in providing that 'the commitment entered into by France in 1974 had two inseparable aspects, namely, on the one hand, an end to nuclear explosions in the atmosphere and, on the other, the shift to a new type of testing, underground testing'.[20] However, had France omitted to mention its intention to carry out underground nuclear testing in 1974, an evolutionary interpretation of the commitment to undertake no further atmospheric tests, at least in principle, would not have been unplausible.

Among the factors to be considered when assessing the possibility for an evolutionary interpretation, one should refer in the first place to the importance that is attached, as a rule, to non-textual elements for the interpretation of unilateral acts that create legal obligations. This distinctive feature of the interpretation of these acts has been confirmed by the ICJ in a number of decisions. In the *Frontier Dispute* case the Court observed that '[i]n order to assess the intentions of the author of a unilateral act, account must be taken of all the factual circumstances in which the act occurred'.[21] In the *Fisheries Jurisdiction* case, it maintained that, in interpreting a State's declaration of acceptance of the Court's jurisdiction, due regard must be had to the intention of the State concerned at the time when it accepted the compulsory jurisdiction of the Court, further specifying that

> the intention of a reserving State may be deduced not only from the text of the relevant clause, but also from the context in which the clause is to be read, and an examination of evidence regarding the circumstances of its preparation and the purposes intended to be served.[22]

The fact that non-textual elements, such as the preparatory works and the circumstances of the adoption of the act, which Article 32 of the VCLT qualifies as 'supplementary means of interpretation', assume greater weight in the context of unilateral acts than in the context of treaties has also been recognised by the ILC, which expressly included these elements in the basic rule of interpretation applicable to unilateral acts. Principle VII of the 2006 Guiding Principles provides that '[i]n interpreting the content of such obligations, weight shall be given first and foremost to the text of the declaration, together with the context and the circumstances in which it was formulated'.[23] Given the importance attached to evidence pertaining to the circumstances of the preparation of the unilateral act and to other non-textual elements indicative of the 'true intention' of the declaring State,

[20] ibid, 300, para 39.

[21] *Frontier Dispute (Burkina Faso v Mali)* (Judgment) [1986] ICJ Rep 554, 574, para 40. See also *Armed Activities in Congo (New Application 2002) (Democratic Republic of Congo v Rwanda)* (Jurisdiction and Admissibility) [2006] ICJ Rep 6, 28.

[22] *Fisheries Jurisdiction (Spain v Canada)* (Jurisdiction of the Court) [1998] ICJ Rep 432, 454, para 49. See *Anglo-Iranian Oil Co (United Kingdom v Iran)* (Jurisdiction) [1952] ICJ Rep 93, 105, which predates the *Fisheries Jurisdiction* case and where the Court, in interpreting the unilateral declaration, gave particular importance to 'the special reasons which led the Government of Iran to draft the Declaration in a very restrictive manner'.

[23] See Guiding Principles applicable to unilateral declarations of States capable of creating legal obligations, *Yearbook of the International Law Commission* 2006, vol II, Part Two, 160.

evidence of this kind must be given an even greater role, particularly if compared to what happens in the context of treaty interpretation, when it comes to determining whether terms used in a unilateral act must be interpreted in an evolutionary manner. This also suggests that greater caution should be used in resorting to an evolutionary interpretation of a unilateral declaration if relying exclusively on the terms employed in the declaration or on other purely textual elements.

Another feature of the interpretation of unilateral acts that may influence the use of evolutionary interpretation is the idea that such acts must be interpreted strictly. This idea seems to find some support in the case law of the ICJ, which, in its judgments in the *Nuclear Tests* cases held that, 'when States make statements by which their freedom of action is to be limited, a restrictive interpretation is called for'.[24] Principle VII of the ILC Guiding Principle endorses such view by providing that '[i]n the case of doubt as to the scope of the obligations resulting from such a declaration, such obligations must be interpreted in a restrictive manner'. Several authors have criticised the view that unilateral acts must be interpreted restrictively, pointing out that a restrictive approach only applies to the determination of whether a legal obligation exists, and not to the issue of interpreting the obligation's scope.[25] Be that as it may, if one accepts the view that unilateral acts must be interpreted restrictively, this would represent a significant departure from the general rules of interpretation applicable to treaties, which only provide a method for interpretation without going to the substance of treaty provisions.[26] Following this approach, recourse to evolutionary interpretation should be assessed by also taking into account the effect that this interpretation would have on the scope of the obligations resulting from the unilateral act. Since the result of an evolutionary interpretation is frequently that of broadening the scope of the obligations deriving from a certain provision or declaration, the overall effect would likely be that of limiting the possibility of resorting to such an interpretation.

IV. Security Council Resolutions

An authoritative description of the method to be applied for the interpretation of resolutions of the Security Council is found in the 2010 *Kosovo* Advisory Opinion. There, the ICJ made clear that

> [w]hile the rules on treaty interpretation embodied in Articles 31 and 32 of the Vienna Convention on the Law of Treaties may provide guidance, differences between Security

[24] *Nuclear Tests (Australia v France)*, above n 4, 267, para 44.

[25] See C Eckart, *Promises of States in International Law* (Oxford, Hart Publishing, 2012) 212–14; Orakhelashvili, above n 7, 467. In *Fisheries Jurisdiction (Spain v Canada)*, above n 22, para 44, the Court specified that there is no reason to interpret restrictively reservations to unilateral declaration accepting the jurisdiction of the Court.

[26] See G Gaja, 'The Protection of General Interests in the International Community' (2014) 364 *Collected Courses of the Hague Academy of International Law* 9, 63–64.

> Council resolutions and treaties mean that the interpretation of Security Council resolutions also require that other factors be taken into account.[27]

In particular, among the elements to be taken into account for the interpretation of Security Council resolutions, the Court referred to

> statements by representatives of members of the Security Council made at the time of their adoption, other resolutions of the Security Council on the same issue, as well as the subsequent practice of relevant United Nations organs and of States affected by those given resolutions.[28]

While this statement only concerned the interpretation of Security Council resolutions, commentators have noted that the arguments used by the Court to distinguish these resolutions from treaties apply more generally to decisions of organs of international organisations.[29]

In the *Kosovo* Advisory Opinion the Court did not elaborate on the differences between treaties and resolutions in the application of the VCLT rules of interpretation. A point that comes out clearly from the Court's Opinion, however, is the greater importance attached to non-textual elements and other supplementary means for the interpretation of resolutions. This specific feature of the Security Council resolutions had already been highlighted by commentators. As one author put it, in the case of Security Council resolutions, the 'Vienna Convention distinction between the general rule and supplementary means has even less significance than in the case of treaties'.[30] In this respect, the method of interpretation of resolutions comes close to the method applicable to unilateral acts of States. This point must be taken into consideration when assessing the possibility of the evolutionary interpretation of resolutions. It implies that textual elements, such as the use of 'generic terms' or terms whose meanings were likely to evolve over time, appear not to have the same importance as in the case of treaty interpretation.[31] Moreover, in order to establish whether the 'true intention' of the Security Council allows for an evolutionary interpretation of the resolution, evidence pertaining to the circumstances of the adoption of the resolution should be given adequate weight.

As already noted, it is rather unlikely that a need for an evolutionary interpretation of a resolution may arise. If there is a need to preserve the effectiveness of a resolution in the face of evolving circumstances, the solution will generally consist in a new Security Council resolution, which will eventually provide the 'authentic' interpretation to be given to the text in question. This does not mean

[27] *Accordance with International Law of the Unilateral Declaration of Independence with Respect to Kosovo* (Advisory Opinion) [2010] ICJ Rep 403, 442, para 94.

[28] ibid.

[29] HG Schermers and NM Blokker, *International Institutional Law*, 6th edn (Leiden, Brill, 2018) 885.

[30] M Wood, 'The Interpretation of Security Council Resolutions' (1998) 2 *Max Planck Yearbook of United Nations Law* 73, 95. See also M Wood, 'The Interpretation of Security Council Resolutions, Revisited' (2016) 20 *Max Planck Yearbook of United Nations Law* 3.

[31] As noted by Wood, 'The Interpretation of Security Council Resolutions', above n 30, 95, 'in general, less importance should attach to the minutiae of language'.

that the interpretation is necessarily fixed at the time of the adoption of the resolution. There is no reason to exclude the possibility that the interpretation of a resolution may not evolve in time.[32] In this respect, it is significant that in the *Kosovo* Advisory Opinion the Court expressly included, among the elements to be taken into account for the interpretation of Security Council resolutions, 'the subsequent practice of relevant United Nations organs and of States affected by those given resolutions'.[33] The weight thus assigned to the subsequent practice appears to suggest that, in interpreting a resolution, the circumstances prevailing at the time of the application of the resolution should also be taken into account. This may include possible changes in the law that takes place after the adoption of the resolution.[34] Recourse to an evolutionary interpretation may also be justified in the light of the importance which is generally assigned to a consideration of the resolution's object and purpose when interpreting it. The Court's approach in the *Kosovo* Advisory Opinion provides a clear illustration of this, given the central role assigned to the object and purpose of resolution 1244 (1999) for determining whether this resolution prohibited the authors of the declaration of 17 February 2008 from declaring independence from the Republic of Serbia.[35] The same approach can also be found in other decisions of international tribunals addressing the problem of the interpretation of Security Council resolutions.[36] Under certain circumstances the use of evolutionary interpretation may be justified as a means for better preserving the resolution's object and purpose.

A last point concerns the presumption that Security Council resolutions must be interpreted restrictively. Unlike unilateral acts of States creating legal obligations, it is hard to find precedents supporting such a presumption. The *Kosovo* Advisory Opinion made no reference to it, although Serbia had advanced an argument to that effect.[37] In this respect, it seems that no opposition to the use of evolutionary interpretation can be possibly grounded on any such presumption.

[32] For the view that 'the terms of a Resolution should be construed in accordance with the meaning they possess at the time of the adoption of the Resolution, since they are rebuttably presumed to convey the collective will of the community at that particular time' see E Papastavridis, 'Interpretation of Security Council Resolutions Under Chapter VII in the Aftermath of the Iraqi Crisis' (2007) 56 *International & Comparative Law Quarterly* 83, 106.

[33] *Accordance with International Law*, above n 27, 442.

[34] According to Wood, 'The Interpretation of Security Council Resolutions, Revisited', above n 30, 34, the impact of other rules of international law for the interpretation of Security Council resolution 'is likely to be less in light of Art 103 of the Charter'. This more limited impact would not exclude the possibility of taking account of changes in the law when interpreting a resolution.

[35] On this point see P Palchetti, 'L'interprétation des résolutions du Conseil de sécurité à la lumière de l'avisde la Cour internationale de Justice sur le Kosovo' in M Arcari and L Balmond (eds), *Questions de droit international autour de l'avis consultatif de la Cour internationale de justice sur le Kosovo* (Milano, Giuffrè, 2011) 162–64.

[36] See International Criminal Tribunal for the Former Yugoslavia, *Prosecutor v Tadić, Decision on the Defence Motion for Interlocutory Appeal on Jurisdiction*, IT-94-1-AR72, paras 77–78; Special Tribunal for Lebanon, *Interlocutory Decision on the Applicable Law: Terrorism, Conspiracy, Homicide, Perpetration, Cumulative Charging*, STL-11-01/1, paras 28–32.

[37] The Special Tribunal for Lebanon expressly excluded the existence of any such presumption. See *Decision on the Defence*, above n 36, para 29.

V. Concluding Remarks

While not uncontroversial, the view that there is no unitary method of interpretation applicable to all international acts is nowadays the one that largely prevails. A progressively increasing body of decisions from international courts and tribunals lends support to such a view, thereby contributing to clarifying the differences in the rules of interpretation applicable to different categories of acts. Inevitably, these differences have an impact on the use of evolutionary interpretation. In the case of treaties, where textual elements carry great weight for the purposes of interpretation, evolutionary interpretation may be justified by relying exclusively on the terms employed and on the consideration of the treaty's object and purpose. Greater caution, instead, is called for in the case of unilateral acts of States and of international organisations. Their interpretation requires an in-depth investigation of the 'true intention', as opposed to the 'declared intention', of the author of the act. Textual and non-textual elements must be carefully balanced one against the other to determine whether the author's intention allows for an evolutionary interpretation of the act in question. In sum, while certainly available, the use of evolutionary interpretation for unilateral acts appears to be subjected to stricter conditions than in the case of treaties.

Apart from the differences between treaties and unilateral acts, there are also differences among various categories of unilateral acts. In this respect, it would be unwise to pretend to construe a general approach to the evolutionary interpretation of unilateral acts. A better course would take into account the specific features of each category of unilateral acts and consider whether and to what extent such features may have an impact on the use of the evolutionary interpretation. This must be done with the awareness that this is an area where the practice available is limited and does not provide a solid basis on which to anchor precise conclusions.

PART III

Evolutionary Interpretation in Human Rights and Environment Law

11

The Strength of Evolutionary Interpretation in International Human Rights Law

GLORIA GAGGIOLI

I. Introduction

Evolutionary interpretation is the hallmark of interpretation in international human rights law. Human rights provisions being rather general and aphoristic, need to be fleshed out through judicial interpretation. The judge's role therefore is key in this branch of international law and human rights law would certainly not be as effective as it is today without dynamic and evolutionary judicial (or quasi-judicial) interpretations.

The propensity of the European Court of Human Rights (ECtHR) to resort to evolutionary interpretation to expand the protective scope of the European Convention has been the subject of much literature[1] and has been skilfully presented in Oliver Dörr's chapter.[2] The strength of evolutionary interpretation is not however limited to the European system of human rights protection. It is a human rights specificity that can be equally found at the universal and regional levels.[3]

[1] See, eg, G Letsas, 'The ECHR as a Living Instrument: Its Meaning and Legitimacy' in A Føllesdal et al (eds), *Constituting Europe: The European Court of Human Rights in a National, European and Global Context* (Cambridge, Cambridge University Press, 2013); A Mowbray, 'The Creativity of the European Court of Human Rights' (2005) 5 *Human Rights Law Review* 57; R Bernhardt, 'Evolutive Treaty Interpretation, Especially of the European Convention on Human Rights' (1999) 42 *German Yearbook of International Law* 11.

[2] See O Dörr 'The Strasbourg Approach to Evolutionary Interpretation', ch 12 in this book.

[3] For the Inter-American case law, see further below. The practice of human rights bodies at the universal and African level also relies on evolutionary interpretation, albeit less frequently and in a less sophisticated manner than the European and Inter-American Courts. See, eg, *Roger Judge v Canada*, CCPR/C/78/D/829/1998, UN Human Rights Committee (HRC), 13 August 2003 (on the requirement, under the right to life, for an abolitionist State to request assurances of non-application of the death penalty before deporting an accused); *Centre for Minority Rights Development (Kenya) and Minority Rights Group International on Behalf of Endorois Welfare Council v Kenya*, 276/04, African Commission on Human and Peoples' Rights, 25 November 2009 (on the right to property of Endorois people).

This chapter will start by providing a few recent examples of the jurisprudence of the Inter-American Court of Human Rights,[4] which is well known for its activism, illustrate the role or impact on human rights protection (part II). It will then discuss why evolutionary interpretation is so present in the human rights field and whether this type of interpretation can be replicated in other fields of international law (part III). Lastly, the chapter will touch upon the delicate question of the limits of evolutionary interpretation in international human rights law (part IV).

II. What is the Impact of Evolutionary Interpretation in International Human Rights Law? The Example of the Inter-American System

Evolutionary interpretation has had a tremendous impact on the Inter-American system of human rights protection, not only in relation to the substance of human rights but also in procedural/jurisdictional matters.[5]

The advisory jurisdiction of the Inter-American Court, in particular, has expanded through evolutionary interpretation. In a 1989 Advisory Opinion,[6] the Inter-American Court has granted itself the right to interpret not only treaties in its advisory opinions, as initially foreseen in the American Convention on Human Rights (ACHR),[7] but also a text such as the American Declaration of the Rights

[4] See also, N Mileva and M Fortuna, 'Environmental Protection as an Object of and Tool for Evolutionary Interpretation', ch 13 in this book, which analyses the following Advisory Opinion of the Inter-American Court in relation to the protection of the environment. See, *The Environment and Human Rights (State obligations in relation to the environment in the context of the protection and guarantee of the rights to life and to personal integrity – interpretation and scope of Articles 4(1) and 5(1) of the American Convention on Human Rights)*, Advisory Opinion OC-23/17, IACHR Series A No 23 (15 November 2017).

[5] See, eg, CE Arévalo Narváez and PA Patarroyo Ramírez, 'Treaties over Time and Human Rights: A Case Law Analysis of the Inter-American Court of Human Rights' (2017) 10 *Anuario Colombiano de Derecho Internacional*, available at: revistas.urosario.edu.co/xml/4295/429552542010/index.html; M De Pauw, 'The Inter-American Court of Human Rights and the Interpretive Method of External Referencing: Regional Consensus v Universality' in Y Haeck, O Ruiz-Chiriboga and CB Herrera (eds), *The Inter-American Court of Human Rights: Theory and Practice, Present and Future* (Cambridge, Intersentia, 2015); L Lixinski, 'Treaty Interpretation by the Inter-American Court of Human Rights: Expansionism at the Service of the Unity of International Law' (2010) 21 *European Journal of International Law* 585; GL Neuman, 'Import, Export and Regional Consent in the Inter-American Court of Human Rights' (2008) 19 *European Journal of International Law* 101.

[6] *Interpretation of the American Declaration of the Rights and Duties of Man Within the Framework of Article 64 of the American Convention on Human Rights*, Advisory Opinion OC-10/89, IACHR Series A No 10 (14 July 1989).

[7] Art 64, para 1, of the ACHR reads as follows: 'The member states of the Organization may consult the Court regarding the interpretation of this Convention *or of other treaties* concerning the protection of human rights in the American states' (emphasis added).

and Duties of Man, which is not a treaty,[8] based on a rather loose legal reasoning that relies heavily on evolutionary interpretation.[9]

The content of numerous rights guaranteed by the ACHR has been fleshed out though evolutionary interpretation. This is not only the case for rights that are prone to evolutionary interpretation, such as the prohibition of torture,[10] but also for less usual suspects. For instance, through evolutionary interpretation, the right to property has been interpreted as including a communal form of collective property of the land in favour of indigenous people.[11] This evolution has had a crucial impact on the rights of indigenous people whose culture, tradition and

[8] The American Declaration was adopted by the Ninth International Conference of American States (Bogotá, 1948) through a resolution adopted by the Conference itself. As admitted by the Inter-American Court itself, '[i]t was neither conceived nor drafted as a treaty'. See Advisory Opinion, above n 6, para 34.

[9] See Advisory Opinion, above n 6, para 37 ff: 'The American Declaration has its basis in the idea that "the international protection of the rights of man should be the principal guide of an evolving American law" (Third Considerandum). This American law has evolved from 1948 to the present; international protective measures, subsidiary and complementary to national ones, have been shaped by new instruments. As the International Court of Justice said: "an international instrument must be interpreted and applied within the overall framework of the juridical system in force at the time of the interpretation" … That is why the Court finds it necessary to point out that to determine the legal status of the American Declaration it is appropriate to look to the inter-American system of today in the light of the evolution it has undergone since the adoption of the Declaration, rather than to examine the normative value and significance which that instrument was believed to have had in 1948 … The General Assembly of the Organization has also repeatedly recognized that the American Declaration is a source of international obligations for the member states of the OAS … Hence it may be said that by means of an authoritative interpretation, the member States of the Organization have signaled their agreement that the Declaration contains and defines the fundamental human rights referred to in the Charter. … it follows that the Court is authorized, within the framework and limits of its competence, to interpret the American Declaration and to render an advisory opinion relating to it whenever it is necessary to do so in interpreting those instruments'.

[10] See, eg, *Bámaca Velásquez v Guatemala*, Merits, IACHR Series C No 70 (25 November 2000).

[11] *Mayagna (Sumo) Awas Tingni Community v Nicaragua*, Merits, Reparations and Costs, IACHR Series C No 79 (31 August 2001) paras 146–48: 'human rights treaties are live instruments whose interpretation must adapt to the evolution of the times and, specifically, to current living conditions … Through an evolutionary interpretation of international instruments for the protection of human rights, taking into account applicable norms of interpretation and pursuant to article 29(b) of the Convention – which precludes a restrictive interpretation of rights, it is the opinion of this Court that article 21 of the Convention protects the right to property in a sense which includes, among others, the rights of members of the indigenous communities within the framework of communal property, which is also recognised by the Constitution of Nicaragua. Among indigenous peoples there is a communitarian tradition regarding a communal form of collective property of the land, in the sense that ownership of the land is not centered on an individual but rather on the group and its community … Indigenous peoples' customary law must be especially taken into account for the purpose of this analysis. As a result of customary practices, possession of the land should suffice for indigenous communities lacking real title to property of the land to obtain official recognition of that property, and for consequent registration'. See also, *Moiwana Communities v Suriname*, Preliminary Objections, Merits, Reparations and Costs, IACHR Series C No 124 (15 June 2005) (effective occupation of the land by indigenous communities as well as the fact that these lands are ancestral indigenous properties suffice to recognise the existence of a right to property); *Yakye Axa Communities v Paraguay*, Merits, Reparations and Costs, IACHR Series C No 125 (17 June 2005) (other international law provisions, including in particular the Convention concerning Indigenous and Tribal Peoples Convention, 1989 (No 169) are taken into account to foster evolutionary interpretation).

survival are intrinsically linked to, and dependent on, the recognition of their right to land.

Evolutionary interpretation has also allowed the Court to tackle new facts, in light of scientific and technological evolutions, which could not have been foreseen at the moment of the adoption of the ACHR, such as IVF treatment. In a case against Costa Rica,[12] the Inter-American Court addressed the question whether a human embryo is a 'person' endowed with the right to life under the ACHR.[13] After a complex legal analysis involving notably a comparative law study to determine the present-day meaning of the term 'person', the Court considered that human embryos have no right to life before being implanted into a woman's womb.[14] As a consequence, prohibiting in-vitro fertilisation, which almost invariably implies the loss of human embryos, as Costa Rica did, could not be justified under the right to life and implied an excessive interference, notably, with the right to private and family life.[15]

Lastly, the Inter-American Court has used evolutionary interpretation as a tool to venture into the area of quasi norm-setting exercises. In an Advisory Opinion concerning migrant children, for instance, the Court conducted an evolutionary interpretation by gathering norms flowing from various human rights and refugee law instruments and then developed on that basis a brand new framework document for an effective protection of migrant children.[16]

In brief, evolutionary interpretation has been the vehicle for an expansion of the Court's competences, a growth in the rights of individuals and collectivities,

[12] *Artavia Murillo and others (In Vitro Fertilization) v Costa Rica*, Preliminary Objections, Merits, Reparations and Costs, IACHR Series C No 257 (28 November 2012).

[13] Art 4, para 1, of the ACHR: 'Every *person* has the right to have his life respected' (emphasis added).

[14] *Artavia Murillo and others (In Vitro Fertilization)*, above n 12, para 245 ff: 'This Court has indicated on other occasions that human rights treaties are living instruments, whose interpretation must keep abreast of the passage of time and current living conditions. This evolving interpretation is consistent with the general rules of interpretation established in Article 29 of the American Convention, as well as in the Vienna Convention on the Law of Treaties. In making an evolutive interpretation, the Court has granted special relevance to comparative law, and has therefore used domestic norms or the case law of domestic courts when analysing specific disputes in contentious cases … Accordingly, the Court observes that the regulatory trends in international law do not lead to the conclusion that the embryo should be treated in the same way as a person, or that it has a right to life'.

[15] ibid, 40–93.

[16] *Rights of Migrant Children in the Context of Migration and/or in Need of International Protection*, Advisory Opinion OC-21/14, IACHR Series A No 21 (19 August 2014). On the role of evolutionary interpretation in the Courts' analysis, see, in particular, para 55 ff: 'In addition, the Court has indicated repeatedly that human rights treaties are living instruments, the interpretation of which must evolve with the times and current living conditions. This evolutive interpretation is consistent with the general rules of interpretation established in Article 29 of the American Convention, as well as those established by the Vienna Convention on the Law of Treaties … Consequently, since this is a matter in which the rights of the child merge with the rights of migrants in the diverse situations that surround migration, in this Advisory Opinion, the Court will interpret and provide content to the rights recognized in the Convention, in keeping with the evolution of the existing international *corpus iuris* concerning the human rights of children and of migrants, and with regard to the international protection that States must provide – specifically international refugee law – bearing in mind that the international community has recognized the need to adopt special measures to ensure the protection of the human rights of these vulnerable groups'.

an update of the ACHR in light of current living conditions, and norm-setting exercises in favour of vulnerable groups at risk of intersecting forms of human rights violations.

III. Why is Evolutionary Interpretation so Prominent in International Human Rights Law and is it Specific to this Field of International Law?

When relying on evolutionary interpretation, human rights courts and bodies often highlight the specificity of human rights treaties as 'living instruments' whose objective is the protection of human beings.[17] They stress the need for evolution in social domains subject to changes. At the same time, references to usual rules of interpretation under the Vienna Convention on the Law of Treaties[18] (VCLT) by human rights courts and bodies are not rare.[19] They often accompany references to evolutionary interpretation.

The conceptualisation of evolutionary interpretation as a stand-alone method of interpretation or rather as deriving from traditional methods of interpretation as foreseen in the VCLT remains fuzzy in human rights case law. The Inter-American Court, for instance, merely highlights that 'evolutive interpretation *is consistent with* the general rules of interpretation established … by the Vienna Convention on the Law of Treaties' (emphasis added).[20] In the European system, the VCLT is mainly invoked when the Court wants to take into account other treaties or instruments of international law in line with Article 31(3), often to support an evolutionary interpretation of the Convention.[21] Legal scholarship

[17] See, eg, *Tyrer v United Kingdom* Series A No 26 (1978) 2 EHRR 1, para 31 (which first referred to the 'living instrument' and which has been followed by numerous subsequent jurisprudence); *The Right to Information on Consular Assistance in the Framework of the Guarantees of the Due Process of Law*, Advisory Opinion OC-16/99, IACHR Series A No 16 (1 October 1999) paras 114–15 (citing the case law of the ECtHR, including *Tyrer v United Kingdom*). See also *Mayagna (Sumo)*, above n 11; *Roger Judge v Canada*, above n 3.

[18] Vienna Convention on the Law of Treaties (adopted 23 May 1969) 1155 *United Nations Treaty Series* 331.

[19] See, eg, previously mentioned case law and relevant paras in footnotes. See also in this sense, *Fragmentation of International Law: Difficulties Arising from the Diversification and Expansion of International Law*, Report of the Study Group of the International Law Commission Finalized by Martti Koskenniemi, A/CN.4/L.682, 13 April 2006, para 164: 'In other words, the European Convention on Human Rights is not, and has not been conceived as a self-contained regime in the sense that recourse to general law would have been prevented. On the contrary, the Court makes constant use of general international law with the presumption that the Convention rights should be read in harmony with that general law and without an *a priori* assumption that Convention rights would be overriding'.

[20] See, eg, *Artavia Murillo and others (In Vitro Fertilization)*, above n 12, para 245; *Rights of Migrant Children*, above n 16, para 55.

[21] See G Letsas, 'Strasbourg's Interpretive Ethic: Lessons for the International Lawyer' (2010) 21 *European Journal of International Law* 509, 521. For case law, see, eg, *Rantsev v Cyprus and Russia* (2010) 51 EHRR 1, paras 272–82 (on the prohibition of human trafficking as derived from the prohibition of slavery); *Demir and Baykara v Turkey* [GC] (2009) 48 EHRR 54, paras 65–68.

also provides conflicting views. Some consider that evolutionary interpretation is proper to human rights treaties as a 'self-contained' regime,[22] while others consider evolutionary interpretation as deriving from general rules of interpretation and therefore applicable throughout international law.[23]

We would adopt an intermediate position. As the various contributions to this book illustrate, evolutionary interpretation is used, to a certain degree, in a number – if not all – branches of public international law. It derives, in many respects, from general rules of interpretation as reflected to a large extent in the VCLT.[24] Even a mere textual interpretation may involve evolution since treaties' terms are not frozen but constantly evolve.[25] Contextual or systematic interpretation (*lato sensu*) is also an obvious vehicle for evolutionary interpretations.[26] True, human rights bodies tend to adopt a broad understanding of 'subsequent practice', which involves at times a comparative law analysis of domestic legislation and practices,[27] or which leads to a fully-fledged amendment of the treaty rather than a simple interpretation of it; [28] but this does not constitute a complete departure from general rules of interpretation. The interpretation rule that treaties must be interpreted in light of 'any relevant rules of international law applicable in the relations between the parties' constitutes one of the main drivers of evolutionary interpretation.[29] It is heavily – and flexibly – relied upon by human rights bodies (which equally take into account non-binding instruments) to ensure coherence of the human rights protection afforded to individuals, as well as to

[22] See, eg, R Bernhardt, 'Thoughts on the Interpretation of Human Rights Treaties' in F Matscher and H Petzold (eds), *Protecting Human Rights: The European Dimension. Studies in Honour of Gérard J Wiarda* (Cologne, Carl Heymanns Verlag, 1988) 70–71; J Velu and R Ergec, *La Convention européenne des droits de l'homme* (Brussels, Bruylant, 1990) 51; Letsas, 'Strasbourg's Interpretive Ethic', above n 21, 538–41.

[23] See, eg, H Waldock, 'The Evolution of Human Rights Concepts and the Application of the European Convention on Human Rights' in *Mélanges offerts à Paul Reuter – Le droit international: unité et diversité* (Paris, Pedone, 1981) 547; J Christoffersen, 'Impact on General Principles of Treaty Interpretation' in MT Kamminga and M Scheinin (eds), *The Impact of Human Rights Law on General International Law* (Oxford, Oxford University Press, 2009); E Bjorge, *The Evolutionary Interpretation of Treaties* (Oxford, Oxford University Press, 2014) 9.

[24] See Arts 31–33 of the VCLT. See also in this sense: G Marceau 'Evolutive Interpretation by the WTO Adjudicator: Sophism or Necessity?' (2018) 21 *Journal of International Economic Law* 791, 812 (who concludes, after having provided a useful typology of changes that may impact treaty interpretation over time, that '[w]hat remains particularly interesting is that it seems that the provisions of the VCLT can integrate and take into account all the changes envisaged at the beginning of this article').

[25] See *British Claims in the Spanish Zone of Morocco* (1925) 2 *Reports of International Arbitral Awards* 722, 725 (providing an evolutionary interpretation of the term 'résidence convenable'); *Dispute Regarding Navigational and Related Rights (Costa Rica v Nicaragua)* (Judgment) [2009] ICJ Rep 213, para 64 (evolving interpretation of the notion of 'commerce').

[26] Art 31(3) of the VCLT. For a typology of context, see, R Kolb, *Interprétation et création du droit international* (Brussels, Bruylant, 2006) 467 (naming Art 31(3) the context '*latissimo sensu*').

[27] See, eg, *Dudgeon v United Kingdom* Series A No 45 (1982) 4 EHRR 149, para 60 (on the fact that the great majority of the member States of the Council of Europe no longer criminalise homosexual practices).

[28] See, eg, *Hassan v United Kingdom* [GC] App no 29750/09 (ECtHR, 16 September 2014) para 101 (discussed below).

[29] Art 31(3(c) of the VCLT.

integrate other branches of public international law such as international humanitarian law.[30] But a broad understanding of context is not limited to the practice of human rights courts.[31] Lastly, teleological interpretation of treaties favours evolutionary interpretation to the extent that it may justify some departure from the text (and narrow intent of the drafters) to meet the demands of the (equally and perhaps more importantly intended) object and purpose of the treaty. Again, while teleological interpretation is certainly predominant in human rights law, it remains a general rule of interpretation.[32]

Notwithstanding this, human rights treaties have characteristics which favour or even require an evolutionary interpretation, in the same way as, among human beings, some are endowed with genetic features that allow them to run faster than others. Three main features are particularly relevant in this regard.

First, human rights treaties are not based on a '*do ut des*' rationale (ie, reciprocal obligations) but are rather akin to constitutional law, which sets up a common objective.[33] In French doctrine, the distinction between '*traités-contrats*' and '*traités-lois*' is often made to categorise treaties.[34] Undoubtedly, human rights treaties are of the second kind. They pursue a humanistic objective, which is to respect, protect and fulfil the human rights of individuals/groups and to protect them from States' arbitrariness. The States become the protectors and guarantors of the rights of individuals within their jurisdiction (vertical relationship) rather than contractors with an equally sovereign State (horizontal relationship). This highest humanistic goal pursued by human rights treaties somehow justifies or legitimises great flexibility for the judge to guarantee an effective protection of human rights.

Second, human rights treaties provisions are broad and general. Indeterminacy not only characterises rights (eg, right to security, right to privacy), but also restrictions to rights.[35] Consider for instance the notions of public order, public safety, morality which may justify limitations to a range of human rights.[36] All these undefined notions are subject to change in interpretation over time. Human rights treaties sometimes also contain certain entry points, or specific rules of interpretation, that facilitate an evolutionary interpretation. For instance, the *pro persona* principle (or *lex favorabilis*, most favourable treatment clause) contained in human rights treaties[37] has been used to justify a broad contextual and

[30] See G Gaggioli, *L'influence mutuelle entre les droits de l'homme et le droit international humanitaire* (Paris, Pedone, 2013) 196.

[31] See Kolb, above n 26, 467–69.

[32] ibid, 570–71.

[33] ibid, 202–03.

[34] ibid, 179.

[35] Bernhardt, 'Evolutive Treaty Interpretation', above n 1, 12.

[36] See, eg, the second paragraphs of Arts 8, 9, 10, 11 of the European Convention on Human Rights (ECHR).

[37] See, eg, Art 29 of the ACHR; Art 53 of the ECHR; Art 5§2 of the International Covenant on Civil and Political Rights.

evolutionary interpretation.[38] Articles 60 and 61 of the African Charter on Human and Peoples Rights, which allow the Commission, to 'draw inspiration from' and 'take into account' sources of international law also deserve a specific mention, as it clearly encourages an integrational and evolutionary approach in interpretation.

Lastly, human rights treaties are endowed with a strong supervision both at the universal and regional levels (Europe, Americas and Africa), including by proper courts and quasi-judicial bodies. These monitoring bodies regularly interpret their founding treaties and thus have the opportunity to update human rights obligations. The existence of regional systems of human rights also implies that the evolution of mentalities and domestic practices can proceed faster in the same direction. The customary law prohibition of the death penalty in Europe, which has led the ECtHR to consider that the capital punishment exception to be found in Article 2.1 of the European Convention has fallen into disuse, is a case in point.[39] Also the fact that various human rights bodies have to pronounce themselves on similar matters at both universal and regional levels, favours the phenomenon of cross-fertilisation and thus a particular dynamism.[40] For instance, the American Court has relied heavily on previous jurisprudence of the ECtHR to support its evolutionary interpretation of the ACHR.[41]

In brief, evolutionary interpretation is particularly vigorous in the field of human rights law because of the characteristics and specificities of human rights treaties, but it is in no way reserved to this body of international law. On the contrary, it is our conviction that given the accelerating pace of technological and other changes in our societies and the evolving needs of the international community, combined with the increasing difficulty to adopt new treaties – at least in certain branches of international law – evolutionary interpretation is the sine qua non condition to ensure the continued relevance and effectiveness of treaties. For instance, while international humanitarian law does not have the same features as human rights law and is traditionally less prone to dynamic and evolutionary interpretations given the sensitivities that are inherent to armed conflict situations, interpreting the 1949 Geneva Conventions in the same way as 60 years ago would make little sense. At the same time, evolutionary interpretation cannot part outright with the classical rules of interpretation and should have some defined limits to be meaningful and acceptable to States.

[38] See, eg, *Mayagna (Sumo)* above n 11; *Artavia Murillo and others (In Vitro Fertilization)*, above n 12; *Rights of Migrant Children* above n 16. Comparatively, the ECtHR is less prone to rely on Art 53 to justify evolutionary interpretation. See D Staes, 'When the European Court of Human Rights Refers to External Instruments to Interpret the European Convention' in *e-legal, Revue de droit et de criminologie de l'ULB*, 1 January 2018, 10, available at: e-legal.ulb.be/volume-n01/theses/when-the-european-court-of-human-rights-refers-to-external- instruments-to-interpret-the-european-convention.

[39] *Al-Saadoon and Mufdhi v United Kingdom* [GC] (2010) 51 EHRR 9.

[40] H Tigroudja, 'L'autonomie du droit applicable par la Cour interaméricaine des Droits de l'Homme: en marge d'arrêts et avis consultatifs récents' (2002) 13 *Revue trimestrielle des Droits de l'Homme* 69, 82; P Wachsmann, 'Les méthodes d'interprétation des Conventions internationales relatives à la protection des Droits de l'Homme' in Société française pour le Droit International, *Colloque de Strasbourg : La protection des Droits de l'Homme et l'évolution du droit international* (Paris, Pedone, 1998) 168.

[41] Neuman, above n 5, 109.

IV. What are the Limits of Evolutionary Interpretation Under Human Rights Law?

The question of the limits of evolutionary interpretation under human rights law is the sore point. Promotors of judicial self-restraint are quick to criticise human rights courts and bodies as going too far, too often. They will accuse them of activism or even judicial imperialism.[42] They will dismiss human rights courts as imposing unrealistic obligations and suggest that if the burden on States' shoulders becomes unbearable, the latter will sadly opt out. They will suggest that human rights courts and bodies lack democratic legitimacy. They will highlight the need for legal security and predictability and remind us of the importance of respecting States' sovereignty.[43] From this perspective, evolutionary interpretation must slow down, and its limits must be acknowledged. Instead, those in favour of evolutionary interpretation will be of the view that raising the question of the limits is a counterproductive endeavour; the right question being how to favour evolutionary interpretation, without giving the impression that States' intentions and general treaty rules of interpretation are simply dismissed.

In our view, limits to evolutionary interpretation derive first and foremost from general rules of interpretation. This is not to say that human rights bodies should strictly abide by the text of Articles 31–33 of the VCLT but rather that general principles of interpretation equally apply under human rights law. For instance, not all treaty terms are subject to evolution and good faith must remain at the centre of any treaty interpretation. The intent of the drafters cannot be set aside. As subtly suggested by Bjorge, evolutionary interpretation is – or should be – based upon the objective establishment of the parties' intention.[44] It is precisely because the drafters of human rights treaties intended rights recognised therein to evolve over time that evolutionary interpretation is so prominent in this branch of international law. The object and purpose of a treaty may also limit the range of possible evolutionary interpretations. We submit that a dynamic interpretation of a human rights treaty, which does not aim at fulfilling the object and purpose of the treaty, does not even deserve the qualification of evolutionary interpretation. For instance,

[42] See also S Garibian 'By Men, not Gods: The (Hidden) Evolutionary Interpretation of International Criminal Law in Light of Extrinsic Sources' (on the issue of hidden judicial activism by international criminal courts and tribunals) (ch 15); MM Mbengue and A Florou, 'Evolutionary Interpretation in Investment Arbitration: About a Judicial Taboo' (on the issue of hidden judicial activism in international investment arbitration) (ch 24); P Van den Bossche, 'Is there Evolution in the Evolutionary Interpretation of WTO Law?' (on the accusations of judicial activism by the WTO dispute settlement system and related crisis) (ch 24); and MC de Andrade, 'Evolutionary Interpretation and the Appellate Body's Existential Crisis' (on the perception of judicial activism of the WTO Appellate Body) (ch 21) in this book.

[43] See F Tulkens, 'What Are the Limits to the Evolutive Interpretation of the Convention?' European Court of Human Rights, *Dialogue between Judges 2011*, 8 (highlighting objections and criticisms towards evolutionary interpretation even with the European. Court), available at: www.echr.coe.int/Documents/Dialogue_2011_ENG.pdf.

[44] Bjorge, above n 23, 188.

in the recent *Hassan* case, the ECtHR opined, in light of State practice and taking into account international humanitarian law, that European States do not need to derogate from the right to liberty under Article 15 of the European Convention in order to administratively detain for security reasons individuals in the context of an international armed conflict.[45] By doing so, the Court added a new ground of detention to Article 5 of the European Convention (ie, administrative detention for security reasons in international armed conflicts) and thus limited the scope of the right to liberty. This type of evolution – taken in the abstract – is particularly worrying: violations of a treaty should not constitute the basis for evolutionary interpretation. In other words, we think that evolution refers not only to chronology (evolution in time) but also to substance, ie, progress in ensuring respect for human rights in line with the object and purpose of human rights treaties.

One can derive two additional limits to the evolutionary interpretation of human rights treaties from the structural characteristics or inherent features of human rights law: (1) The competence of human rights supervisory bodies is circumscribed by their founding treaties.[46] Such treaty bodies do not have a general competence, unlike the International Court of Justice. They cannot apply customary law or a foreign body of international law, such as international humanitarian law.[47] They may – and should – obviously take into account other bodies of law but they cannot apply them directly. As aptly recognised by the Inter-American Court of Human Rights in the *Las Palmeras* case, in relation to the competence of the Court and Commission to apply international humanitarian law, the Convention 'has only given the Court competence to determine whether the acts or the norms of the States are compatible with the Convention itself, and not with the 1949 Geneva Conventions'.[48] In practice, though, there might be a thin line between taking into account other bodies of law, in consonance with Article 31(1)(c) of the VCLT, and applying them.[49] (2) In principle, human rights bodies cannot create additional rights, which do not exist in the founding treaty, through evolutionary interpretation.[50] For instance, the ECtHR could not consider

[45] See *Hassan*, above n 28.

[46] See, eg, Art 32(1) of the ECHR; Arts 33 and 62 of the ACHR.

[47] Gaggioli, above n 30, 190.

[48] *Las Palmeras v Colombia*, Preliminary Objections, IACHR Series C No 67 (4 February 2000) para 33.

[49] *Bámaca-Velásquez v Guatemala*, above n 10, paras 207–28: 'Although the Court lacks competence to declare that a State is internationally responsible for the violation of international treaties that do not grant it such competence, it can observe that certain acts or omissions that violate human rights, pursuant to the treaties that they do have competence to apply, also violate other international instruments for the protection of the individual, such as the 1949 Geneva Conventions and, in particular, common Article 3'. In other words, the Inter-American Court of Human Rights can observe that a State has violated international humanitarian law, but it cannot declare it internationally responsible for that.

[50] See G Cohen-Jonathan, 'La protection des Droits de l'Homme et l'évolution du droit international' in Société française pour le Droit international, *Colloque de Strasbourg: La protection des Droits de l'Homme et l'évolution du Droit international* (Paris, Pedone, 1998) 321: 'the judge does not have at any rate the latitude to create *ex nihilo* completely new rights (this is the function of Additional Protocols) or to go against the clearly expressed intention of States at the moment of the drafting of the founding text; this is true in principle at least' (translated from French).

that economic, social and cultural rights are now part of the European Convention on Human Rights or that the latter now encompasses the rights of animals. In practice, the ECtHR seems to have sometimes circumvented this limitation by expanding the content of rights recognised in the European Convention through evolutionary interpretation.[51]

Another limit, which appears very clearly in the case law of the ECtHR, but less so in the Inter-American system,[52] is related to the existence of a 'consensus' among States parties to the relevant treaty.[53] The notion of consensus does not equate unanimity, but there needs to be a sufficient common denominator, a convergence, or in other words a clear trend in the law or even in mere mentalities. The ECtHR has at times rejected an evolutionary interpretation and justified a margin of appreciation in favour of Member States in the absence of consensus. For instance, in the case *Pretty v United Kingdom*, concerning the assisted suicide of a terminally ill person, the Court refused to recognise a right to die, derived from the right to life, or a positive obligation of Member States to permit euthanasia under Article 3 of the European Convention.[54] Both the overall objectives of the Convention, which is to protect life, and the lack of consensus in Europe on these matters led the Court to reject an evolutionary interpretation of the Convention. Many other cases could be cited to show that even the progressive ECtHR does not consider evolutionary interpretation as an open-ended concept.[55]

Lastly, we believe that to be convincing, legitimate and acceptable to States, evolutionary interpretation should be the result of a strong legal method. It should rely on existing international law instruments, including soft law documents, domestic laws and jurisprudence, not on mere intuitions. A thorough comparative law analysis, in the broad sense of the word, should constitute the basis of most if not all evolutionary interpretation. Evolutionary interpretation could be further

[51] For instance, the right to life has sometimes been interpreted broadly as including a 'right to live', which encompasses the right to food, medical care and the right to a safe environment. See P Currat, *Les crimes contre l'humanité dans le statut de la Cour pénale internationale* (Brussels, Bruylant, Genève, Schulthess, 2003) 153. See also Gaggioli, above n 30, 465. See also, A Volou, 'Evolutive Interpretation: Has the ECtHR Really Gone Too Far? The Case of the Protection of Socio-Economic Rights' Workshop on the ECtHR (Tampere, 2015), available at: blogs.uta.fi/ecthrworkshop/2015/12/14/avolou/.

[52] Neuman, above n 5, 107.

[53] See K Dzehtsiarou, 'Does Consensus Matter? Legitimacy of European Consensus in the Case Law of the European Court of Human Rights' (2011) 12 *German Law Journal* 1730; Tulkens, above n 43, 9.

[54] *Pretty v the United Kingdom* (2002) 35 EHRR 1, paras 54–55: 'While the Court must take a dynamic and flexible approach to the interpretation of the Convention, which is a living instrument, any interpretation must also accord with the fundamental objectives of the Convention and its coherence as a system of human rights protection. Article 3 must be construed in harmony with Article 2, which hitherto has been associated with it as reflecting basic values respected by democratic societies. As found above, Article 2 of the Convention is first and foremost a prohibition on the use of lethal force or other conduct which might lead to the death of a human being and does not confer any right on an individual to require a State to permit or facilitate his or her death … no positive obligation arises under Article 3 of the Convention to require the respondent State either to give an undertaking not to prosecute the applicant's husband if he assisted her to commit suicide or to provide a lawful opportunity for any other form of assisted suicide'.

[55] See, eg, *Banković and others v Belgium* (2007) 44 EHRR SE5, paras 64–66.

legitimised and objectivised by reference to social sciences. Empirical studies can help, for instance, to scientifically analyse the evolution of mentalities and existing trends, which may or may not have already crystallised in domestic or international norms.

V. Conclusion

Evolutionary interpretation has a prominent place in international human rights at both the universal and regional level. Almost all rights have been, or can be, interpreted dynamically to meet the demands of today's societies. Even the competence of human rights courts has been interpreted in an evolutionary manner. The strength of evolutionary interpretation in this field is due to certain specificities of human rights law, notably because of the types of treaties and norms, the humanitarian objective fulfilled by human rights treaties, the regular monitoring by multiple courts and expert bodies. Nevertheless, since evolutionary interpretation is to a large extent the result of classical rules of interpretation as encompassed in the VCLT, it can be applied in other fields of international law. Human rights practice may also gradually render more flexible, malleable, traditional rules of interpretation, and thus impact methods of interpretation in international law more broadly. It is submitted that such a trend is positive, provided that the limits of evolutionary interpretation are clearly defined, taking into account the particular demands of each international law field. As Françoise Tulkens elegantly puts it, 'a balance must be struck between legal certainty and flexibility'.[56] It is submitted that to be legally sound and acceptable to States, evolutionary interpretation should also be grounded in strong legal method, and notably on thorough comparative law analysis. Further research on how to 'objectivise' evolutionary interpretation should be conducted and social sciences may provide useful tools to scientifically analyse social trends and changes of mentalities.

[56] See Tulkens, above n 43, 10.

12

The Strasbourg Approach to Evolutionary Interpretation

OLIVER DÖRR

I. The Two Meanings of Evolutionary Interpretation

When we talk about 'evolutionary interpretation' of treaties in the context of the rules of the Vienna Convention on the Law of Treaties (VCLT), we are in fact talking about two different things that must, from a legal perspective, be distinguished: first, 'evolutionary' refers to the very object of the interpretative process, ie, the content of the treaty provision in question; second, it refers to the instruments used to establish that content.

The first meaning arises when we ask, what moment in time is the interpretation process referring to. This is what the International Court of Justice (ICJ) did, when in the *Namibia* Opinion[1] (1971) it gave a contemporaneous meaning to the phrase 'sacred trust of civilisation', or when in the more recent *Navigational Rights* Judgment[2] (2009), the Court interpreted the term '*comercio*' in a treaty dating from 1858 in the light of its present-day meaning.

The second meaning of 'evolutionary interpretation' refers to the use of dynamic means of interpretation. Some of the methods provided for in Article 31 of the VCLT are per se dynamic, especially those laid down in paragraph 3 of the Article: When it comes to subsequent agreements between the parties (sub-paragraph 3(a)) or their subsequent practice in the application of the treaty (sub-paragraph 3(b)), the term 'subsequent' indicates that the material used for interpretation came into being after the treaty's conclusion and is, thus, in a sense 'evolutionary'. Also, the consideration of 'any relevant rules of international law applicable between the parties', the systemic approach according to sub-paragraph 3(c), is a reference

[1] *Legal Consequences for States of the Continued Presence of South Africa in Namibia (South West Africa) notwithstanding Security Council Resolution 276 (1970)* (Advisory Opinion) [1971] ICJ Rep 16, para 53.

[2] *Dispute Regarding Navigational and Related Rights (Costa Rica v Nicaragua)* (Judgment) [2009] ICJ Rep 213, paras 66–70.

to the rules in force at the time of interpretation, and thus provides yet another dynamic tool of interpretation.

The two meanings of 'evolutionary' do not necessarily coincide, since the dynamic tools of interpretation can also be used to apply the static approach, ie, to establish the meaning of treaty provisions at the time of their conclusion. This approach can be found in the well-known *Corfu Channel* case and in the more recent ICJ *Kasikili/Sedudu Island* case.[3]

II. Evolutionary Interpretation by the European Court of Human Rights

When you look for dynamic approaches to interpretation, the jurisprudence of the European Court of Human Rights (ECtHR) in Strasbourg is usually one of the first candidates that comes to mind. And although the Strasbourg Court very often cites Article 31 of the VCLT to explain and legitimise its approach to interpretation, it appears that the Court makes a very particular, even autonomous, use of those rules.

For over 40 years, starting with the *Tyrer* case in 1978, the Court has referred to the Convention as a 'living instrument which must be interpreted in the light of present-day conditions', in recent case law followed by the phrase: 'and of the ideas prevailing in democratic States today'.[4] Thus, the moment to which any interpretation of the Convention refers has been set to the present, the time of interpretation and application. While in general international law the interpreter can choose between two possible approaches (static or dynamic interpretation), and applies the dynamic method only to generic terms that the parties to the treaty would have wanted to be applied in an evolutionary manner, under the European Convention the dynamic approach is the default rule, and, essentially, is the only permissible approach.

To enhance this approach, the Court uses the dynamic means of interpretation in a way that only loosely resembles the method provided for in Article 31 paragraph 3. As elements of the parties' 'subsequent practice', the Court refers to national legislation or other elements of domestic policies, to establish agreement

[3] *Kasikili/Sedudu Island (Botswana v Namibia)* (Judgment) [1999] ICJ Rep 1045, para 20.

[4] eg, in *Tyrer v United Kingdom* Series A no 26 (1978) 2 EHRR 1, para 31; *Marckx v Belgium* Series A no 31 (1979) 2 EHRR 330, para 41; *Loizidou v Turkey (Preliminary Objections)* Series A no 310 (1995) 20 EHRR 99, para 71; *Öcalan v Turkey* [GC] (2003) 37 EHRR 238, para 193; *Pla and Puncernau v Andorra* (2006) 42 EHRR 25, para 62; *Mamatkulov and Askarov v Turkey* [GC] (2005) 41 EHRR 25 and 41 EHRR 494, para 121; *Siliadin v France* (2006) 43 EHRR 16, para 121; *Demir and Baykara v Turkey* [GC] (2009) 48 EHRR 54, para 68; *Bayatyan v Armenia* [GC] (2012) 54 EHRR 15, para 102; *Hirsi Jamaa et al v Italy* [GC] (2012) 55 EHRR 21, para 175; *X et al v Austria* [GC] 57 EHRR 14, para 139; *Pichkur v Ukraine* App no 10441/06 (ECtHR, 7 November 2013) para 53; *Ternovskis v Latvia* App no 33637/02 (ECtHR, 29 April 2014) para 49; *Meier v Switzerland* App no 10109/14 (ECtHR, 9 February 2016) para 64; *Mitzinger v Germany* App no 29762/10 (ECtHR, 9 February 2017) para 41.

among the Contracting States.[5] As 'relevant rules of international law' it refers to non-binding documents of international soft law[6] or to treaties that are not binding upon all parties to the Convention.[7] Rather than the external 'agreement of the parties', which Article 31 paragraph 3 of the Vienna Convention lays down as the guideline for subsequent practice, the Court, by turning to those documents, seeks to establish a domestic consensus among the national policies of the Contracting Parties and within their societies. It is that legislative and/or societal consensus that seems to play a pivotal role in deciding how dynamic the jurisprudence is going to be and how much room for appreciation and political autonomy is being left to the Contracting Parties.

Even if the Court has acknowledged that its evolutionary approach to the Convention and its protocols has its limits, because it 'cannot, by means of an evolutive interpretation, derive from these instruments a right that was not included therein at the outset',[8] it has nonetheless through its jurisprudential interpretation altered the face of the Convention quite considerably over the last 60 years. What follows are several examples that bear this out, organised according to six categories of evolutionary interpretation that can be identified in the case-law.

The Court interprets two different types of terms used in the Convention in accordance with their present-day meaning. This appears, at first, quite natural with regard to terms whose meaning is from the outset bound to change over time, such as morals (Article 8 paragraph 2, Article 11 paragraph 2) or public order (Article 9 paragraph 2), or the concept of a restrictive measure being 'necessary in a democratic society' (Article 8 paragraph 2), for which the Court requires a 'pressing social need'. When the Convention itself refers to those extra-legal concepts that are intrinsically dynamic, such as the majority views in a national society, they are necessarily meant to be interpreted in an evolutionary manner. In those cases, evolution is taking place not within the law, but outside it, and through normative references it is incorporated into the law. And the Court is expected to implement this development by interpreting the extra-legal concepts in accordance with the changes that have taken place in society.

But this expectation has gone beyond extra-legal terms and is also, secondly, being applied to core elements of the legal guarantees contained in the Convention. Legal terms such as 'degrading', 'privacy' or 'family' and the concepts transported with them have taken on a very different meaning over the last 60 years, and to serve as an effective guarantee for the individual must be interpreted according to their contemporaneous meaning. By taking account of legal

[5] *cf Soering v United Kingdom* Series A no 161 (1989) 11 EHRR 439, para 103; *Öcalan*, above n 4, paras 194–95; *Bayatyan*, above n 4, paras 101–09.

[6] *Al-Adsani v United Kingdom* [GC] (2002) 34 EHRR 11, para 60; *Demir and Baykara*, above n 4, paras 74–75; *Saadi v United Kingdom* [GC] (2008) 47 EHRR 17, para 65; *Bayatyan*, above n 4, para 107.

[7] *cf Demir and Baykara*, above n 4, para 78, with examples given in paras 79–84.

[8] *Johnston et al v Ireland* Series A no 112 (1987) 9 EHRR 203, para 53; *Emonet et al v Switzerland* (2009) 49 EHRR 11, para 66; *Austin and Others v United Kingdom* [GC] App nos 39692/09, 40713/09 and 41008/09 (ECtHR, 15 March 2012) para 53.

developments and legal texts outside the Convention, but also of developments in society, the meaning of a provision, whose wording seemed clear, can thus change over time. This approach is omnipresent throughout the Court's jurisprudence, which is why we confine ourselves to two examples: the prohibition of torture in Article 3 of the Convention uses terms, such as 'inhuman' and 'degrading' that reflect predominant views in a society about how we are not, under any circumstances, supposed to treat other human beings. And since those views are prone to change over time, so is our understanding of the legal prohibition. It is not surprising, therefore, that the *Tyrer* case (1978), which was the first in which the Court explicitly used the 'living instrument'-concept, was about the degrading character of corporal punishment. Another prominent example within the scope of Article 3 is, course, the death penalty. While in the *Soering* case (1989), the Court did not consider that Article 3 generally prohibited the death penalty,[9] it changed its position over the years. In *Öcalan* (2003) the Court observed that the legal position regarding the death penalty had undergone considerable evolution since *Soering*,[10] and in *Al-Saadoon and Mufdhi* (2010) it concluded that Article 2 paragraph 1 of the Convention, explicitly allowing for the death penalty, had been amended by the parties' subsequent practice and that 'inhuman or degrading treatment or punishment' prohibited by Article 3 did indeed encompass capital punishment as such.[11]

An even more dynamic development can be observed in the Court's case law on the term 'family life' in Article 8 of the Convention. Originally based on the idea of a classical ensemble of a married, different-sex couple and their biological children, the term developed over the years to include the relationships of mothers to their children born out of wedlock (*Marckx* 1979);[12] of unmarried couples and their children (*Johnston* 1986);[13] of unmarried fathers and their children who do not live with them;[14] of homosexual couples and adopted children;[15] and of couples with one transsexual partner and their children conceived by means of artificial insemination.[16] As the Court pointed out in *X v Austria*, the State, in its choice of means designed to protect the family and secure respect for family life as required by Article 8,

> must necessarily take into account developments in society and changes in the perception of social, civil-status and relational issues, including the fact that there is not just one way or one choice when it comes to leading one's family or private life.[17]

[9] *Soering*, above n 5, para 103.
[10] *Öcalan*, above n 4, para 195.
[11] *Al-Saadoon and Mufdhi* [GC] (2010) 51 EHRR 9, paras 120–22.
[12] *Marckx v Belgium (Pl)* Series A no 31 (1979), para 31.
[13] *Johnston et al*, above n 8, para 56; *Keegan v Ireland* Series A no 290 (1994) 18 EHRR 342, para 44.
[14] *Keegan*, above n 13, para 45.
[15] *Schalk and Kopf v Austria* (2011) 53 EHRR 20, para 94; *X et al v Austria*, above n 4, para 95.
[16] *X, Y and Z v UK* 1997 (1997) 24 EHRR 143, paras 36–37.
[17] *X et al v Austria*, above n 4, para 139.

A third category of evolutionary interpretation in Strasbourg includes those cases in which the Court, rather than merely interpreting a term used in the Convention in an extensive manner, added new guarantees that are not included in the written text to the legal scope of the Convention. The cause celebre for this category is, of course, the *Golder* case, in which, as early as 1975, the Court held that pursuant to Article 6 paragraph 1 of the Convention, the right to a fair trial, included by necessary implication also the right of access to a court.[18] In 2011, the Court changed its jurisprudence and accepted that Article 9 of the Convention included the right to refuse military service for reasons of conscience and religion, even though Article 4 paragraph 3 explicitly leaves recognition of conscientious objectors to the discretion of States.[19] The Court's main reason for this was that the domestic laws of the majority of European States, along with the relevant international instruments, had evolved to the effect that there was virtually a general consensus on the question in Europe and beyond. As recently as 2016, the Court held in *Magyar Helsinki* that the freedom of expression laid down in Article 10 paragraph 1 of the Convention comprises, under certain conditions, a right of access to State-held information, which is not immediately apparent from the text of that provision.[20] Moreover, it seems that the Court's jurisprudence on Article 8, the right to private life, has extended the scope of the guarantee quite considerably, and this development might be seen as having de facto resulted in creating new rights and inserting them into the Convention, such as the right to physical integrity and self-determination, to a social identity and reputation, to sexual self-determination, to data protection, to a clean local environment, maybe even to a professional career.

Fourth, the Court developed the general scope of the Convention in an evolutionary manner by interpreting the term 'jurisdiction' in Article 1 to include situations that the individuals concerned might confront in third States. This would be relevant if a contracting State were knowingly to hand over an individual to another State when there were substantial grounds for believing that the person concerned faced a real risk of torture or other treatment in violation of Article 3 of the Convention. This principle, developed by the Court in the well-known *Soering* case and subsequently extended in various respects, is now applied to all cases of expulsion, deportation, or extradition. It covers all cases in which an individual faces the real risk of being subjected to the death penalty in the receiving State. Furthermore, the *Soering* principle is now also applied to situations in other Contracting States of the Convention (eg, treatment of refugees in Greece), to the interception of migrants on the high seas[21] and to the risk of grave violations of the procedural guarantees contained in Articles 5 and 6 of the Convention.

[18] *Golder v United Kingdom (Pl)* Series A no 18, paras 31–36 (1975).
[19] *Bayatyan*, above n 4, paras 98–110.
[20] *Magyar Helsinki Bizottság v Hungary* [GC] App no 18030/11 (ECtHR, 8 November 2016) paras 149–70.
[21] *Hirsi Jamaa et al v Italy*, above n 4, paras 175–80.

This jurisprudence not only enlarges de facto the territorial scope of the individual guarantees, but also amends the perspective of the Contracting Parties' legal responsibility: they have to anticipate what is going to happen with the individual concerned when he or she is handed over to the third State.

Referring to the wording of Article 1 of the Convention ('shall secure'), the Court has, fifthly, amended the normative design of the guarantees contained in the Convention by extending their legal scope into positive obligations. States must not only themselves refrain from hassling the individual, they are under an obligation to take appropriate steps to provide protection against an interference with those rights, whether the (potential) interference results from actions of State organs, other individuals, third States, or the forces of nature. Such appropriate measures regularly include taking procedural and organisational precautions, and thoroughly investigating and sanctioning violations by State organs or other individuals.

And, finally, the Court has interpreted in an evolutionary manner the Convention's institutional arrangements, aiming to enhance the functioning of the Convention as an effective instrument of human rights protection. Using the 'living instrument' approach, the Court altered various elements of the Convention's supervisory mechanism. For example, in *Mamatkulov and Askarov* (2005), it referred to the concept to establish the binding force of provisional measures indicated by the Court, which was not explicitly laid down in the Convention or in the Rules of Court.[22] And, beginning in 2004, the Court developed two lines of case law which purport to alter the effect of its judgments for the respondent States, ie, to restrict the discretion of States in implementing the Court's decisions, as it is laid down in Article 46 paragraph 1 of the Convention. First, in cases where the Court finds that the very nature of the violation found is such as to leave no real choice between measures capable of remedying it, it may decide to indicate the measure(s) required for an appropriate implementation of its finding, such as the release of the applicant from detention, a retrial, a criminal investigation, or even the reinstatement of the applicant to a previous post (*Assanidze*). Second, although every judgment is strictly speaking only binding *inter partes*, the Court has taken to indicating general measures required at the national level to execute its judgment, when it finds that a systemic or structural problem affecting a large number of people caused the violation in the respondent State (*Broniowski*). This last approach, usually described as 'pilot-judgment procedure', is by now explicitly provided for in the Rules of Court.

III. Conclusion

To sum up, it is submitted that the 'living instrument' approach of the Strasbourg Court combines the two approaches to evolutionary interpretation provided

[22] *Mamatkulov and Askarov*, above n 4 para 121.

for by international law and moulds them into its own, very specific method of interpretation. The driving force behind that method appears to be, above all, the *effet utile* of the Convention guarantees and its supervisory system. In this respect, the dynamic approach reflects the intention of the parties to the Convention, since, according to paragraph 3 of its preamble, they mean to pursue not only the maintenance, but also the 'further realisation' of human rights in Europe.[23] Prominent in the Court's case law is also the search for consensus among the Contracting Parties and their societies which the Court uses as a criterion to measure the dynamics of its interpretative approach.

Both elements, the *effet utile* and attachment to society, we would submit, reflect the quasi-constitutional role of the Court in the legal order of the Contracting Parties, and of the European Union, which makes it different from other international courts and tribunals. With its particular evolutionary approach, the Court acknowledges that a bill of rights which is implemented by a judicial mechanism, whether on the basis of an international treaty or a constitutional document, is by its very nature bound to evolve with changing social conditions and views. Otherwise, it would lose its ability to function as a legal standard for European democracy and the rule of law.

[23] E Bjorge, 'The Convention as a Living Instrument: Rooted in the Past, Looking to the Future' (2016) 36 *Human Rights Law Journal* (Colloquy in Honour of Judge Paul Mahoney) 243, 244.

13

Environmental Protection as an Object of and Tool for Evolutionary Interpretation

NINA MILEVA AND MARINA FORTUNA

I. Introduction

Evolutionary interpretation covers situations in which an interpretive authority interprets a term or a legal obligation as having a meaning or content capable of evolving.[1] In doctrine, lengthy discussions have taken place to identify the legal bases of evolutionary interpretation. In general, scholars identify the bases for evolutionary interpretation in the intention of the parties,[2] the object and purpose of the instrument being interpreted,[3] or the language used,[4] and evolutionary interpretation can occur in instances of evolution of fact or evolution of law.[5] Recourse to evolutionary interpretation is a growing trend in, among others, the field of environmental law.[6] Moreover, scholars have argued that, absent explicit new

[1] E Bjorge, *The Evolutionary Interpretation of Treaties* (Oxford, Oxford University Press, 2014) 1–2, reflecting on a working definition provided by the International Court of Justice in *Dispute Regarding Navigational and Related Rights (Costa Rica v Nicaragua)* (Judgment) [2009] ICJ Rep 213.

[2] H Thirlway, 'The Law and Procedure of the International Court of Justice 1960–1989 Supplement, 2006: Part Three' (2006) 77 *The British Year Book of International Law* 1, 65–68; J Pauwelyn and M Elsig, 'The Politics of Treaty Interpretation; Variations and Explanations Across International Tribunals' in JL Dunoff and MA Pollack (eds), *Interdisciplinary Perspectives on International Law and International Relations: The State of the Art* (Cambridge, Cambridge University Press, 2012) 451–52; P Merkouris, '(Inter)Temporal Consideration in the Interpretive Process of the VCLT: Do Treaties Endure, Perdure or Exdure?' (2014) 45 *Netherlands Yearbook of International Law* 121; Bjorge, above n 1, 3–4; see also Merkouris, ibid, 139–41 for the argument that these indicators are all actually reflections of the intention of the parties.

[3] Pauwelyn and Elsig, above n 2, 442; Merkouris, '(Inter)Temporal Consideration in the Interpretive Process of the VCLT', above, n 2, 139.

[4] Merkouris, '(Inter)Temporal Consideration in the Interpretive Process of the VCLT', above n 2, 124; C Djeffal, *Static and Evolutionary Treaty Interpretation: A Functional Reconstruction* (Cambridge, Cambridge University Press, 2016).

[5] Merkouris, '(Inter)Temporal Consideration in the Interpretive Process of the VCLT', above n 2, 139–40.

[6] ibid, 140.

legislation by States, international environmental law may be updated in response to new developments through the medium of evolutionary interpretation.[7] Thus, obligations relevant to the protection of the environment may be interpreted evolutively to include new knowledge or developments,[8] and further the objective of environmental protection.

It is against this theoretical background that the chapter addresses two interconnected questions: how has evolutionary interpretation contributed to the development of environmental protection, and, reversely, how has environmental protection furthered our understanding of evolutionary interpretation? These questions are explored using two conceptual categories: (1) environmental protection as an object of evolutionary interpretation; and (2) environmental protection as a tool for evolutionary interpretation. The categories were chosen because they aptly illustrate the relationship between environmental protection and the practice of evolutionary interpretation, where evolutionary interpretation has both contributed to furthering the goal of environmental protection and has been developed in more detail as a result of it. This distinction is of course not a rigid one, and, as will be seen throughout the chapter, interpreters sometimes thread this conceptual line. Thus, the relationship between 'environmental protection as object' and 'environmental protection as tool' may be understood as two sides of the same coin.

The first section of the chapter focuses on environmental protection as an object of evolutionary interpretation, and explores this topic through selected cases from the jurisprudence of the International Court of Justice (ICJ). This section chooses the ICJ jurisprudence as the focus of its analysis for several reasons. First because, as pointed out by scholars, the ICJ practice is one of the standard-setters in the field of interpretation.[9] Thus, its practice can greatly inform the analysis of environmental protection as an object of evolutionary interpretation. Secondly because, in the absence of a permanent international environmental court, the ICJ is currently the only permanent court that can adjudicate environmental cases. Accordingly, its jurisprudence may yield more concrete results as to patterns of evolutionary interpretation compared with arbitral or ad hoc tribunals dealing with the same matter. Finally, because, as will be evident in the analysis, a string of cases in the Court's jurisprudence illustrate a forward-progressing development of environmental protection through the practice of evolutionary interpretation. Thus, the section posits, the ICJ has gradually developed a more open and detailed evolutionary interpretation aimed at environmental protection. The second section of the chapter focuses on environmental protection as a tool of evolutionary interpretation and explores this topic through selected cases from the jurisprudence of the European Court of Human Rights (ECtHR) and the Inter-American Court

[7] M Vordemayer, 'Gardening the Great Transformation: The Anthropocene Concept's Impact on International Environmental Law Doctrine' (2015) 25 *Yearbook of International Environmental Law* 79, 110–11.

[8] ibid, 109.

[9] Djeffal, above n 4, 214.

of Human Rights (IACtHR). The ECtHR is a pioneer in bringing environmental concerns within the realm of human rights. The IACtHR, on the other hand, recently handed down an advisory opinion that is both novel when compared with the Court's earlier jurisprudence, and a detailed example of environmental protection as a tool for evolutionary interpretation. The third section explores recent domestic environmental litigation as an interesting example of a combined approach, ie, environmental protection as both an object of, and tool for, evolutionary interpretation. The chapter includes this brief exploration of domestic cases because the practice of domestic courts is becoming increasingly more significant in the interpretation, application and development of international law. This is particularly evident in what scholars have called 'sectoral regimes' such as environmental law, where regulation taking place on the international level may have a direct bearing on domestic regulation, and vice versa.[10] Thus, the interpretive practices of domestic courts in this regard may directly influence the development of international law as well.[11] Finally, the fourth section briefly comments on the limits of evolutionary interpretation.

The selected cases are by no means an exhaustive exploration of jurisprudence on the topic. They were selected because the authors believe that they aptly illustrate both the contribution of evolutionary interpretation to the protection of the environment, and the reverse influence that the cases have had on our understanding of evolutionary interpretation through the lens of environmental protection as a tool for interpretation. Thus, they offer an illustrative overview of the current state of affairs, and open up fruitful avenues of further research.

II. Environmental Protection as an Object of Evolutionary Interpretation

For the purposes of this section, the protection of the environment may be considered an object of evolutionary interpretation in two scenarios: (i) cases where the relevant interpretive body interpreted a legal obligation to include environmental considerations where there were none envisaged at the time of the original conclusion of that legal obligation; and (ii) cases where legal obligations which were already environmental at the time of their conclusion (including specific environmental obligations stemming from more general, non-environmental treaties) are now interpreted evolutively in the light of new legal or factual circumstances. This latter scenario may at times thread the conceptual line between environmental protection as an object versus environmental protection as a tool, and the section will also make a brief comment on this where such examples arise in the upcoming analysis.

[10] ILA Study Group on Principles on the Engagement of Domestic Courts with International Law, *Mapping the Engagement of Domestic Courts with International Law* (Final Report, 2016) para 10.

[11] ibid, paras 10–14.

One of the first critical examples of environmental protection as the object of evolutionary interpretation in the ICJ's jurisprudence is the judgment in the *Case Concerning the Gabčíkovo-Nagymaros Project of 1997* (*Gabčíkovo-Nagymaros*). In interpreting a broad obligation of environmental protection from a bilateral treaty between the parties concerning the construction and operation of the *Gabčíkovo-Nagymaros* barrage system, the Court found that 'newly developed norms of environmental law are relevant for the implementation of the Treaty, and that the parties could, by agreement, incorporate them through the application of [relevant articles] of the Treaty'.[12] These articles did not contain specific obligations of performance but required the parties to carry out their obligation of environmental protection by taking new environmental norms in consideration. 'By inserting these evolving provisions in the Treaty', the Court argued, 'the parties recognized the potential necessity to adapt the Project. Consequently, the Treaty is not static, and is open to adapt to emerging norms of international law', including new environmental norms.[13] The Court's reasoning provides an example where the Court interpreted an already environmental legal obligation evolutively by emphasising new legal circumstances, namely new environmental norms. The Court however did not point out specific environmental norms which were to be included in the legal obligation, but rather referred generally to 'new environmental norms'. Thus, evolutionary interpretation served the object of environmental protection by including new environmental norms in the parties' legal obligation, but only in a more general manner. Interestingly, in a later point in its analysis, the Court took its evolutionary interpretation progressively forward by referring to sustainable development as a new norm that has to be taken into consideration by States.[14] In doing this, the Court came very close to pronouncing what would amount to a new environmental principle with the potential to affect future interpretation.[15] Nonetheless, here again the Court remained general. Moreover, in a Separate Opinion to the Judgment, Judge Bedjaoui argued for limiting an evolutionary approach, and cautioned against what he considered a potential revision of a treaty via evolutionary interpretation.[16] In *Gabčíkovo-Nagymaros* the Court threaded the conceptual line between protection of the environment as object and as tool, and remained cautious in applying evolutionary interpretation. Nonetheless, the case stands at the beginning of a sequence of interpretative episodes by the ICJ which, this section argues, have furthered the protection of the environment by crystallising legal obligations through the practice of evolutionary interpretation.

The analysis continues with the Judgment in the *Case Concerning Pulp Mills in the River Uruguay* (*Pulp Mills*). Two findings by the Court in *Pulp Mills* are

[12] *Gabčíkovo-Nagymaros Project (Hungary v Slovakia)* (Judgment) [1997] ICJ Rep 7, para 112.
[13] ibid.
[14] ibid, para 140.
[15] Djeffal, above n 4, 262.
[16] *Gabčíkovo-Nagymaros Project*, above n 12, Separate Opinion of Judge Bedjaoui.

relevant to the discussion in this section. The first is the Court's finding concerning the procedural obligation of Uruguay, stemming from the obligation of prevention. According to a 1975 bilateral treaty between Argentina and Uruguay for the rational utilisation of the part of the river Uruguay that constitutes a border between the two States, Uruguay had the obligation to inform CARU[17] when initiating a planned activity on that part of the river. CARU would then make a preliminary finding whether the planned activity would cause significant damage to the other party.[18] With respect to this, the Court pointed out that:

> [T]he principle of prevention, as a customary rule, has its origins in the due diligence that is required of a State in its territory. It is 'every State's obligation not to allow knowingly its territory to be used for acts contrary to the rights of other States'[19] … A State is thus obliged to use all the means at its disposal in order to avoid activities which take place in its territory, or in any area under its jurisdiction, causing significant damage to the environment of another State. This Court has established that this obligation 'is now part of the corpus of international law relating to the environment'.[20,21]

In this paragraph the Court traced the evolution of the principle of prevention from its origin in *Corfu Channel* as a due diligence requirement to its inclusion of environmental considerations in the *Nuclear Weapons* Advisory Opinion and the present case. This reasoning illustrates environmental protection as an object of evolutionary interpretation resulting from the evolution of law. The second observation comes from the Court's finding, when examining whether Uruguay had violated its obligation to prevent pollution, with respect to the notion of an Environmental Impact Assessment (EIA). The Court began by referencing its earlier finding in *Dispute Regarding Navigational and Related Rights* that:

> [T]here are situations in which the parties' intent upon conclusion of the treaty was, or may be presumed to have been, to give the terms used – or some of them – a meaning or content capable of evolving, not one fixed once and for all, so as to make allowance for, among other things, developments in international law.[22]

In this sense, the Court found:

> [T]he obligation to protect and preserve, … has to be interpreted in accordance with a practice, which in recent years has gained so much acceptance among States that it may now be considered a requirement under general international law to undertake an environmental impact assessment where there is a risk that the proposed industrial activity may have a significant adverse impact in a transboundary context, in particular, on a shared resource.[23]

[17] Administrative Commission of the River Uruguay (Comisión Administradora del Río Uruguay).
[18] *Pulp Mills on the River Uruguay (Argentina v Uruguay)* (Judgment) [2010] ICJ Rep 14, para 94.
[19] ibid, para 101, citing *Corfu Channel (United Kingdom v Albania)* (Merits) [1949] ICJ Rep 4, 22.
[20] ibid, citing *Legality of the Threat or Use of Nuclear Weapons* (Advisory Opinion) [1996] ICJ Rep 226, para 29.
[21] ibid, para 101.
[22] ibid, para 204, citing *Dispute Regarding Navigational and Related Rights (Costa Rica v Nicaragua)* (Judgment) [2009] ICJ Rep 213, para 64.
[23] ibid.

The Court thus explicitly relied on evolutionary interpretation to arrive at the conclusion that the obligation of prevention also contains the customary obligation to conduct an EIA. Interestingly, the Court observed that general international law does not specify the exact scope and content of an EIA.[24] In light of this, EIAs may be considered as a customary generic term that may evolve in time and whose content will be open to evolutionary interpretation in future case law.[25]

The analysis culminates in the recent joint judgment of the Court in the *Case Concerning Certain Activities Carried Out by Nicaragua in the Border Area (Costa Rica v Nicaragua)* and *Construction of a Road in Costa Rica along the San Juan River (Nicaragua v Costa Rica)* of 16 December 2015 (hereinafter Joint Judgment). In its judgment the ICJ provided valuable insight into the interpretation of the obligation to conduct an EIA and the obligation to notify and consult. More interestingly however, in addition to interpreting each of these obligations individually, the Court considered them under the wider umbrella of the customary rule of prevention, and thus provided an interpretation of the rule of prevention with these obligations as separate but constitutive components. The Court began by recalling the content of the rule of prevention as delineated in its earlier jurisprudence: 'a state is obliged to use all means at its disposal in order to avoid activities which take place in its territory, … causing significant damage to the environment of another state'.[26] With respect to the obligation to conduct an EIA, the Court recalled its judgment in *Pulp Mills* where it pronounced its customary character. The Court then observed that although *Pulp Mills* concerned specific industrial activities, the underlying principle applies generally to activities that might have a significant adverse transboundary impact. It thus held that:

> [T]o fulfil its obligation to exercise due diligence in preventing significant transboundary environmental harm, a State must, before embarking on an activity having the potential adversely to affect the environment of another State, ascertain if there is a risk of significant transboundary harm, which would trigger the requirement to carry out an environmental impact assessment …
>
> If the environmental impact assessment confirms that there is a risk of significant transboundary harm, the State planning to undertake the activity is required, in conformity with its due diligence obligation, to notify and consult in good faith with the potentially affected State, where that is necessary to determine the appropriate measures to prevent or mitigate that risk.[27]

It seems that the Court lays out a series of steps to be followed in pursuance of prevention. First, a State needs to ascertain whether a planned activity has the

[24] ibid, para 205.

[25] P Merkouris, 'Case Concerning Pulp Mills on the River Uruguay (Argentina v Uruguay): Of Environmental Impact Assessments and Phantom Experts' (2010) 9, available at: www.papers.ssrn.com/sol3/papers.cfm?abstract_id=2378882.

[26] *Certain Activities carried out by Nicaragua in the Border Area (Costa Rica v Nicaragua) and Construction of a Road in Costa Rica along the San Juan River (Nicaragua v Costa Rica)* (Judgment) [2015] ICJ Rep 665, para 104, citing *Pulp Mills*, above n 18, para 101.

[27] ibid, para 104.

potential to cause harm. If it has such a potential, the State then needs to conduct an EIA. If the EIA confirms that there is a risk of significant transboundary harm, the State then needs to notify and consult the other concerned State with a view to finding appropriate measures to prevent or mitigate the harm. This reasoning provides an example of environmental protection as an object of evolutionary interpretation because the Court relies on new developments in the law to arrive at a broader and more specific interpretation of the content of the obligation of prevention. Namely, the Court seems to be interpreting prevention as a substantive obligation, which has as its procedural constituents the customary obligation to conduct an EIA (recently established) and the obligation to notify and consult. Moreover, the Court's evolutionary interpretation is very detailed, as it puts these constituent obligations in a sequential order.

Several observations concerning the contribution of evolutionary interpretation to the protection of the environment can be made on the basis of the above-analysed ICJ jurisprudence. First, as evidenced by *Gabčíkovo-Nagymaros*, jurisprudence sometimes threads the conceptual line between protection as an object of and protection as a tool for evolutionary interpretation. This also seems to be the case in an example of domestic environmental jurisprudence that will be analysed in section III below. This may be owed to the novelty of litigation with the object of environmental protection. To be specific, as this field is still fairly new, interpreters may rely on environmental norms both for the interpretation of a legal obligation (ie, as a tool) and as an end to be achieved or strengthened (ie, as an object). Secondly, as evidenced by *Pulp Mills* and the Joint Judgment, interpreters seem to be relying on customary international law when engaging in evolutionary interpretation with the object of environmental protection. In *Pulp Mills* this was evidenced by introducing the requirement of an EIA as a customary constituent of the obligation of prevention, and in the Joint Judgment this was taken even further by laying out a series of sequential procedural obligations as constitutive elements of the customary rule of prevention. Finally, and perhaps most importantly, it seems that in the time from *Gabčíkovo-Nagymaros* to the Joint Judgment the Court developed a strong jurisprudence of environmental protection through the medium of evolutionary interpretation both by interpreting already environmental obligations to be broader and more detailed, and by interpreting originally non-environmental obligations to include environmental considerations as well. Thus, we observe a forward-progressing development in the Court's practice of evolutionary interpretation, which holds the potential to both clarify and expand legal obligations with a view to environmental protection.

III. Environmental Protection as a Tool for Evolutionary Interpretation

Flipping the coin, this section analyses how international courts and tribunals have used environmental protection as a *tool* for evolutionary interpretation.

For the purposes of this section, the protection of the environment is considered a tool for evolutionary interpretation in cases where a relevant interpretive authority relies on environmental norms and standards to evolutively interpret an originally non-environmental term or obligation to now include environmental considerations as well.

The section focuses on the case law of two regional human rights courts: the IACtHR and the ECtHR. The first part of this section focuses on the case law of the ECtHR[28] to show how the Strasbourg Court has incorporated environmental concerns into the provisions of the European Convention on Human Rights (ECHR), whereas the second part of this section analyses the recent *Inter-American Court of Human Rights Advisory Opinion on Environment and Human Rights.*[29] The final part of this section makes a brief comparison between the way in which the IACtHR engaged in an evolutionary interpretation of human rights norms by reference to environmental protection norms compared with the ECtHR. This comparison aims to further our understanding of the role of environmental norms in evolutionary interpretation, but also of the different extent to which environmental norms can inform the content of human rights norms.

Generally, the mutual influence between the protection of the environment and human rights was explicitly acknowledged in the Stockholm Declaration in 1972.[30] Principle 1 of the Declaration proclaimed man's 'fundamental right to freedom, equality and adequate conditions of life, in an environment of a quality that permits a life of dignity and well-being'.[31] Although the formally proclaimed right to a healthy environment was not endowed with binding force, it caused a ripple effect, manifested differently on the international level compared with the national one. On the domestic level, some States have amended their constitutions by including a right to a healthy environment, while others have given a liberal interpretation to their pre-existing constitutional provisions.[32] On the international

[28] For a more in-depth analysis of evolutionary interpretation in the case law of the ECHR see M Fitzmaurice, 'Dynamic (Evolutive) Interpretation of Treaties, Part I' (2008) 21 *Hague Yearbook of International Law* 101, 121–53.

[29] *The Environment and Human Rights (State obligations in relation to the environment in the context of the protection and guarantee of the rights to life and to personal integrity – interpretation and scope of Articles 4(1) and 5(1) of the American Convention on Human Rights)*, Advisory Opinion OC-23/17, IACHR Series A No 23 (15 November 2017).

[30] Declaration of the United Nations Conference on the Human Environment, Report of the United Nations Conference on the Human Environment, Stockholm, 5–16 June 1972, A/CONF.48/14/Rev.1.

[31] ibid, Principle 1.

[32] Indicatively: *Damodhar Rao v The Special Officer, Municipal Corporation of Hyderabad* AIR 1987 AP 171, available at www.indiankanoon.org/doc/205063/; *MC Mehta v Union of India* AIR 1987 SC 965, available at: www.indiankanoon.org/doc/1599374/; *Subhash Kuimar v State of Uttar Pradesh* 1991 AIR 420, available at: www.indiankanoon.org/doc/1646284/. *Community of Pyrga v Republic of Cyprus* ILDC 1790 (CY 1991) paras 6–16; *Mohiuddin Farooque v Bangladesh* 48 DLR 1996 in United Nations Environment Programme, Compendium of Summaries of Judicial Decisions in Environment Related Cases 90; *Salt Miners Labour Union v The Director, Industries and Mineral Development* 1994 SCMR 2061 para 4; *Gbembre v Shell Petroleum Development Company of Nigeria* ILDC 924 (NG 2005) para 45; *Waweru, Mwangi and Others v Kenya* ILDC 880 (KE 2006) paras 32, 40. For a detailed analysis on the subject see DR Boyd, *The Environmental Rights Revolution. A Global Study of Constitutions,*

level, however, the incorporation of environmental concerns was accomplished, among other means, through the use of evolutionary interpretation.[33]

Among the international courts, the ECtHR was a pioneer in bringing environmental concerns within the realm of human rights. At the moment of the ECHR's conclusion in 1950 the drafters do not seem to have envisaged that an implied right to a healthy environment would be contained in any of the treaty provisions.[34] A first proposal on the conclusion of an additional protocol to the ECHR that would include a right to a healthy environment was made in 1970.[35] The proponents advanced the proposal to include in the ECHR 'a right to reasonably pollution-free air and water, the right to be protected against excessive noise and other nuisances, and the right to reasonable access to coasts, countryside, and mountains'.[36] Interestingly, this proposal was made before the 1973 Stockholm Declaration, which means that the European States were already aware at the time of the interrelationship between the environment and the enjoyment of human rights. After the declaration, another proposal on the inclusion of a right to a healthy environment was formulated by a German jurist, but, similarly to the first proposal, it was rejected.[37] None of this, however, precluded the Court from interpreting evolutively the pre-existing provisions of the Convention in a way that connected environmental degradation with human rights as a result of the growing environmental concerns and legal developments in international environmental law. Article 2, Article 3, Article 5, Article 6, Article 8 and Article 1 of the Additional Protocol 1 to the ECHR have all served as 'points of entry'[38] for environmental concerns and norms into the ECHR.[39] This is due to both the nature of

Human Rights and the Environment (Vancouver, UBC Press, 2012); BE Hill, S Wolfson and Nicholas Targ, 'Human Rights and the Environment: A Synopsis and Some Predictions' (2004) 16 *Georgetown International Law Review* 359, 381–400.

[33] M Burger, 'Bi-Polar and Polycentric Approaches to Human Rights and the Environment' (2003) 28 *Columbia Journal of Environmental Law* 371, 372; J Arato, 'Subsequent Practice and Evolutive Interpretation: Techniques of Treaty Interpretation over Time and Their Diverse Consequences' (2010) 9 *The Law & Practice of International Courts and Tribunals* 443, 456, fn 45.

[34] For instance, the *travaux preparatoires* to Article 8 of the ECHR do not contain any reference to 'environment'. See: www.echr.coe.int/Documents/Library_TP_Art_08_DH(56)12_ENG.PDF.

[35] J-P Jacqué, 'La protection du droit à l'environnement au niveau européen ou régional' in P Kromarek (ed), *Environnement et droits de l'homme* (Paris, Unesco, 1987) 70–71.

[36] D Shelton, 'Human Rights, Environmental Rights, and the Right to Environment' (1991) 28 *Stanford Journal of International Law* 103, 132.

[37] H Steiger and the Working Group for Environmental Law, 'The Right to a Humane Environment: Proposal for an Additional Protocol to the European Human Rights Convention', 27 Beitrfigezur Umweltgestaltung, E Schmidt Verlag, Heft A 13, Berlin (1973) cited in B Van Dyke 'A Proposal to Introduce the Right to a Healthy Environment into the European Convention Regime' (1994) 13 *Virginia Environmental Law Journal* 323, 337.

[38] Merkouris, '(Inter)Temporal Consideration in the Interpretive Process of the VCLT', above n 2, 139–44 uses the notion of 'points of entry' with respect to the provisions of Art 31 of the VCLT.

[39] Indicatively: *Fredin v Sweden (no 1)* Series A no 192 (1991) 13 EHRR 784; *Gorraiz Lizarraga and Others v Spain* (2007) 45 EHRR 45; *Öneryıldız v Turkey* [GC] (2005) 41 EHRR 20; *NA and Others v Turkey* (2007) 45 EHRR 287; *Budayeva and Others v Russia* (2014) 59 EHRR 2; *Mangouras v Spain* [GC] (2012) 54 EHRR 25; *Bursa Barosu Başkanlığı and Others v Turkey* App no 25680/05 (ECtHR, 19 June 2018).

the ECHR, but also to the construction of its provisions in broad and rather vague terms.[40] Most cases, however, concerned the right to respect for private and family life enshrined in Article 8. Article 8 of the ECHR, was first invoked in relation to environmental issues in the 1990 *Powell and Rayner v UK* case.[41] However, it was not until the 1994 *Lopez Ostra v Spain* case that the Strasbourg Court held a State responsible for a violation of Article 8 in an environmental activities related case. From that case onwards, the Strasbourg Court has consistently found Article 8 to be applicable to cases concerning environmentally harmful activities that have impaired or had the potential to impair the right of individuals to enjoy their home and/or their private lives.[42] Moreover, through the course of its case law the Strasbourg Court had not only incorporated environmental concerns in the scope of action of the articles of the Convention, but had also developed more specific environment-related obligations.[43] Since all these cases concerned applicants who lived in proximity to the place where environmentally harmful activities took place,[44] the Court was able, without difficulty, to place their claims inside the textual limits of Article 8, in line with the requirements of Article 31 of the Vienna Convention on the Law of Treaties (VCLT).[45] As the Court stated in *Giacomelli v Italy*:

> breaches of the right to respect for the home are not confined to concrete or physical breaches, such as unauthorised entry into a person's home, but also include those that are not concrete or physical, such as noise, emissions, smells or other forms of interference.[46]

[40] R Bernhardt, 'Evolutionary Treaty Interpretation, Especially of the European Convention on Human Rights' (1999) 42 *German Yearbook of International Law* 11, 12.

[41] *Powell and Rayner v UK* App no 9310/81 (ECtHR, 21 February 1990).

[42] *Guerra and Others v Italy* [GC] (1998) 26 EHRR 357, paras 57, 60; *Hatton and Others v UK* [GC] (2003) 37 EHRR 28, paras 96, 98–99; *Taşkın and Others v Turkey* (2006) 42 EHRR 50, paras 113, 115; *Fadeyeva v Russia* Series A no 25 (2007) 45 EHRR 10, paras 66–70; *Giacomelli v Italy* (2007) 45 EHRR 871, paras 76–79; *Tătar v Romania* App no 67021/01 (ECtHR, 27 January 2008) paras 85–88; *Dubetska and Others v Ukraine* App no 30499/03 (ECtHR, 10 February 2011) paras 105–08. Notwithstanding the use of evolutionary interpretation by the Court in environment-related cases falling under Art 8 of the ECHR, not all the cases where Art 8 was applicable have resulted in the Court finding a violation. This was, however, not because the Court took a step back from evolutionary interpretation, but rather because the Court found that the State acted inside the margin of appreciation afforded to it. For instance, in the *Hatton* case, the Grand Chamber considered that no violation of Art 8 had occurred because the UK had struck a fair balance between the two competing interests: the right to private life and the economic interest of the State. The dissenting judges claimed that the Court, by refusing to recognise a violation of Art 8 of the ECHR, had taken a step backwards and had not 'complied' with the evolutionary and progressive approach that it had taken with regard to claims through which applicants sought protection from pollution and hazardous activities. *Hatton and Others v UK* [GC] (2003) 37 EHRR 28, Joint Dissenting Opinion of Judge Costa, Judge Ress, Judge Türmen, Judge Zupančič and Judge Steiner paras 2, 5.

[43] K Morrow, 'After the Honeymoon: The Uneasy Marriage of Human Rights and the Environment under the European Convention on Human Rights and in UK Law under the Human Rights Act 1998' (2013) 43 *Revue générale de droit* 317, 327.

[44] Indicatively: *Powell and Rayner*, above n 41, para 38; *López Ostra v Spain* Series A no 305 (1995) 20 EHRR 277, para 47; *Guerra and Others*, above n 42, para 69.

[45] For a different opinion see I Buga, *Modification of Treaties by Subsequent Practice* (Oxford, Oxford University Press, 2018) 99–100.

[46] *Giacomelli v Italy*, above n 42, para 76.

The right to respect for private life and home, then, has been evolutively interpreted by the Strasbourg Court to extend to a home's amenities[47] but also, albeit implicitly, to include a certain *quality* of private life and home – a 'characteristic' of home and private life that does not transpire from the explicit intention of the drafters, but is allowed by virtue of the broadness of the term. In evolutively interpreting the provisions of the Convention, the Strasbourg Court, however, made an explicit point that

> the crucial element which must be present in determining whether, in the circumstances of a case, environmental pollution has adversely affected one of the rights safeguarded by paragraph 1 of Article 8 is the existence of a harmful effect on a person's private or family sphere and not simply the general deterioration of the environment.[48]

In other words, the evolutionary interpretation was allowed to go further than the ECHR drafters expressly intended at the moment of its conclusion,[49] but not too far, or at least not as far as recognising an autonomous right to a healthy environment.[50]

Turning to the IACtHR case law, one observes that, aside from the Advisory Opinion further analysed, the jurisprudence on environmental protection as an instrument of evolutionary interpretation is scarce compared with the ECtHR's rich jurisprudence.[51] Most cases where environment-related situations were brought before the Court concerned indigenous communities and were analysed from the angle where protection of the environment per se did not have a central place.[52] In this respect one scholar has pointed to a peculiar approach taken by the Court towards environmental issues – the entanglement of environmental concerns with the protection of indigenous communities.[53] One instance where the Court made reference to UN documents concerning environmental protection and constitutional provisions on the right to a healthy environment, albeit not for purposes of evolutionary interpretation, was in *Kawas-Fernandez v Honduras*.

[47] L Loucaides, 'Environmental Protection Through the Jurisprudence of the European Convention on Human Rights' (2005) 75 *The British Yearbook of International Law* 249, 266.

[48] *Kyrtatos v Greece* (2005) 40 EHRR 16, para 52.

[49] The *travaux préparatoires* to the Convention do not mention discussions on the possible impact of environment-related activities on human rights. For *travaux préparatoires* of the ECHR see: www.echr.coe.int/Documents/Library_TravPrep_Table_ENG.pdf.

[50] *Hatton and Others*, above n 42, para 96; *Kyrtatos v Greece*, above n 48, para 52.

[51] On use of other international law norms for the purposes of an evolutionary interpretation of the ACHR see L Burgorgue-Larsen and A Ubeda de Torres, *The Inter-American Court of Human Rights: Case Law and Commentary* (Oxford, Oxford University Press, 2011) 375–80; CE Arevalo Narvaez and PA Patarroyo Ramirez 'Treaties Over Time and Human Rights: A Case Law Analysis of the Inter-American Court of Human Rights' (2017) 10 *Annuario Colombiano de Derecho Internacional* 295, 316–23.

[52] *Community of San Mateo de Huanchor v Peru*, IACHR Report No 69/04 (15 October 2004); *Case of the Saramaka People v Suriname*, IACHR Series C No 172 (28 November 2007); *Case of the Indigenous Community Yakye Axa v Paraguay*, IACHR Series C No 142 (6 February 2006); *Case of the Kichwa Indigenous People of Sarayaku v Ecuador*, IACHR Series C No 245 (27 June 2012).

[53] L Lixinski, 'Treaty Interpretation by the Inter-American Court of Human Rights: Expansionism at the Service of the Unity of International Law' (2010) 21 *European Journal of International Law* 585, 594.

In this case, concerning freedom of association, the Inter-American Court emphasised the 'undeniable link between the protection of the environment and other human rights'.[54]

Considering this reluctance of the Court to use environmental protection as a tool for evolutionary interpretation, the *Advisory Opinion on Environment and Human Rights*[55] comes as a breath of fresh air. At the basis of the Advisory Opinion is a question submitted by Colombia. This State party to the American Convention on Human Rights (ACHR) asked the IACtHR to elucidate how the provisions of the Convention should be interpreted in light of treaty and customary law environmental norms when there was a risk that large infrastructure works may affect the marine environment and, as a result, the inhabitants of the coastal States' enjoyment of the rights guaranteed by the Convention.[56] At the outset, the Court expressly acknowledged that it would be engaging in evolutionary interpretation.[57] It stated that the use of evolutionary interpretation was justified by the nature of the treaty (a human rights treaty) and that it had to accompany the evolution of times and living conditions.[58] Further on, the Court stated expressly that

> another consequence of the interdependence and indivisibility between human rights and environmental protection is that, in the determination of these [human rights law] State obligations, the Court can make use of the principles, rights and obligations of international environmental law, which as part of the international *corpus iuris* contribute decisively to set the scope of the obligations derived from the American Convention in this area.[59]

In using the environmental law provisions for the purposes of interpretation, the Court drew two main conclusions: (1) that the jurisdiction of State parties to the Convention to respect and ensure human rights is applicable to situations of transboundary environmental damage, whenever a State party exercised effective control over the source of pollution;[60] and (2) that the right to life and the right to personal integrity interpreted by reference to the principle of prevention, principle of cooperation and the precautionary principle oblige States to undertake certain environment-related obligations to ensure citizens' full enjoyment of the rights guaranteed in the Convention.[61]

Returning to the case law of the Strasbourg Court, one can make the following observations: the practice of the two regional courts in using environmental

[54] *Kawas-Fernandez v Honduras*, IACHR Series C No 196 (3 April 2009) para 148.
[55] Advisory Opinion OC-23/17, above n 29.
[56] ibid, para 1.
[57] ibid, para 43.
[58] ibid.
[59] ibid, para 55, unofficial translation provided by the Environmental Law Alliance in Summary of Advisory Opinion OC-23/17, 26 February 2018, available at: www.elaw.org/system/files/attachments/publicresource/IACHR_summary_ELAW.pdf.
[60] ibid, para 82.
[61] ibid, para 242.

norms and concerns as tools for evolutionary interpretation is in some aspects similar, whereas in others quite different. Both the ECtHR and the IACtHR have included environment-related obligations as a means to ensure the fulfilment of the express human rights duties contained in the Convention. At the same time, while the ECtHR requires a certain minimum threshold of harm to trigger the applicability of the Convention, the American Court states that any damage is significant damage and is sufficient to determine the applicability of the provisions of the Convention.[62] This may be due to the *pro persona* interpretative principle contained in Article 29 of the Convention,[63] or the Court's especially strong commitment to the full and effective enjoyment of human rights. Nonetheless, regardless of the reasons behind the Court's reasoning, it shows that the use of environmental concerns as tools for evolutionary interpretation in the hands of the IACtHR goes a bit further than in the case of the ECHR. Needless to say, the American Court went much further that the ECHR when deciding that the Convention contains an autonomous and *justiciable* right to live in a healthy environment, with a basis not only in the San Salvador Protocol, but also in Article 26 of the Convention,[64] while at the moment of the conclusion of the San Salvador Protocol the right to a healthy environment contained in Article 11 was not among the rights enumerated by Article 19(6) that gave the right of individual petition to the Commission or the Court.

On the basis of the aforementioned analysis, two important things can be concluded. First, that environmental protection can be an efficient tool for evolutionary interpretation because, as seen in the *Advisory Opinion on Environment and Human Rights*, it can expand considerably the scope of other international law norms, especially human rights norms. Such an expansion of human rights norms allows this field of law to develop in line with the evolution of other 'special regimes' of international law. At the same time, it is important that courts keep within the 'natural limits' of evolutionary interpretation,[65] such as the general rule of interpretation enshrined in Article 31 of the VCLT. Going beyond these limits puts the courts at a risk of backlash from States, on which the courts' legitimacy depends.[66] Secondly, that environmental protection norms and environmental concerns can be used in different ways as instruments of evolutionary interpretation, depending on the Court that is engaged in the interpretative exercise – even when the courts have jurisdiction in the same 'special area' of international law. Finally, environmental protection as a tool for evolutionary interpretation is useful in bringing together different fields of international law and, thus, in overcoming

[62] ibid, para 140.

[63] ibid, para 42.

[64] ibid, para 55.

[65] On the limits of evolutionary interpretation see Merkouris, '(Inter)Temporal Consideration in the Interpretive Process of the VCLT', above n 2, 150; JE Helgesen, 'What are the Limits to the Evolutive Interpretation of the European Convention on Human Rights?' (2011) 31 *Human Rights Law Journal* 275.

[66] A Brysk and M Stohl (eds), *Expanding Human Rights. 21st Century Norms and Governance* (Cheltenham, Edward Elgar Publishing, 2017) 170.

the problem of fragmentation. This is especially relevant with regard to human rights and environmental law. As transpires from the IACtHR *Advisory Opinion on Environment and Human Rights*, there is a 'natural' connection between human rights and environmental protection, which both justifies and *requires* the adjudicator to interpret them together.

IV. Environmental Protection as Both an Object and a Tool for Evolutionary Interpretation

As stated in the introduction, on closer scrutiny, the 'environmental protection as an object' and the 'environmental protection as a tool' for the purposes of evolutionary interpretation are not two completely separate and separable interpretative exercises. There are cases where the line between the two is blurred, so much so in fact that the claim could be made that they make up two sides of the same coin. The most recent case in this regard is the *Urgenda* case brought before the Dutch national courts. This case is relevant in an analysis of international law because the Court both interpreted international law provisions and relied on these provisions for the purposes of interpretation of domestic law.

The *Urgenda* case arose from a claim brought by a Dutch foundation against the Netherlands in which it asked the Court to order the State to limit the annual greenhouse gas emissions by at least 25 per cent by 2020, compared with 1990.[67] The dispute revolved around two main questions. First, whether in pursuing a reduction target lower than 25 per cent by 2020, the State was breaching its duty of care enshrined in Article 21 of the Dutch Constitution and the provisions of the Dutch Civil Code,[68] especially in light of the Netherlands international obligations and its high rate of greenhouse gas emissions per capita. Secondly, whether the State, by setting a target of less than 25 per cent, acted in contradiction to the provisions of Article 2 and Article of the ECHR.

The first instance court held that it could not analyse Urgenda's claim based on Article 2 and Article 8 of the ECHR, since the foundation did not satisfy the victim requirements provided for by Article 34 of the European Convention. It analysed the claim by reference to the duty of care contained in domestic legal sources, but in interpreting the scope of the duty of care it relied on the provisions of Article 2 and Article 3 of the UN Climate Change Framework Convention, the no harm principle, and Article 2 and Article 8 of the ECHR.[69] The first instance court interpreted the environmental duty of care evolutively by reference to both international norms on climate change and international human rights norms – an instance of

[67] *Urgenda Foundation v The State of the Netherlands*, Case no 200.178.245/01, Hague District Court, Judgment (24 June 2015) para 3.2.

[68] Book 6, Section 162 and Book 5, Section 37 of the Dutch Civil Code.

[69] *Urgenda Foundation v Netherlands*, above n 67, paras 4.46, 4.52, 4.55, 4.63.

environmental protection as an object of evolutionary interpretation. In light of international environmental norms, the Court constructed the constitutional duty of care – an obligation of means that is usually quite broad – narrowly and, as a result, reached the conclusion that the State 'has acted negligently and therefore unlawfully towards Urgenda by starting from a reduction target for 2020 of less than 25% compared to the year 1990'.[70] In the appellate proceedings of the same case,[71] environmental protection norms took on a different role – that of shaping the contents of Article 2 and Article 8 of the ECHR. The Court used the precautionary principle to extend the applicability of Article 2 and Article 8 of the ECHR to the threats posed by climate change – an instance of evolutionary interpretation. While in the ECHR's jurisprudence the presence of a real, imminent and foreseeable threat to identifiable victims is crucial to determine the applicability of the Convention's provisions, the Dutch domestic courts went beyond these limits set by the ECHR's authoritative interpretations. Although the reality of the threat of catastrophic consequences on the lives of individuals caused by climate change is difficult to dispute, the foreseeability and imminence to particular, identifiable individuals is open to question. This is one of the reasons why scholars have argued that bringing climate change related claims in front of the ECHR has a very low chance of success.[72] This Dutch domestic court's approach brings a new dimension to the way evolutionary interpretation is exercised when it comes to the issue of environmental protection. Since the domestic court interpreted the imminence requirement in a more expansive way than the ECtHR, it would be interesting to observe whether this approach could affect how the ECtHR interprets imminence in the future. Similarly, it might be interesting to observe whether environmental considerations more generally affect how evolutionary interpretation is employed by the ECtHR and other relevant interpretive bodies.

Similar cases, relying on a combination of domestic obligations and obligations stemming from human rights and general international law, are currently under way against the governments of Ireland,[73] the United States[74] and Belgium.[75] Unfortunately, at the time of writing, these cases are still ongoing and have not yielded any definitive judgments to be analysed for the purposes of this chapter. Nonetheless, the cases indicate a growing trend of domestic litigation aimed at environmental protection and it will be interesting to observe whether these cases, like *Urgenda*, rely on evolutionary interpretation to read environmental protection into States' obligations, and thus further the goal of environmental protection on a global level.

[70] ibid, para 4.93.

[71] *The State of the Netherlands v Urgenda*, Case no 200.178.245/01, The Hague Court of Appeal, Judgment (9 October 2018).

[72] S Humphreys and M Robinson, *Human Rights and Climate Change* (Cambridge, Cambridge University Press, 2009) 76.

[73] Climate Case Ireland, available at: www.climatecaseireland.ie/climate-case/.

[74] Our Children's Trust, 'Juliana v US – Climate Lawsuit', available at: www.ourchildrenstrust.org/us/federal-lawsuit.

[75] Klimaatzaak, 'De rechtszaak', available at: www.klimaatzaak.eu/nl/the-case.

V. The Limits of Evolutionary Interpretation

While this chapter has largely focused on the positive application of evolutionary interpretation with respect to the protection of the environment, mention must be made of the limits of this practice, as well as the dangers of expanding evolutionary interpretation beyond what is envisaged in Articles 31 and 32 of the VCLT.

In his Separate Opinion to the *Gabčíkovo-Nagymaros* Judgment, Judge Bedjaoui laid out what he considered should be the precautions taken when engaging in evolutionary interpretation. His observation was prompted by an earlier finding of the Court in the *Namibia* Advisory Opinion, which stated that a treaty should be interpreted within the framework of the entire legal system prevailing at the time of the interpretation, and which was relied upon by Hungary in its arguments in the present case.[76]

Taken literally and in isolation [Judge Bedjaoui argued] there is no telling where this statement may lead. The following precautions must be taken:

- an '*evolutionary interpretation*' can only apply in the observation of the general rule of interpretation laid down in Article 31 of the Vienna Convention of the Law of Treaties;
- the '*definition*' of a concept must not be confused with the '*law*' applicable to that concept;
- the 'interpretation' of a treaty must not be confused with its '*revision*'.[77]

With respect to Article 31 of the VCLT, Judge Bedjaoui further clarified that evolutionary interpretation must respect the principle of *pacta sunt servanda* unless there is incompatibility with *jus cogens*,[78] and must comply with the parties' intention as expressed at the time of the conclusion of the treaty.[79] Along similar lines, he stressed that the interpretation of the 'negotiated and approved text' may never result in its substitution with a 'completely different text which has neither been negotiated nor agreed'. This, Judge Bedjaoui argued, would amount to a distorted revision.[80] Scholars have made similar observations concerning the limits of evolutionary interpretation, stressing that the interpretative process can never result in a contravention to *jus cogens* norms, that evolutionary interpretation is limited by the principle of non-retroactivity, and that evolutionary interpretation may never amount to a revision of the treaty being interpreted.[81] The most important limitation outlined in scholarship, however, is that evolutionary interpretation should always observe the general rule laid down in Article 31 of the VCLT, and in particular the text of the provision being interpreted, its context, and the intention

[76] *Gabčíkovo-Nagymaros Project*, above n 12, Separate Opinion of Judge Bedjaoui, para 4.
[77] ibid, para 5.
[78] ibid, para 6.
[79] ibid, para 7.
[80] ibid, para 12.
[81] Merkouris, '(Inter)Temporal Consideration in the Interpretive Process of the VCLT', above n 2, 150.

of the parties.[82] Taking this last observation under consideration, it may be argued that this is the most important limitation because by respecting the parameters laid down in Article 31 of the VCLT, interpreters would ensure that none of the other identified limits of evolutionary interpretation were breached.

Having identified the limits of evolutionary interpretation, it might be worth looking back at what interpreters invoke as the basis for engaging in this practice. As indicated in the chapter's introduction, the parties' intention, the object and purpose of the instrument being interpreted, or the language used have been identified as possible bases for evolutionary interpretation. In other words, it may be observed that the basis for evolutionary interpretation is once again found within Article 31 of the VCLT. Evolutionary interpretation does not exist as a separate method of interpretation outside the VCLT and the customary law interpretative edifice, but is rather the result of a proper application of the usual means of interpretation, through which the intention of the parties is established.[83]

In light of the above discussion, when it comes to the limits of evolutionary interpretation, the following two conclusions seem to hold true. On the one hand, the limits as to how much a term or legal obligation may evolve through interpretation are dictated by the parameters expressed in Articles 31 and 32 of the VCLT. On the other hand, evolutionary interpretation itself, when applied appropriately, finds its basis and justification in those same parameters. Therefore, similar to the 'object' and 'tool' categories discussed throughout this chapter, the limits posed on evolutionary interpretation by Articles 31 and 32 of the VCLT, and the justification for it found in the same provisions, seem to operate as two sides of the same coin.

VI. Conclusion

This chapter examined the contribution of evolutionary interpretation to the development of environmental protection, and reversely the contribution of environmental protection to our understanding of evolutionary interpretation. The relationship was examined through the conceptual categories of environmental protection as 'object' and as 'tool', and the chapter relied on jurisprudence from the ICJ, regional human rights courts and domestic courts, which have recently dealt with environmental litigation. Through these examples the chapter identified a general forward-progressing development of environmental protection through the practice of evolutionary interpretation. In the ICJ jurisprudence, environmental protection was an object achieved through the medium of evolutionary interpretation, and over time the Court increasingly relied on evolutionary interpretation both to interpret environmental obligations expansively and in more detail, and to interpret originally non-environmental obligations to include

[82] ibid, 150–51; Helgesen, above n 65.
[83] Bjorge, above n 1, 3.

environmental considerations as well. In the jurisprudence of human rights bodies, on the other hand, environmental protection played the role of a tool for evolutionary interpretation, and environmental principles were relied on by courts to interpret human rights expansively to also include environmental considerations. Finally, in domestic courts, the chapter traced a convergence of the 'object' and 'tool' categories, and courts both engaged in evolutionary interpretation aimed at environmental protection and relied on environmental standards to evolutively interpret legal obligations.

These cases illustrate that evolutionary interpretation holds the potential to clarify and even modify legal obligations with a view to environmental protection. This is particularly pertinent in the face of increasing environmental litigation in the field of climate change, and in particular the fast developing field of domestic climate litigation. Nevertheless, it must be observed that evolutionary interpretation does not provide interpreters with a carte blanche to modify or create legal obligations. Both judges and scholars have cautioned against the expansion of evolutionary interpretation beyond what is envisaged for the practice of interpretation in Article 31of the VCLT. Thus, having discovered the Janus-faced character of environmental protection as both object and tool for evolutionary interpretation, as well as some of its limitations, it remains to be seen how interpreters learn from these practices and develop them further.

14

The European Court of Human Rights and the Right to a Clean Environment: Evolutionary or Illusory Interpretation?

MALGOSIA FITZMAURICE*

I. Introduction

This chapter will focus on the human right to a clean environment within the context of the European Convention on Human Rights (ECHR). The ECHR does not include such a right. Therefore, such a right could only be given effect through an evolutionary interpretation of the Convention's provisions. The hypothesis of this chapter is that an analysis of the recent case law of the European Court of Human Rights (ECtHR) has evidenced that the Court has not acknowledged the existence of such a right, through evolutionary interpretation of the Convention's provisions, and moreover has applied very strict standards in cases of environmental harm to individuals.

This chapter will be structured as follows: first it will explain in general terms the human right to a clean environment; there will be an introduction to interpretation under the Vienna Convention on the Law of Treaties (VCLT), including a brief explanation of the general meaning of evolutionary interpretation (as this topic will be dealt with elsewhere in this publication). Lastly, the case law of the ECtHR will be considered in relation to environmental matters.

II. The Human Right to a Clean Environment

After many decades of debates and doubts, there is at present a widely shared view, by the majority of both scholars and practitioners, that a human right to a

* Professor Fitzmaurice would like to express her thanks to Professor Gabrielle Marceau, Professor Georges Abi-Saab and Mr Clément Marquet for the organisation of such an intellectually stimulating conference and a resulting publication. She also would like to extend her thanks to Mr Marquet for his excellent ideas concerning her chapter.

clean environment exists. This is largely supported by the inclusion of such a right in international conventions (see below) and international case law. However, in contrast to this general trend, the recent judicial practice of the ECtHR is an exception, as will be explained below.

The most compelling evidence of the existence of such a right was the recent Advisory Opinion of the Inter-American Court of Human Rights,[1] which made a very strong link between general human rights and environmental degradation, including the possibility of the extra-territorial application of environmental human rights in the case of environmental harm. Admittedly, such a right does not have a clearly defined substance, even when it is contained in international conventions, and therefore, may be said to be rather nebulous. This right was invoked in a few judicial and quasi-judicial proceedings, not as a self-standing ground for the litigation but in conjunction with other rights, such as the right to life, exemplified in the decision in the *Ogoniland* case based on the African Charter.[2]

This chapter will not be devoted to an exhaustive discussion on the right to a clean environment but will confine itself to giving examples of such a right where it has been expressly included in certain conventions, in contrast to the ECHR, where such a right is not included.

The first treaty to accord a direct right to a clean and healthy environment was the African Charter. Article 24 provides peoples with a right to 'a general satisfactory environment favourable to their development'.

Although the decision in the *Ogoniland* case is truly remarkable, particularly as it confirms the justiciable nature of Article 24, the African Commission's restricted regulatory powers and the poor record of compliance with its recommendations limit the practical usefulness of its attempts to remedy environmental degradation in the African region.

The second convention is Article 11 of the San Salvador Protocol to the American Convention on Human Rights, which provides for a right to a healthy environment:

> 1. Everyone shall have a right to live in a healthy environment and to have access to basic public services.
> 2. The States Parties shall promote the protection, preservation, and improvement of the environment.

However, the Inter-American human rights institutions have limited powers under this right. They can only receive annual reports from States on how they observe

[1] *The Environment and Human Rights (State obligations in relation to the environment in the context of the protection and guarantee of the rights to life and to personal integrity – interpretation and scope of Articles 4(1) and 5(1) of the American Convention on Human Rights)*, Advisory Opinion OC-23/17, IACHR Series A No 23 (15 November 2017).

[2] Communication 155/96, The Social and Economic Rights Action Centre and the Centre for Economic, and Social Rights/Nigeria, available at: www.achpr.org/files/sessions/30th/comunications/155.96/achpr30_155_96_eng.pdf.

this right as there is no provision for individual applications to the Inter-American Commission or Court.

III. The Classic Rule of Treaty Interpretation as Reflected in the Vienna Convention on the Law of Treaties and the Evolutionary Interpretation

This section presents briefly a necessary background to general rules of treaty interpretation, in order to distinguish the interpretation of human rights treaties and the specific issue of evolutionary interpretation.

A. The General Rule of Treaty Interpretation

The general rule of treaty interpretation is contained in Article 31 of the VCLT. This provision merges the principles of textuality, ordinary meaning and integration, as well as well as the teleological principle of the 'object and purpose', which is itself regarded as incorporating the principle of effectiveness (all these principles preceded the VCLT).[3] Even though these principles are presented in an order that may signify some primacy to the text, a hierarchy among the various components of Article 31 is far from categorically or even clearly expressed. The main feature, which has been emphasised in literature, is that the rule of interpretation adopted in Article 31 is the 'crucible approach', whereby the various interpretative elements are thrown together in a 'single combined operation'.[4] This approach signifies, it may be suggested, that the VCLT rules are not step-by-step formulas producing a conclusive interpretation in each and every case. The interpretative method, instead, indicates factors or elements that should be taken into account, including text, preamble, annexes, related agreements and preparatory work. Although the rules of interpretation contain a certain logical sequence, they should not necessarily be used in each and every case, nor should they always be sequentially applied.[5] All international courts and tribunals, including the International Court of Justice (ICJ) and national courts, have endorsed the Article 31 method of interpretation. Commentators have remarked that the ICJ's application of the VCLT rule of interpretation is 'virtually axiomatic'.[6] The ICJ's starting point in relation to interpretation is the ordinary meaning of the text, taking into account 'all the

[3] G Fitzmaurice, 'The Law and Procedure of the International Court of Justice: Treaty Interpretation and Certain Other Treaty Points' (1951) 28 *The British Year Book of International Law* 1.
[4] R Gardiner, *Treaty Interpretation*, 2nd edn (Oxford, Oxford University Press, 2015) 31.
[5] ibid.
[6] ibid.

consequences which normally and reasonably flow from that text'.[7] The ordinary meaning is not an abstract notion, but instead must be interpreted in the light of the 'place which that phrase occupies in the text to be interpreted'.[8] Article 31(2) defines the context of the treaty. Much analysis has been devoted to the question of the role of the intention of the parties to the treaty in its interpretation. The text of Article 31 is silent on the parties' intention. The prevailing view is that the parties' intention is one of the elements to be taken into account in the interpretative process, as it is reflected in the text of treaty 'and the other relevant factors in terms of interpretation', as stated by the ICJ.[9] As explained by Bjorge, the intention of the parties to the treaty, while not explicitly one of the elements of the means of interpretation, is included by means of an objectivised procedure.[10] However, such a neat and seemingly straightforward procedure is often impossible to follow, considering that in a world with nearly 200 States drawing up and adhering to treaties, the task of finding the parties' common intention has become increasingly difficult, if not impossible. Thus, 'a search for the common intention of the parties can be likened to a search for the pot of gold at the end of the rainbow'.[11] Be that as it may, the intention of the parties remains, as elusive as it is, a crucial factor in interpretation, with a focus on a battle between the objective (textual) and the subjective (intent) schools.[12] Adhering to the 'intention of the parties' is still one of the final litmus tests of traditional interpretative techniques.

The incorporation of the principle of integration has broadened the scope of 'ordinary meaning'; this is of great importance in human rights treaty interpretation. Article 31(2) adds to this, defining the context so that it extends beyond the treaty text (including its preamble and annexes) to also include other related agreements. The use of the *travaux préparatoires* (Article 32) is yet another divisive question in international law, as evidenced by, for example, the ICJ case law.[13]

The 'ordinary meaning' as an interpretation tool can appear to be deceptively simple. However, in relation to human rights treaties, there are many different abstract concepts and principles, which may acquire different meanings in different contexts. There are also other interpretative tools whose use may prove to be contentious and divisive, such as the principles of 'contemporaneity' and the 'object and purpose'. The terms used in treaties change their meaning with use and the passage of time. A commonly held view suggests that the meaning of a treaty's

[7] I Sinclair, *The Vienna Convention on the Law of Treaties*, 2nd edn (Manchester, Manchester University Press, 1984) 1.

[8] ibid, 121.

[9] *Dispute Regarding Navigational and Related Rights (Costa Rica v Nicaragua)* (Judgment) [2009] ICJ Rep 213, 237.

[10] See on this E Bjorge, *The Evolutionary Interpretation of Treaties* (Oxford, Oxford University Press, 2014) 2–3.

[11] ibid, 130.

[12] M Waibel, 'Demystifying the Art of Interpretation' (2011) 22 *European Journal of International Law* 571, 572.

[13] *Maritime Delimitation and Territorial Questions between Qatar and Bahrain (Qatar v Bahrain)* (Jurisdiction and Admissibility) [1995] ICJ Rep 6. In this respect, see Judge Schwebel's Dissenting Opinion.

'object and purpose' is established from an examination of its preamble. However, the inherent uncertainty surrounding this concept requires, at times, further investigation, which is not merely confined to the preamble of the treaty, as has been evidenced by the *Oil Platforms* case. In this case, the ICJ took into account the whole context of the treaty, not just its Article 1, to establish its object and purpose.[14] The object and purpose is also related to the doctrine of effectiveness, captured in the maxim *ut res magis valeat quam pereat*, ie, treaties are presumed to have legal force and effect. A treaty therefore may be interpreted expansively in order to ensure that all of its provisions have an independent meaning (*effet utile*).[15]

B. The Interpretation of Human Rights Treaties and Evolutionary Interpretation: General Outline

The usefulness of the VCLT interpretative regime is not at all clear in relation to human rights treaties. The provisions of human rights treaties are at times perceived as requiring more expansive interpretation than is permitted under the terms of the VCLT; but views vary considerably on this issue, from approaching the VCLT as a 'straitjacket' that has no use in a contemporary world;[16] to being the only instrument that prevents an interpreter making 'illegal' interpretations.[17] For example, according to a classical rule of interpretation, the notion of a treaty's object and purpose should be treated with caution, in the view of many authors, as in extreme cases it can lead to meanings that extend beyond the bounds of treaty interpretation.[18] However, other scholars and judges are of the view that reliance on a treaty's object and purpose is not only fully in accordance with Article 31(1) of the VCLT, but is particularly appropriate in the context of human rights obligations.[19]

One important tool in human rights treaty interpretation is the so-called systemic interpretation.[20] This tool was largely dormant until the *Oil Platforms*

[14] *Case Concerning Oil Platforms (Islamic Republic of Iran v United States of America)* (Preliminary Objections) [1996] ICJ Rep 803, para 31. On object and purpose see, eg, I Buffard and K Zemanek, 'The "Object and Purpose of a Treaty": An Enigma?' (1998) 3 *Austrian Review of International and European Law* 311.

[15] Fitzmaurice, 'The Law and Procedure of the International Court of Justice', above n 3, 211.

[16] JHH Weiler, 'Prolegomena in a Meso-Theory of Treaty Interpretation at the Turn of the Century (III)' International Legal Theory Colloquium (New York, 2008), available at: www.iilj.org/courses/iilj-colloquium/iilj-colloquium-2008.

[17] B Schlütter, 'Aspects of Human Rights Interpretation by the UN Treaty Bodies' in H Keller and G Ulfstein (eds), *Human Rights and Treaty Bodies: Law and Legitimacy* (Cambridge, Cambridge University Press, 2012) 317.

[18] Sinclair, above n 7, 33.

[19] L Caflisch and AA CançadoTrindade, 'Les conventions américaine et européenne des droits de l'homme et le droit international général' (2004) 108 *Revue générale de droit international public* 5, 12.

[20] P Merkouris, *Article 31(3)(c) VCLT and the Principle of Systemic Integration: Normative Shadows in Plato's Cave* (Leiden, Brill/Nijhoff, 2015).

case, and a few of the World Trade Organization cases, which have brought about its renaissance. There is already a vast body of literature on this subject, which, however, remains rather elusive and not very well defined (often being confused with evolutionary interpretation). This principle is based on the premise that no treaty exists in a legal vacuum but has to be interpreted in the wider context of international law, taking account both of relevant treaties and the norms of customary international law (Article 31(3)(c)).

The other somewhat puzzling aspect of treaty interpretation is evolutionary interpretation, which, despite many attempts at clarification, remains a mysterious concept, in particular the limits of its interpretation, the role of the parties' intention and the principle of good faith. It plays, however, an important role in the ECtHR's jurisprudence. It can be defined as a situation in which an international court or tribunal approaches the terms of a treaty on the basis that it is capable of evolving, as treaties are not permanently fixed, and new developments in international law can be taken into account.[21] The ICJ has embraced evolutionary interpretation in its jurisprudence, most notably, in the *Namibia* Advisory Opinion[22] and the *Navigational Rights* case.[23] The Court has opined that in an evolutionary interpretation the terms to be interpreted 'must be understood to have the meaning it bears on each occasion on which the Treaty is to be applied, and not necessarily their original meaning'.[24]

Although evolutionary interpretation is an established element of the ICJ's interpretative arsenal, the jurisprudence of the human rights courts has developed it in a more sophisticated and nuanced manner (although this remains controversial). Gerald Fitzmaurice has strongly advocated the view that a treaty interpreter may only adopt such a method of interpretation if the parties to the treaty intended it and that such an intention cannot be presumed. Any contrary practice, according to him, amounts to judicial legislation.[25] This statement clearly evidences the inherent problem with establishing the parties' intention when using an evolutionary interpretation, absent an explicit expression to this effect in the treaty. Arato also expressed some concerns regarding establishing the parties' intention, ie, whether it must be explicit, or if not, what evidence might provide the basis for asserting the evolutionary character of a treaty.[26] These are, in the view of the present author, the crucial questions pertaining to evolutionary interpretation. There is a view that the concoction of a principle of evolutionary interpretation is, at times, totally redundant because the evolutionary

[21] Bjorge, above n 10, 59.

[22] *Legal Consequences for States of the Continued Presence of South Africa in Namibia (South West Africa) notwithstanding Security Council Resolution 276 (1970)* (Advisory Opinion) [1971] ICJ Rep 16.

[23] *Navigational and Related Rights*, above n 9, para 63.

[24] ibid, para 70.

[25] G Fitzmaurice, 'The Law and Procedure of the International Court of Justice 1951–54' (1957) 33 *The British Year Book of international Law* 203, 225.

[26] J Arato, 'Subsequent Practice and Evolutive Interpretation: Techniques of Treaty Interpretation over Time and Their Diverse Consequences' (2010) 9 *The Law & Practice of International Courts and Tribunals* 445, 466.

development of treaty provisions could be achieved without it on the basis of an interpretation of the plain meaning of the text read in good faith – for instance in the case of treaties drafted in generic terms.[27] However, such an approach, even if justifiable in some cases, is not applied uniformly and is somewhat esoteric. It does not take into account the different, or even at times capricious, approaches of judicial bodies to treaty interpretation. It may be said that the evolutionary method of interpretation is still developing through the practice of international courts and tribunals, along with its relationship to other means of interpretation. The nature of evolutionary interpretation is not yet fully understood and there remain several unresolved issues, such as its relationship to subsequent agreement and practice and the textual limits of such an interpretation. The most complex tool in the context of interpretation by the ECtHR is the much-analysed doctrine of 'margin of appreciation'.[28] There is no reference to this doctrine in the Convention's text, but the approach was initiated in the Court's case law.[29] Suffice it to say that this doctrine is rooted in the Court's need to balance its subsidiary role in safeguarding human rights application against the fundamental and primary function of national authorities in this respect. The national authorities, being better equipped to deal with the implementation of human rights, therefore have a 'margin of appreciation', or discretion, which varies, but is not unlimited. The ECtHR exercises a supervisory function, which 'concerns both the aim of the necessary measure challenged and its necessity' viewed in context.[30] The margin of appreciation doctrine is still debated; and the Court is frequently challenged regarding the manner in which it applies it, and its lack of consistency. The margin of appreciation is very relevant as an interpretative tool in relation to a possible right to a clean environment.

IV. The European Convention on Human Rights and the Right to a Clean Environment

The ECHR does not contain a direct substantive environmental human right and the first few cases regarding environmental degradation were regarded as inadmissible. For example, the case of *X and Y v Federal Republic of Germany* was deemed

[27] Bjorge, above n 10, 191–92.

[28] See, eg, Y Shany, 'All Roads Lead to Strasbourg? Application of the Margin of Appreciation Doctrine by the European Court of Human Rights and the UN Human Rights Committee' (2018) 9 *Journal of International Dispute Settlement* 180; E Benvenisti, 'Margin of Appreciation, Consensus and Universal Standards' (1999) 32 *Journal of International Law and Politics* 843; M Saul, 'The European Court of Human Rights' Margin of Appreciation and the Processes of National Parliaments' (2015) 15 *Human Rights Law Review* 745.

[29] *Lawless v Ireland* Series A no 2 (1961) 1 EHRR 15; *Handyside v United Kingdom* Series A no 6 (1976) 1 EHRR 737.

[30] *Handyside*, above n 29, para 48.

inadmissible by the ECHR on the basis that the ECHR did not include a right to the preservation of nature.[31]

In the intervening years, the Court has given effect to environmental considerations indirectly through its interpretation of the protections accorded to other rights set out within the ECHR, in particular Article 8 (the right to respect for private and family life). Dealing with environmental degradation in this manner is particularly challenging as there is competition between those rights explicitly protected by the ECHR and the protection of the environment which is not. The right protected by Article 8 is qualified and may be restricted if this is 'necessary in a democratic society', requiring that 'the interference corresponds to a pressing social need and … is proportionate to the legitimate aim pursued. The reasons given to justify the interference must be "relevant" and "sufficient"'.[32] However, as will be explained, the Court has changed its initial positive policy towards the existence of such a right, dashing many hopes, which had arisen after the first batch of cases.

A. The Relevant Case Law

The first 'environmental' case brought before the ECtHR concerned noise pollution from aircraft arriving and leaving London airports. In *Powell and Raynor v UK*, the Court balanced the competing interests of the individuals who were disturbed by flights to and from Heathrow airport and those of the community at large, including the economic importance of the airport as a source of employment and the development of trade and communications. The ECtHR concluded that although the applicants' quality of life had been disturbed, this was necessary for the wellbeing of the community.[33]

Lopez Ostra v Spain, concerning toxic fumes, originating from a solid and liquid waste treatment plant located a few metres away from the applicant's home, was considered to be a groundbreaking case.[34] The ECtHR held that environmental pollution, even without causing serious damage to health, could affect the wellbeing of individuals and impede the enjoyment of private and family lives. Spain had not struck a proper balance between the wellbeing of the applicant and the general economic benefits brought by the waste treatment plant. It was the first time that the ECtHR had found a violation of the ECHR on the basis of environmental pollution.

However, the 2003 case of *Hatton v UK*, which also concerned noise pollution from aircraft was a disappointment from the point of view of environmental

[31] *X and Y v The Federal Republic of Germany*, App No 7407/76, Decision on the Admissibility of the Application, 13 May 1976, 5 DR 161 (1976). In general on the ECtHR's method of interpretation, see O Dörr, 'The Strasbourg Approach to Evolutionary Interpretation', ch 12 in this book.

[32] *Olsson v Sweden* Series A no 130 (1988) 11 EHRR 259.

[33] *Powell and Rayner v UK* Series A no 172 (1990) 12 EHRR 335.

[34] *López Ostra v Spain* Series A no 305 (1995) 20 EHRR 277.

protection and human rights, as the Court reversed its position. The ECtHR adopted a very restrictive approach to the link between environmental degradation and human rights, exhibiting a more deferential attitude towards States than in the *Lopez Ostra* case. The *Hatton* case was first heard by a Chamber of the Court in 2001.[35] Referring to the 'fair balance' that must be struck between the competing interests of the individual and the community as a whole, the Chamber admitted that the State enjoyed a certain margin of appreciation in determining the steps to be taken to ensure compliance with the ECHR. The Chamber found that despite the margin of appreciation left to the UK government, the implementation of the noise quota scheme failed to strike a fair balance between the country's economic wellbeing and the applicants' effective enjoyment of their right to respect for home and family life; therefore, violating Article 8 of the ECHR. The UK government requested the referral of the case to the Grand Chamber.

In contrast to previous cases, the Grand Chamber stated clearly that 'there is no explicit right under the Convention to a clean and quiet environment' and that only 'where the individual is directly and seriously affected by noise or other pollution' may an issue arise under Article 8.[36] Finding that there was no violation of Article 8, the Grand Chamber reiterated the fundamentally subsidiary role of the Court: national authorities have direct democratic legitimacy and are better placed than an international tribunal to assess local needs and conditions. In matters of general policy, which may involve different opinions in a democratic society, the actions of domestic policymakers to ensure compliance with the ECHR should be given a wide margin of appreciation.

This judgment initiated a new phase in the case law of the ECtHR in relation to environmental matters, which clearly indicates that the Court has not recognised a self-standing right to a clean environment through the interpretation of its provisions.

A minority of judges appended a powerful joint dissenting opinion.[37] The dissenting judges argued that an 'evolutive' interpretation of the ECHR leads to the construction of an environmental human right on the basis of Article 8. They asserted that the ECtHR has confirmed on several occasions, including in *Lopez Ostra*, that Article 8 embraces the right to a healthy environment:

> [T]he Convention and the Court have increasingly taken the view that Article 8 embraces the right to a healthy environment, and therefore to protection against nuisance caused by harmful chemicals, offensive smells, agents which precipitate respiratory ailments, noise and so on.[38]

They felt that, unfortunately, the Grand Chamber Judgment in *Hatton* appeared to deviate from these developments, appearing to take a step backwards, and that

[35] *Hatton and Others v UK* (2001) EHRR 565.

[36] *Hatton and Others v UK* [GC] (2003) 37 EHRR 28, para 96.

[37] ibid, Joint Dissenting Opinion of Judge Costa, Judge Ress, Judge Türmen, Judge Zupančič and Judge Steiner, above n 36.

[38] ibid, para 2.

the UK government had not sufficiently substantiated the economic importance of Heathrow airport for the country.

From the 2003 *Hatton* case onwards, the ECtHR has adopted a very restrictive and deferential view towards States' positions regarding environmental human rights and the possibility of redressing environmental degradation. The Court took into consideration the fact that the UK government had acted in conformity with national laws concerning night flights. By contrast, in *Lopez Ostra* the authorities had failed to comply with domestic law, as there was no licence for the tannery.

This line of reasoning was also present in *Fadeyeva v Russia* in which the Court noted the breach of national laws by the defendant State. The European Court clarified in *Fadeyeva v Russia* that not every instance of environmental degradation will constitute a breach of Article 8 of the ECHR.[39] The case concerned air pollution from a Soviet steel plant which had been privatised. In order for the pollution to raise an issue under Article 8, the Court reiterated the principles it had set out in its earlier cases. First, the deleterious effects of the pollution must directly affect the applicant's home, family, or private life; and, second, the adverse effects must have reached a certain minimum level if they are to fall within the scope of Article 8. The minimum level to be reached is not general but relative and depends on all the circumstances, including the intensity and duration of the nuisance, its physical or mental effects, and the general environmental context (eg, there would be no claim under Article 8 if the harm complained of was negligible in comparison to the environmental hazards inherent to life in every modern city). The Court held that the emissions from the industrial plant had affected the applicant's health, making her more vulnerable to various diseases, as well as affecting the enjoyment of her home. Taken together, the effects of the pollution were of a level to bring it within the scope of Article 8. A violation of Article 8 was found as the State had made no efforts to provide the applicant with an effective solution to the dangers of the steel plant's emissions.

V. Concluding Remarks

The earlier judicial practice of the ECtHR in relation to the existence of environmental rights based on an evolutionary interpretation of the ECHR appears to have been reversed. The Court now accords a wide margin of appreciation to States in such cases, which also differs from the first judgments relating to the so-called environmental right.

It is obvious from the ECtHR's case law that the numerous requirements that 'an environmental claim' must fulfil to fall under the scope of Article 8 ECHR are challenging. It would be overstating the case to consider that there is a substantive environmental right under the ECHR. Some ECtHR judges, such as

[39] *Fadeyeva v Russia* Series A no 25 (2005) 45 EHRR 10,

Judge Greve in the 2001 *Hatton* case, have already expressed their concern as to the far-reaching evolutionary interpretation of the ECHR in order to give effect to an environmental human right. She noted that even treating the Convention as a living instrument,

> there are limits as to the kind of environmental problems – pollution in the widest sense of the word – which people will have to accept before these problems give rise to a violation of Article 8. These environmental rights are nonetheless of a different character from the core right not to have one's home raided without a warrant.[40]

She also advocated a wide margin of appreciation in such matters.

It may be added that there were many suggestions to add a right to a clean environment to a catalogue of human rights protected by the ECHR and its protocols, such as the first attempt in 1973, when a German working group proposed a protocol to the ECHR, Article 1(1) of which read: 'No one should be exposed to intolerable damage or threats to his health or to intolerable impairment of his well-being as a result of adverse changes in the natural conditions of life' and lately in 1999, 2003 and 2009, the Parliamentary Assembly of the Council of Europe adopted recommendations in which the Assembly called upon the Committee of Ministers to draw up an additional protocol to the ECHR, recognising the right to a healthy and viable environment. However, all of these recommendations and suggestions were not acknowledged and implemented by the Committee of Ministers.[41]

In light of the relevant case law, it may be concluded that there is no right to a clean environment under the ECHR and that the Court is not applying an evolutionary method of interpretation in order to interpret the relevant provisions of the Convention to give an effect to such a right.

[40] *Hatton v UK*, Partly Dissenting Opinion of Judge Greve, above n 35.

[41] J Verschuuren, 'Contribution of the Case Law of the European Court of Human Rights to Sustainable Development in Europe' in W Scholtz and J Verschuuren (eds), *Regional Environmental Law: Transregional Comparative Lessons in Pursuit of Sustainable Development* (Cheltenham, Edward Elgar Publishing, 2015) 384–85.

15

By Men, not Gods: The (Hidden) Evolutionary Interpretation of International Criminal Law in Light of Extrinsic Sources

SÉVANE GARIBIAN*

> It is, however, important to appreciate why, apart from [the] dependence on language as it actually is, with its characteristics of open texture, we should not cherish, even as an ideal, the conception of a rule so detailed that the question whether it applied or not to a particular case … never involved, at the point of actual application, a fresh choice between open alternatives. Put shortly, the reason is that the necessity for such choice is thrust upon us because we are men, not gods.[1]

I. Introduction

Ever since its inception, and throughout the long process of its formation, international criminal law has fundamentally been constructed around the thorny issue of its reconciliation with the principles of State sovereignty and legality.[2] The need for legality in criminal law, which is what interests us here, has three corollaries: the principles of *nullum crimen/nulla poena sine lege*, the non-retroactivity of criminal law, and its strict interpretation. A priori, the latter principle stands in opposition to an evolutionary, or dynamic interpretation.

From a legalistic point of view, setting up a system of international criminal law was made all the more difficult by the fact that, prior to the creation of the (only) permanent International Criminal Court (ICC) in 1998, the establishment

* The author is grateful to Aurore Peirolo and Olivier van den Brand for their assistance in legal research and editing work.

[1] HLA Hart, *The Concept of Law*, 2nd edn (Oxford, Clarendon Press, 1994) 128.

[2] See generally S Garibian, *Le crime contre l'humanité au regard des principes fondateurs de l'Etat moderne. Naissance et consécration d'un concept* (Genève, Schulthess, 2009).

of ad hoc tribunals had been reliant on non-conventional legal arrangements. These tribunals' statutes derived from an agreement between the victorious States from a global conflict (the military tribunals held in Nuremberg in 1945 and Tokyo in 1946), from a resolution of the UN Security Council (the International Criminal Tribunals for the former Yugoslavia, ICTY, in 1993 and for Rwanda, ICTR, in 1994) or from negotiated agreements between the United Nations and the States concerned (internationalised or mixed criminal tribunals created subsequently). Furthermore, these statutes are far from precise and lack any definition of international criminal legality or of the specific rules to be followed regarding interpretation in this area. In this chapter, we will focus on the work of the International Criminal Tribunals (ICTs), and specifically that of the ICTY. The latter's jurisprudential output has not only been rich, but in many ways pioneering. It is also particularly revealing with regard to the questions of interpretation and legality for the simple reason that it has had to function within a normative framework which is considerably vaguer than that of the ICC, whose statute is conventional, 'legalistic' and much more elaborate.[3]

The 'open' nature of the statutes of the ad hoc jurisdictions cited above and of international criminal law more generally – echoing the idea of *open texture* developed by Herbert Hart[4] – offers judges a decisive role.[5] They are obliged to call upon *extrinsic sources* (sources not forming part of their statutes) at various stages of their reasoning to assist them in the considerable interpretative task they are asked to perform, while at the same time being required to adhere to a strict interpretation of the applicable law.

At first, following the Nuremberg Tribunal experience, there seemed to be a general consensus among commentators – including the French judge Henri Donnedieu de Vabres, in several texts published at the time[6] – that, while necessary, this exceptional international criminal law was nevertheless only a preliminary stage. It was an ad hoc law that was novel, retroactive and imperfect: a law

[3] The ICC Statute (Rome Statute) entered into force on 1 July 2002, comprises a preamble and 13 parts (128 articles in total), including specific provisions on its jurisdiction *ratione temporis* (Art 11), the applicable law (Art 21) and the principle of legality (Arts 22–24). It is notably completed by the Elements of crimes adopted in 2002 to assist the Court in interpreting and applying Arts 6–8bis of the Statute (which establish the crimes within the jurisdiction of the ICC). As a matter of comparison, the ICTY Statute comprises 34 articles and the ICTR Statute comprises 32 articles. Let us recall that the ICTY completed its mandate in 2017, and the ICTR in 2015.

[4] Hart, above n 1, 124 ff.

[5] In this regard, Mireille Delmas-Marty emphasised the importance of controlling their work by suggesting the creation of a *recours en interprétation* before the International Court of Justice (whose role would thus be upgraded in criminal matters) or the ICC (whose criminal specialisation would facilitate the task). See M Delmas-Marty, 'Droit comparé et droit international: interactions et internormativité' in M Chiavario (ed), *La justice pénale internationale entre passé et avenir* (Paris, Dalloz, 2003) 11, 26.

[6] H Donnedieu de Vabres, 'Le jugement de Nuremberg et le principe de légalité des délits et des peines' (1946–47) 27 *Revue de droit pénal et de criminologie* 813; H Donnedieu de Vabres, 'Le procès de Nuremberg' (1947) *Revue de science criminelle et de droit pénal comparé* 171; H Donnedieu de Vabres, 'Le procès de Nuremberg devant les principes modernes du droit pénal international' (1947) 70 *Recueil des cours de l'Académie de droit international de La Haye* 477.

in progress born of the laws of war, which 'are not static, but by continual adaptation follow the needs of a changing world';[7] a law that illustrated the '*caractère évolutif de la jurisprudence pénale internationale*',[8] 'the evolutionary character' of the international criminal case law which was coming into being. The unprecedented experience at Nuremberg[9] obliged legal doctrine to give serious thought for the first time to the meaning and scope of the principle of legality in the context of international law and, by extension, the question of interpretation in *international criminal* matters. Most authors – including such celebrated upholders of legal positivism as Hans Kelsen[10] – were prepared, in this special context, to put the principle of legality in perspective and to limit it by what they termed higher principles on the basis of arguments of a jusnaturalistic nature.[11] This 'elastic' approach[12] to legality sought to justify the necessarily creative and innovative work of the Nuremberg judges, in the name of morality, justice and equity. It would also, soon afterwards, lead to the drafting of Articles 7(2) of the European Convention on Human Rights (ECHR, 1950) and 15(2) of the International Covenant on Civil and Political Rights (ICCPR, 1966), both of which provide for an exception to the principle of legality in the name of the general principles of law recognised by 'civilised nations' and 'the community of nations'.

Subsequently, the Cold War saw the expansion of international human rights law, the adoption of the 1969 Vienna Convention on the Law of Treaties (VCLT), and increasing activity on the part of the UN Security Council. All of this led to the creation of new legal tools that would serve the second generation of ad hoc international criminal tribunals established by the executive organ of the United Nations in the early 1990s. This new flourishing followed almost half a century of drought in the field of international criminal repression. It is important to note that the ad hoc judges who have followed their Nuremberg and Tokyo predecessors have mainly called on international public law and principles of human rights law in their search for elements that would allow them, first, to provide a sound basis for the creation, not to mention the competence, of their tribunals; secondly, to define the constitutive elements of the crimes falling within their competence; and, finally, to justify *a posteriori* their interpretation, which is de facto evolving

[7] *Nuremberg War Crimes Trials* (1947) 1 *Trial of the Major War Criminals* 221 (cited in Judgment, *Kunarac et al* (IT-96-23 & 96-23/1-A) Appeals Chamber, 12 June 2002, para 67).

[8] Donnedieu de Vabres, 'Le jugement de Nuremberg et le principe de légalité', above n 6, 817.

[9] *cf* G Acquaviva, 'At the Origins of Crimes Against Humanity: Clues to a Proper Understanding of the *Nullum Crimen* Principle in the Nuremberg Judgement' (2011) 9 *Journal of International Criminal Justice* 881.

[10] H Kelsen, 'The Rule Against Ex Post Facto Laws and the Prosecution of the Axis War Criminals' (1945) 2 *The Judge Advocate Journal* 8, 8–12 and 46; H Kelsen 'Will the Judgment in the Nuremberg Trial Constitute a Precedent in International Law?' (1947) 1 *International Law Quarterly* 153.

[11] See S Garibian, 'Crimes Against Humanity and International Legality in Legal Theory After Nuremberg' (2007) 9 *Journal of Genocide Research* 93; as well as *Le crime contre l'humanité*, above n 2, 149 ff.

[12] Donnedieu de Vabres, 'Le procès de Nuremberg devant les principes modernes', above n 6, 512.

and dynamic, of the applicable law. It is on this last point – the jurisdictional justification of a creative interpretation – that we will concentrate here.

In interpreting their statutes, these judges claim that they are simply bringing to light a pre-existing, albeit hidden meaning intended by the 'international legislator' (in other words, sovereign States), made explicit by means of a purely cognitive activity which thereby guarantees that the principle of legality is respected. Their approach to interpretation-as-knowledge involves adopting a position not only with regard to the rules applicable in this area (section II), but also to the very definition of legality within the international criminal law (section III). Their denial that this interpretative work has a creative aspect is accompanied by a dynamic use of extrinsic legal sources, thus illustrating the 'holistic'[13] nature of the process at work here.

II. A 'Reasonable' Interpretation Through an Analogic Application of the Rules of the Vienna Convention on the Law of Treaties

The ICTs legitimise their interpretative work by systematically denying its creative character, in order to counter the criticisms inherited from the Nuremberg trials experience and to bolster the validity of their own existence.[14] In this way, the judges make use of the fiction that they hold no power.[15] Associated with the cognitive theory of interpretation as an act of *knowledge* (as opposed to interpretation as an act of will), this fiction carries the idea that judges abstain from any form of normative creation, thereby protecting the legal security of individuals.[16] It holds that judges merely exercise a competence that is linked to the application of pre-existing international norms – norms that are nevertheless customary,[17]

[13] We borrow this term from G Marceau, 'Evolutive Interpretation by the WTO Adjudicator: Sophism or Necessity?' (2018) 21 *Journal of International Economic Law* 791.

[14] See also the recommendations of the UN Secretary-General in the *Report Pursuant to Paragraph 2 of Security Council Resolution 808 (1993)* UN Doc S/25704: 'It should be pointed out that, in assigning to the International Tribunal the task of prosecuting persons responsible for serious violations of international humanitarian law, the Security Council would not be creating or purporting to "legislate" that law. Rather, the International Tribunal would have the task of applying existing international humanitarian law' (para 29); '[t]he application of the principle *nullum crimen sine lege* requires that the international tribunal should apply rules of international humanitarian law which are beyond any doubt part of customary law' (para 34, emphasis in the original). A similar question is also discussed in other chapters: MM Mbengue and A Florou, 'Evolutionary Interpretation in Investment Arbitration: About a Judicial Taboo' (ch 23); P Van den Bossche, 'Is there Evolution in the Evolutionary Interpretation of WTO Law?' (ch 20); and MC de Andrade, 'Evolutionary Interpretation and the Appellate Body's Existential Crisis' (ch 21) in this book.

[15] See especially Judgment, *Zejnil Delalic et al* (IT-96-21) Trial Chamber II, 16 November 1998, paras 159–60. See also, notably, the Dissenting Opinion of Judge Rodrigues (para 40) annexed to the Judgment, *Zlatko Aleksovski* (IT-95-14/1) Trial Chamber I, 25 June 1999.

[16] For developments, see Garibian, *Le crime contre l'humanité*, above n 2, 312 ff.

[17] Judgment, *Zejnil Delalic et al* Trial Chamber II, above n 15, para 310.

which is a situation that appears difficult to reconcile with a strictly legalistic approach. In this view, they are thus beholden to

> the well-recognised paramount duty of the judicial interpreter, or judge, to read into the language of the legislature, honestly and faithfully, its plain and rational meaning and to promote its object …: [t]his rule would appear to have been founded on the firm principle that it is for the legislature and not the court or judge to define a crime and prescribe its punishment.[18]

Indeed, according to the cognitive theory of interpretation developed by the 'Ecole de l'Exégèse', interpreting amounts to uncovering the objective meaning of a norm, a meaning already assigned by the legislator and empirically verifiable, and which simply needs to be *described*, not determined.

These judges pointed out in particular that their area of *ratione materiae* competence is set by international customary law as it existed at the time of the facts in question, and that this limitation of their competence is due to a desire to respect the principle of legality, in line with the UN Secretary-General's recommendations.[19] They added that said principle 'does not prevent a court from interpreting and clarifying the elements of a particular crime', nor does it prevent it from relying on previous decisions[20] or 'preclude the progressive development of the law by the court'.[21] However,

> under no circumstances may the court create new criminal offenses after the act charged against an accused either by giving a definition to a crime which had none so far …, or by criminalising an act which had not until the present time been regarded as criminal,[22]

'since the essence of interpretation is to discover the true purpose and intent of the statute in question, invariably, the search of the judge interpreting a provision under whichever system, is necessarily the same'.[23] Finally, they stated that '[i]t cannot be disputed that the cornerstone of the theory and practice of statutory interpretation is to ensure the accurate interpretation of the words used in

[18] ibid, paras 408 ff. This case law is also quoted in the decision of the same Trial Chamber in *Enver Hadzihasanovic et al* (IT-01-47) Trial Chamber II, 12 November 2002, para 60.

[19] *cf* Judgment, *Mitar Vasiljevic* (IT-98-32) Trial Chamber II, 29 November 2002, para 197 and above n 14.

[20] Judgments, *Zlatko Aleksovski* (IT-95-14/1) Appeals Chamber, 24 March 2000, paras 126–27; and *Zejnil Delalic et al* (IT-96-21) Appeals Chamber, 20 February 2001, para 173. See also Judgment, *Mitar Vasiljevic* Trial Chamber II, above n 19, para 196, as well as Decision, *Milan Milutinovic et al* (IT-99-37) Appeals Chamber, 21 May 2003, para 38.

[21] Judgment, *Mitar Vasiljevic* Trial Chamber II, above n 19, para 196 also quoted, notably, in Decision, *Milan Milutinovic et al* Appeals Chamber, above n 20, para 38. On this matter, the Trial Chamber referred to the following case law of the European Court of Human Rights (ECtHR): *Kokkinakis v Greece* Series A no 260-A (1994) 17 EHRR 397, paras 36 and 40; *SW v United Kingdom* Series A no 355-B (1996) 21 EHRR 363, paras 35–36; *CR v United Kingdom* Series A no 335-C (1996) 21 EHRR 363, para 34; *Ecer and Zeyrek v Turkey* (2002) 35 EHRR 672, para 52. See also the decision of the same Trial Chamber, *Enver Hadzihasanovic et al* Trial Chamber II, above n 18, para 58.

[22] Judgment, *Mitar Vasiljevic* Trial Chamber II, above n 19, para 196.

[23] Judgment, *Zejnil Delalic et al* Trial Chamber II, above n 15, para 159.

the statute as the intention of the legislation'.[24] While the primary task of judicial interpretation is to 'ascertain the meaning' of a provision, '[i]n cases of ambiguity, however, all legal systems consider methods for determining how to give effect to the legislative intention'.[25]

Exactly which rules or methods of interpretation are applicable remains to be determined, given that none are cited either in Security Council resolutions or in the preparatory work or statutes of the ICTs. Judges have resolved this question by considering that, even though their statutes are not international treaties in the sense of Article 2(1)(a) of the VCLT, the rules of interpretation set out by the latter in Articles 31–33 apply by analogy.[26] To justify this analogic application they have used two main arguments:[27] first, the ICTs' statutes, which were created on the basis of Security Council resolutions, have their legal basis in the 1945 Charter of the UN, that is to say in an international treaty to which the VCLT rules apply, even retroactively; for, their second argument goes, the latter Convention codifies international custom as far as interpretation is concerned, given that custom derives from rules which are generally accepted by States in the context of their own national law.[28] The justification of the analogic application of the VCLT to these statutes employs what is by any standard an extensive approach to these international texts. Such an approach, along with international rules governing interpretation, is in and of itself enough – notwithstanding the incompleteness (the lack of 'quality') of the international texts in question to ensure the practical impossibility of strict interpretation.

International criminal judges have, to date,[29] made near-systematic use of the rules contained in Articles 31 and 32 of the VCLT, whether this is

[24] ibid, para 160.

[25] ibid, paras 160–61.

[26] See especially, the Joint Separate Opinion presented by Judges McDonald and Vohrah (paras 3 ff) annexed to Judgment, *Drazen Erdemovic* (IT-96-22) Appeals Chamber, 7 October 1997; Judgment, *Zejnil Delalic et al* Trial Chamber II, above n 15, para 1161; Dissenting Opinion of Judge Shahabuddeen (pp 21–22) annexed to Judgment, *Joseph Kanyabashi* (ICTR-96-15) Appeals Chamber, 3 June 1999; as well as the Joint Separate Opinion presented by Judges McDonald and Vohrah (para 15) in the same judgment; Judgment, *Goran Jelisic* (IT-95-10) Trial Chamber I, 14 December 1999, para 61; Decision, *Enver Hadzihasanovic et al* Trial Chamber II, above n 18, para 63.

[27] *cf* notably the above Opinions of Judges McDonald and Vohrah, as well as the Opinion of Judge Shahabuddeen. See also, eg, Judgment, *Goran Jelisic* Trial Chamber I, above n 26, para 61.

[28] This argument aims at justifying the retroactive application of the VCLT (considering that Art 28 of the VCLT establishes the principle of non-retroactivity of treaties).

[29] See, eg, in the case law of the ICC: annex I of the Decision, *Thomas Lubanga Dyilo* (ICC-01/04-01/06-102) Pre-Trial Chamber I, 15 May 2006, para 1; Judgment, *Thomas Lubanga Dyilo* (ICC-01/04-168) Appeals Chamber, 13 July 2006, paras 6, 33 and 40; Decision, *Thomas Lubanga Dyilo* (ICC-01/04-01/06-803) Pre-Trial Chamber I, 29 January 2007, paras 276 and 283; Separate Opinion of Judge Georghios M Pikis (para 15) annexed to Judgment, *Thomas Lubanga Dyilo* (ICC-01/04-01/06-824) Appeals Chamber, 13 February 2007; Decision, *Thomas Lubanga Dyilo* (ICC-01/04-01/06-926) Appeals Chamber, 13 June 2007, para 8; Judgment, *Germain Katanga and Mathieu Ngudjolo* (ICC-01/04-01/07-522) Appeals Chamber, 27 May 2008, para 38; Decision, *Germain Katanga and Mathieu Ngudjolo* (ICC- 01/04-01/07-384) Pre-Trial Chamber I, 9 April 2008, paras 6–7; Judgment, *Thomas Lubanga Dyilo* (ICC-01/04-01/06-1432) Appeals Chamber, 11 July 2008, paras 55–56; Decision, *Omar Hassan Ahmad Al Bashir* (ICC-02/05-01/09) Pre-Trial Chamber I, 4 March 2009, paras 44 and 126; Decision, *Jean-Pierre Bemba Gombo* (ICC-01/05-01/08-424) Pre-Trial Chamber II, 15 June 2009,

acknowledged or not.[30] Priority is generally given to semiotic interpretation, as applied to language in its 'ordinary sense', which these judges generally term a 'literal' interpretation.[31] However, they also combine this, more often than not, with a 'logical' (or systemic) and 'teleological' (or functional) interpretation. Reference is also made to the preparatory work of the statutes (including that of the ICC) and the draft Codes of the International Law Commission as customary norms in the process of crystallisation (in cases covered by Article 32 of the VCLT, as complementary means of interpretation).[32] The logical and teleological forms of interpretation are the most interesting processes insofar as they involve calling on a very extensive series of texts, in the sense of the list set out in Article 31(2) and (3) of the VCLT, thus going well beyond the 'legalist' recommendations of the UN Secretary-General and involving considerable normative activity on the part of judges. These texts constitute what we term *extrinsic sources*, separate from the law of the ICTs' statutes, which reveal the substantial evolution of international customary law since Nuremberg.

The judges' interpretative work is thus legitimised by the way in which it is defined (uncovering and indicating a pre-existing, yet hidden meaning intended by the legislator) and by the rules employed in the process itself (rules of interpretation set out in the VCLT). The latter rules – literal, logical and teleological interpretations – are, again according to the judges, 'winners' insofar as they guarantee a 'reasonable interpretation'[33] which, while it may not correspond exactly to the principle of strict interpretation in criminal matters as understood in national legal systems, is nevertheless compatible with the principle of legality as conceived at an international level.

paras 361 and 364; Decision, *William Samoei Ruto et al* (ICC-01/09-01/11-373) Pre Trial Chamber II, 23 January 2012, para 289; Judgment, *Thomas Lubanga Dyilo* (ICC-01/04-01/06-2842) Trial Chamber I, 14 March 2012, paras 601 and 979; Decision, *Unnamed applicant* (ICC-RoR216-01/14-2) Presidency, 28 February 2014, paras 22–23; Judgment, *Germain Katanga* (ICC-01/04-01/07-3436) Trial Chamber II, 7 March 2014, paras 43–49; Judgment, *Jean-Pierre Bemba Gombo* (ICC-01/05-01/08-3343) Trial Chamber III, 21 March 2016, para 86.

[30] For an example of the application of those rules of interpretation without the express mention of the 1969 Convention, see Decision, *Dusko Tadic* (IT-94-1) Appeals Chamber, 2 October 1995, paras 71 ff (on literal, teleological, logical and systematic interpretation of the ICTY Statute).

[31] On the confusion made by the judges in between the literal interpretation and the ordinary meaning, see W Schabas, 'Interpreting the Statutes of the Ad Hoc Tribunals' in LC Vohrah et al (eds), *Man's Inhumanity to Man. Essays on International Law in Honour of Antonio Cassese* (The Hague, Kluwer Law International, 2003) 847, 855 ff.

[32] For jurisprudential illustrations of each point, see Garibian, *Le crime contre l'humanité*, above n 2, 317–18.

[33] Judgment, *Zejnil Delalic et al* Trial Chamber II, above n 15, para 170. See also Decision, *Milan Milutinovic et al* Appeals Chamber, above n 20, para 38 where the judges underlined that the principle of legality 'does prevent a court from creating new law or from interpreting existing law *beyond the reasonable limits of acceptable clarification*' (emphasis added). This latter case law was cited in Appeal Judgment, *Kaing Guek Eav alias 'Duch'* (ECCC/SC-001/18-07-2007) Supreme Court Chamber, 3 February 2012, para 95; as well as Judgment, *Case 002/01* (ECCC-002/19-09-2007) Trial Chamber, 7 August 2014, para 16.

III. An 'Elastic' Legality Through a Flexible Application of the Criteria of the European Human Rights Case Law

Since the principle of legality is likewise absent from their statutes, the judges need to define it on the basis, mainly, of the case law of the European Court of Human Rights (ECtHR).[34] The fiction of their lack of power is here based not only on the legitimisation of interpretation, but also on a particular approach – once again 'elastic'[35] – to the principle of legality in international criminal law. The judgments in the *Delalic*, *Vasiljevic* and *Ojdanic* cases are particularly revealing in this respect.

Here, international criminal judges have for the first time taken a position on the question of the definition of the legality from the point of view not just of the *existence* of norms (the legality of the incriminations) but also of their *content* (the legality of the definitions of the crimes) – in other words, of their applicability or opposability to individuals. It was the *Delalic* case which first provided the Trial Chamber of the ICTY with the opportunity to restate the meaning attached to the principle of legality in the 'world's major criminal justice system'.[36] It was subsequently added that

> [it] is not certain to what extent [this principle has] been admitted as part of international legal practice, separate and apart from the existence of the national legal systems … essentially because of the different methods of criminalisation of conduct in national and international criminal justice systems.[37]

It was only later, with the *Vasiljevic* case, that the Trial Chamber judges of the ICTY would refine their positions, beginning with an acknowledgement of the importance of the principle of legality in international criminal law.[38] In it they stressed that the mere fact that incriminations exist under pre-existing international customary law does not make up for the absence of a precise definition

[34] For a critical analysis of the influence of the ECtHR's case law on (international) criminal law, see the symposium co-edited by R Roth and F Tulkens (2011) 9 *Journal of International Criminal Justice* 571. By contrast, on the influence of international criminal law on the work of the European Court, see G Gaggioli, 'The Relevance of International Criminal Law for Interpreting and Applying Human Rights Treaties: A Study of the Case Law of the European Court of Human Rights' in R Kolb and D Scalia (eds), *Droit international pénal*, 2nd edn (Bâle, Helbing Lichtenhahn, 2012).

[35] Above n 12.

[36] Judgment, *Zejnil Delalic et al* Trial Chamber II, above n 15, para 402.

[37] ibid, para 403. See also paras 404–06 on the differences, briefly listed, between national legal systems and the international criminal justice system without expanding on the meaning, per se, of international criminal legality.

[38] The same Chamber affirmed, shortly before, in the Decision, *Enver Hadzihasanovic et al* Trial Chamber II, above n 18, the importance of the principle of legality as a 'fundamental principle' in 'international human rights law' (para 56). The Chamber concluded in the same decision that the Tribunal must comply with this principle, even though its statute 'does not contain a specific article stating this general principle of law' (para 57).

of the crime at the time it occurred:[39] '[the] requirement of sufficient clarity of the definition of a criminal offense [under customary international law] is in fact part of the *nullum crimen sine lege* requirement, and it must be assessed in that context';[40] and 'anything contained in the statute of the court in excess of existing customary international law would be a utilisation of power and not of law'.[41] In spite of this condition, however, it would not be possible to ignore the 'specificity of international law'.[42] For,

> [o]nce it is satisfied that a certain act or set of acts is indeed criminal under customary international law, the Trial Chamber must satisfy itself that this offence with which the accused is charged was defined with sufficient clarity *under customary international law* for its general nature, its criminal character and its approximate gravity to have been sufficiently foreseeable and accessible.[43]

The judges concluded by stating that

> [a] criminal conviction should indeed never be based upon a norm which an accused could not reasonably have been aware of at the time of the acts, and this norm must make it sufficiently clear what act or omission could engage his criminal responsibility.[44]

The applicability of an international criminal norm would thus appear to depend upon the satisfaction of two criteria derived from European case law on matters of legality: namely, the *foreseeability* and the *accessibility* of the law upon which is based the reponsibility of the individual, who is thereby in a position to be cognisant of the criminal nature of his action. The judges consider these criteria to be compatible with the function of the principle of legality in the international legal order, namely to maintain 'a balance between the preservation of justice and fairness towards the accused and taking into account the preservation of world order'.[45]

[39] Judgment, *Mitar Vasiljevic* Trial Chamber II, above n 19, para 195.
[40] ibid, para 201. The judges referred to the case law of the ECtHR related to the principle of legality: *Sunday Times v United Kingdom* Series A no 30 (1979–80) 2 EHRR 245, para 49; *Kokkinakis v Greece*, above n 21, para 52; *Ecer and Zeyrek v Turkey*, above n 21, para 51; as well as Decision of the European Commission of Human Rights, *X v Austria* (1981) 22 DR 140.
[41] Judgment, *Mitar Vasiljevic* Trial Chamber II, above n 19, para 202.
[42] ibid, para 201.
[43] ibid (emphasis in the original). See also para 193.
[44] ibid, para 193. The Tribunal quoted the following European case law: *Kokkinakis v Greece*, above n 21; *G v France* Series A no 325-B (1996) 21 EHRR 288; *SW v United Kingdom* Series, above n 21.
[45] Judgment, *Zejnil Delalic et al* Trial Chamber II, above n 15, para 405, recalled in the Decision, *Enver Hadzihasanovic et al* Trial Chamber II, above n 18, para 60. This approach reminds us of the one adopted by the ECtHR in the judgments, *Streletz, Kessler and Krenz v Germany* [GC] (2001) 33 EHRR 31 and *K-H W v Germany* [GC] (2003) 36 EHRR 59, which not only confirmed the extensive and constructive interpretation of the principle of legality under the ECHR, but also underlined the limitations of the principle of non-retroactivity in criminal matters when confronted with the transition towards democracy. On this case law, see P Tavernier, 'L'affaire du "Mur de Berlin"' devant la Cour européenne. La transition vers la démocratie et la non rétroactivité en matière pénale' (2001) 48 *Revue trimestrielle des droits de l'homme* 1159. *cf* also above on international criminal legality in the aftermath of Nuremberg.

They have subsequently been clearly confirmed[46] and set out explicitly[47] in the context of the *Ojdanic* case.

In the latter case, the Appeals Chamber began by noting that, according to the ECtHR's case law, the criteria of foreseeability and accessibility applying to a given norm depend upon a certain number of factors. In this sense, these criteria are highly relative – as, the Chamber observed, is the principle of non-retroactivity in international criminal law.[48] Digging deeper into this idea, the appeal judges went on to list three distinct types of factors to take into consideration when checking the applicability of an international customary norm, by which is meant the foreseeability and accessibility from the point of view of the individual:[49] the position of the national law of the accused party's country with respect to the incrimination in question; the extent to which comparable precedents can be found in international law; and the 'atrocious nature' of the crimes committed.[50]

It was thus established that the legality of the definitions contained in the law of the ICTs' statutes is to be examined in the light of extrinsic legal sources, which are both national (the first factor) and international (the second factor). As far as the third factor is concerned, although 'the immorality of the appalling character of an act is not a sufficient factor to warrant its criminalisation under international customary law', it 'may in fact play a role …, insofar as it may refute any claim by the Defense that it did not know of the criminal nature of the acts'.[51] On this point, the Appeals Chamber referred to one of its previous rulings (made during the *Delalic* case), which called upon the 'general principles of law recognized by the community of nations' in the sense of Article 15(2) of the ICCPR to counter an argument made on the grounds of illegality by the defense.[52] The nature of the crimes, in the final analysis, merely allows recourse to the general principles of law as justification for the applicability of an international norm, even when the latter is 'textually' incomplete, vague or retroactive. This process of *positivising* a naturalist argument is not new: the premises for it are to be found in the work of the judges at Nuremberg[53] and in the subsequent doctrine relating thereto.[54]

To conclude, then, it would seem that the quality – in the sense of the textual precision – of international criminal law matters little, provided that the

[46] Decision, *Milan Milutinovic et al* Appeals Chamber, above n 20, paras 21 and 37–38.

[47] ibid, paras 38 ff.

[48] ibid, para 39. See also the Separate Opinion of Judge Sidhwa (para 72) annexed to the Decision, *Dusko Tadic* Appeals Chamber, above n 30.

[49] Decision, *Milan Milutinovic et al* Appeals Chamber, above n 20, paras 41–42.

[50] This notion seems to echo the old concept of *mala in se* which designates the acts that are 'bad *per se*', wrongful and illegal by their very nature (in opposition to acts that are *mala prohibita*, wrongful and illegal because they are prohibited by the law). See MS Davis, 'Crimes *Mala in Se*: An Equity-Based Definition' (2006) *Criminal Justice Policy Review* 270.

[51] Decision, *Milan Milutinovic et al* Appeals Chamber, above n 20, para 42.

[52] Judgment, *Zejnil Delalic et al* Appeals Chamber, above n 20, para 173.

[53] Garibian, *Le crime contre l'humanité*, above n 2, 134 ff.

[54] Garibian, 'Crimes Against Humanity and International Legality in Legal Theory After Nuremberg', above n 11.

incriminations are foreseeable and accessible. These very criteria, which are rooted in the case law of the Strasbourg Court, are understood in a flexible manner by the Appeals Chamber of the ICTs.[55] The latter confirmed in its ruling of 16 July 2003 that it is enough, in order to fulfil the first of these, that the accused 'be able to appreciate that the conduct is criminal in the sense generally understood, without reference to any specific provision' and, in order to fulfil the second, that in the case of an international tribunal reliance be 'placed on a law which is based on custom'.[56] The foundations of these principles are to be found in extrinsic legal sources, acknowledged from the outset in the *Ojdanic* case through the reference made to the different factors governing the applicability of an international norm.[57] What therefore appears to be the essential element in monitoring the legality of the contents of incriminations, that is to say, the definitions of the crimes set out in the ICTs' statutes which are then 'applied' by judges, is in fact nothing more than the contents of similar definitions found in extrinsic sources.[58]

IV. Conclusion

What we can say for sure is that, aside from the acknowledgement of the evolving character of the law by judges,[59] the actual notion of *evolutionary interpretation* is not, unsurprisingly, referred to explicitly in international criminal case law. A hint of the recognition of its presence can however be found in a ruling by the Appeals Chamber of the Special Tribunal for Lebanon,[60] in which the judges

[55] See also P Manzini, 'Le rôle du principe de la légalité dans la détermination des sources du droit international pénal' in M Delmas-Marty, E Fronza and E Lambert-Abdelgawad (eds), *Les sources du droit international pénal. L'expérience des tribunaux pénaux internationaux et le statut de la Cour pénale internationale* (Paris, Société de législation comparé, 2004) 267.

[56] Decision, *Enver Hadzihasanovic et al* (IT-01-47) Appeals Chamber, 16 July 2003, para 34.

[57] The Appeals Chamber referred to its Decision, *Milan Milutinovic et al* Appeals Chamber, above n 20, paras 37 ff.

[58] For recent confirmation by other international criminal jurisdictions: Appeal Judgment, *Kaing Guek Eav alias 'Duch'* Supreme Court Chamber, above n 33, paras 90–96; Dissenting Opinion of Judge Baragwanath (paras 13 ff) annexed to the *decision on Badreddine Defence Interlocutory Appeal of the 'Interim Decision on the Death of Mr Mustafa Amine Badreddine and Possible Termination of Proceedings'* (STL-11-01) Appeals Chamber, 13 July 2016; Appeal Judgment, *Nuon Chea and Khieu Samphân* (ECCC-002/19-09-2007) Supreme Court Chamber, 23 November 2016, paras 758 ff.

[59] See Separate Opinion of Judge Abi-Saab (point 1) annexed to the Decision, *Dusko Tadic* Appeals Chamber, above n 30; Judgment, *Goran Jelisic* Trial Chamber I, above n 26, para 61; Judgment, *Alfred Musema* (ICTR-96-13-A) Trial Chamber I, 27 January 2000, para 228; Judgment, *Kunarac et al* Appeals Chamber, above n 7, para 67; Dissenting Opinion of Judge Schomburg (para 17) annexed to the Judgment, *Blagoje Simic* (IT-95-9-A) Appeals Chamber, 28 November 2006.

[60] Decision, *Akhbar Beirut SAL Ibrahim Mohamed Ali Al Amin* (STL-14-06/PT/AP/AR126.1) Appeals Panel, 23 January 2015, paras 60 ff where the judges referred to: Decision, *Dusko Tadic* Appeals Chamber, above n 30, paras 96–136 (for a progressive interpretation of war crimes committed in international as well as non-international armed conflicts); Judgment, *Dusko Tadic* (IT-94-1-A) Appeals Chamber, 15 July 1999, paras 163–66 (for a progressive interpretation of the term 'nationals'); and Decision, *Enver Hadzihasanovic* Appeals Chamber, above n 56, paras 10–36 (for a progressive interpretation of command responsibility in non-international armed conflicts).

distinguished between analogy (*analogia legis*), which is rejected, and 'progressive interpretation' (*analogia juris*) – or a 'progressive approach to legal interpretation' – which is considered to be valid. Crucially, this approach is presented as a means of filling the gaps 'by resorting to general principles of international criminal law, or to general principles of criminal justice, or to principles common to the major legal systems of the world'[61] within the limits set, in particular, by the ECHR. Obviously, the objective of such an approach is to avoid a *non liquet*. It is nevertheless possible to consider, along with those who do not agree with the 'gap theory' (which is associated with the cognitive theory of interpretation),[62] that the function of the general principles used in exceptional circumstances to fill in gaps is in fact normative,[63] albeit concealed.

Furthermore, the ICTs have only very rarely invoked the principle of *strict interpretation* and, when they did so, it was above all to affirm that, in criminal cases, the version most favourable to the accused must be accepted. In the *Delalic* case,[64] the judges defined what they termed 'strict construction', according to which the interpreter 'can only determine whether the case is within the intention of a criminal statute by construction of the express language of the provision'. The effect of this is that 'where an equivocal word or ambiguous sentence leaves a reasonable doubt of its meaning which the canons of construction fail to solve, the benefit of the doubt should be given to the subject and against the legislature which has failed to explain itself'; '[t]his is why ambiguous criminal statutes are

[61] A Cassese et al (eds), *Cassese's International Criminal Law*, 3rd edn (Oxford, Oxford University Press, 2013) 34, quoted by the judges at para 63 of Decision, *Akhbar Beirut SAL Ibrahim Mohamed Ali Al Amin* Appeals Panel, above n 60.

[62] See especially H Kelsen, *General Theory of Law and State* (trans Anders Wedberg) (Cambridge, MA, Harvard University Press, 1945) 146 ff; H Kelsen, *Pure Theory of Law* (trans Max Knight), 2nd edn (Clark, NJ, Lawbook Exchange, 2009) 245 ff.

[63] On the link between the so-called gap theory and the function of general principles, see H Kelsen, *The Law of the United Nations. A Critical Analysis of Its Fundamental Problems*, 2nd edn (London, Stevens & Sons Limited, 1951) 533–34; H Kelsen, *Principles of International Law*, 2nd edn (New York, Holt, Rinehart and Winston Inc, 1966) 529; also A Verdross, 'Les principes généraux de droit dans le système des sources du droit international public' in *Recueil d'Etudes de Droit international en hommage à Paul Guggenheim* (Genève, Faculté de Droit de l'Université de Genève, Institut Universitaire de Hautes Etudes Internationales, 1968) 527 ff. For developments, see Garibian, *Le crime contre l'humanité*, above n 2, 350 ff. On the incompatibility with the need of strict construction, see Concurring Opinion of Judge Christine Van den Wyngaert (para 16) annexed to Judgment, *Mathieu Ngudjolo Chui* (ICC-01/04-02/12-4) Trial Chamber II, 18 December 2012, who is 'firmly of the view that treaty interpretation cannot be used to fill perceived gaps in the available arsenal of forms of criminal responsibility'.

[64] Judgment, *Zejnil Delalic et al* Trial Chamber II, above n 15, paras 410 ff. This reference was mentioned in several international criminal cases, eg, see Judgment, *Stanislav Galic* (IT-98-29-T) Trial Chamber I, 5 December 2003, para 93; Declaration of Judge Shahabuddeen (para 3) annexed to Judgment, *Limaj and al* (IT-03-66-A) Appeals Chamber, 27 September 2007; Decision, *Ieng Thirith* (ECCC-002/19-09-2007) Trial Chamber, 17 November 2011, para 80. See also: Decision, *Milan Milutinovic et al* Appeals Chamber, above n 20, para 28; Partial Dissenting Opinion of Judge Shahabuddeen (para 12) annexed to Decision, *Enver Hadzihasanovic et al* Appeals Chamber, above n 56; Decision, *William Samoei Ruto and al* (ICC-01/09-01/11) Trial Chamber II, 5 April 2016, Reasons of Judge Eboe-Osuji, para 433.

to be construed *contra proferentem*'. However, this approach derives neither from Articles 31–32 of the VCLT, nor from the usual interpretative practice engaged in by the ICTs.[65]

Finally, following on from this, while this practice of appealing to international human rights law in the ICTs work is 'quantitatively' significant, 'qualitatively' speaking[66] it is limited by the problem of its transposability into international criminal law. For, while judges have maintained a degree of 'fruitful porousness' ('*porosité fructueuse*') between these two 'conjoined' branches ('*branches siamoises*') of law,[67] they remained conscious of the structural differences between their objects and their purposes.[68] This question of 'transposability' is partially solved by Article 21(3) of the ICC Statute which, in a way, turns the situation on its head: it grants a higher authority to international human rights law, although the latter is considered as a subsidiary source for international criminal law. In this way, it establishes a general condition for the application *and* (more importantly) the interpretation of the applicable law by the ICC, namely the compatibility of this applicable law with 'internationally recognised human rights', in the sense of an enhanced protection of the rights of the accused.[69]

Along much the same lines, the ICC Statute – in a first for international criminal law – formally enshrines the principle of legality (Article 22 *et seq*), in particular the principle of strict interpretation and, in those cases where ambiguity arises, the principle of *in dubio pro reo* (Article 22(2)),[70] thus imposing 'a clear and

[65] *cf* William Schabas who explains that most of the time, judges preferred an interpretation much more favourable to prosecution than to defence, except in very few cases (W Schabas, 'Droit pénal international et droit international des droits de l'homme: faux frères' in M Henzelin and R Roth (eds), *Le droit pénal à l'épreuve de l'internationalisation* (Paris, LGDJ, 2002) 170–71).

[66] See E Lambert-Abdelgawad, 'Les Tribunaux pénaux pour l'ex-Yougoslavie et le Rwanda et l'appel aux sources du droit international des droits de l'homme' in M Delmas-Marty, E Fronza and E Lambert-Abdelgawad (eds), *Les sources du droit international pénal. L'expérience des tribunaux pénaux internationaux et le statut de la Cour pénale internationale* (Paris, Société de législation comparée, 2004) 115.

[67] P Tavernier, 'Les Tribunaux pénaux internationaux et le droit international des droits de l'homme' in M Delmas-Marty, E Fronza and E Lambert-Abdelgawad (eds), *Les sources du droit international pénal. L'expérience des tribunaux pénaux internationaux et le statut de la Cour pénale internationale* (Paris, Société de législation comparée, 2004) 402.

[68] *cf* Art 31(1) of the 1969 Vienna Convention. For developments, see Garibian, *Le crime contre l'humanité*, above n 2, 329 ff.

[69] Judgment, *Thomas Lubanga Dyilo* (ICC-01/04-01/06-772) Appeals Chamber, 14 December 2006, para 36 (also cited in Judgment, *Thomas Lubanga Dyilo* Trial Chamber I, above n 29, para 602); Judgment, *Thomas Lubanga Dyilo* (ICC-01/04-01/06-773) Appeals Chamber, 14 December 2006, paras 20 and 50; Decision, *Germain Katanga* (ICC-01/04-01/07-257) Pre-Trial Chamber I, 10 March 2008, 7; Judgment, *Germain Katanga* Trial Chamber II, above n 29, para 50; Judgment, *Jean-Pierre Bemba Gombo* Trial Chamber III, above n 29, para 82. See also G Bitti, 'Article 21 and the Hierarchy of Sources of Law before the ICC' in C Stahn (ed), *The Law and Practice of the International Criminal Court* (Oxford, Oxford University Press, 2015). More generally, see E Fronza, 'Human Rights and Criminal Law: Reference to the Case Law of Human Rights Bodies by International Criminal Tribunals' in R Kolb and D Scalia (eds), *Droit international pénal*, 2nd edn (Bâle, Helbing Lichtenhahn, 2012).

[70] See especially Decision, *Thomas Lubanga Dyilo* Pre-Trial Chamber I, above n 29, para 303; Judgment, *Germain Katanga* Trial Chamber II, above n 29, para 50 ff; Judgment, *Jean-Pierre Bemba Gombo* Trial Chamber III, above n 29, paras 83–84.

explicit restriction on all interpretative activity'.[71] Some believe that interpretation in the light of the rules of the VCLT – and in particular teleological interpretation entailing consideration of the need to end impunity for the perpetrators – could be antithetical to the principle of legality and its corollaries.[72] Nevertheless, the ICC considered it 'self-evident that the aim of the Statute … can under no circumstance be used to create a body of law extraneous to the terms of the treaty or incompatible with a purely literal reading of its text'.[73] And it affirmed that the VCLT 'provides for a method of interpretation which is both circumscribed and rigorous and which leaves little scope for any risk of misinterpretation of the Statute'.[74]

All things considered, what the judges of the ICTs – and above all the ICTY – have been constructing is, a 'nested' mechanism of interpretation that dynamically puts norms into action through a 'network'. This network is a set of extrinsic sources within which international human rights law occupies a prime position when it comes to contextualising, clarifying and occasionally supplementing, their statute. It nevertheless remains the case that what we have here is in fact evolutionary interpretation hiding its true colours. To paraphrase the legal theorist Michel Troper, following Herbert Hart, it is precisely the negation of the creative character of judicial activity which provides judges with the means to create.[75] They adopt the classical, mechanistic conception of interpretation-as-knowledge to justify their work. However, one inevitably needs to ponder the real nature of their power and to bring into question the ideal of the permanence, completeness and certainty of law. The open texture of law, in particular of an international criminal law in progress, is intrinsically bound up with the very nature of language and the endless new realities to be dealt with. More fundamentally, perhaps, the '[c]anons of 'interpretation' cannot eliminate, though they can diminish, these uncertainties; for these canons are themselves general rules for the use of language, and make use of general terms which themselves require interpretation' – interpretation by men, not gods.[76]

[71] Judgment, *Germain Katanga* Trial Chamber II, above n 29, para 51.

[72] The ICC itself recalled it (ibid, para 54) referring to D Robinson, 'The Identity Crisis of International Criminal Law' (2008) 21 *Leiden Journal of International Law* 933; L Grover, 'A Call to Arms: Fundamental Dilemmas Confronting the Interpretation of Crimes in the Rome Statute of the International Criminal Court' (2010) 21 *European Journal of International Law* 550; D Jacobs, 'Positivism and International Criminal Law: The Principle of Legality as a Rule of Conflict of Theories' in J d'Aspremont and J Kammerhofer (eds), *International Legal Positivism in a Post-Modern World* (Cambridge, Cambridge University Press, 2014). The Court also referred to the Concurring Opinion of Judge Christine Van den Wyngaert (paras 16–18) annexed to Judgment, *Mathieu Ngudjolo Chui* Trial Chamber II, above n 63.

[73] Judgment, *Germain Katanga* Trial Chamber II, above n 29, para 55.

[74] ibid, para 56.

[75] M Troper, *La théorie du droit, le droit, l'Etat* (Paris, PUF, 2001) 170. See also Hart, above n 1, 135–36.

[76] Hart, above n 1, 126 and 128.

PART IV

Evolutionary Interpretation in WTO Law

A. Systemic Approaches to Evolutionary Interpretation

16

Understanding the Choice for Evolutionary Interpretation

ISABELLE VAN DAMME

I. Introduction

This contribution will discuss elements that may affect whether international courts and tribunals, and in particular the World Trade Organization (WTO) dispute settlement system, refer to or make use of so-called evolutionary interpretation.

The choice for evolutionary interpretation can be broadly understood as meaning an interpreter's decision on whether it is necessary to interpret a term or phrase in a treaty in a manner that takes account of either legal or factual developments subsequent to a treaty's conclusion, meaning developments not known to the treaty drafters at the time of the treaty's conclusion and/or that might not have been known by judges who had previously interpreted the same term or phrase.[1] Evolutionary interpretation might therefore also result in reversing previous judgments.

In practice, what is described as evolutionary interpretation is in essence often an effort to ensure that the treaty remains relevant and effective over time. In other words, evolutionary interpretation may often be understood as a choice, at the time of the interpretation of a treaty (and thus not necessarily at the time of its conclusion), to give meaning to a treaty taking into account developments subsequent to the conclusion of the treaty. Those developments might be factual or legal.[2] Different legal bases might be invoked (possibly in combination) in order to justify or, for that matter, to reject that choice. Those bases include the treaty text, its context, its object and purpose, other rules of international law and the principle of effectiveness.

[1] For an overview of different understandings of the notion of 'evolutionary interpretation', see, eg, E Bjorge, *The Evolutionary Interpretation of Treaties* (Oxford, Oxford University Press, 2014) esp ch 3.3; G Marceau, 'Evolutive Interpretation by the WTO Adjudicator: Sophism or Necessity?' (2018) 21 *Journal of International Economic Law* 791; C Djeffal, *Static and Evolutive Treaty Interpretation: A Functional Reconstruction* (Cambridge, Cambridge University Press, 2016) esp ch 7.

[2] See, eg, Marceau, above n 1; R Kolb, 'Evolutionary Interpretation in International Law: Some Short and Less than Trail-Blazing Reflections', ch 3 in this book.

The choice for evolutionary interpretation is controlled, though not exclusively, by the principles codified in Articles 31–33 of the 1969 Vienna Convention on the Law of Treaties (VCLT).[3] Few would probably dispute that treaty interpretation always involves the intention of the parties. However, the debate continues on where that intention is to be found. Is the controlling element the text of a treaty, its object and purpose (in whatever manner that might be established), its origins or some other feature?[4] There continue to be many perspectives on what the concept of the intention of the parties means and where it can (or should) be found. It is undoubtedly true that all of those principles might be relevant to an interpreter's choice of whether it is necessary to interpret a treaty term or phrase in a manner that takes account of either legal or factual developments subsequent to a treaty's conclusion. Thus, we do not take issue with the proposition that evolutionary interpretation is not a separate method of interpretation but can result from applying the principles codified in Articles 31–33 of the VCLT. However, it appears to us that those principles as such are not necessarily exclusive in controlling the decision of an international court or tribunal on whether to interpret a treaty in a manner that takes account of developments, whether or not specifically tied to the treaty being interpreted, that were not known to the treaty drafters at the time of the treaty's conclusion.[5] We therefore have some reservations regarding a thesis that establishes the acceptability of, and justification for, evolutionary interpretation entirely on the notion of the intention of the parties as apparent from the application of Articles 31–33 of the VCLT.[6] We do not consider that the matter can be simplified in this manner. In any event, as we have explained elsewhere, the interpretive practices of international courts and tribunals cannot easily be analysed into distinct schools of interpretation, such as textual, teleological or evolutionary interpretation.[7]

The principles of treaty interpretation codified in the VCLT offer various tools for interpreters to take into account legal or factual developments subsequent to a treaty's conclusion. Those tools include the text and context of the treaty, the object and purpose of the treaty, subsequent practice and agreements, other rules of international law and even supplementary means of interpretation. However, despite the function of those provisions as a possible basis of evolutionary and other approaches to interpretation, international courts and tribunals exercise a certain degree of discretion in deciding to rely on those elements and possibly, based thereon, to identify or construct the intention of the parties.

[3] Vienna Convention on the Law of Treaties (adopted 23 May 1969) 1155 *United Nations Treaty Series* 331.

[4] See also D McRae, 'Evolutionary Interpretation: The Relevance of Context', ch 7 in this book.

[5] See also I Van Damme, 'Is Evolutionary Interpretation Only a Matter of Finding the Parties' Intentions?' EJIL Book Discussion, 17 December 2014, available at: www.ejiltalk.org/is-evolutionary-interpretation-only-a-matter-of-finding-the-parties-intentions.

[6] See E Bjorge, 'Time Present and Time Past: The Intention of the Parties and the Evolutionary Interpretation of Treaties', ch 5 in this book.

[7] See I Van Damme, *Treaty Interpretation by the WTO Appellate Body* (Oxford, Oxford University Press, 2009) 35–37.

Whether it is a matter of method of interpretive reasoning or judicial policy, the fact is that international courts and tribunals do not always make the same interpretive choices including whether to take account of factual and legal developments subsequent to the conclusion of the treaty that they have jurisdiction to interpret and apply. Elements outside the principles of treaty interpretation codified in Articles 31–33 of the VCLT might also affect interpretive choices. This is not a novel proposition. International courts and tribunals have always produced case law within a specific context (which may be institutional) and against a historical background.[8] Both elements affect what is considered to be acceptable and justified in terms of judicial interpretation in the context of a particular dispute submitted for adjudication by a third party. The interpretive practices of, for example, the WTO dispute settlement bodies or the Court of Justice of the European Union are deeply rooted in the features of the legal systems created by each organisation and the respective (often evolving) roles of each adjudicator therein as well as their origins.[9]

Therefore, factors explaining how that discretion is exercised, taking into account the principles of treaty interpretation codified in Articles 31–33 of the VCLT, are relevant too in understanding the reasons for the choice for or against evolutionary interpretation. It is not particularly revealing to state that every interpretation of a text with authority as law starts with the wording of that text because that text is the result a consensus. However, that position does not necessarily resolve, for example, how an international court or tribunal in practice moves from one element to another in every case of treaty interpretation (taking into account the content and the logic of Articles 31–33) and eventually opts for an evolutionary interpretation.

II. Elements Affecting the Choice for Evolutionary Interpretation

Against that background, we now turn to exploring four elements that might affect the choice for evolutionary interpretation in the particular context of WTO dispute settlement.

First, if it is accepted that the notion of evolutionary interpretation itself presupposes that it is possible to know what was, in the absence of subsequent

[8] See, eg, G Shaffer, M Elsig and S Puig, 'The Law and Politics of WTO Dispute Settlement' in W Sandholtz and C Whytock (eds), *Research Handbook on the Politics of International Law* (Chelthenham, Edward Elgar Publishing, 2017); A Sennekamp and I Van Damme, 'A Practical Perspective on Treaty Interpretation: The Court of Justice of the European Union and the WTO Dispute Settlement System' (2014) 3 *Cambridge Journal of International and Comparative Law* 1.

[9] See, eg, K Lenaerts and JA Gutiérrez-Fons, 'To Say What the Law of the EU Is: Methods of Interpretation and the European Court of Justice' (2013) EUI Working Papers AEL, available at cadmus.eui.eu/bitstream/handle/1814/28339/AEL_2013_09_DL.pdf?sequence=1; Sennekamp and Van Damme, above n 8.

legal and factual developments, the meaning of a treaty term at the time of the conclusion of the treaty, then it might be particularly difficult to identify what is evolutionary interpretation in context of the WTO dispute settlement system.

The WTO covered agreements are multilateral agreements that were concluded for an indefinite period of time[10] and with an increasing number of parties. The General Agreement on Tariffs and Trade 1994 (GATT, 1994) is in essence the same treaty as that to which, in 1947, a total of 23 Contracting Parties became a party. That same treaty was then, in essence, incorporated in the WTO covered agreements to which, in 1994, 128 WTO Members became a party.[11] Presently, there are 164 WTO Members.

WTO Members became a party to a complex set of agreements that are collectively called the WTO covered agreements. To characterise an interpretation as evolutionary, it is typically assumed that an interpreter can ascertain the treaty's meaning at the time of its conclusion and the original intention of the parties. With a large set of multilateral agreements such as the WTO covered agreements, having a rich history and a growing set of diverse parties, it appears more difficult to ascertain the so-called original meaning as compared with that of, for example, a bilateral agreement. In that context, Gabrielle Marceau has rightly remarked that '[t]he issue of "changes" is particularly relevant in the context of the WTO Treaty, because it combines long-standing provisions with other, more recent ones, adopted simultaneously'.[12]

For example, the Appellate Body's interpretation in *US – Shrimp* of the phrase 'exhaustible natural resources' in Article XX(g) of the GATT 1994 is typically cited as an instance of evolutionary interpretation. This is, in part, because the Appellate Body itself appeared to declare that it was engaging in an evolutionary interpretation. In particular, the Appellate Body stated that '[f]rom the perspective embodied in the preamble of the WTO Agreement, we note that the generic term "natural resources" in Article XX(g) is not "static" in its content or reference but is rather "by definition, evolutionary"'.[13] Therefore, it was 'pertinent to note that

[10] See, eg, WTO Appellate Body Report, *China – Measures Affecting Trading Rights and Distribution Services for Certain Publications and Audiovisual Entertainment Products (China – Publications and Audiovisual Products)* adopted 19 January 2010, WT/DS363/AB/R, para 397: 'More generally, we consider that the terms used in China's GATS Schedule ("sound recording" and "distribution") are sufficiently generic that what they apply to may change over time. In this respect, we note that GATS Schedules, like the GATS itself and all WTO agreements, constitute multilateral treaties with continuing obligations that WTO Members entered into for an indefinite period of time, regardless of whether they were original Members or acceded after 1995'.

[11] See further, eg, J Pauwelyn and I Van Damme, 'The World Trade Organization' in MJ Bowman and D Kritsiotis (eds), *Conceptual and Contextual Perspectives on the Modern Law of Treaties* (Cambridge, Cambridge University Press, 2018); JH Jackson, 'The Evolution of the World Trading System – The Legal and Institutional Context' in D Bethlehem, D McRae, R Neufeld and I Van Damme (eds), *The Oxford Handbook of International Trade Law* (Oxford, Oxford University Press, 2009) 30–37.

[12] Marceau, above n 1, 792.

[13] WTO Appellate Body Report, *United States – Import Prohibition of Certain Shrimp and Shrimp Products (US – Shrimp)* adopted 6 November 1998, WT/DS58/AB/R, para 130.

modern international conventions and declarations make frequent references to natural resources as embracing both living and non-living resources'.[14] However, the Appellate Body itself recognised in that report that two GATT 1947 panel reports had, prior to the conclusion of the Agreement Establishing the World Trade Organization (WTO Agreement), accepted in adopted reports that that provision also covered fish and thus living organisms.[15] At the time of the WTO Agreement's conclusion, WTO Members did not seek to react against that interpretation by modifying the text of the relevant provision or adopting any other type of decision to that effect. Instead, they included the principle of sustainable development in the preamble to the WTO Agreement. Thus, the Appellate Body's interpretation was evolutionary if the GATT 1947 is taken as a starting point but it was not evolutionary compared with the view of WTO Members at the time of the conclusion of the WTO Agreement.[16] For similar reasons, it is debatable whether the interpretation of Article XX(g) of the GATT 1994 in light of the principle of sovereignty over natural resources in the panel report in *China – Raw Materials* is an instance of evolutionary interpretation. That panel considered it appropriate, taking into account Article 31(3)(c) of the VCLT, to interpret Article XX(g) of the GATT 1994 (which corresponds with the text of the same provision in the GATT 1947) in light of the fundamental principle of international law that is 'the principle of state sovereignty, denoting the equality of all States in competence and independence over their own territories and encompassing the right to make laws applicable within their own territories without intrusion from other sovereign states'.[17] An element of that sovereignty, relevant to the interpretation of Article XX(g) of the GATT 1994 advanced by China in that case, was a State's sovereignty over its natural resources. The development of that principle well predated the GATT 1994, as the panel documented.[18]

Second, unlike many other international agreements, the WTO Agreement comprises a large number of international agreements which, according to the Appellate Body, must be interpreted as a whole and harmoniously.[19] That has

[14] ibid, para 130.

[15] ibid, para 131.

[16] For another explanation of why this interpretation is not evolutionary, see, eg, G Cook, 'The Illusion of "Evolutionary Interpretation" in WTO Dispute Settlement', ch 17 in this book.

[17] WTO Panel Reports, *China – Measures Related to the Exportation of Various Raw Materials* (*China – Raw Materials*) adopted 22 February 2012, WT/DS394/R / WT/DS395/R / WT/DS398/R / Add.1 and Corr.1, paras 7.377 and 7.378.

[18] ibid, paras 7.380–7.383.

[19] See, eg, WTO Appellate Body Report, *Argentina – Safeguard Measures on Imports of Footwear (Argentina – Footwear (EC))* adopted 12 January 2000, WT/DS121/AB/R, para 81; WTO Appellate Body Report, *Korea – Definitive Safeguard Measure on Imports of Certain Dairy Products (Korea – Dairy)* adopted 12 January 2000, WT/DS98/AB/R, para 81; also WTO Appellate Body Report, *United States – Standards for Reformulated and Conventional Gasoline (US – Gasoline)* adopted 20 May 1996, WT/DS2/AB/R, 23; WTO Appellate Body Report, *Japan – Taxes on Alcoholic Beverages (Japan – Alcoholic Beverages II)* adopted 1 November 1996, WT/DS8/AB/R / WT/DS10/AB/R / WT/DS11/AB/R, 106; WTO Appellate Body Report, *India – Patent Protection for Pharmaceutical and Agricultural Chemical Products (India – Patents (US))* adopted 16 January 1998, WT/DS50/AB/R, para 4;

often meant that the legal standard under a provision of one agreement evolves in tandem with the case law regarding the meaning of a provision's legal standard in another agreement, irrespective of any considerations of what the parties' intention might have been with respect to the first agreement. Thus, a panel or the Appellate Body might often consider the evolving case law regarding the meaning of a particular legal standard at the time when it is applied, even if that case law related to a different WTO agreement. For example, the interpretation of the Agreement on Technical Barriers to Trade (TBT Agreement) has evolved in light of the case law regarding Article III:4 of the GATT 1994.[20]

This element also underlies the Appellate Body's position in *China – Publication and Audiovisual Products* that

> interpreting the terms of the GATS specific commitments based on the notion that the ordinary meaning to be attributed to those terms can only be the meaning that they had at the time the schedule was concluded would mean that very similar or identically worded commitments could be given different meanings, content, and coverage depending on the date of their adoption or the date of a Member's accession to the treaty.[21]

The Appellate Body thus considered that evolutionary interpretation was justified in order to achieve the objectives of 'the predictability, security, and clarity of GATS specific commitments, which are undertaken through successive rounds of negotiations'.[22]

Third, unlike the interpretation of (for example) a bilateral agreement on an ad hoc basis, panels and the Appellate Body interpret the WTO covered agreements in a defined institutional context. That institutional context is marked by a particular balance of powers between, on the one hand, the WTO dispute settlement bodies and other bodies in the WTO and, on the other hand, the WTO as an organisation and its Members. This balance of powers is related to the notions of 'judicial policy' and 'judicial function' (notions which are discussed in greater detail by Professor Abi-Saab's contribution to this book) and the context within which the WTO dispute settlement bodies interpret the covered agreements.[23]

WTO Appellate Body Report, *United States – Subsidies on Upland Cotton (US – Upland Cotton)* adopted 21 March 2005, WT/DS267/AB/R, paras 547–49; WTO Appellate Body Report, *United States – Continued Existence and Application of Zeroing Methodology (US – Continued Zeroing)* adopted 19 February 2009, WT/DS350/AB/R, para 268.

[20] See, eg, WTO Appellate Body Report, *United States – Measures Affecting the Production and Sale of Clove Cigarettes* (*US – Clove Cigarettes*) adopted 24 April 2012, WT/DS406/AB/R, paras 109–11. See further, eg, Pauwelyn and Van Damme, above n 11, 820–23.

[21] *China – Publications and Audiovisual Products*, above n 10, para 397.

[22] ibid.

[23] See, MC de Andrade, 'Evolutionary Interpretation and the Appellate Body's Existential Crisis', ch 21 in this book. See also, eg, Sennekamp Van Damme, above n 8; G Abi-Saab, 'The Appellate Body and Treaty Interpretation' in G Sacerdoti, A Yanovich and J Bohanes (eds), *The WTO at Ten – The Contribution of the Dispute Settlement System* (Cambridge, Cambridge University Press, 2006) 460–62.

That institutional context must also be considered together with the processes through which WTO law is made and the means through which WTO law may evolve outside the context of WTO dispute settlement. Thus, for example, so-called treaty rigidity might make it more acceptable for the WTO dispute settlement system to 'update' the treaty so as to retain its relevance and thus effectiveness.[24] Although effective interpretation and evolutionary interpretation are usually regarded as distinct methods of interpreting treaties, they can equally mutually support their application. The principle of effective interpretation also means that 'the treaty must remain effective rather than ineffective', thus the treaty language may need to be put into practice to ensure its continued effect. The panel's reasoning in *Mexico – Telecoms* illustrates well this relationship between the principles of effective and evolutionary interpretation:

> Just as the interpretation and application of GATT provisions have dynamically evolved in response to the several hundred GATT dispute settlement proceedings since 1948, so the interpretation and clarification of GATS provisions is likely to evolve over time. The diverse backgrounds of the panellists, and the assistance granted by the Secretariat pursuant to Article 27.1 of the DSU, have ensured that this Panel was fully aware of the legal and technical complexity of the regulation of telecommunications services, including their rapid technological evolution and the drafting history of GATS provisions to which both parties to this dispute referred extensively.[25]

Gregory Schaffer and others have written extensively on the importance of that institutional context and the values of transparency, accountability and legitimacy that are connected with it.[26] It suffices to note, for the purposes of this contribution, that that context and those values result in the fact that the WTO dispute settlement system is an appropriate case study for considering, in the context of discussions on evolutionary interpretation, the question of who should decide on whether the meaning of a treaty term has evolved over time. Is it the WTO panels and the Appellate Body? Is it the WTO Members? Is it other international organisations on which the WTO covered agreements confer some powers?

The WTO Agreement is increasingly read in light of declarations, decisions, guidelines and other products of the activities within other WTO bodies. Through those instruments, WTO Members often agree on how to apply or interpret parts of the treaty text and thereby further develop existing rules. Increasingly, panels and the Appellate Body acknowledge the interpretive relevance of such instruments and seek a basis in the VCLT for that approach. In that context, the Appellate Body in *US – Tuna II (Mexico)* decided that a Technical Barriers to Trade Committee Decision on Principles for the Development of International

[24] See also, P Van den Bossche, 'Is there Evolution in the Evolutionary Interpretation of WTO Law?', ch 20; and M Fitzmaurice, 'European Court of Human Rights and the Right to a Clean Environment: Evolutionary or Illusory Interpretation?', ch 14 in this book.

[25] WTO Panel Report, *Mexico – Measures Affecting Telecommunications Services (Mexico – Telecoms)* adopted 1 June 2004, WT/DS204/R, para 7.2.

[26] See, eg, Shaffer, Elsig and Puig, above n 8.

Standards, Guides and Recommendations was a subsequent agreement between the parties regarding the interpretation of the TBT Agreement and therefore could, based on Article 31(3)(a) of the VCLT, be used to interpret Article 2.4 of that agreement.[27] In another report, the Appellate Body construed the Doha Ministerial Declaration as a 'subsequent agreement' to guide its interpretation of a 'reasonable interval' in Article 2.12 of the TBT Agreement.[28]

Those reports signal that the Appellate Body is willing to endorse the position that the meaning of the complex treaty structure agreed upon in the Uruguay Round needs constant revision and 'updating' as a result of action of WTO Members in various committees and other bodies – even though the mechanism in question cannot be characterised as a formal waiver, an authoritative interpretation or an amendment adopted pursuant to the procedures explicitly provided for in the WTO Agreement itself (outside the context of WTO treaty negotiations). Thus despite the fact that the WTO treaties are difficult to amend, some case law suggests that those norms must be read against the background of an increasing production of instruments by either the WTO itself or its Members which, while not constituting treaty law or secondary legislation, assume varying degrees of normative relevance – in terms of the day-to-day implementation and operation of WTO law as well as of WTO dispute settlement.[29] However, not all WTO Members agree with this development in the case law.[30]

It is nonetheless the case that, from one perspective, that case law could be characterised as evolutionary whereas, from another perspective, it could be seen as the Appellate Body deciding to defer to an action taken by WTO Members themselves.

Both perspectives are also relevant to understanding the interpretation of 'public morals' under Article XX(a) of the GATT 1994 or Article XIV(a) of the General Agreement on Trade in Services (GATS) in the case law of panels and the Appellate Body. The panel in *US – Gambling* interpreted the term 'public morals' to 'denote[] standards of right and wrong conduct maintained by or on behalf of a community or nation'.[31] The term 'public order' was understood to 'refer[] to the preservation of the fundamental interests of a society, as reflected in public policy and law'.[32] That panel also accepted that 'the content of these concepts for Members can vary in time and space, depending upon a range of factors, including

[27] WTO Appellate Body Report, *United States – Measures Concerning the Importation, Marketing and Sale of Tuna and Tuna Products (US – Tuna II (Mexico))* adopted 13 June 2012, WT/DS381/AB/R, paras 371–78.

[28] *US – Clove Cigarettes*, above n 20, paras 256–68.

[29] See also J Pauwelyn and I Van Damme, 'World Trade Organization', above n 11, 831; G Schaffer and J Trachtman, 'Interpretation and Institutional Choice at the WTO' (2011) 52 *Virginia Journal of International Law* 103.

[30] See, eg, WTO, Minutes of Meeting held on 13 June 2012, WT/DSB/M/317 (31 July 2012) para 16.

[31] WTO Panel Report, *United States – Measures Affecting the Cross-Border Supply of Gambling and Betting Services (US – Gambling)* adopted 20 April 2005, WT/DS285/R, para 6.465.

[32] ibid, para 6.467.

prevailing social, cultural, ethical and religious values' and that 'Members should be given some scope to define and apply for themselves the concepts of "public morals" and "public order" in their respective territories, according to their own systems and scales of values'.[33] This interpretation thus envisages that what constitutes public morals may change over time but defers to WTO Members' choices in that regard.[34]

Fourth, the extent to which evolutionary interpretation may result from taking into account subsequent legal developments, including in other areas of international law, its acceptance appears to be tied to the understanding of the role of panels and the Appellate Body. Some WTO Members consider that panels and the Appellate Body must resolve interpretive questions within the context of the four corners of the WTO covered agreements. Others seem more willing to accept that, to ensure an overall coherence of WTO Members' obligations under the WTO covered agreements and other international agreements and to guarantee that the WTO covered agreements remain effective, it might be acceptable for panels and the Appellate Body to take into account such subsequent developments outside the WTO.

III. Conclusion

We do not argue that these four elements form an exhaustive list or that a single element might explain why a panel or the Appellate Body rejects or chooses evolutionary interpretation. However, the interaction between all of these elements might assist in better understanding why, taking into account the principles in the VCLT, evolutionary interpretation is either chosen or rejected. In practice, whether panels and the Appellate Body opt for evolutionary interpretation is often tied to whether the treaty drafters offered some sort of mandate (eg, by referring to the objective of sustainable development) to the interpreter to look outside the WTO covered agreements and at later developments. Typically, where the Appellate Body takes into account subsequent legal and factual developments, there is some 'textual hook' in the text of the treaties. It is less common that panels and the Appellate Body make that choice acting of their own motion.

[33] ibid, para 6.461.

[34] See, eg, Appellate Body Reports, *European Communities – Measures Prohibiting the Importation and Marketing of Seal Products* (*US – Seal Products*) adopted 18 June 2014, WT/DS400/AB/R / WT/DS401/AB/R, para 5.200 and the case law cited. See also, eg, Cook, above n 16.

17

The Illusion of 'Evolutionary Interpretation' in WTO Dispute Settlement

GRAHAM COOK

I. Introduction

The International Court of Justice (ICJ) speaks of cases in which it confronted treaty terms 'whose meaning had evolved since the conclusion of the treaty at issue'. It says that it sometimes 'adhered to the original meaning', and that other times it went with 'the present meaning'.[1] It has gone so far as to contemplate the possibility of changes to 'the meaning acquired by the terms in question *upon each occasion on which the treaty is to be applied*' (emphasis added).[2] The International Law Commission (ILC) has likewise referred to evolutionary interpretation in terms of 'a meaning which is capable of evolving over time'.[3] While there is no authoritative definition of 'evolutionary interpretation', Gardiner notes 'the gist is that the meaning of treaty terms may change over time'.[4]

It may be useful to disambiguate this notion of evolutionary interpretation from other notions of 'evolutionary interpretation' used more loosely in some of the other chapters in this book. First, the progressive clarification of vague treaty terms through legal standards subsequently developed by adjudicators is an unavoidable exercise in clarification aimed at giving meaning to the terms, not an evolutionary interpretation in the sense above.[5] Second, when a tribunal

[1] *Dispute Regarding Navigational and Related Rights (Costa Rica v Nicaragua)* (Judgment) [2009] ICJ Rep 213, see, eg, paras 63–64, 70.

[2] ibid, paras 63 and 64.

[3] International Law Commission, *Report of the International Law Commission: Sixty-eighth Session* (2 May–10 June and 4 July–12 August 2016), UN Doc A/71/10 (2016) 182–83, conclusion 8(3), and associated commentary at 181.

[4] R Gardiner, *Treaty Interpretation*, 2nd edn (Oxford, Oxford University Press, 2015) 467.

[5] To take one example, the vague concept of a non-violation 'nullification or impairment' of a 'benefit' in the context of Art XXIII of the GATT has given rise to the formulation of legal standards that probably could not have been verbalised by the drafters at the time of the treaty's conclusion. See G Cook, 'The Legalization of the Non-Violation Concept in the GATT/WTO System' (24 October 2018), available at: ssrn.com/abstract=3272165). However, when WTO adjudicators developed and applied these legal standards, they were not in any intelligible sense making a choice between the 'original' or 'present' meaning of the terms.

deviates from a legal standard developed in its earlier case law, it does so because it considers that earlier interpretation to be erroneous. It would rarely concede that the interpretation it is rejecting corresponded to the 'original meaning' as understood by the drafters.[6] Third, when a modern tribunal adopts reasoning that places a greater explicit emphasis on notions such as 'balance' or 'sustainable development', or which takes into account other rules of international law or practice post-dating the conclusion of the treaty, this does not in itself represent any change in the meaning of the term being interpreted.[7]

As articulated by the ICJ and other leading authorities, the concept of 'evolutionary interpretation' comprises the arresting notions that: (i) the meaning of words used in treaty provisions changes over time; (ii) when this happens, it is in principle legitimate for the adjudicator to substitute their contemporary meaning over the original meaning. The prevailing discourse celebrates the notion of 'evolutionary interpretation' as a means of ensuring that old rules adapt to the modern times. In the context of World Trade Organization (WTO) dispute settlement, *US – Shrimp* and *China – Publications and Audiovisual Services* are often held up as examples of such progressive 'evolutionary interpretation'.

There is nothing controversial or objectionable in the idea that the written words of laws adopted many decades or centuries ago must, in some way, be capable of continuously adapting to changed societal values, new technologies, and other subsequent evolutions in the law. However, this chapter argues that there is a better analytical tool than the notion of 'evolving meaning' to achieve that end. The next part of this chapter explains the distinction between 'evolutionary interpretation' and 'evolutionary application'.

II. Distinguishing Evolutionary Interpretation from Evolutionary Application

The distinction between evolutionary interpretation and application is not an original idea. It has been articulated many times before, in varying terminology, in the context of both domestic and international legal interpretation.

In 'The Elasticity of the Constitution', published more than 100 years ago, Professor Machen set out several principles regarding the relationship between the fixed US Constitution and an ever-changing society. One of the main principles,

[6] For example, the earliest WTO panel and Appellate Body reports interpreted the term 'like products' in a way that rejected the approach taken by some GATT-era panels which had applied an 'aims and effects' test; and at about the same time, the Appellate Body rejected the restrictive interpretation of Art XX followed by some GATT-era panels in relation to regulations directed at non-product related process and production methods. In no sense did the Appellate Body consider the interpretations developed by the GATT-era panels, which it regarded as erroneous, to correspond to the 'original meaning' of the terms of the GATT 1947.

[7] These appear to be two of the four different types of evolutionary interpretation that serve as the analytical framework in J Grigorova, 'Energy Trade in the WTO, Yesterday, Today and Tomorrow: The Role of Evolutionary Interpretation', ch 22 in this book.

he explained, was that the abstract meaning of the original legal principles embodied in the Constitution does not change, but that the facts to which those principles are applied are constantly changing. Professor Machen rejected the 'heresy' of a varying construction of the law, letting the notion of 'application' do the work of ensuring that the written law adapts to infinitely various facts:

> The separation of the law from the facts is a difficult but transcendentally important task. For while *denying* in the most unqualified terms the notion that the Constitution is capable of *a varying construction*, we may often be swayed by the same arguments advanced in favour of that *heresy*, and even reach the same results, but in a perfectly *legitimate* way, simply by a careful discrimination between *matters of law and fact*. The *law* of the Constitution remains *forever unchanging*: the *facts* to which it must be *applied are infinitely various* (emphasis added).[8]

In an article published 100 years later entitled 'The Meaning of Original Meaning', the authors provide an extended discussion on the distinction between 'meaning' and 'application', and how it informs the way we should think about the originalism versus non-originalist debate in US constitutional law. For present purposes, we will confine ourselves to quoting their explanation that:

> One way to see that meaning and applications must be different is to recognize that over time *the meaning of a word can stay the same while the set of things to which it is applied changes*. For example, through advances in microscope technology, we could come to realize that organisms not previously recognized to be viruses were in fact viruses. Or, new viruses could evolve and come to be recognized as viruses. In either case, the things to which speakers applied the word 'virus' could change while the word's meaning stayed the same. Similarly, people in the past sometimes applied 'gold' to fool's gold, but that did not prevent them from meaning 'gold'; rather, the meaning of 'gold' has remained constant while its applications have changed.
>
> There is of course a close relation between meaning and application, which is one reason why they are sometimes conflated (emphasis added).[9]

The distinction between evolutionary interpretation and application finds reflection outside the United States. For instance, according to *Driedger on the Construction of Statutes*, the leading Canadian text on statutory interpretation, it can be argued that:

> [E]ven though *the meaning of a word remains constant, the things or events that fall within its ambit may change dramatically over time*. Understanding the original meaning as the original sense or definition of words allows for a dynamic approach to interpretation. New inventions, changes in institutions or the environment and the evolution of new ideas may all be taken into account, provided they do not depend on an expansion of the original definition of the word (emphasis added).[10]

[8] AW Machen, 'The Elasticity of the Constitution (pts 1 & 2)' (1900) 14 *Harvard Law Review* 200, 273.

[9] MD Greenberg and H Litman, 'The Meaning of Original Meaning' (1998) 86 *Georgetown Law Journal* 569, 588.

[10] R Sullivan and E Driedger, *Driedger on the Construction of Statutes*, 3rd edn (Toronto, Butterworths, 1994) 110.

In *Statutory Interpretation in Australia*, reference is made to a High Court case in which the question arose whether a reference to the powers of a council to supply 'gas' included the supply of liquefied petroleum gas. When the Act was passed, coal gas was the only type of gas then available. Justice Barwick, writing for the majority, stated that he could 'see no reason why, whilst the *connotation* of the word "gas" will be *fixed*, its *denotation* cannot change with changing technologies' (emphasis added).[11]

In his 1976 lectures to The Hague Academy of International Law concerning the Vienna Convention rules of interpretation, Yasseen (who was a member of the ILC involved in drafting those rules) explained how words like 'convenient' and 'appropriate' do not change over time in a linguistic sense, but that the things that are *characterised* as convenient or appropriate will naturally change over time. In his view, it would be artificial to impute to the parties to a treaty an intention to have, from a 'linguistic' point of view, employed words in an 'evolutive' sense.[12] He considered, however, that

> [s]i le *sens* de ces termes reste *le même*, ce qui *est* convenable ou approprié peut par contre *changer* dans le temps. Par conséquent, ce qui *est* convenable ou approprié au moment de la conclusion du traité peut ne pas l'être au moment de son *application* (emphasis added).[13]

In a more recent article entitled 'Evolutive Treaty Interpretation: Legality, Semantics and Distinctions', Helmersen defines 'evolutive interpretation' as 'an interpretation where a term is given a meaning that changes over time', and notes that 'the evolutive *interpretation* of a term is distinct from its *application*. A term that is applied to new circumstances while its meaning remains constant is not being interpreted evolutively' (emphasis original).[14]

III. WTO Case Law from the Prism of the Evolutionary Interpretation/Application Distinction

A. The Appellate Body Report in *US – Shrimp*

In *US – Shrimp*, the Appellate Body famously found that the term 'natural resources' in Article XX(g) of the General Agreement on Tariffs and Trade (GATT)

[11] DC Pearce and RS Geddes, *Statutory Interpretation in Australia*, 5th edn (Chatswood, NSW, Butterworths, 2001) 95.

[12] MK Yasseen, 'L'interprétation des traités d'après la Convention de Vienne sur le droit des traité' (1976) 3 *Recueil des Cours de l'Académie de Droit International* 1, 26–27, para 7.

[13] ibid, para 9.

[14] ST Helmersen, 'Evolutive Treaty Interpretation: Legality, Semantics and Distinctions' (2013) 6 *European Journal of Legal Studies* 127, 128. See also M Milanovic, 'The ICJ and Evolutionary Interpretation' (*EJIL Talk!*, 14 July 2009), available at: www.ejiltalk.org/the-icj-and-evolutionary-treaty-interpretation/.

covers not only non-living resources, such as minerals, but also living resources, such as sea turtles. The Appellate Body stated that the generic term 'natural resources' is 'by definition, evolutionary',[15] and concluded that 'it is too late in the day to suppose that Article XX(g) of the GATT 1994 may be read as referring only to the conservation of exhaustible mineral or other non-living natural resources'.[16] However, the Appellate Body did not say that the meaning of the term 'natural resources' had evolved, or changed. What it said is that the generic term 'natural resources' is not static 'in its content or reference'.[17] While this formulation may accommodate different understandings of what is meant by 'evolutionary', saying that a term is not static in its 'reference' is consistent with the idea that the meaning of the concept may be fixed, but that '*the things or events that fall within its ambit may change*' (emphasis added).[18] What appeared to have changed over time was the extent of people's knowledge, in the light of 'modern biological sciences', about *which* resources are 'susceptible of depletion, exhaustion and extinction' (ie, 'exhaustible').

Assuming for the sake of argument that the meaning of the term 'natural resources' in 1947 was even relevant to the interpretative issue before the Appellate Body,[19] it never endorsed the complaining parties' assertion that, back in 1947, the meaning of 'natural resources' excluded living resources. To the contrary, multiple elements of the Appellate Body's reasoning establish that the terms had *always* meant living and non-living natural resources: first and foremost, the Appellate Body stressed that '[t]extually, Article XX(g) is *not* limited to the conservation of "mineral" or "non-living" natural resources';[20] the Appellate Body also stated that the drafting history did *not* support the complainant's restrictive reading of these terms.[21] The Appellate Body further noted that two adopted GATT 1947 panel reports had already confirmed that fish were 'natural resources'.[22]

Furthermore, the Appellate Body invoked the notion of an 'evolutionary' interpretation merely as a legal hook for justifying its consideration of non-WTO conventions and instruments post-dating the conclusion of the GATT 1947, not as an argument for finding that the meaning of the terms of Article XX(g) had changed since that time. After stating that the generic term 'natural resources' in Article XX(g) is not 'static' in its content or reference but is rather 'by definition,

[15] WTO Appellate Body Report, *United States – Import Prohibition of Certain Shrimp and Shrimp Products (US – Shrimp)* adopted 6 November 1998, WT/DS58/AB/R, para 130.

[16] ibid, paras 130–31.

[17] ibid, para 130.

[18] Sullivan and Driedger, above n 10, 110.

[19] The Appellate Body was interpreting Art XX(g) of the GATT 1994, which comprises part of the Uruguay Round Agreements that entered into force on 1 January 1995. Thus, the 'original meaning' of the terms would have been the meaning they carried in 1995, not the meaning they carried in 1947. For a similar view, see D McRae, 'Evolutionary Interpretation: The Relevance of Context', ch 7; and I Van Damme, 'Understanding the Choice for Evolutionary Interpretation', ch 16 in this book.

[20] WTO Appellate Body Report, *US – Shrimp*, above n 15, para 128.

[21] ibid, fn 114.

[22] ibid, para 128.

evolutionary', the Appellate Body continued by stating that '*[i]t is, therefore, pertinent to note that* modern international conventions and declarations make frequent references to natural resources as embracing both living and non-living resources' (emphasis added).[23]

It is interesting that the Appellate Body never directly discussed the meaning of the word 'resources', and whether the particular living creatures at issue (sea turtles) are actually 'resources'. The ordinary meaning of the word 'resource' denotes something that we *use*, and a relevant dictionary definition is 'a stock or reserve which can be drawn on when necessary'.[24] The second prong of Article XX(g) presupposes that there is 'consumption' and 'production' of the exhaustible natural resources that it covers; likewise, the preamble to the WTO Agreement refers to the 'use' of the world's resources. In the 1994 GATT panel proceeding on *US – Tuna (EEC)*, the EEC had argued that since the Convention on International Trade in Endangered Species ensured that there was no trade in dolphin species, 'one could question whether dolphins were *resources* in any economic sense of the term' (emphasis added).[25]

However, sea turtles arguably qualify as 'resources' even under the narrowest possible economic definition of what constitutes a 'resource'. A variety of products made from sea turtles were bought and sold on the open market going back centuries (the reader who wishes to know more can Google 'turtle soup'). Even today, as endangered species that cannot be bought and sold on the open market, sea turtles are still bought and sold – most notably, to aquariums, zoos and other conservation habitats. In any event, the ordinary meaning of the term is wider, and embraces things that we *use*, in the sense of being 'a stock or reserve which can be drawn on when necessary';[26] it is not confined to stocks or reserves that

[23] ibid, para 130.

[24] *Shorter Oxford English Dictionary*, 5th edn, Vol II, 2550.

[25] GATT Panel Report, *United States – Restrictions on Imports of Tuna* (*US – Tuna (EEC)*) 16 June 1994, unadopted, DS29/R, para 3.52. The Panel found that dolphin are 'exhaustible natural resources', but did not expressly address the EEC argument, ibid, para 5.13.

[26] This is from the 2002 edition of the *Shorter Oxford English Dictionary*. See also the 1947 dictionary definitions of 'resource' which are quoted in ST Helmersen, 'The Evolutionary Treaty Interpretation by the WTO Appellate Body', ch 19 in this book, and which are either identical or to the same effect. In 'Prospective Linguistics and Trade: The Art of the Deal', ch 18 in this book, Marquet argues that the choice to use a current dictionary when interpreting a treaty provision reflects a choice towards evolutionary interpretation, because a current dictionary 'already reflects an evolution of language, and departs from the meaning of words at the time of the conclusion of the treaty'. This seems to assume that it is common for the abstract, semantic meaning of words changes across successive editions of the same dictionary. However, if that was so, one would expect that, in many dispute settlement proceeding where the meaning of a treaty provision was contested, one party would rely on definitions from older dictionary editions that supported its interpretation, while the other would rely on definitions from more recent editions that supported its opposing interpretation. But one is hard pressed to think of a single WTO case in which a panel or the Appellate Body was confronted with a problem of recourse to old versus new dictionary definitions, or any pronouncement at all on this issue. This is the jurisprudential equivalent of the dog that didn't bark, and a very strong indication that the abstract, semantic meaning of words does not change in the way that is contemplated by the doctrine of evolutionary interpretation.

are *bought and sold*. In this vein, the panel in *US – Gasoline* accepted that clean air (which is used, but not something capable of being bought or sold) is a 'resource' because it has 'value'.[27] In sum, rather than constituting a stealthy evolutionary reinterpretation of what constitutes a 'resource', the Appellate Body's interpretation in *US – Shrimp* rightly takes for granted that sea turtles were and are 'resources'.

It is difficult to find any angle from which the Appellate Body's reasoning or conclusion in *US – Shrimp* can be viewed as an example of the WTO Appellate Body rejecting the 'original meaning' of treaty terms, in favour of their 'contemporary' or 'present-day' meaning. Approached from the prism of the interpretation/application distinction, it falls squarely on the side of evolutionary application (as opposed to any change in meaning of the terms). The term 'natural resources' has always included both living and non-living resources, and endangered species like sea turtles have always been 'exhaustible natural resources' within the meaning of Article XX(g) of the GATT. The fact that people in 1947 might not have known that this was (or would in the future be) the case does not establish a change in the meaning of the term 'natural resources'.

B. Other WTO Panel and Appellate Body Reports

Moving beyond *US – Shrimp*, the distinction between 'meaning' and 'application' is evident in other pronouncements and practice of WTO adjudicators, including in relation to two recurring issues: (1) other cases examining the extent to which old exceptions in the GATT and the GATS may apply to contemporary concerns, knowledge, and needs; and (2) the extent to which old treaty terms cover new products, services and forms of intellectual property exploitation.

i. The Extent to Which Exceptions May Apply to Contemporary Concerns, Knowledge and Needs

In *India – Solar Cells*, the panel interpreted the scope of 'products in general or local short supply' in the general exception in Article XX(j) of the GATT. It offered the following textbook illustration of the distinction between evolutionary interpretation and application:

> [I]t follows from the absence of any textual limitation or qualification that it would cover shortages arising from these or any other causes, insofar as it is a shortage of the kind covered by Article XX(j) … [W]e agree with India insofar as it suggests that the types of measures that are 'essential' to address situations of general or local short supply may need to be seen in the context of contemporary concerns of a country and the international community. For example, we consider that the types of measures

[27] WTO Panel Report, *United States – Standards for Reformulated and Conventional Gasoline (US – Gasoline)* adopted 20 May 1996, WT/DS2/AB/R, para 6.37.

> that may have existed in 1947 for acquiring or distributing products in short supply may not be the same as the types of measures that exist today for achieving the same purpose …
>
> However, *we do not consider that the applicable legal standard for what it means to be a 'product in general or local short supply' has changed over time.* We consider that, even if a consequence of globalization and trade liberalization were the elimination of all product shortages in the world, such that the factual circumstance for invoking Article XX(j) would no longer exist and the provision would no longer have any sphere of operation, it would *not be open to a treaty interpreter to change the applicable legal standard* for what it means to be a 'product in general or local short supply' in the name of 'evolutionary interpretation' or ensuring that there would continue to be factual circumstances triggering the application of this provision (emphasis added).[28]

In several other cases involving general exceptions or carve-outs, panels have characterised what they were doing in terms that might seem similar to 'evolutionary interpretation', but upon closer inspection these too were cases of evolutionary application.

For instance, Article XX(a) establishes a general exception for measures necessary for the protection of 'public morals'. The panel in *US – Gambling* considered that the 'content of' the concept of 'public morals' can 'vary in time and space, depending upon a range of factors, including prevailing social, cultural, ethical and religious values'.[29] However, the notion that the 'content' of these concepts can 'vary in time', and the likelihood that certain issues found to concern 'public morals' might not have been characterised as such by the drafters of the GATT in 1947,[30] does not imply that the meaning of the words 'public morals' has changed over time. Just as the forms of the conduct that may offend 'public morals' will change over time, it is equally true that they vary 'in space'. That is to say, at any one point in time, different countries and communities across the world may hold different and sometimes diametrically opposed views on whether certain types of conduct (eg, criticising the government, promoting acceptance of same sex-partnerships) do or do not offend 'public morals'. This does not mean that, at this point in time, there is a multitude of different interpretations, or different meanings, of 'public morals'.

By way of analogy, consider the prevailing interpretation of the term 'like products' which calls for a conclusion based on an examination of the degree of competition between two products in a given market. Under that legal standard,

[28] WTO Panel Report, *India – Certain Measures Relating to Solar Cells and Solar Modules (India – Solar Cells)* adopted 14 October 2016, WT/DS456/R, paras 7.232–7.233.

[29] WTO Panel Report, *United States – Measures Affecting the Cross-Border Supply of Gambling and Betting Services (US – Gambling)* adopted 20 April 2005, WT/DS285/R, para 6.461.

[30] Policies covered under the public morals exception in past WTO cases have addressed a grab-bag of issues such as money laundering, organised crime, fraud, underage gambling and pathological gambling; content review to prevent the dissemination of cultural goods with a content that has a negative impact on a Member's public morals; public concerns related to seal welfare; and even bridging the digital divide to promote social inclusion.

it is foreseeable that the same two products compete in one country, but not in another with different consumer preferences. That could lead to the conclusion that, under the prevailing meaning of 'like products', the same products may be characterised as 'like products' in eg the United States but not Japan – not to the conclusion that the term 'like products' carries a different meaning in the United States and Japan, amounting to proof of some fallacious, alien interpretative principle of 'inter-spatial' or 'inter-geographical' treaty interpretation.[31]

As another example, Paragraph 2(a) of the Annex on Financial Services provides that no WTO Member is prevented from taking measures for 'prudential reasons, including for the protection of investors, depositors, policy holders or persons to whom a fiduciary duty is owed by a financial service supplier, or to ensure the integrity and stability of the financial system'. In interpreting the prudential measures carve-out, the panel in *Argentina – Financial Services* considered that '[t]he nature and scope of financial regulation at different times reflect the knowledge, experience and scales of values of governments at the moment in question'.[32] In that sense, the panel indicated that the concept of 'prudential reasons' has an 'evolutionary nature'.[33] The panel was clearly not saying that the meaning or definition of 'prudential reasons' has changed over time.

ii. The Extent to Which Treaty Terms Cover New Products, Services and Forms of Intellectual Property Exploitation

a. New Products

In the 1950s, Greece imposed an import duty of 70 per cent on so-called 'long-playing gramophone records', much higher than the specific bound duty for 'gramophone records, etc' in its schedule (which formed an integral part of the GATT). When challenged by Germany in the GATT, Greece justified its decision on the basis that such records had not existed at the time when the concession in its schedule was made. For Greece, it followed that the scope of the concession did not cover those new products. The Group of Experts established by the GATT concluded otherwise, given that 'when this item was negotiated the parties concerned did not place any qualification upon the words "gramophone record"'.[34] There was no recourse to any legal construct of 'evolutionary interpretation' to justify this straightforward conclusion.

[31] Those who are committed to the prevailing notion of evolutionary interpretation might not agree that this would be fallacious. Indeed, if one adheres to the concept of evolutionary interpretation, then exactly how does one avoid doubling down and buying into the intellectual construct of 'inter-spatial' or 'inter-geographical' treaty interpretation?

[32] WTO Panel Report, *Argentina – Measures Relating to Trade in Goods and Services (Argentina – Financial Services)* adopted 9 May 2016, WT/DS453/R, para 7.871.

[33] ibid, para 7.873.

[34] GATT Group of Experts Report, *Greek Increase in Bound Duty*, 9 November 1956, unadopted, L/580.

Fast forward 50 years to the WTO *EC – IT Products* case. That dispute concerned the tariff treatment of flat-panel display devices (FPDs) capable of receiving and reproducing video signals both from automatic data-processing machines (eg, computers) and other sources (eg, DVD players). The panel noted that 'generic terms were used to cover a wide range of products and technologies', and that certain related technologies existed, and were known to negotiators, at the time of the relevant negotiations.[35] However, the panel added that:

> [T]here is no need to consider further the particular status of technology at the time of negotiating the concession in assessing the scope of the concession before us … [T]he Panel does not consider the fact that DVI [Digital Visual Interface] was developed after the conclusion of the ITA [Information Technology Agreement] operates to exclude FPDs with DVIs from the scope of the concession. As explained, we have established on the terms of the concession that 'flat panel display devices' incorporating a wide range of characteristics and technologies are covered.[36]

In the accompanying footnote, the panel clarified that '[w]e also do not consider it necessary to resort to *any form of evolutionary interpretation* of the terms, in light of our conclusion on the ordinary meaning of the terms' (emphasis added).[37] This is significant and revealing, because the panel was clarifying that it did not need to invoke any concept of 'evolutionary interpretation' to reach the conclusion that the (unchanged) meaning of 'flat-panel display devices' extended to FPD devices using DVI technology developed only after the negotiations.

b. New Services and Forms of Service Supply

Other technology-related issues have also arisen in WTO dispute settlement relating to digital methods of transmission or delivery in trade in services.[38] For instance, in *China – Publications and Audiovisual Services*, the question in dispute was whether a GATS commitment in China's services schedule concerning 'sound recording distribution services' covered network music services provided in *intangible* (ie, digital) form over the internet or mobile networks (eg, Apple iTunes), or only the distribution of sound recordings in *physical* form (eg, tapes, compact discs, DVDs). The Appellate Body concluded, following a detailed textual analysis, that the term 'sound recording distribution services' extends to the distribution of non-physical products. Ultimately, the Appellate Body stated that the terms used in China's GATS Schedule 'are sufficiently generic that

[35] WTO Panel Reports, *European Communities and its member States – Tariff Treatment of Certain Information Technology Products (EC – IT Products)* adopted 21 September 2010, WT/DS375/R / WT/DS376/R / WT/DS377/R, para 7.599.

[36] ibid, para 7.600.

[37] ibid, fn 807.

[38] See World Trade Organization, *World Trade Report 2018: The future of world trade: How digital technologies are transforming global commerce*, Section D, paras 168–70.

what they apply to may change over time' (emphasis added).[39] By its terms, this formulation concerns the evolutionary *application* of the terms. To speak of this case as one involving the 'evolutionary interpretation' of the *meaning* of the relevant terms wrongly implies that the Appellate Body accepted China's argument that 'sound recording distribution services' *originally* meant only the distribution of sound recordings embodied in tangible, *physical* products (a proposition that virtually the entirety of the Appellate Body's textual analysis is dedicated to refuting), and that the meaning subsequently changed at some point.[40]

c. New Forms of Intellectual Property Exploitation

In the context of intellectual property rights and dispute settlement under the Trade-Related Aspects of Intellectual Property Rights (TRIPS) Agreement, several panels have highlighted how legal rights and obligations are applied to changing circumstances and practice.

The panel in *Canada – Pharmaceutical Patents* considered the term 'normal exploitation' in the context of Article 30 of the TRIPS Agreement. After articulating a general principle, the panel discussed how specific *forms* of exploitation 'are not static':

> The normal practice of exploitation by patent owners, as with owners of any other intellectual property right, is to exclude all forms of competition that could detract significantly from the economic returns anticipated from a patent's grant of market exclusivity. The specific forms of patent exploitation are not static, of course, for to be effective exploitation must adapt to changing forms of competition due to technological development and the evolution of marketing practices.[41]

In *China – Intellectual Property Rights*, the panel took a very similar approach when considering the term 'commercial scale' in Article 61 of the TRIPS Agreement. However, this panel was even more explicit in trying to separate 'considerations relevant to the interpretation of the terms used' from their 'application' in 'different situations'. The panel stated:

> [T]he terms used in the first sentence of Article 61, in particular 'commercial', are technology-neutral. A 'commercial scale' can apply to various forms of commerce

[39] WTO Appellate Body Report, *China – Measures Affecting Trading Rights and Distribution Services for Certain Publications and Audiovisual Entertainment Products (China – Publications and Audiovisual Services)* adopted 19 January 2010, WT/DS363/AB/R, para 396.

[40] Helmersen also makes the point that it would have involved a degree of circular reasoning for the Appellate Body to ground its interpretation on the basis of an 'evolutionary interpretation'. See ST Helmersen, 'The Evolutionary Treaty Interpretation by the WTO Appellate Body', ch 19 in this book.

[41] WTO Panel Report, *Canada – Patent Protection of Pharmaceutical Products* (*Canada – Pharmaceutical Patents*) adopted 7 April 2000, WT/DS114/R, para 7.55. To the same effect, and in similar terms, see WTO Panel Report, *United States – Section 110(5) of the US Copyright Act* (*US – Section 110(5) Copyright Act*) adopted 27 July 2000, WT/DS160/R, para 6.187 (examining the phrase 'normal exploitation' in the context of Art 17).

> and, hence, various means of infringement. The specific *forms* of commerce are not static but *adapt* to changing forms of competition due to technological development and the evolution of marketing practices. The Panel sees no reason why those *forms* of commerce should be limited to the forms of commerce that existed at the time of negotiation of the TRIPS Agreement. Accordingly, the *application* of the term 'commercial scale' can *adjust to different situations*, and refer to a different relative magnitude or extent, degree or proportion, depending on the facts. *However*, subsequent technological developments *do not alter the considerations relevant to the interpretation of the terms* used in Article 61 (emphasis added).[42]

IV. Conclusion

The illusion of evolutionary interpretation is created by conflating the notions of legal interpretation and factual application under the rubric of 'meaning'.[43] Once the distinction between these notions is collapsed, it may appear that applying an old legal standard to new factual circumstances constitutes some kind of change in the meaning of the legal standard itself – or, conversely, it may appear that adhering to the original meaning of a legal standard requires an interpreter to undermine the effectiveness of a treaty provision by confining the scope of its application to the factual circumstances as they existed at the time of the treaty's conclusion.

There is a better way to think about and describe the adaptation of written legal instruments to evolving values, technologies and legal developments. As the UK House of Lords stated in a judgment concerning the UN Convention on Refugees, it is 'plain that the Convention must be seen as a living instrument in the sense that while its *meaning* does not change over time its *application* will'.[44] There is probably no substantive difference between the approach taken by WTO adjudicators as compared with the approach followed by the ICJ,[45] but there is an appreciable difference in the way they describe what they are doing. WTO adjudicators have maintained a much clearer distinction and separation between 'evolutionary interpretation' and 'evolutionary application', which yields greater analytical clarity, and also greater coherence among various principles of interpretation and adjudication. It also creates less exposure to the charge of judicial

[42] WTO Panel Report, *China – Measures Affecting the Protection and Enforcement of Intellectual Property Rights (China – Intellectual Property Rights)* adopted 20 March 2009, WT/DS362/R, para 7.657.

[43] As discussed in the introduction to this chapter, the illusion is further reinforced by using the terminology of 'evolutionary interpretation' to describe changes in case law relating to the meaning of a term, notwithstanding that such changes do not reflect or constitute any change in the objective meaning of the treaty term, let alone the substitution of a 'present' meaning for an 'original' meaning.

[44] *Sepet v Secretary of State for the Home Department* [2003] UKHL 15, para 6.

[45] See P Van den Bossche, 'Is there Evolution in the Evolutionary Interpretation of WTO Law?', ch 20 in this book.

activism by adjudicators[46] – or, conversely, to the charge that international treaties necessarily become outdated or obsolete as the world changes and new circumstances emerge.

There is to date no example of the Appellate Body or any WTO panel adopting an 'evolutionary interpretation', in the sense of rejecting the 'original meaning' of a treaty term in favour of its 'contemporary meaning'. However, as set forth above there are many examples of WTO panels and the Appellate Body accepting the evolutionary application of provisions to adapt to changing factual circumstances. It may be that WTO adjudicators are not very adventurous, and highly reluctant to veer away from the vocabulary and conceptual framework for treaty interpretation expressly codified in Articles 31 and 32 of the Vienna Convention (which do not refer to 'evolutionary interpretation'). Whatever the reason, this body of WTO panel and Appellate Body jurisprudence constitutes a useful contribution to public international law, and to the progressive clarification of the legal concept of 'evolutionary interpretation'.

[46] As some contributions in this book have observed, the notion of evolutionary interpretation operates at a rhetorical level, in a way that risks fostering negative perceptions of judicial activism. See, eg, MC de Andrade, 'Evolutionary Interpretation and the Appellate Body's Existential Crisis', ch 21 in this book.

18

Prospective Linguistics and Trade: The Art of the Deal

CLÉMENT MARQUET

I. Introduction

Claiming that international trade is currently facing troubled times would be a euphemism. Be it through the turmoil caused by Brexit, the multiple deadlocks at the WTO or the looming trade wars, only one thing seems certain: uncertainty. In this context, trade agreements seem to be the way forward towards normalising trade relations. The equilibrium might very well change from the one that prevailed in the past decades, but ultimately, new trade deals ought to be concluded to increase predictability in international trade.

Previous chapters have argued that evolutionary interpretation is, to a variable extent, used to interpret trade deals, in particular the World Trade Organization (WTO) agreements. For this chapter, we suggest applying this understanding to future trade relations, with an exercise edging towards legal science fiction. In other words, we will assess whether and how evolutionary interpretation could be used – or abused – in trade negotiations. Can governments exploit the notion to gain an edge further down the road in a treaty's life? How legitimate would it be? These questions will lead us to question the very notion of evolutionary interpretation.

In an attempt at an answer, we will first turn to the way 'ordinary meaning' is usually established in the interpretation process. One peculiar point will be underlined regarding the use of current dictionaries. We will then turn to how governments could use this to their advantage, through not so fictitious science. Finally, we will discuss the impact of these considerations on the very notion of evolutionary interpretation.

A preliminary point needs to be made here, regarding the meaning of 'evolutionary interpretation' discussed in this text. While aware of the different meanings attributed to the notion, as evidenced by the chapters of this book, we will focus on a very specific part of it: the society-driven evolution of language. This type of change can have a significant impact on the interpretative process, in particular in the context of trade law.

II. The 'Ordinary Meaning' in the Interpretative Process

The first element warranting a closer look in this analysis is the use of 'textual interpretation', as it is one of the ways to assess the ordinary meaning.[1] This requires looking into a long-standing debate regarding interpretation in international law: the determination of its true objective. Should the ultimate purpose of interpretation be the assessment of the subjective intention of the parties, or should it rather be an analysis of that intention as embodied by the objective text of a treaty? Such is the debate that animates the tenants of subjectivism and objectivism in interpretation.[2]

At the risk of reinventing the wheel, we will argue in the same direction as Eirik Bjorge did earlier in the book.[3] In our view, two elements speak against the subjectivist approach. The first touches upon the ontological possibility of a 'common intention of the parties'. By definition, an intention can only be common where two or more parties would be in complete agreement not only on the formal negotiated result – the text of the treaty – but also on the underlying reasoning, the *ratio legis*. We argue that such a common intention cannot exist. Because every country is in a different situation, politically and economically, there will necessarily exist some differences in the objectives they are pursuing through a trade agreement.

Additionally, the true extent of the parties' intention poses a question of evidence. States might not wish to disclose all their negotiating objectives. They may believe parts of their policy might be easier to reach if hidden rather than disclosed to the other party.[4] In this situation, relying on the preparatory work to a treaty would not amount to recourse to the subjective intention of the parties, as the two could be distinct notions. For these reasons, trying to assess a subjective common intention of the parties would not only be misguided, but simply illusory.

[1] On the notion, see A Bianchi, 'Textual Interpretation and (International) Law Reading: The Myth of (in) Determinacy and the Genealogy of Meaning' in PHF Bekker, R Dolzer and M Waibel (eds), *Making Transnational Law Work in the Global Economy: Essays in Honour of Detlev Vagts* (Cambridge, Cambridge University Press, 1996).

[2] E Menezes de Carvalho, *Semiotics of International Law: Trade and Translation* (Dordrecht, Springer, 2011) 150–52. See also D McRae, 'Evolutionary Interpretation: The Relevance of Context' (ch 7); E Bjorge, 'Time Present and Time Past: The Intention of the Parties and the Evolutionary Interpretation of Treaties' (ch 5); C Djeffal, 'An Interpreter's Guide to Static and Evolutive Interpretations: Solving Intertemporal Problems According to the VCLT' (ch 4); K Magraw, 'Role of State Party Pleadings in the Evolutionary Interpretation of International Investment Agreements' (ch 24); and S Garibian, 'By Men, not Gods: The (Hidden) Evolutionary Interpretation of International Criminal Law in Light of Extrinsic Sources' (ch 15) in this book, all discussing the question of objectivity versus subjectivity in interpretation.

[3] Bjorge, 'Time Present and Time Past', above n 2.

[4] Even though this might not be the ideal negotiating tactic, R Fischer B Patton and W Ury, *Getting to Yes: Negotiating Agreement Without Giving In*, 2nd edn (New York, Penguin Books, 1991) 40–43.

Following this reasoning, the only option left is the objectivist one, whereby an interpreter would consider the text as the embodiment of the parties' intention. In other words, while intention remains the core of the reasoning, it is accessed through a proxy: the actual vocabulary used. This approach is at the core of the WTO Appellate Body's interpretative methodology.[5] However, this reliance on the text does not solve the issue of interpretation. To the contrary, it gives birth to a further problem: the assessment of the 'objective' meaning of a word – if such a thing even exists.

In this regard, the Appellate Body relies heavily on a tool extrinsic to the field of law: a dictionary. It could be argued that this is the best way to remove oneself from the debate on evolutionary interpretation. Indeed, what more objective and timeless source of meaning for a word than a language dictionary? However, this approach already entails a choice, a preference for current meaning. Indeed, if evolutionary interpretation is to be opposed to the doctrine of intertemporal law,[6] what justifies using a modern-day dictionary rather than one reflecting language at the time of the conclusion of the treaty? The former already reflects an evolution of language, and departs from the meaning of words at the time of the conclusion of the treaty. Using a current dictionary is already a choice towards evolutionary interpretation.

Various examples of this problem can be invoked. Let us assume a seventeenth-century trade treaty grants market access in the field of 'broadcasting services'. A modern-day dictionary reading would most likely lead to market access for radio and television services, for it is how the term is currently used.[7] However, this would disregard the fact that at the time of conclusion of the treaty, the proper meaning of the word was limited to sowing seeds around.[8] Similarly, a few centuries ago, 'meat' referred to any sort of food, while the current sense is limited to the edible flesh of an animal.[9] These examples go to show that what might be seen as an obvious, 'objective' meaning is sometimes far from what had been envisioned by the treaty's drafters. Even though dictionary use can be limited to a status of starting point,[10] subtle changes in meaning could go undetected. In turn, adjudicating bodies relying on such tools would make the new meaning of a word prevail.

[5] D Pavot, 'The Use of Dictionary by the WTO Appellate Body: Beyond the Search of Ordinary Meaning' (2013) 4 *Journal of International Dispute Settlement* 29.

[6] The doctrine of intertemporal law suggests that interpretation should take place according to the understanding of a term or phrase prevailing at the time of conclusion of the treaty. Its most prominent expression can be found in the *Island of Palmas* case, *Island of Palmas (Netherlands v USA)* (1928) 2 *Reports of International Arbitral Awards* 829, 845.

[7] *Shorter Oxford English Dictionary on Historical Principles*, 6th edn, vol 1 (Oxford, Oxford University Press, 2007) 295.

[8] ibid.

[9] The former use is now considered 'archaic', *Shorter Oxford English Dictionary on Historical Principles*, above n 7, 1736–37.

[10] WTO Appellate Body Report, *United States – Measures Affecting the Cross-Border Supply of Gambling and Betting Services (US – Gambling)* adopted 20 April 2005, WT/DS285/AB/R, para 164.

Interestingly, this reliance on modern-day dictionaries is not solely the Appellate Body's prerogative. Even though it remains the herald of this process,[11] other courts and tribunals have adopted a similar approach. While their reliance on dictionaries in assessing meaning is less heavy, all adjudicating bodies nevertheless turn to current ones rather than explore past semantics.[12] This approach seems somewhat undisputed in jurisdictional practice.

III. The Use of Evolutionary Interpretation When Negotiating a Trade Deal

The observation above leads to a logical question: is it possible to take advantage of this mechanism? Can States abuse the tendency of courts and tribunals to rely on recent dictionary meaning? While the question could be asked in the context of any treaty negotiation, trade agreements stand apart due to their objectives. Where a human rights treaty could well entail acrimonious negotiations, trade deals are the ones where governments try to outmanoeuvre their counterparts. Corollary to the notion of *traité-contrat*,[13] trade agreements reflect the desire of each party to get the better deal and most positive outcome for its own economy. As Malgosia Fitzmaurice puts it, '[n]ormative … treaties are considered to further community interests', while '[c]ontractual … treaties, on the other hand, are seen to further the individual interests of the participating States'.[14] While the relevance of this Manichean view of treaties has been doubted,[15] it is nevertheless a useful tool here. Trade agreements are probably the closest to *traités-contrats*. Hence, the unilateral benefit sought through them justifies a closer look at evolutionary interpretation as a tool to gain an edge in negotiations.

Examining the use of evolutionary interpretation in negotiations requires stepping out of legal considerations to turn to the realm of linguistics. There, some questions asked as if novel in the legal field are long-standing ones with a plethora of existing literature in linguistics.[16] A simple example is the distinction between

[11] G Abi-Saab, 'The Appellate Body and Treaty Interpretation' in O Elias, M Fitzmaurice and P Merkouris (eds), *Treaty Interpretation and the Vienna Convention on the Law of Treaties: 30 Years On* (Leiden, Martinus Nijhoff, 2010) 106.

[12] See for instance *Oil Platforms (Islamic Republic of Iran v United States of America)* (Preliminary Objections) [1996] ICJ Rep 803, para 45; *Tulip Real Estate and Development Netherlands BV v Republic of Turkey*, ICSID Case No ARB/11/28, Decision on Annulment, 30 December 2015, para 192, fn 168; *Luedicke, Belkacem and Koç v Germany* Series A no 29 (1980) 2 EHRR 149, para 40.

[13] On the difference between *traité-loi* and *traité-contrat*, see also G Gaggioli, 'The Strength of Evolutionary Interpretation in International Human Rights Law', ch 13 in this book.

[14] M Fitzmaurice, 'Treaties' in *Max Planck Encyclopedia of Public International Law* (February 2010) para 8, available at: www.opil.ouplaw.com/view/10.1093/law:epil/9780199231690/law-9780199231690-e1481 (accessed 14 December 2018).

[15] G Abi-Saab, 'Cours général de droit international public' (1987) 207 *Collected Courses of The Hague Academy of International Law* 9, 428.

[16] As already discussed in J Wyatt, 'Using Intertemporal Linguistics to Resolve the Problem at the Origin and Core of the Evolutionary Interpretation Debate', ch 6 in this book.

signe and *signifié* identified by Ferdinand de Saussure, which can serve as a canvas for the whole discussion on 'ordinary meaning'. This theory, dating back to the early twentieth century, splits words into two elements: their specific combination of characters and the meaning they carry.[17] This distinction can act as a background to the issue identified above, whereby a word physically remains the same, while its meaning evolves. Its *signe* remains, while the *signifié* changes.[18]

Much more recently, however, a new type of linguistic research emerged, with predictive implications. A first category of research laid out the groundwork by focusing on modelling the evolution of word meaning. This evolution is mapped on an individual word basis at first, before more recent attempts at defining broader rules. This allows the creation of retrospective patterns of changes to the semantics of a word. It is, therefore, possible to obtain a sort of time line of meanings. Katrin Erk's work shines in this regard, as it tackles the important task of creating 'gold data', or data that allows a clear analysis.[19] This remains an important hurdle in research, as material is not readily available, and reaching statistically significant results requires substantial computing power. Researchers need access to large databases in which a given term is repeatedly used through time, in order to process it electronically and obtain a relevant output. While this remains a challenge, progress in data-processing technology has allowed tremendous advances between 2011 and now.[20] For instance, a recent research by Katrin Erk and Alex Rosenfeld proposes a precise mapping of the evolution of the term 'gay', which used to mean 'lively' and now is mainly used to mean a 'homosexual'.[21]

These considerations could seem to take us far from the topic at hand. However, this is where the second leg of linguistic research comes into play. Once a proper mapping of language evolution over a statistically significant number of words is reached, a new inductive phase of research begins. From this data, theories of the evolution of language have recently started to emerge.[22] While none of them seems to lead the race at the moment, interesting approaches have been suggested. For instance, some have argued that semantic change through time could depend on

[17] A third element exists, the *signifiant*, but it is not relevant for this argument, F de Saussure, *Cours de linguistique générale* (Genève, Payot, 1995) 97–100.

[18] A similar approach, although on a different level of interpretation, is discussed in G Cook, 'The Illusion of "Evolutionary Interpretation" in WTO Dispute Settlement', ch 17 in this book.

[19] K Erk and A Rosenfeld, 'Deep Neural Models of Semantic Shift' (2018) *Proceedings of North American Chapter of the Association for Computational Linguistics: Human Language Technologies* 474, 475.

[20] One could compare the progress between the clearing in M Baroni and K Gulordava, 'A Distributional Similarity Approach to the Detection of Semantic Change in the Google Books Ngram Corpus' (2011) *Proceedings of the GEMS 2011 Workshop on Geometrical Models of Natural Language Semantics* 67 and the meta analysis offered in Erk and Rosenfeld, above n 19.

[21] Erk and Rosenfeld, above n 19.

[22] H Dubossarsky, E Grossman and D Weinshall, 'Outta Control: Laws of Semantic Change and Inherent Biases in Word Representation Models' (2017) *Proceedings of the 2017 Conference on Empirical Methods in Natural Language Process* 1147, 1147.

the degree to which a given word reflects the broader lexical field in which it fits ('theory of prototypicality').[23] The closer to the centre of a semantic field, the less likely it is a given word would evolve.[24] Other patterns have been identified. For instance, the 'law of conformity' posits that frequent use of a word is inversely correlated with its semantic change,[25] and the 'law of innovation' suggests that polysemous words tend to change meaning faster than others.[26] The purpose of this chapter is not to list all the possibilities, but these suggested theories illustrate some possibilities for modelling semantic evolution. As debated as they are,[27] they are the first bricks of a larger building that is starting to take shape, and will allow for prediction of future changes in word meaning.

It remains to be seen whether and how these theories are relevant in trade negotiations. Given the recourse to dictionary meaning underlined above, predictive linguistics could become a useful tool. Indeed, once reliable rules have been identified: it is only a matter of time before some elements of the evolution of language can be anticipated. We will not go as far as to suggest that the precise meaning of a word at a given time in the future could be foreseen. That type of research is probably not realistic in the near future, if it even is possible at any point. However, the sheer ability to predict that a word's meaning could change is already an incredible edge in negotiations. For instance, the choice of a specific word in the drafting process could seem innocuous to one party, while the other had specifically chosen it for its potential to change meaning and expand the other party's commitments in the future.

While we have discussed above the question of current use of dictionaries by adjudicating bodies, an open question remains as to the legitimacy of the use of such predictive linguistics. More specifically, the problem does not so much revolve around the use of this tool in negotiations, but rather the adoption of the desired new meaning by a court or a tribunal. Is it proper for judges to fulfil the wishes of the government anticipating a semantic change? In our view, various arguments lead to an affirmative answer.

The first one mimics the issue of subjective interpretation underlined above. Should a government obfuscate its use of predictive linguistics, the judges would have no means to position themselves in relation to it. In other words, they would adopt the desired new meaning through a normal interpretative process, ignorant of the underlying reasoning of one of the parties. Because the judge has no way of

[23] ibid, 1152–53.

[24] The authors offer the example of the word *robin*, which is considered more representative of *bird* than the word *parrot*. Therefore, the word *robin* is less likely to evolve through time, ibid.

[25] WL Hamilton, J Leskovec and D Jurafsky, 'Diachronic Word Embeddings Reveal Statistical Laws of Semantic Change' (2018) para 4.3, available at: www.arxiv.org/abs/1605.09096.

[26] ibid, para 4.4.

[27] A Kutuzov et al, 'Diachronic Word Embeddings and Semantic Shifts: A Survey' (2018) *Proceedings of the 27th International Conference on Computational Linguistics* 1384, 1390–91.

knowing that predictive linguistics have been used, there is no reason to question the legitimacy of the interpretation.

Another argument goes back to the idea of *traité-contrat* invoked earlier. As mentioned, an international trade agreement is a way for each party to attempt to maximise its gains. Consequently, information asymmetry should come as no surprise to an observer. Nothing in international law requires both parties to a negotiation to disclose every bit of information they have. Rather, information asymmetry is a frequent element in any negotiation of this type.[28] Pushing the analogy with contracts further, this is also a standard situation in commercial negotiations, and unless specific transparency rules exist, nothing compels one party to disclose an informational advantage to the other.[29] Similarly, a hunch that a certain type of good will become highly demanded in the near future is part of the gamble that a party might be taking in its negotiating tactics. Unless rules are created to require that each party discloses everything it knows, good faith in negotiations is the only limiting factor to information asymmetry.[30] In other words, recourse to predictive models of linguistics would only become a tool at the disposal of a government, as much as having well-trained lawyers and negotiators would be. The ultimate goal would simply be to reward better anticipation. Obviously, an argument could be made against the fairness of such negotiations, but it would be a more general one, reflecting the broader issue of asymmetric relations in international politics, be it because of informational, economic or military power.[31]

Realistically, such use of predictive linguistics is probably at the very least a few years away. The process of identifying meta-rules of the evolution of language is still ongoing, and they will be a prerequisite before any robust tool can be built using these rules. However, one should not discard such use as pure fiction. The economic stakes of trade negotiations mean that a small edge in a given domain can be leveraged into large financial gains.[32] It is therefore likely that the evolution of language, as a component of evolutionary interpretation, will be used in a proactive way by governments when negotiating future trade agreements.

[28] D Tussie and M Saguier, 'The Sweep of Asymetric Trade Negotiations: Introduction and Overview' in S Bilal, P De Lombaerde and D Tussie (eds), *Asymmetric Trade Negotiations* (Farnham, Ashgate, 2011) 5.

[29] D Kästle-Lamparter, 'Pre-contractual Information Duties' in N Jansen and R Zimmermann (eds), *Commentaries on European Contract Laws* (Oxford, Oxford University Press, 2018) 386.

[30] R Kolb, *La bonne foi en droit international public* (Geneva, Graduate Institute Publications 2000) 579–81; K Wellens, *Negotiations in the Case Law of the International Court of Justice* (Farnham, Ashgate, 2014) 43.

[31] C Chatterjee, *International Law and Diplomacy* (London, Routledge, 2010) 90–101.

[32] This has happened in the past with high-frequency trading in the world of finance for instance, see FS Lhabitant and GN Gregoriou, 'High-Frequency Trading: Past, Present and Future' in GN Gregoriou (ed), *The Handbook of High Frequency Trading* (London, Academic Press, 2015).

IV. The Subjectivity of Evolutionary Interpretation

All these developments raise, however, a peculiar question regarding the core of the notion of evolutionary interpretation. More specifically, it adds confusion to its exact definition. Two distinct arguments can be made in this regard. The first relates to the conflation of 'evolutionary' with 'progressive'; and the second concerns the point of view adopted when analysing evolutionary interpretation.

Regarding the first element, the developments above underline that future language variations could be predicted. However, evolutionary interpretation is usually approached through its 'progressive' implications.[33] That is to say, the current practice of evolutionary interpretation tends to widen the scope of previous commitments, by including new technological, social or environmental concerns. This was the case for the well-known disputes involving evolutionary interpretation. For instance, *US – Shrimp* led to a seemingly broader definition of 'exhaustible natural resources', through the lens of environmental factors.[34] Similarly, the ICJ's *Namibia* Advisory Opinion reflected new social values, which could be deemed 'progressive' or 'liberal' as they capture the decolonisation process.[35] However, the possible use of evolutionary interpretation highlighted in this chapter is not an approach that tends to a specific 'progressive' goal. Rather, it becomes a tool for governments using it, to become able to shape the evolution to suit their objectives. In other words, they could also use predictive linguistics to prevent evolution, or to shape evolution towards a narrowing of the scope of certain commitments.[36] There is no fateful end towards which this type of evolutionary interpretation would invariably lean.

Examples of this other dynamic already exist. For instance, the US Trade Representative, Robert Lighthizer, has recently argued that the Appellate Body's approach to interpretation departs too much from the text of the WTO agreements.[37] Here, recourse to a predictive model could lead the US into choosing words less likely to evolve over time. Evolutionary interpretation would simply be avoided. Another option could even be to choose terms likely to evolve towards a narrower meaning. This would still be a type of evolution, but not towards a wider coverage of the undertakings. In sum, it is not because vocabulary evolves that its evolution

[33] This point could be debated depending on the field in which the evolution is taking place, see Gaggioli, above n 13.

[34] WTO Appellate Body Report, *United States – Import Prohibition of Certain Shrimp and Shrimp Products (US – Shrimp)* adopted 6 November 1998, WT/DS58/AB/R, paras 130–31.

[35] *Legal Consequences for States of the Continued Presence of South Africa in Namibia (South West Africa) notwithstanding Security Council Resolution 276 (1970)* (Advisory Opinion) [1971] ICJ Rep 16, para 53. The term 'progressive' must be used with caution, as it reflects a subjective system of values.

[36] In this direction, see R Kolb, 'Evolutionary Interpretation in International Law: Some Short and Less than Trail-Blazing Reflections', ch 3 in this book.

[37] Center for Strategic & International Studies, 'US Trade Policy Priorities: Robert Lighthizer, United States Trade Representative' (18 September 2017), available at: www.csis.org/analysis/us-trade-policy-priorities-robert-lighthizer-united-states-trade-representative.

serves any sort of 'progressive' or 'liberal' purpose by default.[38] Society remains largely the creator of meaning and ruler of its evolution. Piggybacking on the latter simply means that any policy choice could be fulfilled by negotiators. Should they desire a narrowing of commitments, it is up to them to guide their drafting in this direction. Conflating 'progress' and 'evolution' would lead to brand this a 'devolutionary interpretation'.

The second element that questions evolutionary interpretation itself revolves around the point of view adopted. We have shown above that future semantic changes could be anticipated. Should it happen, will the variation in meaning still be considered 'evolutionary' interpretation? An example can illustrate the question. One of the central cases when looking at evolutionary interpretation in trade law is *US – Shrimp*. There, what was considered to have evolved was the meaning of 'exhaustible natural resources', to include 'both living and non-living resources'.[39] However, this does not tell the whole story. In particular, a titbit from GATT negotiations is worth mentioning. In 1947, concerned about its sheep exports, Australia wanted to retain the ability to impose export restrictions. In that context, the Belgian representative 'felt that the institution of export prohibitions on marino [sic] sheep … would be permissible … [T]he case could be covered by the provision elsewhere in the Charter permitting the use of restrictions to safeguard *exhaustible natural resources*' (emphasis added).[40] That is to say, at the time some governments already envisioned an interpretation that would be deemed 'evolutionary' half a century later.

Similarly, recourse to prospective linguistics could lead to one side of the negotiations having anticipated a change later enshrined by an adjudicating body, while it would come as a surprise to the other party. Could this still be considered evolutionary interpretation? If, internally, one government had considered from the outset that upon interpretation, an X word would have changed to mean Y, the situation has hardly evolved in its eyes. Here, the classification as 'evolutionary' could seem relevant for the surprised party only. This casts doubts over the possibility to define 'evolutionary interpretation' from an objective point of view.

V. Conclusion

George Orwell thought that '[p]eople can foresee the future only when it coincides with their own wishes'.[41] Through this brief piece, almost touching upon legal

[38] In the same direction, see E Bjorge, *The Evolutionary Interpretation of Treaties* (Oxford, Oxford University Press, 2014) 84.

[39] *US – Shrimp*, above n 34, para 130.

[40] ECOSOC 'Second Session of the Preparatory Committee of the United Nations Conference on Trade and Employment' E/PC/T/A/SR/40(1) (15 August 1947) 1–2.

[41] G Orwell, *The Collected Essays, Journalism, and Letters of George Orwell: As I please, 1943–1945* (New York, Harcourt, Brace & World, 1968) 297.

science fiction, we have made governments' wishes coincide with the future they could be shaping. Any ability to anticipate future events or evolutions will necessarily be accompanied by a desire to shape this very future. It would be illusory to expect that governments would disregard tools that could potentially increase their country's wealth or wellbeing.

Three main conclusions arise from this chapter. The first regards the use of dictionaries by adjudicating bodies. Recourse to modern-day language and meaning already entails an evolutionary choice. It is not a trivial point, and an underlying conception of international law can be discerned through the use of such tools. The second conclusion highlights that this mechanism of interpretation could be used or abused. Over a few short years, research in the field of diachronic linguistics has progressed tremendously, and modelling of language evolution is on an encouraging path. It is therefore realistic to suggest that in the near future, predictive tools will start to emerge. Where power and large amounts of money are at stake, the existence of a possibility to gain an edge creates a vacuum, which will lead to the creation of predictive linguistics services.

However, the opening of these possibilities leads to a third conclusion, in the form of a question. Ultimately, where change can be predicted, is there still room for such a thing as 'evolutionary' interpretation? Or is evolutionary interpretation only in the eye of the beholder?

B. Evolutionary Interpretation in Practice

19

The Evolutionary Treaty Interpretation by the WTO Appellate Body

SONDRE TORP HELMERSEN*

I. Introduction

The World Trade Organization (WTO) Appellate Body has used evolutionary interpretations in two cases: *US – Shrimp* and *China – Publications and Audiovisual Products*.[1] These cases are discussed in section II below. Section III identifies commonalities between them: their adherence to the Vienna Convention on the Law of Treaties (VCLT) rules on interpretation, the absence of any mention of the parties' intention, the evolutionary interpretations being superfluous, and the use of evolutionary interpretations to resolve vagueness rather than ambiguity. Section IV is a conclusion.

There are other Appellate Body reports that could be discussed.[2] In *US – FSC (Article 21.5 – EC)*, the Appellate Body used 'bilateral [and] multilateral tax treaties' and model conventions when interpreting the phrase 'foreign source income'.[3] While many of the instruments that the Appellate Body used were created after the WTO)agreements that the Appellate Body was interpreting, that did not make the Appellate Body's interpretation evolutionary. Similarly, in *EC – Tariff Preferences*, the Appellate Body interpreted the term 'needs' in the Enabling Clause paragraph 3(c), and mentioned 'multilateral instruments adopted by international organizations'.[4] Such multilateral instruments could be more recent than

* I thank Professor Geir Ulfstein for numerous useful comments on the manuscript.

[1] E Bjorge, *The Evolutionary Interpretation of Treaties* (Oxford, Oxford University Press, 2014) 126.

[2] WTO Panel Reports are discussed, eg, by P Van den Bossche, 'Is there Evolution in the Evolutionary Interpretation of WTO Law?', ch 20 in this book.

[3] WTO Appellate Body Report, *United States – Tax Treatment for "Foreign Sales Corporations" – Recourse to Article 21.5 of the DSU by the European Communities (US – FSC (Article 21.5 – EC))* adopted 29 January 2002, WT/DS108/AB/RW, para 141.

[4] WTO Appellate Body Report, *European Communities – Conditions for the Granting of Tariff Preferences to Developing Countries (EC – Tariff Preferences)* adopted 20 April 2004, WT/DS246/AB/R, para 163.

the Enabling Clause, but again, that is not enough to make the interpretation evolutionary, if that is defined as 'an interpretation where a term is given a meaning that changes over time'.[5] In *China – Rare Earths*, the Appellate Body referred to *US – Shrimp*, and noted that that report interpreted '"natural resources" … evolutionary'.[6] However, the Appellate Body did not use an evolutionary interpretation in that report.

The Appellate Body's operation is governed by the Dispute Settlement Understanding (DSU), which is annexed to the Agreement Establishing the World Trade Organization. The DSU Article 3.2 obliges the Appellate Body to apply 'customary rules of interpretation of public international law'. Article 3.2 also states that '[r]ecommendations and rulings of the DSB cannot add to or diminish the rights and obligations provided in the covered agreements'. Article 19.2 contains a similar phrase.

It could be argued that evolutionary interpretations 'add to or diminish the rights and obligations', since an evolutionary interpretation of a provision means that its content (its rights and obligations) will change over time.[7] The Appellate Body did not raise this question in *US – Shrimp* or *China – Publications and Audiovisual Products*. In both cases the Appellate Body merely highlighted an awareness of Article 3.2, and in *US – Shrimp* it even scorned the panel for not having been sufficiently faithful to the 'customary rules of interpretation'.[8]

Generally, most judicial interpretations, not just evolutionary ones, can be said to 'affect' the law in some way.[9] However, merely interpreting the agreements cannot suffice to 'add to or diminish' rights and obligations. Thus, the Appellate Body has stated that it has 'difficulty in envisaging circumstances in which a panel could add to the rights and obligations of a Member of the WTO if its conclusions reflected a correct interpretation and application of provisions of the covered agreements'.[10] This must be the correct conclusion: as long as the Appellate Body's methodology is in line with general rules on interpretation, there is no violation of Article 3.2 of the DSU.[11] Therefore it is significant that the

[5] ST Helmersen, 'Evolutive Treaty Interpretation: Legality, Semantics and Distinctions' (2013) 6 *European Journal of Legal Studies* 127, 128. Similarly, C Djeffal, 'An Interpreter's Guide to Static and Evolutive Interpretations: Solving Intertemporal Problems According to the VCLT', ch 4 in this book.

[6] WTO Appellate Body Reports, *China – Measures Related to the Exportation of Rare Earths, Tungsten and Molybdenum* (*China – Rare Earths*) adopted 29 August 2014, WT/DS431/AB/R / WT/DS432/AB/R / WT/DS433/AB/R, para 5.89.

[7] eg, MC de Andrade, 'Evolutionary Interpretation and the Appellate Body's Existential Crisis', ch 21 in this book.

[8] WTO Appellate Body Report, *United States – Import Prohibition of Certain Shrimp and Shrimp Products (US – Shrimp)* adopted 6 November 1998, WT/DS58/AB/R, para 114.

[9] eg, I Van Damme, *Treaty Interpretation by the WTO Appellate Body* (Oxford, Oxford University Press, 2009) 28.

[10] WTO Appellate Body Report, *Chile – Taxes on Alcoholic Beverages* (*Chile – Alcoholic Beverages*) adopted 12 January 2000, WT/DS87/AB/R; WT/DS110/AB/R, para 79.

[11] eg, R Howse, 'The Most Dangerous Branch? WTO Appellate Body Jurisprudence on the Nature and Limits of the Judicial Power' in T Cottier and PC Mavroidis (eds), *The Role of the Judge in International Trade Regulation: Experience and Lessons for the WTO* (Ann Arbor, MI, University of Michigan Press, 2003) 15.

Appellate Body's evolutionary interpretations follow the rules set out in the VCLT, as explained in section III.A below.

II. The Reports

A. *US – Shrimp*

US – Shrimp concerned a ban on imports of shrimp and shrimp products enacted by the US in 1989.[12] The ban aimed to protect sea turtles, and it excepted imports from nations whose governments had a regulatory programme for enforcing the use of 'turtle excluding devices'. India, Malaysia, Pakistan and Thailand challenged the import ban in the WTO. A panel report, which found that the ban violated Article XI of the General Agreement on Tariffs and Trade (GATT), and could not be justified under Article XX, was appealed to the Appellate Body. The US did not challenge the finding that its ban violated Article XI. The Appellate Body found that the ban was covered by paragraph (g) of Article XX of the GATT, but that the requirements of the Article's chapeau had not been met, and thus that the measure could not be justified.

When considering Article XX, the Appellate Body had to decide whether the protection of sea turtles was covered by any of the alternatives listed in paragraphs (a)–(j). The US primarily invoked paragraph (g) ('relating to the conservation of exhaustible natural resources'), and alternatively paragraph (b) ('necessary to protect … animal … life or health').[13] When examining paragraph (g), the Appellate Body had to consider whether sea turtles were an 'exhaustible natural resource'. The Appellate Body's approach to that question can be divided into three parts: the interpretation of 'exhaustible' (*US – Shrimp* paragraph 128)' the interpretation of 'natural resources' (paragraphs 129–30); and the interpretation of 'exhaustible natural resources' as a whole (paragraph 131).

The term 'exhaustible' was interpreted 'textually', with no other arguments used. The conclusion was that living resources (such as sea turtles) can be 'exhaustible'.[14]

'Natural resources' was given an evolutionary interpretation, justified by the observation that the term is 'generic' and that the WTO Agreement's preamble mentions 'the objective of sustainable development'. Four 'modern conventions and declarations' were used to elucidate the current meaning of 'natural resources', the conclusion being that the term covers living resources.[15]

When interpreting the term 'exhaustible natural resources' as a whole, the Appellate Body noted that this 'must be read … in the light of contemporary

[12] *US – Shrimp*, above n 8, para 3.
[13] ibid, para 125.
[14] ibid, para 129.
[15] ibid, para 130.

concerns of the community of nations about the protection and conservation of the environment'.[16] Three additional arguments were used to back up the conclusion that living resources were covered by 'exhaustible natural resources': the GATT 1947's drafting history, the principle of effectiveness in treaty interpretation, and two adopted GATT 1947 panel reports.[17] These three were supporting arguments, as they were added on after a tentative conclusion had already been arrived at.

Table 1 is a visual representation of the Appellate Body's reasoning. The table is read from left to right, with arguments to the left and conclusions to the right.

Table 1 Overview of the Reasoning in *US – Shrimp*

<table>
<tr><td colspan="2">Textually</td><td>'Exhaustible' does not exclude living resources</td><td rowspan="8">'Exhaustible natural resources' includes living resources</td></tr>
<tr><td colspan="3">'Exhaustible natural resources' must be read 'in the light of contemporary concerns'</td></tr>
<tr><td>Generic term</td><td rowspan="2">'Natural resources' is evolutive</td><td rowspan="3">'Natural resources' includes living resources</td></tr>
<tr><td>Preamble</td></tr>
<tr><td>Modern conventions and declarations speak of 'living' natural resources</td><td>The current meaning of 'natural resources' includes living resources</td></tr>
<tr><td colspan="3">Effectiveness</td></tr>
<tr><td colspan="3">Two GATT 1947 reports</td></tr>
<tr><td colspan="3">The drafting history</td></tr>
</table>

B. *China – Publications and Audiovisual Products*

The dispute in *China – Publications and Audiovisual Products* was over measures in (the People's Republic of) China regulating the importation and distribution of a wide range of cultural products, including 'reading materials' (books, newspapers, etc), 'audiovisual home entertainment products' (most importantly DVDs), 'sound recordings' and 'films for theatrical release'.[18] The US challenged the measures in the WTO. It claimed that the measures violated China's Accession Protocol and Accession Working Party Report, the General Agreement on Trade in Services (GATS) Articles XVI and XVII, and the GATT 1994 Article III:4.

[16] ibid, para 129.

[17] ibid, para 131.

[18] WTO Appellate Body Report, *China – Measures Affecting Trading Rights and Distribution Services for Certain Publications and Audiovisual Entertainment Products (China – Publications and Audiovisual Products)* adopted 19 January 2010, WT/DS363/AB/R, para 1.

A panel report found that China had violated the above-mentioned obligations, and that the violations were not justifiable under Article XX(a) of the GATT. China appealed this to the Appellate Body, which upheld all the panel's conclusions.[19] The Appellate Body proceedings focused on three issues: (1) The applicability of China's trading rights commitments to measures pertaining to films for theatrical release and unfinished audiovisual products; (2) China's defence under Article XX(a) of the GATT; and (3) the scope of China's GATS Schedule entry 'Sound Recording Distribution Services'.

Under the final issue, the Appellate Body had to decide whether the scope of 'Sound Recording Distribution Services' included 'the distribution of sound recordings in non-physical form, notably through electronic means'.[20] China and the US put forward two possible interpretations (although the Appellate Body could also have made an independent choice and had another interpretation). One possibility was that 'Sound Recording' referred to 'sound recordings in physical form' embedded with sound, and that 'distribution' referred to their physical distribution.[21] The other was that a 'sound recording' is the (intangible) sound content, and that 'distribution' refers to any form of distribution, including on physical records and by electronic means.[22]

The Appellate Body first held that the 'ordinary meaning' of 'recording' cannot be limited to sound embedded on physical media, and that 'distribution' can be understood as 'the dispersal of things of value', which may involve 'tangible or intangible goods'.[23]

Relevant 'context' included the rest of China's GATS Schedule, which provided support for non-physical media being included in 'sound recording', and provisions of the GATS and GATS schedules of other members, neither of which supported a different interpretation.[24]

Reviewing the rules' 'object and purpose', the Appellate Body did not find guidance in any of the objectives listed in the GATS preamble.[25] However, in reply to China's argument that the terms 'sound recording' and 'distribution' should be interpreted according to their meaning at the time of China's accession to the WTO (ie, 2001), the Appellate Body noted that a consequence of China's argument would be that similarly worded obligations were given different meanings, and that this would undermine (the objects and purposes of) 'predictability, security, and clarity', mentioned in Article 3.2 of the DSU.[26] In light of this, the Appellate Body found that what the terms 'apply to' could 'change over time', ie, that they

[19] ibid, paras 414–16.
[20] ibid, para 338.
[21] ibid, para 349.
[22] ibid, para 350.
[23] ibid, paras 350–51.
[24] ibid, paras 372, 380 and 384.
[25] ibid, para 393.
[26] ibid, para 397.

were evolutionary. This conclusion was supported by the facts that the terms were 'generic' and that the WTO agreements were of 'indefinite' duration.[27]

The Appellate Body went on to conclude that 'Sound Recording Distribution Services', and thus China's commitment, extended to 'recordings distributed in non-physical form'.[28]

Since the conclusion under Article 31 was clear, the Appellate Body did not need to examine Article 32.[29] Nevertheless it did so, prompted by an argument by China. It endorsed the panel's finding that 'certain circumstances' at the conclusion of the treaty 'did not exclude the possibility' that the commitment extended to electronic distribution.[30]

Table 2 is a visual representation of the Appellate Body's reasoning. The table is read from left to right, with arguments to the left and conclusions to the right.

Table 2 Overview of the Reasoning in *China – Publications and Audiovisual Products*

<table>
<tr><td rowspan="7">The VCLT Art 31</td><td rowspan="2">Ordinary meaning</td><td>'Sound Recording' cannot be limited to physical media</td><td rowspan="6">'Sound Recording Distribution Services' extends to sound recordings distributed in non-physical form</td></tr>
<tr><td>'Distribution' can be understood as involving tangible or intangible products</td></tr>
<tr><td rowspan="3">Context</td><td>China's GATS Schedule provides support for non-physical products being included</td></tr>
<tr><td>Provisions of the GATS do not support a different interpretation</td></tr>
<tr><td>GATS schedules of other members do not point to a different interpretation</td></tr>
<tr><td rowspan="2">Object and purpose</td><td>None of the objectives in the GATS preamble provide specific guidance</td></tr>
<tr><td>Predictability, security, and clarity demand that Schedule obligations evolve</td><td rowspan="3">'Sound recording' and 'distribution' are evolutive</td></tr>
<tr><td colspan="3">'Sound recording' and 'distribution' are generic</td></tr>
<tr><td colspan="3">The WTO agreements are of indefinite duration</td></tr>
<tr><td>The VCLT Art 32</td><td colspan="3">Preparatory works do not exclude the interpretations reached on the basis of Art 31</td></tr>
</table>

[27] ibid, para 396.
[28] ibid, para 398.
[29] ibid, para 400.
[30] ibid, para 409.

III. Patterns in the Appellate Body's Approach

A. Adherence to the VCLT Rules

In *US – Shrimp*, the Appellate Body found that 'natural resources' was 'by definition' evolutionary. 'Defining' a term is to determine its 'ordinary meaning', according to Article of the VCLT 31(1). This holds even though the Appellate Body's interpretation may be called 'expansive'.[31] The Appellate Body read the term 'from the perspective' of the WTO Agreement's preamble. That is a contextual interpretation, as mentioned in Article 31(1) and 31(2). It is also an example of interpretation in light of a provision's 'object and purpose' as mentioned in Article 31(1). Securing sustainable development is an object of the WTO system,[32] and thus of Article XX(g) of the GATT, and the evolutionary interpretation furthered that objective.

As for the evolutionary interpretation in *China – Publications and Audiovisual Products*, the Appellate Body analysed whether the terms 'sound recording' and 'distribution' were 'generic', which is part of finding their 'ordinary meaning' (Article 31(1)). It also noted that the treaties were of indefinite duration, which reflects their 'object and purpose' (Article 31(1)). When a treaty is intended to last for a long time, its 'purpose' is presumably to be relevant in the future as well as the present. 'Predictability, security, and clarity', which the Appellate Body also mentioned, were part of the 'object and purpose' as well. These goals are important for the practical functioning of schedules and other WTO agreements, and disregarding them would risk undermining the smooth functioning of the WTO system.

The interpretation in *US – Shrimp* was also aided by references to four 'modern conventions and declarations'. These do not fit well under Article 31(3)(b) of the VCLT because it seems unlikely that they '[implied] agreement on the interpretation', which, in a treaty system with a high number of parties and pronounced political differences, must be a threshold.[33] The conventions and declarations are also difficult to subsume under Article 31(3)(c), since only two (the United Nations Convention on the Law of the Sea and the Convention on Biological Diversity) qualify as 'rules of international law', and only one (the United Nations

[31] eg, DM McRae, 'GATT Article XX and the WTO Appellate Body' in M Bronckers and R Quick (eds), *New Directions in International Economic Law: Essays in Honour of John H Jackson* (The Hague, Kluwer Law International, 2000) 227.

[32] eg, J Waincymer, *WTO Litigation: Procedural Aspects of Formal Dispute Settlement* (London, Cameron May, 2002) 446.

[33] J Pauwelyn, *Conflict of Norms in Public International Law: How WTO Law Relates to Other Rules of International Law* (Cambridge, Cambridge University Press, 2003) 252.

Convention on the Law of the Sea)[34] would be binding on 'the parties', regardless of whether this refers to the treaty as a whole or to the specific dispute.[35] The Appellate Body only cited Article 31(3)(c) much later, on a separate question.[36] In connection with the evolutionary interpretation, the Appellate Body did quote a passage from the International Court of Justice's (ICJ) *Namibia* Opinion, saying that 'an international instrument has to be interpreted and applied within the framework of the entire legal system'.[37] While that is most likely a reference to Article 31(3)(c),[38] it does not seem that the Appellate Body itself meant to apply that provision as part of the evolutionary interpretation. Even though the Appellate Body's approach does not fit within Article 31(3)(b) of the VCLT or Article 31(3)(c), the approach was not contrary to the VCLT as such. Invoking these types of instruments is permitted if it helps clarify the meaning of a treaty, under Article 31(1) of the VCLT, even if the specific requirements for using Article 31(3) are not fulfilled.[39]

The Appellate Body referred to 'drafting history' in both its reports. According to Article 32 of the VCLT, this is a 'supplementary' means of interpretation. It can be used freely to 'confirm' an interpretation reached by other means, but can only be used to 'determine' the meaning of terms when their interpretation in light of Article 31 'leaves the meaning ambiguous or obscure' or 'leads to a result which is manifestly absurd or unreasonable'. In *US – Shrimp*, the Appellate Body's reference to drafting history was confined to a footnote, began with the word 'furthermore', and confirmed an interpretation already reached.[40] It is thus clear that the Appellate Body was not using drafting history to 'determine' meaning. In *China – Publications and Audiovisual Products*, preparatory works and circumstances of the treaty's conclusion were used, but only to confirm that they did not contradict the interpretation of 'Sound Recording Distribution Services' already reached.[41] The Appellate Body's approach is therefore in line with Article 32 of the VCLT.[42]

[34] *US – Shrimp*, above n 8, fn 110.

[35] eg, R Gardiner, *Treaty Interpretation*, 2nd edn (Oxford, Oxford University Press, 2015) 302–04; compare Pauwelyn, above n 33, 261.

[36] *US – Shrimp*, above n 8, fn 157.

[37] ibid, fn 109.

[38] eg, U Linderfalk, *On the Interpretation of Treaties: The Modern International Law as Expressed in the 1969 Vienna Convention on the Law of Treaties, Law and Philosophy Library* (Dordrecht, Springer, 2007) 83.

[39] eg, WTO Panel Reports, *European Communities – Measures Affecting the Approval and Marketing of Biotech Products (EC – Approval and Marketing of Biotech Products)* adopted 21 November 2006, WT/DS291/R / WT/DS292/R / WT/DS293/R, paras 7.92–7.94.

[40] *US – Shrimp*, above n 8, fn 114.

[41] *China – Publications and Audiovisual Products*, above n 18, paras 401–11.

[42] The point that the Appellate Body has stuck to the VCLT in its evolutionary interpretations is also made by Van den Bossche, above n 2; and de Andrade, above n 7.

B. No Mention of the Intentions of the Parties

An interesting aspect of the Appellate Body's evolutionary interpretations is that the Appellate Body does not justify its interpretations by referring to the (supposed) intentions of the parties to the treaties. The Appellate Body has been content with declaring that terms 'are' evolutionary and must be interpreted accordingly. The closest the Appellate Body gets to acknowledging an intention for evolution is the statement in *US – Shrimp* that the drafting history does not 'demonstrate an intent' to exclude living natural resources from Article XX(g) of the GATT,[43] and in *China – Publications and Audiovisual Products* that GATS schedules are 'entered into for an indefinite period of time'.[44]

By contrast, all evolutionary interpretations by the ICJ have concluded that the parties are presumed to have 'intended' terms to evolve.[45]

The absence is especially notable considering previous Appellate Body statements. In *EC – Computer Equipment*, released three months prior to *US – Shrimp*, the Appellate Body held that the 'purpose of treaty interpretation under Article 31 of the Vienna Convention is to establish the common intention of the parties to the treaty'.[46] In *India – Patents (US)* it similarly noted that 'the duty of a treaty interpreter is to examine the words of the treaty to determine the intentions of the parties'.[47]

However, a common assumption is that when the VCLT Articles 31–33 are properly applied, the final interpretation will, by definition, be the interpretation that the parties (are assumed to have) intended.[48] The Appellate Body's approach therefore seems to be a convenient shortcut rather than a fundamental break with its own and the ICJ's practice on treaty interpretation.

C. The Evolutionary Interpretations were Superfluous

Another common pattern seen in the Appellate Body's use of the two evolutionary interpretations is that neither was necessary to resolve the case.

[43] *US – Shrimp*, above n 8, fn 114. Bjorge, *The Evolutionary Interpretation of Treaties*, above n 1, 93 interprets *China – Publications and Audiovisual Products*, above n 18, as a reference to intention, but that is implicit at best.

[44] *China – Publications and Audiovisual Products*, above n 18, para 396.

[45] Helmersen, above n 5, 134–35.

[46] WTO Appellate Body Report, *European Communities – Customs Classification of Certain Computer Equipment* (*India – Patents (US)*) adopted 5 June 1998, WT/DS62/AB/R / WT/DS67/AB/R / WT/DS68/AB/R, para 84.

[47] WTO Appellate Body Report, *India – Patent Protection for Pharmaceutical and Agricultural Chemical Products (India – Patents (US))*, adopted 16 January 1998, WT/DS50/AB/R, para 45.

[48] *Dispute Regarding Navigational and Related Rights (Costa Rica v Nicaragua)* (Judgment) [2009] ICJ Rep 213, para 48. The same point is made, eg, by E Bjorge, 'Time Present and Time Past: The Intention of the Parties and the Evolutionary Interpretation of Treaties', ch 5; and D McRae, 'Evolutionary Interpretation: The Relevance of Context', ch 7 in this book.

The Appellate Body found that between the conclusion of the GATT 1947 or the WTO Agreements of 1994 and 1998, when *US – Shrimp* was decided, 'natural resources' had evolved to include living resources in addition to non-living.[49] This assumes that 'natural resources' initially, ie, by 1947 or 1994, covered only non-living resources.

Dictionaries dating from the period of the GATT 1947 drafting do not confirm this assumption. According to the *Pocket Oxford Dictionary* of 1947, 'natural' meant 'provided by nature',[50] while 'resources' were 'stock that can be drawn on' or 'means of supplying a want'.[51] Sea turtles, and other living creatures, occurred in 'nature' in 1947, and many of them 'could be drawn on' and 'supply a want'. The 'ordinary meaning' (Article 31(1) of the VCLT) of 'natural resources' – read in isolation, ie, without 'exhaustible' – already included both living and non-living resources in 1947. If that is correct, the evolutionary interpretation used by the Appellate Body was not necessary to justify the inclusion of sea turtles in 'natural resources'.[52] The Appellate Body could have achieved the same result by a simple textual interpretation.

The real obstacle was the term 'exhaustible'. According to the same dictionary, to 'exhaust' means to 'consume', 'use up', or 'empty'.[53] It is plausible that the use of 'exhaustible' was intended to exclude creatures that can reproduce from the provision, since such creatures are not finite and thus cannot (at least in one sense) be 'consumed' or 'used up'.[54] The Appellate Body disagreed with that understanding, holding that 'textually', living resources are 'in certain circumstances susceptible of … exhaustion' and thus 'exhaustible'.[55]

It is striking that the Appellate Body used evolutionary interpretation, which was an unusual mode of interpretation, to justify the part of the interpretation that hardly needed justification, while using only a 'textual' basis for the more controversial interpretation of 'exhaustible'. A different approach would have been to interpret 'natural resources' textually, to include living resources, and to admit that 'exhaustible' indicates the exclusion of living resources, but interpret it in light of the WTO Agreement's preamble and contemporary concerns so as to include them. That approach, which would not contain any evolutionary interpretations, reaches the same result, and would arguably be more coherent.

In *China – Publications and Audiovisual Products*, when interpreting 'sound recording distribution services' based on Article 31 of the VCLT, the Appellate

[49] *US – Shrimp*, above n 8, para 131.

[50] FG Fowler et al, *Pocket Oxford Dictionary* (Oxford, Clarendon Press, 1947) 521.

[51] ibid, 693.

[52] Similar points are made by I Van Damme, 'Understanding the Choice for Evolutionary Interpretation', ch 16; G Cook, 'The Illusion of "Evolutionary Interpretation" in WTO Dispute Settlement', ch 17; and de Andrade (ch 21), above n 7, in this book.

[53] *Pocket Oxford Dictionary*, above n 50, 278.

[54] S Charnovitz, 'Exploring the Environmental Exceptions in GATT Article XX' (1991) 25 *Journal of World Trade* 37, 45.

[55] *US – Shrimp*, above n 8, para 128.

Body considered the terms 'ordinary meaning', 'context' and 'object and purpose'. In its consideration of 'ordinary meaning' and 'context', the Appellate Body found several arguments in favour of the conclusion that digital recordings were covered by 'sound recording', and none against it. 'Object and purpose' did not provide any counter-arguments either. These findings, which did not include an evolutionary interpretation, were sufficient to reach a conclusion. An evolutionary interpretation was therefore not necessary.[56]

In fact, not only was the evolutionary interpretation not *necessary*, it could not have contributed towards the main conclusion at all. Using an evolutionary interpretation to resolve the main interpretative issue would have been circular. The Appellate Body found that the meaning of 'sound recording' could 'change over time'. This is, however, only true if 'sound recording' means 'recorded material'. 'Recorded material' used to be inseparably embedded in its medium, in the form of grooves in a vinyl disc or pits in a compact disc. Today, the information can exist independently of its medium, as a small digital file on a vast hard drive, or as a sequence of 1s and 0s transmitted over the internet. Back when sound recordings did not exist independently of physical media, mere information (such as 1s and 0s) would presumably not have been considered 'sound recordings'. This means that the term has changed its meaning over time, and is evolutionary. If so, 'distribution' is also an evolving term; it used to refer only to distribution of physical goods, but because of its open-ended nature it now applies equally to, for example, delivery of digital information over the internet. By contrast, 'recording material' may encompass new types of physical media as technology advances. Some of these new forms of media would not have been conceivable earlier. Nevertheless, they would still be physical media embedded with sound, and thus be covered by the term's original meaning. The term would not be capable of evolving. Again, the same is true for 'distribution'. With time, physical media are distributed in novel ways, but none that would not have been 'distribution' according to the term's original meaning. Therefore, the evolving meaning of 'sound recordings' had to be chosen – by interpretation – before the term could be labelled 'evolutionary'.

It is also notable that in paragraph 395 of the report, the Appellate Body noted that the terms 'sound recording' and 'distribution' already covered digital distribution of digital recordings by 2001. The terms had thus not evolved between the drafting of the instrument and the date of the Appellate Body's decision. This is another reason why an evolutionary interpretation was not necessary.

The two evolutionary interpretations are thus similar in that they were not necessary to resolve their respective cases.[57] They are nonetheless different, in that the *US – Shrimp* interpretation was used in the resolution of the case, whereas the

[56] A similar view is held by de Andrade, above n 7.

[57] Bjorge, *The Evolutionary Interpretation of Treaties*, above n 1, 141 makes the same point for other cases, including *Navigational and Related Rights*, above n 48.

interpretation in *China – Publications and Audiovisual Products* interpretation was not. In other words, the *China – Publications and Audiovisual Products* interpretation was an *obiter*, while the *US – Shrimp* interpretation was part of the *ratio*. One reason for including the obiter was presumably effectiveness, by ensuring that the instrument will continue to evolve in the future.[58] Another, more tangible reason why the obiter was included was to refute an argument made by China, namely that since 'progressive liberalisation' is an objective of the WTO system, the terms in the GATS schedule should be interpreted according to their meaning at the time of accession (ie, 2001).[59]

D. The Evolutionary Interpretations were Used to Resolve Vagueness, Not Ambiguity

When interpreting texts, it is possible to distinguish between 'vagueness' and 'ambiguity': 'A vague word has one meaning (and its application is unclear in some cases); an ambiguous word has more than one meaning (and it may be unclear, in some cases, which is in use)'.[60] Evolutionary interpretations are suited to resolve vagueness, but not ambiguity.[61] In line with this, both of the Appellate Body's evolutionary interpretations were used to resolve vagueness.

In *China – Publications and Audiovisual Products*, 'sound recording' had to mean either 'recording material' or 'recorded material'.[62] These two different interpretations of 'sound recording' were entirely different concepts; one referred to tangible items, the other to intangible entities. Finding the correct meaning was therefore a matter of resolving ambiguity rather than vagueness. This interpretation was resolved before the evolutionary interpretation was used. As noted above, the Appellate Body looked at 'ordinary meaning', 'context' and 'object and purpose', and concluded that 'sound recording distribution services' encompassed non-physical forms of sound recording. The evolutionary interpretation was invoked only after this conclusion was drawn and the ambiguity was resolved, as an obiter (as argued above).

The (evolutionary) interpretation of 'natural resources' in *US – Shrimp* concerned vagueness. The parties agreed on a basic level what 'natural resources' were, but not completely on what the term encompassed. A good definition of 'natural resources' is 'materials or substances occurring in nature which can be exploited for economic gain'.[63] Over time, its definition has encompassed (and will

[58] T Voon and A Mitchell, 'Open For Business? China's Telecommunications Service Market and the WTO' (2010) 13 *Journal of International Economic Law* 321, 370–71.

[59] *China – Publications and Audiovisual Products*, above n 18, para 390.

[60] TAO Endicott, *Vagueness in Law* (Oxford, Oxford University Press 2000) 54.

[61] Helmersen, above n 5, 142–44.

[62] *China – Publications and Audiovisual Products*, above n 18, para 350.

[63] Oxford Dictionaries Online, 'natural resources', available at: en.oxforddictionaries.com/definition/natural_resources.

encompass) vastly different kinds of materials. Whether a material or substance is exploitable or not depends on the available technology, which is constantly developing. There was a time when neither oil nor rivers were exploitable, a time when flint stone was a valuable natural resource, and there may come a time when asteroid belts and the likes can be exploited by humans. The term's content changes, and it is thus evolutionary (but not ambiguous).

IV. Conclusion

This chapter has discussed two cases where the WTO Appellate Body used evolutionary interpretations. When doing so, the Appellate Body adheres to the VCLT rules on interpretation, but does not mention the intention of the parties. Another point of note is that the two evolutionary interpretations used were not necessary to resolve the cases. Finally, the Appellate Body used the evolutionary interpretations to resolve vagueness rather than ambiguity.

As of December 2018, the Appellate Body has released a total of 148 reports, of which only two contain evolutionary interpretation. While the Appellate Body's third evolutionary interpretation may be forthcoming, evolutionary interpretation seems unlikely to become a staple in its interpretative repertoire.[64]

Predicting what terms may be subject to evolutionary interpretations is difficult,[65] but candidates include 'public morals' and 'human … life or health' in the GATT 1994 Article XX and the GATS Article XIV;[66] 'public morals' and 'essential security interests' in the GATT 1994 Article XX and Article XXI;[67] 'telecommunications services' in the GATS annexes;[68] the treaty references in the TRIPS footnote 2;[69] 'development, financial and trade needs' in the Enabling Clause paragraph 3(c);[70] and 'like products' in the GATT 1994 Article III.[71]

[64] Although compare Pauwelyn, above n 33, 268.

[65] eg, Van Damme, *Treaty Interpretation by the WTO Appellate Body*, above n 9, 370.

[66] eg, F Francioni, 'WTO Law in Context: The Integration of International Human Rights and Environmental Law in the Dispute Settlement Process' in G Sacerdoti, A Yanovich and J Bohanes (eds), *The WTO at Ten – The Contribution of the Dispute Settlement System* (Cambridge, Cambridge University Press, 2006) 151.

[67] Pauwelyn, above n 33, 267.

[68] Voon and Mitchell, above n 58, 369.

[69] Pauwelyn, above n 33, 265–66

[70] T Voon, *Cultural Products and the World Trade Organization* (Cambridge, Cambridge University Press, 2007) 137.

[71] AE Appleton, 'Shrimp/Turtle: Untangling the Nets' (1999) 2 *Journal of International Economic Law* 477, 482.

20

Is there Evolution in the Evolutionary Interpretation of WTO Law?

PETER VAN DEN BOSSCHE

I. Introduction

The existence of the World Trade Organization (WTO) dispute settlement system, the most active system for the resolution of disputes between States, is under threat. By the end of 2019 it may be unable to hear and decide any new appeals and quickly wither away thereafter. At the core of this existential crisis is the accusation that, particularly in recent years, the Appellate Body has been guilty of judicial activism in interpreting and applying WTO law. As evolutionary interpretation is often associated with judicial activism, it is in the context of the current crisis appropriate to examine whether WTO panels and the Appellate Body have engaged in evolutionary interpretation that would amount to judicial activism, and, if so, whether they have done so more and/or differently over the years. Hence, the title of this contribution: 'Is there Evolution in the Evolutionary Interpretation of WTO Law?'

II. The Nature of Evolutionary Interpretation

There is a considerable body of literature on evolutionary interpretation or, as it is also referred to, evolutive or dynamic interpretation of international law. This literature reflects the wide variety of views on evolutionary interpretation and on the role it can play in interpreting and applying international law, and in particular treaty law. The challenge facing the international community is how to ensure that international law takes account of the ever-changing circumstances in which it is applied. The changes referred to include, but are by no means limited to (geo-)political changes, changes in societal values pursued by the international community or its members, changes in technology, and changes in scientific knowledge. It is important, if not vital, that international law takes account of these changes if it wishes to remain relevant in today's world. Obviously, the most appropriate way of doing so would be through the constant updating of existing international agreements and the conclusion of new agreements. However, this approach is often not available. Negotiating and concluding updated or new agreements, which take on board new (geo-)political, societal, technological and scientific realities, is at best time-consuming and arduous, and in many cases, for a myriad of reasons, not feasible. Unfortunately, WTO law is an excellent example of international law's limited ability to adapt to change through the updating of existing agreements or the conclusion of new agreements. The question then arises whether and, and if so, to what extent international adjudicators can adapt the law they (must) apply to the factual circumstances as the latter change over time. Can an international adjudicator adapt 'old' rules to modern times so that these rules remain relevant in today's world? Or, in other words, can an international adjudicator apply an evolutionary interpretation to a treaty's terms or concepts to adapt the treaty to modern-day realities?

The International Court of Justice (ICJ) has struggled with this question and in its 1970 Advisory Opinion in the *Namibia* case held:

> Mindful as it is of the primary necessity of interpreting an instrument *in accordance with the intentions of the parties at the time of its conclusion*, the Court is bound to take into account the fact that the concepts embodied in Article 22 of the Covenant – 'the strenuous conditions of the modern world' and 'the well-being and development' of the peoples concerned – were not static, but were by definition *evolutionary*, as also, therefore, was the concept of the 'sacred trust' … Moreover, an international instrument has to be interpreted and applied within the framework of *the entire legal system prevailing at the time of the interpretation* (emphasis added).[1]

The ICJ thus allowed for the evolutionary interpretation of a treaty's terms, albeit on the strict condition that the interpretation was to be 'in accordance with the intentions of the parties at the time of its conclusion'. In reaching its decision, the ICJ considered it essential that the concepts requiring interpretation, namely 'the strenuous conditions of the modern world', 'the well-being and development' and 'sacred trust' were 'not static but … by definition evolutionary', and thus fit for evolutionary interpretation. The ICJ confirmed this approach to evolutionary interpretation in the 1978 *Aegean Sea Continental Shelf* case. In its judgment, the ICJ repeated that the interpretation of the treaty terms must be based on the intention of the parties to the treaty at the moment of its conclusion, and that the use of 'generic terms' in the treaty reflected the parties' intention 'to follow the evolution of the law'.[2] Most recently, in 2009 and in 2010, the ICJ reaffirmed its position on evolutionary interpretation in the *Costa Rica v Nicaragua* case and the

[1] *Legal Consequences for States of the Continued Presence of South Africa in Namibia (South West Africa) notwithstanding Security Council Resolution 276 (1970)* (Advisory Opinion) [1971] ICJ Rep 16, para 53.

[2] *Aegean Sea Continental Shelf (Greece v Turkey)* (Judgment) [1978] ICJ Rep 3, para 77.

Pulp Mills case respectively. In the former case, the ICJ ruled on the meaning of the term '*comercio*' (commerce) in the 1858 Treaty of Limits between Costa Rica and Nicaragua:

> It is true that the terms used in a treaty must be interpreted in light of what is determined to have been the parties' common intention, which is, by definition, contemporaneous with the treaty's conclusion … This does not however signify that, where a term's meaning is no longer the same as it was at the date of conclusion, no account should ever be taken of its meaning at the time when the treaty is to be interpreted for purposes of applying it.[3]

In the *Pulp Mills* case, the ICJ repeated and emphasised a statement already made in *Costa Rica v Nicaragua* that

> there are situations in which the parties' intent upon conclusion of the treaty was, or may be presumed to have been, to give the terms used – or some of them – a meaning or content capable of evolving, not one fixed once and for all, so as to make allowance for, among other things, developments in international law.[4]

The ICJ has thus repeatedly endorsed the evolutionary interpretation of treaty terms, albeit on the condition that the intention of the parties to the treaty remains the basis for the interpretation. When the ICJ made its evolutionary interpretation in the four cases referred to above, it stayed within the framework of the rules of interpretation set out in Articles 31 and 32 of the Vienna Convention on the Law of Treaties (VCLT). It set out to establish the ordinary meaning of the generic, non-static terms at issue, in their context and in light of the object and purpose of the agreement at issue. The generic, non-static nature of the terms at issue allowed for their evolutionary interpretation in accordance with the intention of the parties to the agreement. As Eirik Bjorge has commented, evolutionary interpretation, as endorsed and applied by the ICJ, is not so much an interpretative rule but rather 'the result of a proper application of the usual means of interpretation, as a means by which to establish the intention of the parties'.[5] While not without reservations and/or expressions of concern, the ICJ's approach to evolutionary interpretation has found significant support in the literature.[6]

[3] *Dispute Regarding Navigational and Related Rights (Costa Rica v Nicaragua)* (Judgment) [2009] ICJ Rep 213, para 63–64.

[4] *Pulp Mills on the River Uruguay (Argentina v Uruguay)* (Judgment) [2010] ICJ Rep 14, para 204. See *Navigational and Related Rights*, above n 3, para 64.

[5] E Bjorge, *The Evolutionary Interpretation of Treaties* (Oxford, Oxford University Press, 2014) 2.

[6] See, *inter alia*, G Marceau, 'L'interprétation évolutive par le juge OMC: sophisme ou nécessité?' (2018) 122 *Revue générale de droit international public* 23; J Wyatt, An Original or Modern-Day Meaning for Treaty Terms? The Problem of Intertemporal Linguistics in the Case Law of International Courts and Tribunals' (University of Geneva, 2017, 846–47; Bjorge, above n 5, 2; I Van Damme, 'Is Evolutionary Interpretation Only A Matter of Finding the Parties' Intentions?' EJIL Book Discussion, 17 December 2014, available at: www.ejiltalk.org/is-evolutionary-interpretation-only-a-matter-of-finding-the-parties-intentions; P Palchetti, 'Interpreting "Generic Terms": Between Respect for the Parties' Original Intention and the Identification of the Ordinary Meaning' in N Boschiero, T Scovazzi, C Pitea and C Ragni (eds), *International Courts and the Development of International Law: Essays in*

III. The WTO's Approach to 'Evolutionary' Interpretation

Since 1 January 1995, when the WTO dispute settlement system became operational, and as of 15 February 2019, the Appellate Body and WTO panels have circulated in total 140 and 239 reports respectively. In only a few of these reports does the Appellate Body or a panel either adopt or reject an evolutionary interpretation. The most frequently cited Appellate Body report in this respect is US – Shrimp. Here, the Appellate Body adopted a broad, 'evolutionary' interpretation of the term 'exhaustible natural resources' in Article XX(g) of the GATT 1994. The complainants (India, Malaysia, Pakistan and Thailand) considered that the general exception provided for in Article XX(g) was limited to measures related to the conservation of 'mineral' or 'non-living' natural resources. Their principal argument was rooted in the notion that 'living' natural resources are 'renewable' and therefore cannot be 'exhaustible' natural resources. The Appellate Body disagreed:

> We do not believe that 'exhaustible' natural resources and 'renewable' natural resources are mutually exclusive. One lesson that modern biological sciences teach us is that living species, though in principle, capable of reproduction and, in that sense, 'renewable', are in certain circumstances indeed susceptible of depletion, exhaustion and extinction, frequently because of human activities. Living resources are just as 'finite' as petroleum, iron ore and other non-living resources (emphasis added).[7]

The Appellate Body further noted with regard to the appropriate interpretation of the term of 'exhaustible natural resources':

> The words of Article XX(g), 'exhaustible natural resources', were actually crafted more than 50 years ago. They must be read by a treaty interpreter in the light of *contemporary concerns of the community of nations* about the protection and conservation of the environment. While Article XX was not modified in the Uruguay Round, the preamble attached to the WTO Agreement shows that the signatories to that Agreement were, in 1994, fully aware of the importance and legitimacy of environmental protection as a goal of national and international policy. The preamble of the WTO Agreement – which informs not only the GATT 1994, but also the other covered agreements – explicitly acknowledges 'the objective of sustainable development'.

Honour of Tullio Treves (The Hague, Springer, 2013) 91–92; A Pellet, 'L'adaptation du droit international aux besoins changeants de la société internationale' (2007) 329 *Collected Courses of The Hague Academy of International Law* 17; A Boyle and C Chinkin, *The Making of International Law* (Oxford, Oxford University Press, 2007) 244; T Georgopoulos, 'Le droit intertemporel et les dispositions conventionnelles évolutives' (2004) 108 *Revue générale de droit international public* 123, 130; B Stern, *20 ans de jurisprudence de la Cour international de Justice: 1975–1995* (The Hague, Martinus Nijhoff, 1998) 80–81; R Jennings and A Watts (eds), *Oppenheim's International Law*, 9th edn, Vol I (Aylesbury, Longman's, 1992) 1282; E Jimenez de Arechaga, 'International Law in the Past Third of a Century' (1978) 159 *Collected Courses of The Hague Academy of International Law* 1, 49.

[7] WTO Appellate Body Report, *United States – Import Prohibition on Certain Shrimp and Shrimp Products (US – Shrimp)* adopted 6 November 1998, WT/DS58/AB/R, para 128.

> … From the perspective embodied in the preamble of the WTO Agreement, we note that the *generic term of 'natural resources'* in Article XX(g) is *not 'static'* in its content or reference *but is rather 'by definition, evolutionary'*. It is, therefore, pertinent to note that modern international conventions and declarations make frequent references to natural resources as embracing both living and non-living resources (emphasis added).[8]

In a footnote to the last paragraph quoted above, the Appellate Body explicitly referred to the ICJ's 1971 Advisory Opinion in the *Namibia* case, discussed above, and recalled the ICJ's ruling that where concepts embodied in a treaty are 'by definition, evolutionary', their 'interpretation cannot remain unaffected by the subsequent development of law … Moreover, an international instrument has to be interpreted and applied within the framework of the entire legal system prevailing at the time of the interpretation'.[9] In the same footnote, the Appellate Body also referred to the ICJ's judgment in the 1978 *Aegean Sea Continental Shelf* case in further support of its 'evolutionary interpretation' of the term 'exhaustible natural resources'.

The second report where the Appellate Body had recourse to evolutionary interpretation was *China – Publications and Audiovisual Products*. In this case, China contended on appeal that the panel had erred in interpreting its General Agreement on Trade in Services (GATS) schedule entry 'Sound recording distribution services' according to the contemporary meaning of that term, ie, also covering the electronic distribution of sound recordings, a distribution service that did not exist in 2001 when China joined the WTO and its GATS schedule was concluded. According to China, the GATS principle of progressive liberalisation does not allow for the expansion of the scope of the commitments of a WTO Member by interpreting the terms used in the schedule based on the meaning of those terms at the time of interpretation.[10] Disagreeing with China, the Appellate Body ruled that: 'The terms used in China's GATS Schedule ("sound recording" and "distribution") are *sufficiently generic* that what they apply to may change over time'(emphasis added).[11] As the Appellate Body further explained:

> [I]nterpreting the terms of GATS specific commitments based on the notion that the ordinary meaning to be attributed to those terms can only be the meaning that they had at the time the Schedule was concluded would mean that very similar or identically worded commitments could be given different meanings, content, and coverage depending on the date of their adoption or the date of a Member's accession to the treaty. Such interpretation would undermine the predictability, security, and clarity of GATS specific commitments, which are undertaken through successive rounds of negotiations, and which must be interpreted in accordance with customary rules of interpretation of public international law.[12]

[8] ibid, paras 129 and 130.
[9] ibid, para 129, fn 109.
[10] WTO Appellate Body Report, China – *Measure Affecting Trading Rights and Distribution Services for Certain Publications and Audiovisual Entertainment Products (China – Publications and Audiovisual Products)* adopted 19 January 2010, WT/DS363/AB/R, para 390.
[11] ibid, para 396.
[12] ibid, para 397.

The Appellate Body justified its recourse to evolutionary interpretation in this case by referring to the 2009 ICJ judgment in the *Costa Rica v Nicaragua* case, discussed above.[13]

WTO panels have also had recourse to evolutionary interpretation in a number of cases. In *Mexico – Telecoms*, the panel emphasised the importance of it being fully aware of the 'rapid technological evolution' regarding telecom services since 'some of the telecommunication provisions seem to be technology-specific and may no longer reflect prevailing industry practices'.[14] The technological evolution was thus to be considered in interpreting the GATS provisions on telecom services. In *US – Gambling*, one of the issues before the panel was whether gambling services provided over the internet, ie, services that did not exist in 1994 when the United States made its market access and national treatment commitments concerning gaming services, were nevertheless covered by these commitments. The panel found that they were and gave the following justification for this finding:

> Article I:2(a) of the GATS defines 'mode 1', otherwise referred to as 'cross-border', as the supply of a service 'from the territory of one Member into the territory of any other Member'. The definition does not contain any indication as to the means that can be used to supply services cross-border. This indicates, in our view, that the GATS does not limit the various technologically possible means of delivery under mode 1.[15]

In *EC – IT Products*, the question arose whether the European Union's tariff concession for flat-panel display devices (FPDs) applied to FPDs receiving and reproducing video signals from DVD players (the common technology when the concession was made in 1996) *as well as* to FPDs receiving and reproducing video signals from automatic data-processing machines (ie, computers) (an existing but still uncommon technology in 1996). The panel did not examine in depth the status of the technology at the time the concession was made,[16] but found that: 'In the case of this concession, … *generic terms* were used to cover a wide range of products and technologies' (emphasis added).[17] It thus established, based on the concession's terms, that FPDs incorporating a wide range of characteristics and technologies were covered, including both types of FPDs at issue.[18] Interestingly, the panel stated in a footnote that: 'We also do not consider it necessary to resort to any form of evolutionary interpretation of the terms, in light of our conclusion on the ordinary meaning of the terms'.[19]

[13] See ibid, para 397, fn 705.

[14] WTO Panel Report, *Mexico – Measures Affecting Telecommunication Service (Mexico – Telecoms)* adopted 1 June 2004, WT/DS204/R, para 7.2, fn 799.

[15] WTO Panel Report, *United States – Measures Affecting the Cross-Border Supply of Gambling and Betting Services (US – Gambling)* adopted 20 April 2005, WT/DS285/R, para 6.281.

[16] WTO Panel Reports, *European Communities and its member States – Tariff Treatment of Certain Information Technology Products (EC – IT Products)* adopted 21 September 2010, WT/DS375/R / WT/DS376/R / WT/DS377/R, para 7.600.

[17] ibid, para 7.599.

[18] See ibid, para 7.600.

[19] ibid, para 7.600, fn 807.

This statement seems to reflect a different understanding of 'evolutionary interpretation' than that adopted by the Appellate Body and the ICJ, discussed above. The panel report in *EC – IT Products* was not appealed.

In *Canada – Pharmaceutical Patents* and *US – Section 110(5) Copyright Act*, panels considered the term 'normal exploitation' in Articles 17 and 30 of the TRIPS Agreement and in *China – Intellectual Property Rights* the panel analysed the term 'commercial scale' in Article 61 of that Agreement. The panels found that the specific forms of exploitation or commerce covered by these terms are 'not static' but 'adapt to changing forms of competition due to technological development and the evolution of marketing practices'.[20]

Panels explicitly declined to give an evolutionary interpretation to WTO provisions in *EC – Approval and Marketing of Biotech Products*[21] and in *India – Solar Cells*.[22] In the latter case, the panel observed:

> [A]s the Appellate Body found with respect to the provisions of Article XX(g), the terms 'products in general or local short supply' in Article XX(j) are not static in their 'content or reference', but are 'sufficiently generic that what they apply to may change over time'.[23]

However, it subsequently concluded:

> [W]e do not consider that the applicable legal standard for what it means to be a 'product in general or local short supply has changed over time. We consider that, even if a consequence of globalization and trade liberalization were the elimination of all product shortages in the world, such that the factual circumstance for invoking Article XX(j) would no longer exist and the provision would no longer have any sphere of operation, it would not be open to a treaty interpreter to change the applicable legal standard for what it means to be a 'product in general or local short supply' in the name of 'evolutionary interpretation' or ensuring that there would continue to be factual circumstances triggering the application of this provision.[24]

This finding by the panel in *India – Solar Cells* was not appealed.

IV. Conclusion

As already observed above, WTO panels and the Appellate Body have not had frequent recourse to evolutionary interpretation, and the discussion above

[20] See WTO Panel Report, *China – Measures Affecting the Protection and Enforcement of Intellectual Property Rights (China – Intellectual Property Rights)* adopted 20 March 2009, WT/DS362/R, para 7.657. See also WTO Panel Report, *Canada – Patent Protection of Pharmaceutical Products (Canada – Pharmaceutical Patents)* adopted 7 April 2000, WT/DS114/R, para 7.55; and WTO Panel Report, *United States – Section 110(5) of the US Copyright Act (US – Section 110(5) Copyright Act)* adopted 27 July 2000, WT/DS160/R, para 6.187.

[21] WTO Panel Reports, *European Communities – Measures Affecting the Approval and Marketing of Biotech Products (EC – Approval and Marketing of Biotech Products)* adopted 21 November 2006, WT/DS291/R / WT/DS292/R / WT/DS293/R, paras 7.92–7.96.

[22] WTO Panel Report, *India – Certain Measures Relating to Solar Cells and Solar Modules (India – Solar Cells)* adopted 14 October 2016, WT/DS456/R, paras 7.232–7.233.

[23] ibid, para 7.232.

[24] ibid, para 7.233.

reveals that when they did, the approach taken was generally in line with the ICJ's approach to evolutionary interpretation. When giving an evolutionary interpretation to terms and concepts in WTO law, the Appellate Body and panels have stayed within the framework of the rules of interpretation set out in Articles 31 and 32 of the VCLT. They set out to establish the ordinary meaning of the generic, non-static terms and concepts at issue, in their context (broadly understood) and in light of the object and purpose of the WTO agreement at issue. Evolutionary interpretation, as endorsed and applied by the Appellate Body, is not a distinct rule of, or approach to, interpretation but the result of a proper application of the VCLT rules of interpretation, as a means by which to establish the intention of the parties to the WTO agreement at issue. In all the instances of evolutionary interpretation discussed above, it was the generic, non-static nature of the terms and concepts at issue that allowed for an evolutionary interpretation. The fact that generic, non-static terms and concepts were used in a WTO agreement reflects the intention of the parties to allow the rights and obligations under that agreement to evolve with the changing circumstances and situations in which they were to be applied. The approach of WTO adjudicators to evolutionary interpretation has been prudent and cannot be considered to reflect judicial activism. Moreover, their approach has not changed since the Appellate Body report in *US – Shrimp*. Accordingly, there has been no evolution in the evolutionary interpretation of WTO law. Such evolution was neither called for nor desirable.

21

Evolutionary Interpretation and the Appellate Body's Existential Crisis

MARIANA CLARA DE ANDRADE

I. Introduction

The crown jewel of the World Trade Organization (WTO), namely its dispute settlement system and most notably its Appellate Body, has been challenged with internal legitimacy problems. This is partly due to unaddressed discontents with certain Appellate Body practices, including some related to treaty interpretation, which have resulted in accusations that the organ has indulged in undue judicial activism.[1] The present contribution examines whether the Appellate Body's use of the evolutionary approach as an interpretative tool can reinforce these accusations of judicial activism. Among these criticisms, two are of interest for the present purposes: the claims that the Appellate Body has engaged in interpretative exercises which add to or diminish the rights and obligations of the parties; and the allegations that some of its findings are unnecessary to the resolution of the dispute, thus exceeding its mandate according to the Understanding on Rules and Procedures Governing the Settlement of Disputes (DSU).

Because of their generality[2] and the ever-changing aspect of global relations, there are treaty terms which are 'capable of evolving over time':[3] evolutionary interpretation takes these changes into account. Stating that the meaning of a treaty provision or term has changed may arguably amount to undue law-making which departs from the original intention of the parties.[4]

[1] See generally R McDougall, 'The Crisis in WTO Dispute Settlement: Fixing Birth Defects to Restore Balance' (2018) 52 *Journal of World Trade* 867.

[2] See U Linderfalk, *On the Interpretation of Treaties: The Modern International Law as Expressed in the 1969 Vienna Convention on the Law of Treaties, Law and Philosophy Library* (Dordrecht, Springer, 2007) 67 ff; ST Helmersen, 'Evolutive Treaty Interpretation: Legality, Semantics and Distinctions' (2013) 6 *European Journal of Legal Studies* 127.

[3] G Nolte, *Fifth report on subsequent agreements and subsequent practice in relation to the interpretation of treaties* (28 February 2018) UN Doc A/CN.4/715, 21.

[4] As Thirlway expressed it, the principle of contemporaneity (which is closely related to the evolutionary approach to treaty interpretation) states that 'Provided that, where it can be established that it

This chapter is divided into two sections. The first section briefly reviews the *US – Shrimp* and *China – Publications and Audiovisual Products* reports, in which the Appellate Body has used an evolutionary approach. It also describes the reception of the reports upon their circulation in the Dispute Settlement Body (DSB) meetings. The purpose is to shed light on Members' immediate reactions to the Appellate Body's reasoning. The second section addresses the Appellate Body's reasoning and the comments to the organ's reports made by the WTO membership in these meetings. This contribution also considers whether the perceptions of judicial activism are influenced by how individual WTO Members view the Appellate Body's judicial function – either as a mere arbitrator for the resolution of disputes or as an international court – whose role is also to clarify (and arguably develop) the law.

II. The Case Law on Evolutionary Interpretation and the Response from WTO Members

A. *US – Shrimp*

In *US – Shrimp*, the Appellate Body had to determine whether sea turtles could be considered 'exhaustible natural resources' under the exception of Article XX(g) of the General Agreement on Tariffs and Trade (GATT). The complainants had claimed that the drafting history of Article XX(g) indicated that 'exhaustible natural resources' meant finite, non-living resources such as raw materials and minerals.[5]

The Appellate Body considered that:

> The words of Article XX(g), 'exhaustible natural resources', were actually crafted more than 50 years ago. They must be read by a treaty interpreter in the light of contemporary concerns of the community of nations about the protection and conservation of the environment … [T]he generic term 'natural resources' in Article XX(g) is not 'static' in its content or reference but is rather 'by definition, evolutionary'. It is, therefore, pertinent to note that modern international conventions and declarations make frequent references to natural resources as embracing both living and non-living resources.[6]

was the intention of the parties that the meaning or scope of a term or expression used in the treaty should follow the development of the law, the treaty must be interpreted so as to give effect to that intention' (H Thirlway, *The Law and Procedure of the International Court of Justice: Fifty Years of Jurisprudence*, Vol I (Oxford, Oxford University Press, 2013) 305). See also PM Dupuy, 'Evolutionary Interpretation of Treaties: Between Memory and Prophecy' in E Cannizzaro (ed), *The Law of Treaties Beyond the Vienna Convention* (Oxford, Oxford University Press, 2011) 127.

[5] WTO Panel Report, *United States – Import Prohibition of Certain Shrimp and Shrimp Products (US – Shrimp)* adopted 6 November 1998, WT/DS58/R, para 3.238.

[6] WTO Appellate Body Report, *United States – Import Prohibition of Certain Shrimp and Shrimp Products* (*US – Shrimp*) adopted 6 November 1998, WT/DS58/AB/R, para 129–30, fns omitted.

The evolutionary approach adopted in this report is thus characterised by the attention given to 'contemporary concerns' to inform the interpretation of a provision that was 'crafted more than 50 years ago'. The Appellate Body took into account the preamble of the WTO Agreement and other international legal instruments[7] to conclude that there was a 'recent acknowledgement by the international community of the importance of concerted bilateral or multilateral action to protect living natural resources'.[8]

B. *China – Publications and Audiovisual Products*

In *China – Publications and Audiovisual Products*, the scope of China's entry on 'Sound recording distribution services' under its *China – Publications and Audiovisual Products* (GATS) schedule was in dispute. China contended it did not include sound recordings in non-physical form, in particular because at the time of its accession, in 2001, the scope given to this entry was limited to physical forms of sound recording distribution devices. The panel disagreed with this interpretation.

On appeal, China argued that the panel had interpreted the entry according to the contemporary meaning of the words, and this had amounted to an expansion of the scope of the commitments of a WTO Member.[9] China's argument was that this entry should be interpreted according to its meaning at the time of its accession to the WTO.[10]

To delimit the scope of China's commitment under its schedule, the Appellate Body followed Article 31 of the Vienna Convention on the Law of Treaties (VCLT). China's claims on the temporal scope of the entry were addressed as part of the 'object and purpose' of the GATS. The Appellate Body found that 'the terms used in China's GATS Schedule ("sound recording" and "distribution") are sufficiently generic that what they apply to may change over time'.[11] The Appellate Body also concluded that interpreting Members' commitments according to the time of their accession to the WTO 'would mean that very similar or identically worded commitments could be given different meanings, content, and coverage depending on the date of their adoption or the date of a Member's accession to the treaty'.[12]

'By definition, evolutionary' was a reference to the International Court of Justice's *Namibia* Advisory Opinion: *Legal Consequences for States of the Continued Presence of South Africa in Namibia (South West Africa) notwithstanding Security Council Resolution 276 (1970)* (Advisory Opinion) [1971] ICJ Rep 16.

[7] Including the United Nations Convention on the Law of the Sea, Convention on Biological Diversity, and the Agenda 21 (ibid, 48–49).

[8] WTO Appellate Body Report, *US – Shrimp*, above n 6, para 131.

[9] WTO Appellate Body Report, *China – Measures Affecting Trading Rights and Distribution Services for Certain Publications and Audiovisual Entertainment Products (China – Publications and Audiovisual Services)* adopted 19 January 2010, WT/DS363/AB/R, para 390.

[10] ibid, para 395.

[11] ibid, para 396.

[12] ibid, para 397.

C. Members' Perceptions of the Appellate Body Reports as Expressed in DSB Meetings

It is not surprising that those Appellate Body findings that were characterised by an evolutionary interpretation displeased Members whose interests were affected by the outcome of this approach. In *US – Shrimp*, Thailand, India and Pakistan (complainants in the dispute) criticised the 'evolutionary approach', arguing that it was a 'recipe for adding to and diminishing the rights and obligations of Members'.[13] 'Evolutionary interpretation' was also regarded as an overstepping of WTO jurisdiction by the complaining parties in this dispute.[14] The main criticism was that taking into account 'contemporary concerns' had resulted in an 'amendment or authoritative interpretation' by the Appellate Body, which was not permitted under its mandate.[15] This interpretative approach had, in turn, undermined the predictability of the multilateral trading system.

On the other hand, the United States 'was pleased' that the Appellate Body had emphasised the importance of considering contemporary concerns in international relations in ascertaining the applicability of Article XX of the GATT.[16] Although the DSB meeting minutes do not show the United States as having made any express mention of evolutionary interpretation, this declaration can be interpreted as an endorsement of the Appellate Body's approach.

Similarly, in *China – Publications and Audiovisual Products*, the United States welcomed the finding that China's services included electronic distribution of sound recordings, and stated that '[a] contrary finding would have diminished significantly the value of services commitments in an ever-innovating world'.[17] It is also possible to infer here an (at least tacit) endorsement of the evolutionary approach.

Interestingly, China did not make any substantive remarks regarding the findings on the scope of a Member's entry under the GATS schedule. Other third parties also did not comment on the issue; they focused their comments on other findings by the adjudicators.

This difference in how the concerned Members received these two reports can intuitively be explained by different factors, but the speculative nature of these explanations does not allow for extended scrutiny here. Still, one possibility is worth a comment: the perception of activism may have been influenced by the interpretative process indicated in the report. When the evolutionary approach is

[13] Minutes of Meeting Held in the Centre William Rappard on 6 November 1998 (14 December 1998) WT/DSB/M/50, 5.

[14] See, eg, Pakistan's view (ibid, 5).

[15] ibid, 9.

[16] ibid, 11.

[17] Minutes of Meeting Held in the Centre William Rappard on 19 January 2010 (9 March 2010) WT/DSB/M/278, 15, para 78.

less evident, as in *China – Publications and Audiovisual Products* when compared with *US – Shrimp*, Members focus less on this interpretative aspect as a point of criticism. Generally speaking, stating that the original intention of the parties must be read in light of new concerns is an easy target for accusations of adding to or diminishing rights and obligations by concerned Members.

III. Evolutionary Interpretation by the Appellate Body: How Far Should it Go?

This section examines the Appellate Body's use of an evolutionary approach in the aforementioned reports and whether such use may contribute to criticisms of judicial overreach.[18] At the outset, it is argued that these criticisms can be influenced by the view on the Appellate Body's role as a judicial organ. With this consideration in mind, the subsequent part examines whether the use of the evolutionary approach in those reports amounted to judicial overreach. Finally, this section addresses whether this interpretative tool is a useful one from a policy perspective, and whether it can be employed in a more nuanced manner by WTO adjudicators.

A. Two Views on the Judicial Function of the Appellate Body

The crisis in WTO dispute settlement can partly be explained by the divergence of views on the function that its adjudicators should perform.[19] On one side of the spectrum, there is the view that WTO adjudicators should address questions only to the extent necessary to resolve a dispute.[20] On the other side, there is the view that they should contribute to the clarification of WTO rules[21] and even, in some cases, compensate for the fact that there is a deadlock in the negotiation of

[18] Van den Bossche submits in his contribution to this book that WTO adjudicators have not been activist in their resort to evolutionary interpretation. The problem examined here is of a different nature: it focuses on the *perception* by WTO Members towards the Appellate Body's interpretative practice when applying the evolutionary approach. For a detailed consideration on whether this approach is indeed activist or not (and a defence for a negative reply, see P Van den Bossche, 'Is there Evolution in the Evolutionary Interpretation of WTO Law?', ch 20 in this book.

[19] See McDougall, above n 1, 883. For general considerations on judicial activism and the function of adjudicators, see F Zarbiyev, 'Judicial Activism in International Law – A Conceptual Framework' (2012) 3 *Journal of International Dispute Settlement* 247, 257–59.

[20] This is the view taken by the United States. See 'Statements by the United States at the Meeting of the WTO Dispute Settlement Body Geneva, December 2018, Statements by the United States at the Meeting of the WTO Dispute Settlement Body, Geneva, December 18, 2018', available at: geneva.usmission.gov/2018/12/19/statements-by-the-united-states-at-the-december-18-2018-dsb-meeting/ (18 December 2018 Statements).

[21] See, eg, R Howse, 'Adjudicative Legitimacy and Treaty Interpretation in International Trade Law: The Early Years of WTO Jurisprudence' in JHH Weiler (ed), *The EU, the WTO, and the NAFTA: Towards a Common Law of International Trade?* (Oxford, Oxford University Press, 2000) 51 ff.

new agreements at the multilateral trading system and that amendment is difficult under WTO procedural rules.[22]

'Resolving the dispute' was the approach traditionally taken in GATT dispute settlement, which was strongly influenced by diplomatic considerations.[23] To some extent, this tradition has been kept by the WTO.[24] But for reasons that fall outside the scope of this chapter, WTO dispute settlement undertook a more 'judicial' approach to the detriment of a 'diplomatic' one.[25] Focusing on adjudication with the view of settling disputes would give less margin for findings that are unnecessary to solve the specific dispute or that result in judicial law-making – including, one could argue, 'evolutionary interpretations'.

'Clarifying the law' as part of the judicial function is a double-edged sword. On the one hand, clarifying the meaning of terms and provisions by means of judicial decisions can provide legal certainty for future disputes. On the other hand, according to the Appellate Body's critics, unnecessary interpretative elements exceed the mandate of WTO adjudicators.[26] These clarifications, so-called unnecessary obiter dicta,[27] may then acquire precedential value, another point of critique towards the Appellate Body practice.[28]

To better understand these concerns, it should also be kept in mind that the Appellate Body is not allowed to 'add to or diminish the rights and obligations' in the covered agreements.[29] This means that, if the WTO adjudicators clarify 'too much' of WTO provisions, their report can be regarded by Members as an overstepping of their mandate. In this vein, the idea of avoiding an unnecessary interpretative exercise is related to the belief that the Appellate Body should not engage in findings that are not needed to solve the dispute, and which, in particular, may amount to adding to or diminishing rights and obligations of WTO Members.

[22] See, eg, S Peng, 'Regulating New Services through Litigation? Electronic Commerce as a Case Study on the Evaluation of "Judicial Activism" in the WTO' (2014) 48 *Journal of World Trade* 1189.

[23] J Hillman, 'Moving Towards an International Rule of Law? The Role of the GATT and the WTO in its Development' in G Marceau (ed), *A History of Law and Lawyers in the GATT/WTO: The Development of the Rule of Law in the Multilateral Trading System* (Cambridge, Cambridge University Press, 2015) 66.

[24] For instance, Art 3.7 of the DSU indicates that 'The aim of the dispute settlement mechanism is to secure a positive solution to a dispute. A solution mutually acceptable to the parties to a dispute and consistent with the covered agreements is clearly to be preferred'.

[25] Jackson describes this transition in detail. See JH Jackson, *Sovereignty, the WTO and Changing Fundamentals of International Law* (Cambridge, Cambridge University Press, 2006) ch 5.

[26] See 18 December 2018 Statements, above n 20.

[27] This terminology is used by the United States in its statements (ibid). For a discussion on obiter dicta by the WTO Appellate Body, see, eg, H Gao, 'Dictum on Dicta: Obiter Dicta in WTO Disputes' (2018) 17 *World Trade Review* 509; and G Sacerdoti, 'A Comment on Henry Gao, "Dictum on Dicta: Obiter Dicta in WTO Disputes"' (2018) 17 *World Trade Review* 535.

[28] See 18 December 2018 Statements, above n 20, 16 ff.

[29] Art 3.2 of the DSU states that 'The Members recognize that it serves to preserve the rights and obligations of Members under the covered agreements, and to clarify the existing provisions of those agreements in accordance with customary rules of interpretation of public international law. Recommendations and rulings of the DSB cannot add to or diminish the rights and obligations provided in the covered agreements'.

B. The Evolutionary Approach: Substance and Method

As previously described, WTO Members' dissatisfaction with the 'evolutionary approach' as expressed in DSB meetings was that the Appellate Body had engaged in findings that 'added to or diminished rights and obligations' found in the covered agreements. The validity of these concerns can be ascertained in two ways. First, the merits of the findings: is there ground for the claim that the findings amounted to a modification of the rights and obligations of WTO Members? Second, the method employed: were the interpretative steps followed by the Appellate Body when engaging in the evolutionary approach necessary in reaching a conclusion on the interpretation of the provision?

The first element relates to the substance of the finding. One of the problems relating to the underpinnings of an evolutionary approach to interpretation is the belief that such an approach contradicts the original intent of the treaty's signatories and thus creates new rights or obligations.

In *US – Shrimp*, the Appellate Body noted that the provisions under contention 'were actually crafted more than 50 years ago' and that they should be 'read by a treaty interpreter in the light of contemporary concerns'.[30] With this phrasing, the adjudicators virtually acknowledged that the drafters of the GATT did not have in mind the interpretation that was ultimately given to the meaning of 'exhaustible natural resources' in that report. This arguably amounts to expanding the scope of Article XX(g) (thus 'adding to a right' of those who invoke it, and 'diminishing the rights' of those affected by the measure).

In *China – Publications and Audiovisual Products*, a central part of China's argument was that when it acceded to the WTO, it did not consider electronic forms of sound recordings. Following this logic, deciding otherwise would go against China's initial consent. The Appellate Body could thus not circumvent an evaluation of whether China's entry on its services schedule included sound recordings in electronic form or not. This was a matter of interpretation of the entry. Whether it added to or diminished the rights of the parties depends on whether one agrees that China did not intend non-physical forms of sound recordings to be covered by the entry.[31]

In both cases, the Appellate Body mentioned the term was 'generic',[32] a statement that can potentially give more leeway to judicial activism. Still, the Appellate

[30] WTO Appellate Body Report, *US – Shrimp*, above n 6, para 129.

[31] This problem is accompanied by another question: how far can the parties to a treaty foresee the contours the words they agree on will take with the passage of time? For a take on this matter, see C Marquet, 'Prospective Linguistics and Trade: The Art of the Deal', ch 18 in this book.

[32] WTO Appellate Body Report, *US – Shrimp*, above n 6, para 130; *China – Publications and Audiovisual Products*, above n 9, para 396. For an analysis on the relation between 'generic terms' and evolutionary interpretation, see P Palchetti, 'Interpreting "Generic Terms": Between Respect for the Parties' Original Intention and the Identification of the Ordinary Meaning' in N Boschiero, T Scovazzi, C Ragni and C Pitea (eds), *International Courts and the Development of International Law: Essays in Honour of Tullio Treves* (The Hague, Springer, 2013).

Body had to interpret the meaning of the terms (Article XX(g) and China's GATS Schedule entry) to settle the dispute. In this sense, the findings were not 'unnecessary'. What may have been 'unnecessary' obiter dicta was the statement that the terms under scrutiny could change over time – ie, the rhetoric adopted in the reasoning.[33] In this sense, the second element that should be considered is the method by which the Appellate Body resorted to the evolutionary approach.

In *US – Shrimp*, the Appellate Body acknowledged the international developments that had taken place in more recent decades, and mentioned the preamble of the WTO Agreement and other international conventions to determine the meaning of 'exhaustible natural resources'. As Howse points out, the Appellate Body could have reached the same conclusion resorting only to the preamble and previous GATT decisions, without leaving the WTO framework. In this sense, he argues that perhaps the Appellate Body was 'making a statement' that the relationship between trade and environment should consider the interests of the international community.[34] Considering that the Appellate Body could have adopted a more WTO and VCLT-oriented rhetoric, the findings do seem to amount to unnecessary obiter dicta. The adjudicators chose to state that 'natural resources' was a term, 'by definition, evolutionary'. The ensuing reasoning may thus have enhanced the perception that adjudicators have indulged in activism, while following another interpretative method could have led to the same result.

In *China – Publications and Audiovisual Products*, the Appellate Body resorted to a more nuanced choice of words to assess China's claim that 'sound recording distribution services' did not cover non-physical elements by the time of China's accession. For instance, the report does not explicitly refer to 'evolutionary interpretation'. Furthermore, the adjudicators considered this argument only after going through a number of other interpretative elements (ordinary meaning, object and purpose, and context) when ascertaining the scope of the GATS schedule entry.

However, the Appellate Body still found it useful to point out that adopting China's argument regarding intertemporal interpretation 'would undermine the predictability, security, and clarity of GATS specific commitments, which are undertaken through successive rounds of negotiations'.[35] In this sense, perhaps the Appellate Body was also 'making a statement', one that could have been discarded if the only objective of the report was to ensure the resolution of the dispute rather than the clarification of the law.

[33] Arguing in greater detail that the Appellate Body's recourse to the evolutionary approach in both cases was unnecessary to resolve the case, see ST Helmersen, 'The Evolutionary Treaty Interpretation by the WTO Appellate Body', ch 19 in this book.

[34] R Howse, 'The Use and Abuse of Other "Relevant Rules of International Law" in Treaty Interpretation: Insights from WTO Trade/Environment Litigation' (2007) 1 Institute for International Law and Justice Working Paper 16.

[35] *China – Publications and Audiovisual Products*, above n 9, para 397.

C. Should WTO Adjudicators Avoid an Evolutionary Approach?

A central question to be asked is to what extent WTO adjudicators should actually *avoid* applying the evolutionary approach. With several provisions crafted many years or decades ago, and with the deadlock of new negotiations, it may actually be desirable that panels and the Appellate Body take into consideration the changes that the meaning of a term may have gone through.

Two factors may justify resorting to an evolutionary interpretation. First, new concerns in the international sphere and inside a particular treaty regime may arise, but these can be hard to address since multilateral treaties are difficult to modify.[36] This is particularly so in the case of the WTO legal system, with a membership of 164 State and non-State entities.[37] One can claim that these factors make treaty interpretation all the more important.[38]

Second, the intentions of the parties, regardless of whether they drafted a certain provision as a result of a compromise in negotiations or did not foresee a different applicability to it in the first place, may also change over time. The multilateral trading system comprises provisions that were drafted over five decades ago, during several rounds of negotiations until the creation of the WTO in 1994. In addition, nearly 25 years of changes and developments add to this history.

The desirability of a judicial body – more specifically, the Appellate Body – making findings on the evolution of a term in relation to the parties' original intention may depend on the judicial function one believes such a judicial body should perform. If one sides with the view which defends the strict settlement of disputes, the systemic impact of considering current concerns within the scope of old texts may be undesirable. On the other hand, the evolutionary approach may serve as a valuable tool to clarify the law in light of the changes in the international background – such as environmental concerns.[39] In this sense, if one believes the judicial function is to also clarify (and even develop) the law for the benefit of the entire system, the evolutionary approach may serve as a valuable tool.

Therefore, evolutionary interpretation may be desirable to clarify WTO law and to address the rise of new, originally unforeseen concerns. On the other hand, from a legitimacy point of view, it may be unwelcome when viewed as judicial activism. In the context of the WTO that can be the case if, in the view of the

[36] A Aust, *Modern Treaty Law and Practice*, 3rd edn (Cambridge, Cambridge University Press, 2013) 232.

[37] Art X of the Agreement Establishing the World Trade Organization sets out the procedure for amendment of the WTO agreements.

[38] See G Marceau, 'Evolutive Interpretation by the WTO Adjudicator: Sophism or Necessity?' (2018) 21 *Journal of International Economic Law* 791.

[39] For other instances of how evolutionary interpretation can take into consideration unforeseen concerns, see J Grigorova, 'Energy Trade in the WTO, Yesterday, Today and Tomorrow: The Role of Evolutionary Interpretation', ch 22 in this book.

membership, it either adds to or diminishes rights and obligations of the Members or amounts to unnecessary findings.

To some extent, the perception of judicial activism can be regulated by the reasoning expressed in the reports. As Marceau submits, there are different 'categories' under which an evolutionary approach can be advanced in the adjudicator's reasoning.[40] An evolutionary interpretation can be taken by means of more nuanced hermeneutics than, for instance, explicitly asserting that the meaning of the terms changed over time.[41] Van den Bossche explains in his contribution to this volume that the evolutionary approach has been applied by the Appellate Body as a 'result of a proper application of the VCLT rules of interpretation'.[42] Nevertheless, even when based on VCLT rules of treaty interpretation, adjudicators can resort to different approaches that can lead to an evolutionary interpretation

A subtler rhetoric should focus on the ordinary meaning, object and purpose, and context (the general rule of interpretation in Article 31 of the VCLT), while references to the parties' intention according to a treaty's drafting history should serve only as a supplementary means of interpretation (Article 32 of the VCLT).[43] In other words, interpretation based on the text of the WTO agreements should be given priority, while contrasting the 'new' meaning and the one which could have been envisaged at the time of the drafting should be avoided.[44] Among the elements to be considered according to this textual approach are other WTO provisions, the preamble, as well as dictionary-based readings of the ordinary meaning.

Moreover, there is also a variation of subjectivity within the elements of the general rule of Article 31 of the VCLT. As an illustration, the approach taken by the *US – Shrimp* report was perhaps more subject to criticism by the concerned parties than the one in *China – Publications and Audiovisual Products* because of

[40] Marceau, 'Evolutive Interpretation by the WTO Adjudicator', above n 38. She identifies four methods by which WTO adjudicators have advanced the evolutionary approach: i. generic terms in connection with the intention of the parties; ii. the ordinary meaning of the terms in their 'context'; iii. treaty object and purpose; iv. in relation to related (subsequent agreements and practice) and relevant international law.

[41] See E Bjorge, *The Evolutionary Interpretation of Treaties* (Oxford, Oxford University Press, 2014) ch 3.

[42] See Van den Bossche, above n 18.

[43] As Djeffal argues in this book, 'the travaux préparatoires carry by definition less argumentative weight'. The author also submits that the technique codified by the VCLT makes it 'possible to avoid the difficult questions and intricacies in the debate between objective and subjective interpretation that have existed for a long time'. Put differently, following the general rule of interpretation allows the treaty interpreter to circumvent having to state that it is opting for a subjective or objective approach. See C Djeffal, 'An Interpreter's Guide to Static and Evolutive Interpretations: Solving Intertemporal Problems According to the VCLT', ch 4 in this book.

[44] In the same sense, Palchetti elucidates that 'The presumed intention is deduced from objective factors which are substantially the same factors on which one should rely when interpreting a treaty according to the general criterion stated in the Vienna Convention' (Palchetti, above n 32, 104). On the different 'schools of interpretation' and WTO practice, see generally I Van Damme, *Treaty Interpretation by the WTO Appellate Body* (Oxford, Oxford University Press, 2009) ch 2.

the Appellate Body's choice of words ('generic terms' which were 'by definition, evolutionary'), and reference to non-WTO law (Article 31(3)(c)).[45] If the WTO adjudicator focuses on the ordinary meaning of a word by means of a dictionary approach, for example, instead of how this meaning can be ascertained in light of other non-WTO law and 'contemporary concerns', the perception of activism may be lessened.[46]

IV. Conclusion

Evolutionary interpretation is not explicitly listed as one of the Appellate Body practices that has contributed to the legitimacy crisis surrounding this organ. However, the choice of words in the reasonings examined here may have contributed, directly or indirectly, to the perception that the Appellate Body is overstepping its mandate and being activist in its findings.

Whether it is desirable to adopt an evolutionary interpretation is a question open to debate. It was argued here that while it may be desirable for policy reasons, it is also possible to address such reasons through a more nuanced interpretative approach than explicitly resorting to the evolutionary one. WTO Members may perceive explicit references to evolutionary interpretation as a statement that the parties' original intention should be relativised. This is a critical assumption given the reasons triggering the crisis in the WTO dispute settlement.

This contribution examined one aspect of treaty interpretation among many that may have given rise to the discontent towards the WTO Appellate Body. Regardless of the future of WTO dispute settlement, it is clear that there is a general need to overhaul the decision-making process beyond written procedural limits.

The solution to this problem is also a question of approach to the judicial function of the Appellate Body: should the Appellate Body 'merely' settle disputes between the parties or should it also clarify the law of the multilateral trading system by taking into account systemic concerns (such as the relationship between trade and environment and trade and new technologies)? Irrespective of one's theoretical view of the WTO dispute settlement function, the practice of

[45] For an analysis of how international tribunals make their 'interpretative choice', see H Lauterpacht, 'Restrictive Interpretation and the Principle of Effectiveness in the Interpretation of Treaties' (1949) 26 *The British Year Book of International Law* 48; J Pauwelyn and M Elsig, 'The Politics of Treaty Interpretation: Variations and Explanations Across International Tribunals' in JL Dunoff and MA Pollack (eds), *Interdisciplinary Perspectives on International Law and International Relations: The State of the Art* (Cambridge, Cambridge University Press, 2012). For the particular context of WTO dispute settlement on the matter, see I Van Damme, 'Understanding the Choice for Evolutionary Interpretation', ch 16 in this book.

[46] On the role of subsequent practice for an evolutionary approach by the WTO Appellate Body, see G Nolte, 'Subsequent Practice as a Means of Interpretation in the Jurisprudence of the WTO Appellate Body' in E Cannizzaro (ed), *The Law of Treaties Beyond the Vienna Convention* (Oxford, Oxford University Press, 2011) 144.

any international court must find support from its addressees. If this element is ignored, its legitimacy will be undermined and its existence may be threatened.

While in its early years it may have been useful for the Appellate Body to issue a 'declaration of independence' in relation to the trade law community,[47] now it is certainly more prudent to follow a more restrained rhetoric of treaty interpretation. One may conclude that, in fact, perhaps the role of an international court vis-a-vis its addressees is also, 'by definition, evolutionary'.

[47] See R Howse, 'The World Trade Organization 20 Years On: Global Governance by Judiciary' (2016) 27 *European Journal of International Law* 9.

22

Energy Trade in the WTO, Yesterday, Today and Tomorrow: The Role of Evolutionary Interpretation

JENYA GRIGOROVA*

I. Introduction

Energy trade is a polarised topic. Energy resources are unevenly distributed, but universally needed. Cross-border trade in energy materials and products, and in electricity, is crucial for resource-rich, energy-importing and transit countries alike.

The energy sector is subject to intense regulation at the domestic level, often in pursuit of secure and affordable access to energy, combined with environmental policy objectives. At the international level, energy trade is a field of unavoidable cooperation. Thus, energy issues touch the very heart of a nation's sovereignty.[1]

Policy choices in the sector reflect a combination, ideally a balance, between environmental, social, political and security concerns. *Environmental* concerns disfavour trade in fossil fuels, and in goods manufactured or transported using fossil fuels, and promote alternative energy sources, environmental goods and high energy standards. *Social and political* concerns explain political economy choices with respect to fair competition on the energy market and access to affordable energy. *Energy security* concerns govern the quest for diversification of supplies (ie, the availability of energy at the place of final consumption at affordable prices, in sufficient quantities and at the moment of need, so that the economic and social development of the country is not halted), or of export markets.[2] The pursuit of

* The author is grateful to Professor Gabrielle Marceau for the invaluable support and reviews, and to Svetlana Chobanova, Dr Dominic Coppens, Clément Marquet, Dr Bregt Natens, Edoardo Stoppioni and Dr Claus Zimmermann for their input and reviews of earlier drafts.

[1] See J Pauwelyn, 'Global Challenges at the Intersection of Trade, Energy and the Environment: An Introduction' in J Pauwelyn (ed), *Global Challenges at the Intersection of Trade, Energy and the Environment* (Geneva, The Graduate Institute, 2010).

[2] The concept of energy security reflects 'the availability of usable energy supplies, at the point of final consumption, at economic price levels and in sufficient quantities and timeliness, so that, given

these objectives often leads to sophisticated domestic policies and measures that may be difficult to reconcile with the objectives of free trade.

For a long time, the General Agreement on Tariffs and Trade (GATT) and World Trade Organization (WTO) dispute settlement systems only rarely dealt with disputes directly related to energy measures,[3] although they did deal with multiple disputes regarding natural resources, some of which concerned energy-related products.[4] Recently, however, WTO Members have started challenging the compatibility of energy measures with various WTO agreements. The WTO panels and Appellate Body (collectively, WTO adjudicator) have to apply the existing provisions, which, arguably, were not negotiated with the specificities of the energy sector in mind.[5]

This chapter suggests that in addressing its task, the WTO adjudicator has – more or less consciously – used an evolutionary approach in interpreting WTO rules and applying them to the energy sector.

The chapter refers to 'trade in energy', or 'energy trade' in a broad sense, covering trade in energy resources (fossil fuels and renewables) and electricity. It focuses on the energy sector as an example, because energy trade is illustrative of the interactions between the objectives of free trade, on the one hand, and sector-specific environmental, policy and security objectives, on the other hand. When considering the compatibility of energy-related measures with WTO rules and disciplines, the adjudicator interprets, in very concrete terms, how these concerns interact with the objective of free trade.

This chapter starts with an analysis of the way the WTO adjudicator addresses energy-related concerns today, with a focus on detecting traces of evolutionary interpretation or application (section II). It then tentatively suggests that in the absence of energy-specific rules, in the future an evolutionary approach to the interpretation and application of the general WTO rules to energy trade might assist the WTO adjudicator in the difficult task of adjusting the application of these rules to the specificities of energy trade (section III).

due regard to encouraging energy efficiency, the economic and social development of a country is not materially constrained' (United Nations Economic Commission for Europe, *Emerging Global Energy Security Risks* (2007) 8).

[3] During the GATT-era and the first years of the WTO, only three cases directly concerned energy trade: GATT Panel Reports, *United States – Taxes on Petroleum and Certain Imported Substances*, adopted 17 June 1987, L/6175 – 34S/136, and *United States – Taxes on Automobiles*, unadopted, circulated 11 October 1994, DS31/R; and WTO Appellate Body Report, *United States – Standards for Reformulated and Conventional Gasoline* (*US – Gasoline*) adopted 20 May 1996, WT/DS2/AB/R.

[4] See WTO Panel Reports, *China – Measures Related to the Exportation of Various Raw Materials* (*China – Raw Materials*) adopted 22 February 2012, WT/DS394/R / WT/DS395/R / WT/DS398/R, fn 607 to para 7.381.

[5] See G Marceau, 'The WTO in the Emerging Energy Governance Debate' (2010) 5 *Global Trade and Customs Journal* 93.

II. Energy Trade in the WTO Today

A. Lack of Energy-Specific Rules

The recent surge of energy-related cases in the WTO shows that energy trade undoubtedly falls within the scope of WTO law,[6] although this has been debated in the past.[7] WTO rules apply to energy trade, but the way in which sectoral specificities are or should be reflected in the application of these rules is still subject to discussions. Some have argued that WTO rules are not necessarily adapted to tackle energy-specific issues.[8]

However, the WTO system currently contains no energy-specific rules. To the extent that energy resources are products, energy trade falls within the ambit of the general rules on trade in goods, including those on subsidies.[9]

To the extent that energy-related activities are services, they are covered by the disciplines of the General Agreement on Trade in Services (GATS) (except those supplied in the exercise of governmental authority). An additional hurdle in applying the GATS to the energy sector lies in the lack of a distinct comprehensive category for energy services. The generally accepted classification of services in the Sectoral Classification List (W/120) contains only subsectors which are either directly related to energy activities,[10] or could potentially cover such activities.[11] This lack of a comprehensive category for 'energy services' creates uncertainty in the application of the specific obligations due to the difficulties in identifying and interpreting the specific commitments covering each energy-related activity.[12]

[6] See WTO Appellate Body Reports, *Canada – Certain Measures Affecting the Renewable Energy Generation Sector / Canada – Measures Relating to the Feed-in Tariff Program (Canada – Renewable Energy / Canada – Feed-In Tariff Program)* adopted 24 May 2013, WT/DS412/AB/R / WT/DS426/AB/R; WTO Appellate Body Report, *India – Certain Measures Relating to Solar Cells and Solar Modules (India – Solar Cells)* adopted 14 October 2016, WT/DS456/AB/R; WTO Panel Report, *European Union and its member States – Certain Measures Relating to the Energy Sector (EU – Energy Package)* circulated 10 August 2018, WT/DS476/R.

[7] See, eg, WC Shih, 'Energy Security, GATT/WTO, and Regional Agreements' (2009) 49 *Natural Resources Journal* 433, 439; or E Harks, 'The International Energy Forum and the Mitigation of Oil Market Risks' in A Goldthau and JM Witte (eds), *Global Energy Governance: The New Rules of the Game* (Global Public Policy Institute and Brookings Institution Press, 2010) 248.

[8] For discussions on this point, see, eg, Y Selivanova, 'The WTO Agreements and Energy' in K Talus (ed), *Research Handbook on International Energy Law* (Cheltenham, Edward Elgar Publishing, 2014); or Marceau, above n 5.

[9] See Marceau, above n 5, 84.

[10] Namely, services incidental to mining, services incidental to energy distribution, and the pipeline transportation of fuels.

[11] For instance, road, rail or maritime transport, distribution, construction, engineering and consulting.

[12] For further details on this point, see M Cossy, 'Energy Services Under the General Agreement on Trade in Services' in Y Selivanova (ed), *Regulation of Energy in International Trade Law: WTO, NAFTA and Energy Charter* (United Kingdom, Wolters Kluwer, 2011); I Muselli and S Zarrilli, 'Oil And Gas

It is also worth noting that some energy-related issues have been dealt with in the context of accession negotiations, with acceding countries undertaking commitments with respect to export duties,[13] transit,[14] or, to some extent, dual pricing.[15]

B. Energy Trade Before the WTO Adjudicator: Evolutionary Approaches

In order to address the issues before it in an energy-related case, the WTO adjudicator has to interpret and apply the relevant rules, and in this process needs to accommodate the specificities of the energy sector and the multilayered rationales behind energy measures. On some of these occasions, an evolutionary approach allows the adjudicator to 'ensure that international law takes account of the ever-changing circumstances in which it is applied'.[16]

Today, it is undisputed that energy trade falls within the ambit of WTO law. This was probably not envisaged at the time of drafting of the GATT. Neither the rules of the GATT, nor those introduced upon the creation of the WTO were initially designed to address energy issues per se.[17] Nevertheless, the WTO adjudicator has applied the general rules to energy trade in a series of cases.

In *US – Gasoline*, the panel and the Appellate Body asserted the applicability of the general rules on non-discrimination, in particular Article III:4 of the GATT 1994, to US regulations aimed at controlling toxic and other pollution caused by the combustion of gasoline. The Appellate Body took a further step towards ensuring that the general rules are adjusted to the underlying rationales of energy policies, when it held that clean air is an exhaustible natural resource within the meaning of Article XX(g) of the GATT.[18] This finding can be attributed to a value-driven evolutionary interpretation of the legal texts, leading to a broader integration of energy-related environmental concerns. It would allow

Services – Market Liberalization and the Ongoing GATS Negotiations' (2005) 8 *Journal of International Economic Law* 551.

[13] See WTO, *World Trade Report 2010: Trade in Natural Resources* (WTO, 2010) 184; and P Milthorp and D Christy, 'Energy Issues in Selected WTO Accessions' in Y Selivanova (ed), *Regulation of Energy in International Trade Law: WTO, NAFTA and Energy Charter* (United Kingdom, Wolters Kluwer, 2011).

[14] See M Cossy, 'Energy Trade and WTO Rules: Reflexions on Sovereignty over Natural Resources, Export Restrictions and Freedom of Transit' (2012) *European Yearbook of International Economic Law* 281, 300.

[15] Dual pricing was one of the key issues discussed during Russia's accession negotiations. See V Pogoretskyy and S Melnyk, 'Russian Energy and the WTO: Overview of the Accession Negotiations of the Russian Federation and Final Commitments' (2018) 1 *Oil, Gas & Energy Law*.

[16] See P Van den Bossche, 'Is there Evolution in the Evolutionary Interpretation of WTO Law?', ch 20 in this book.

[17] Marceau, above n 5, 83.

[18] WTO Appellate Body Report, *US – Gasoline*, above n 3, 15–18.

governments, in the context of climate change programmes, to treat differently products that are otherwise similar, by introducing appropriate regulatory distinctions based on environmental considerations such as the CO_2 content level.[19]

In *China – Rare Earths* and *China – Raw Materials* the panels and the Appellate Body further acknowledged that Articles III and XI of the GATT 1994, as well as the exceptions of Article XX of the GATT 1994, apply to energy-related products.

More recently, in *Canada – Renewable Energy/Feed-in Tariff*, the WTO adjudicator acknowledged the relevance of the GATT 1994 and the Agreement on Subsidies and Countervailing Measures to trade in electricity. In this case, the Province of Ontario was buying electricity from generators at a favourable price if these generators had purchased part of their energy equipment from local suppliers. The panel and the Appellate Body first accepted to apply the relevant WTO rules to trade in electricity. This choice can be attributed to an evolutionary interpretation of the generic term 'goods'. At the time of negotiation of the GATT, energy resources, like oil or natural gas, and energy-related products and materials, like petrochemicals, were already considered goods. However, the same cannot be said for electricity. Without engaging in this debate, the panel and Appellate Body in *Canada – Renewable Energy/Feed-in Tariff* considered that the Feed-in Tariff Programme at issue, which concerned the purchase of *electricity*, could potentially be qualified as a government purchase of *goods*.[20]

In the context of identifying market benchmarks to determine whether a benefit was conferred, the panel and the Appellate Body faced a situation where the market was entirely created by government intervention. The Appellate Body held that '[w]here a government creates a market, it cannot be said that the government intervention distorts the market, as there would not be a market if the government had not created it'.[21] This approach can also be characterised as evolutionary: such a market entirely created by government intervention might not have been conceivable at the time of conclusion of the GATT, but the WTO adjudicator needed to give consideration to this situation in order to uphold the object and purpose of the GATT.

Finally, the panel report in *EU – Energy Package* provides the most recent example of the WTO adjudicator applying the general rules to energy trade. In this case, the European Union (EU) sought to ensure a separation of the functions of natural gas transmission, production and supply. The panel's struggle to adjust

[19] Marceau, above n 5, 84.

[20] WTO Panel Reports, *Canada – Certain Measures Affecting the Renewable Energy Generation Sector/ Canada – Measures Relating to the Feed-in Tariff Program (Canada – Renewable Energy/Canada – Feed-In Tariff Program)* adopted 24 May 2013, WT/DS412/R / WT/DS426/R, para 7.136, on a point confirmed by the Appellate Body.

[21] WTO Appellate Body Reports, *Canada – Renewable Energy / Feed-in Tariff Program*, above n 6, para 5.188. See for further details HB Asmelash, 'Energy Subsidies and WTO Dispute Settlement: Why Only Renewable Energy Subsidies Are Challenged' (2015) 18 *Journal of International Economic Law*, 272.

the application of the general rules to the specificities of the energy sector was clear in its approach to the GATS and the GATT 1994 exceptions.

First, the EU raised an Article XIV(a) of the GATS defence in response to Russia's claim that the requirement for a 'security of energy supply' assessment prior to the certification of third-country transmission system operators, but not domestic ones ('third-country certification measure'), constituted a breach of Article XVII of the GATS. The EU claimed that security of energy supply is a 'fundamental interest of society', covered by the concept of 'public order' in Article XIV(a) of the GATS, as clarified by footnote 5.[22] Russia argued that the EU's definition of energy security was too unclear and inconsistent, and did not allow the WTO adjudicator to assess whether it amounted to a fundamental interest of society.[23] The panel disagreed, and by doing so, seems to have laid the grounds for future evolutionary interpretation. It held that 'a certain minimum level of clarity is required to meaningfully assess whether a stated interest can be considered fundamental', but that the required level of clarity should not be 'overly demanding'.[24] This balancing exercise might lead future panels (if they choose to follow it) to an interpretation of the term 'fundamental' giving a generic word such as 'fundamental' a broader meaning than the one originally envisaged by the negotiators.

The panel, however, was reluctant to pursue an evolutionary approach further. In particular, the EU suggested references to definitions of energy security from other fora (International Energy Agency, United Nations Economic Commission for Europe), thus calling for an evolutionary interpretation of footnote 5. The panel, however, chose a different path, and focused mainly on the specific characteristics of the gas sector.[25] The panel also had an opportunity to interpret in an evolutionary manner the term 'threat'. The EU claimed there was a potential threat that foreign governments may have incentives to undermine the security of energy supply when their interests conflict.[26] This claim could have served as a starting point to interpret the word 'threat', at least in the energy context, giving it a very broad sense not envisaged by the GATT negotiators, in order to preserve the effectiveness of the object and the purpose of the provisions applied to energy trade. While cautiously distancing itself from a suggestion that the right of a foreign government to act in the best interests of its citizens, in and of itself, should be considered a threat to the EU's energy security, the panel agreed that the EU's concern was not mere conjecture or speculation.[27]

Second, in *EU – Energy Package*, the EU also raised a security-related defence with respect to the TEN-E (Trans-European Networks for Energy) measure, which

[22] fn 5 reads as follows: 'The public order exception may be invoked only where a genuine and sufficiently serious threat is posed to one of the fundamental interests of society'.

[23] WTO Panel Report, *EU – Energy Package*, above n 6, para 7.1149.

[24] ibid, para 7.1153.

[25] ibid, para 7.1179.

[26] ibid, para 7.1175.

[27] ibid.

provided incentives for infrastructure projects of common interest. The EU argued that this measure was essential to the acquisition or distribution of products in short supply and was justified under Article XX(j) of the GATT. This provision allows for measures 'essential to the acquisition or distribution of products in general or local short supply', if they are 'discontinued as soon as the conditions giving rise to them have ceased to exist' and 'consistent with the principle that all contracting parties are entitled to an equitable share of the international supply of such products'.

Relying on the Appellate Body's recent holding in *India – Solar Cells* that Article XX(j) requires 'a careful scrutiny of the relationship between supply and demand based on a holistic consideration of trends in supply and demand as they evolve over time, as well as whether the conditions giving rise to short supply have ceased to exist',[28] the panel in *EU – Energy Package* focused on the specific characteristics of the gas sector and adopted a very broad interpretation of 'short supply'.[29] Although the panel referred to energy security as a possible rationale behind a measure potentially justifiable under Article XX(j) of the GATT, here again, the panel's holding fell short of an evolutionary interpretation of the words 'short supply', which would have allowed for incorporating into the reading of the words 'short supply' an element of risk that might not have been initially associated with the concept of shortage.[30] In light of the volatilities of the energy market, the interdependence of the actors, and the risk of shortages due to political crises, such an evolutionary interpretation might have allowed for greater flexibilities.

These examples prove that the WTO adjudicator is no stranger to evolutionary interpretation (in its broadest sense) when it comes to applying the WTO rules and disciplines to energy trade. Keeping an open mind for potential evolutionary interpretation of the existing provisions might be the best, if not the only, way to accommodate the rapidly changing landscape of varied energy policies and to ensure that these policies remain in harmony with WTO obligations.

III. Energy Trade in the WTO Tomorrow

A. Negotiating Energy-Specific Rules

In the absence of energy-specific rules, the WTO adjudicator interprets the general rules and applies them to energy trade. However, it has been suggested that it may

[28] WTO Appellate Body Report, *India – Solar Cells*, above n 6, para 5.70.

[29] WTO Panel Report, *EU – Energy Package*, above n 6, para 7.1344.

[30] Art XX(j) was drafted to achieve the equitable distribution of products in short supply after the end of the war, rather than to address future risks of short supply (see GATT Analytical Index (pre-1995) 592).

be advisable to adopt a separate agreement in the sector. Recent proposals, essentially in legal scholarship, include a 'General Agreement on Trade in Energy',[31] a 'Framework Agreement on Energy within WTO law',[32] or – more restrictively – a 'Sustainable Energy Trade Agreement'.[33] It has also been suggested that energy services require additional disciplines on domestic regulation and competition.[34]

Very few of these proposals have been sufficiently laid out, proving that there is a long way to go before energy-specific rules are negotiated and included in the WTO framework, if ever. In the meanwhile, the main role is left to the WTO adjudicator who, it seems, will be called upon ever more often to assess the compatibility of energy measures with the general rules of the WTO.

B. The Inevitable Role of the WTO Adjudicator in the Energy Debate

The WTO adjudicator plays an active role in the energy debate. This might create tensions and meet reluctance from WTO Members, deeply attached to the political aspects of the sector. Admittedly, the combination of environmental, policy and security concerns characterising energy trade was conceivable at the time of the conclusion of the WTO agreements. However, evolutionary interpretation can also reflect the growing role of judges, in areas that were previously considered outside their sphere of influence. Indeed, WTO Members are bringing an increasing number of energy-related cases before the WTO adjudicator, with fully-fledged arguments focused entirely on measures reflecting sensitive choices in the area of energy policy. Although energy was never excluded from the ambit of the multilateral trading system, it is only now that the WTO adjudicator is being called upon to examine energy policies on such a large scale.

The WTO adjudicator is, though, only an interpreter, 'someone who tries to explain what other people have drafted',[35] and Article 3.2 of the Dispute Settlement Understanding is there 'to avoid the Appellate Body members incurring the temptation to become legislators'.[36] Recourse to evolutionary interpretation can thus serve as a tool for auto-control, whereby the WTO adjudicator attentively

[31] Pauwelyn, 'Global Challenges at the Intersection of Trade, Energy and the Environment: An Introduction' above n 1, 7.

[32] T Cottier et al, 'Energy in WTO Law and Policy' in T Cottier and P Delimatsis (eds), *The Prospects of International Trade Regulation* (United Kingdom, Cambridge University Press, 2011).

[33] J Bacchus, 'A Way Forward for the WTO' in R Melender-Ortiz, C Bellmann and M Rodriguez-Mendoza (eds), *The Future And The WTO: Confronting The Challenges (A Collection Of Short Essays)* (Geneva, ICTSD, 2012).

[34] Marceau, above n 5, 84.

[35] LO Baptista, 'Interpretation and application of WTO Rules: Florentino Feliciano and the First Seven' in S Charnovitz, D Steger and P Van den Bossche (eds), *Law in the Service of Human Dignity: Essays in Honour of Florentino Feliciano* (Cambridge, Cambridge University Press, 2005) 130.

[36] ibid, 129.

takes into consideration the multifaceted and politically sensitive nature of energy policies. This would in turn guarantee that their immersion in energy-related questions is less controversial, and more acceptable to the WTO membership.

An interesting example of this would be the approach to border tax adjustments in the energy sector. Energy policies aimed at reducing use of fossil fuels often take the shape of carbon taxes or emission trading systems (ETS).[37] These systems work on a 'cap and trade' principle. Within the 'cap', ie, the total amount of certain greenhouse gases that can be emitted, companies receive or buy emissions allowances. At the end of a certain period, companies are then required to surrender enough allowances to cover their emissions. If they reduce their emissions, they can sell the allowances ('trade'). This creates a market for allowances, which, much as the market for renewable electricity generation, is created entirely by governmental intervention.

Although the EU's ETS has not yet been subject to border tax adjustments, some commentators have discussed the possibility.[38] Article II:2(a) of the GATT allows for border tax adjustments under certain conditions. For this provision to cover ETS, an evolutionary interpretation of the terms 'charge' and 'internal tax' would be required. Traditionally, a tax is seen as a compulsory contribution imposed by the government for which taxpayers receive nothing identifiable in return,[39] while a 'charge' is 'a 'pecuniary burden' and a 'liability to pay money laid on a person'.[40] An ETS consists rather of an allocation of allowances, coupled with a requirement to surrender the same, or lower, quantity at the end of a set period. Such a system did not exist at the time of the negotiation of the GATT, and would probably not be what the negotiators considered a 'tax'. In fact, companies have enough flexibility to adjust their compliance costs by using different strategies leading to different costs.[41] It can, however, be argued that the cost associated with the obligation to surrender allowances, and the associated fines if the obligation is not met, could qualify as a tax.[42] If the WTO adjudicator were to accept such a logic, this would involve an evolutionary interpretation of the term 'tax'.

[37] See, eg, Directive 2003/87/EC of the European Parliament and of the Council of 13 October 2003 establishing a scheme for greenhouse gas emission allowance trading within the Community and amending Council Directive 96/61/EC.

[38] See K Holzer, 'Proposals on Carbon-related Border Adjustments: Prospects for WTO Compliance' (2010) 51 *Carbon & Climate Law Review* 51, 56; J De Cendra, 'Can Emissions Trading Schemes be Coupled with Border Tax Adjustments? An Analysis vis-à-vis WTO Law' (2006) 15 *Review of European, Comparative & International Environmental Law* 131; F Sindico, 'The EU and Carbon Leakage: How to Reconcile Border Adjustments with the WTO?' (2008) *European Energy and Environmental Law Review* 328, 332.

[39] J Pauwelyn, 'US Federal Climate Policy and Competitiveness Concerns: The Limits and Options of International Trade Law' (2007) Nicholas Institute for Environmental Policy Solutions, Duke University, NI Working Paper WP 07-02, 21, referring to R Ismer and K Neuhoff, 'Border Tax Adjustments: A Feasible Way to Address Nonparticipation in Emission Trading' (2004) 36 *CMI Working Paper* 1, 11.

[40] WTO Panel Report, *Argentina – Measures Affecting the Export of Bovine Hides and the Import of Finished Leather (Argentina – Hides and Leather)* adopted 16 February 2001, WT/DS155/R, para 11.143.

[41] See Holzer, above n 38, 57.

[42] Pauwelyn, 'US Federal Climate Policy and Competitiveness Concerns', above n 39, 21.

IV. Conclusion

In the absence of energy-specific rules in the WTO framework, the WTO adjudicator interprets and applies the general WTO rules to the field of energy. It is argued that in this context, the WTO adjudicator has already adopted a de facto evolutionary approach, asserting that energy trade falls within the scope of these rules. Pursuing such an approach might allow for further flexibilities and stabilise the growing role of the WTO adjudicator in the energy debate. Ultimately, this would reflect an effort to ensure that WTO law remains 'relevant and effective over time',[43] when applied to energy trade.

[43] I Van Damme, 'Understanding the Choice for Evolutionary Interpretation', ch 16 in this book.

PART V

Evolutionary Interpretation in ISDS Law

23

Evolutionary Interpretation in Investment Arbitration: About a Judicial Taboo

MAKANE MOÏSE MBENGUE AND AIKATERINI FLOROU

I. Introduction

The evolutionary interpretation of treaties is a phenomenon that has marked the practice of international courts and tribunals. A classic case where the International Court of Justice (ICJ) engaged in evolutionary interpretation is the *Costa Rica v Nicaragua* case.[1] In interpreting the phrase 'for the purposes of commerce' in the 1858 Treaty of Limits between Costa Rica and Nicaragua, the Court equalled evolutionary interpretation with temporal variations of treaty terms based on the parties' intent. Disagreeing with Nicaragua's contemporaneity argument, the Court held that, because the parties had used generic terms in their treaty, they had been aware that the meaning of those terms would evolve over time. Thus, their intention must have been to update such meaning every time the treaty is applied. Moreover, the Court considered this intent to be buttressed by the object of the treaty, which was to resolve the parties' territorial disputes permanently.[2]

Generic terms are also widespread in international investment agreements (IIAs). Provisions regarding the 'promotion', 'protection' and 'treatment' of investments, or 'umbrella clauses', all include generic terms. For instance, in *Daimler v Argentina*, an International Centre for Settlement of Investment

[1] *Dispute Regarding Navigational and Related Rights (Costa Rica v Nicaragua)* (Judgment) [2009] ICJ Rep 213.

[2] ibid, paras 64, 66, 70, 79. The ICJ's evolutionary interpretative approach was confirmed in the *Pulp Mills* case. See *Pulp Mills on the River Uruguay (Argentina v Uruguay)* (Judgment) [2010] ICJ Rep 14, para 204. See also P Van den Bossche, 'Is there Evolution in the Evolutionary Interpretation of WTO Law?', ch 16 in this book.

Disputes (ICSID) tribunal was confronted with the generic nature of the word 'treatment'.[3] On the one hand, the majority adopted the principle of contemporaneity to establish the meaning of the term holding that

> treatment was likely meant by the two State Parties, at the time of the conclusion of the BIT, to refer to the host State's direct treatment of the investment and not to the conduct of any international arbitration arising out of that treatment.[4]

On the other hand, Judge Charles Brower issued a Dissenting Opinion, disagreeing with the majority's construction of the term, counter-arguing that the relationship between an investor's treatment by the host State and dispute settlement is *today* well established both under the World Bank's Guidelines and under general international law.[5]

If generic terms are widely used in IIAs, why have investment tribunals been reluctant to admit that they often engage in an evolutionary interpretation of these terms? This chapter aims to shed some light on the phenomenon of evolutionary interpretation in international investment arbitration by proceeding as follows: the first section sketches out the reasons why arbitral tribunals avoid making references to evolutionary interpretation. The second section explores the drivers behind evolutionary interpretation and its different types in the context of investment arbitration. Last, the third section maps out the effects that this interpretative approach has in international investment arbitration.

II. Evolutionary Interpretation as a 'Taboo' in International Investment Arbitration?

To date, there has been no comprehensive scholarly work dealing with the evolutionary interpretation of IIAs by arbitral tribunals. This is perhaps mainly because investment tribunals have scarcely dealt with evolutionary interpretation in practice. It is therefore legitimate to wonder why arbitral tribunals are reluctant to refer to the concept, although evolutionary interpretation does sometimes occur in this context, and one may even say that it is an inherent feature of investment treaty interpretation.

There are two main reasons why arbitral tribunals are not keen on admitting that they engage in evolutionary interpretation.

First, they want to convince themselves that they are exercising judicial restraint, that they are deferential to the *loi des parties*, and do not lapse into judicial activism.[6] By doing so, they attempt at pre-empting criticism by a tribunal

[3] *Daimler Financial Services AG v Argentine Republic*, ICSID Case No ARB/05/1, Award, 22 August 2012.

[4] ibid, para 224.

[5] ibid, Dissenting Opinion of Judge Charles Brower, paras 19–20.

[6] On this point, see also MC de Andrade, 'Evolutionary Interpretation and the Appellate Body's Existential Crisis', ch 21 in this book.

member who might not want to subscribe to the majority position of his or her co-arbitrators. For instance, in his Dissenting Opinion in the *Abaclat* case,[7] Professor Abi-Saab criticised the tribunal for judicial innovation and improvisation for asserting jurisdiction over class actions and devising *proprio motu* procedural rules to address such claims.[8]

Pedro Nikken also wrote a dissenting opinion accusing an investment tribunal of disguised recourse to evolutionary interpretation in the *Aguas Argentinas* case.[9] Arbitrator Nikken disagreed with the tribunal's (and previous tribunals') interpretation of the fair and equitable treatment standard (FET) as encompassing the 'legitimate expectations' of the investor, arguing that such interpretation goes beyond the normal meaning of the terms of the BITs and the intention of the parties. He also pointed in this regard to the interpretative statement of the North American Free Trade Agreement (NAFTA) State parties as a reaction to what they considered an incorrect interpretation by some tribunals of the FET standard.[10]

Secondly, there is another – more technical – reason why tribunals are reluctant to admit that they often adopt an evolutionary interpretation of the treaty at stake in an investment arbitration case. Investment awards can be subject to annulment under the ICSID Convention or be challenged before domestic courts when they result from ad hoc arbitral proceedings as in the case of arbitration conducted under United Nations Commission on International Trade Law (UNCITRAL) rules. As opposed to the judgments of other international adjudicatory bodies, like the ICJ or the International Tribunal for the Law of the Sea, the risk with arbitral awards is that they might be set aside or annulled because of a failure to state reasons, should the tribunals 'confess' that they engaged in evolutionary interpretation not based on detailed reasoning, thus exceeding their powers.

As a result, instead of admitting that they resort to evolutionary interpretation, arbitral tribunals prefer to use more neutral language. For example, in addition to the three traditional international law criteria of 'investment', ie, contribution of capital, risk, and duration, several tribunals have added as a fourth criterion the significant contribution to the economic development of the host State. In particular the *Salini* tribunal, considering that the three-prong test left the definition of 'investment' incomplete, added the fourth prong after examination of the ICSID Convention's preamble, which makes specific reference to the role of

[7] *Abaclat and Others v Argentine Republic*, ICSID Case No ARB/07/5, Decision on Jurisdiction and Admissibility, 4 August 2011.

[8] ibid, Dissenting Opinion of Professor Georges Abi-Saab, para 4.

[9] *Suez, Sociedad General de Aguas de Barcelona SA, and Vivendi Universal SA v The Argentine Republic*, ICSID Case No ARB/03/19, Decision on Liability, 30 July 2010.

[10] ibid, Separate Opinion of Arbitrator Pedro Nikken, paras 2 and 6. For a detailed discussion of the role of interpretative statements by means of State party pleadings, see K Magraw, 'Role of State Party Pleadings in the Evolutionary Interpretation of International Investment Agreements', ch 24 in this book.

foreign direct investment in the host States' economic development.[11] This fourth criterion has, thus and without doubt, been the result of case law interpreting the term 'investment' in an evolutionary manner.

However, the Annulment Committee in *Mitchell v Congo* did not admit subscribing to an evolutionary interpretation of the term 'investment', holding instead that the concept of investment was 'somewhat broadened'.[12] More specifically, in deciding to annul the arbitral award for failure to state reasons, the Committee noted that

> while it is true that in some cases, where explicit reference was made to the contribution to the economic development of the host State, the concept of investment *was somewhat broadened*, this does nothing to alter the fundamental nature of that characteristic (emphasis added).[13]

It is not clear why the Committee would prefer to use such neutral language instead of simply admitting that the concept of investment has been subject to evolutionary interpretation by several arbitral tribunals.

In light of the above, it is safe to conclude that evolutionary interpretation may be perceived generally as a 'taboo' in investment arbitration.

The decision on jurisdiction in *RosInvestCo UK Ltd v The Russian Federation* – a case before the Stockholm Chamber of Commerce (SCC) – is emblematic in this respect. *In casu*, the claimant, in its written and oral arguments, had urged the tribunal to adopt a 'dynamic'[14] approach to the interpretation of the Agreement between the Government of the United Kingdom and the Government of the USSR for the Promotion and Reciprocal Protection of Investments (IPPA) in order to find jurisdiction. In particular, the claimant advanced that the tribunal should not be confined by the circumstances against which the Contracting Parties reached agreement on the IPPA at the time, but should instead give full weight, for the purposes of giving meaning to its terms, to events and attitudes as they have developed since then, notably the dissolution of the USSR, the emergence of the Russian Federation as its legal continuation, and the radically different economic, trading and investment policies adopted by the Russian Federation as that period went on.[15] This invitation to engage into evolutionary interpretation was diplomatically but strongly rejected by the tribunal. The reasoning of the latter was as follows:

> The Tribunal is unable to agree … The cases cited by the Claimant relate almost in their entirety to human rights treaties and to the constituent instruments of international

[11] *Salini Costruttori SpA and Italstrade SpA v Morocco*, ICSID Case No ARB/00/4, Decision on Jurisdiction, 23 July 2001.

[12] *Patrick Mitchell v Congo, the Democratic Republic of the*, ICSID Case No ARB/99/7, Decision on the Application for Annulment of the Award, 1 November 2006, para 30.

[13] ibid, paras 30, 41.

[14] *RosInvestCo UK Ltd v The Russian Federation*, SCC Case No 079/2005, Award on Jurisdiction, October 2007, para 37.

[15] ibid.

> organizations. It is however plain that both of these are special cases: the former (human rights) because they represent the very archetype of treaty instruments in which the Contracting Parties must have intended that the principles and concepts which they employed should be understood and applied in the light of developing social attitudes (as has repeatedly been held by national as well as international judicial bodies); the latter (international organizations) because it is generally understood that, given the changing nature of the problems and circumstances international organizations have to confront, a degree of evolutionary adaptation is the only realistic approach to realizing the underlying purposes of the organization as laid down in its constituent instrument. It is difficult to see what bearing any of this might have on the jurisdiction of an arbitral tribunal, which remains, as it always has been, a matter of specific consent by the parties.[16]

In the tribunal's view, evolutionary interpretation is surely not inherent to the process of interpretation of a bilateral investment treaty (BIT) and cannot be used as a general rule of treaty interpretation; evolutionary interpretation can and should be based on a specific provision in a BIT that would allow such an approach. In the case of the IPPA, the tribunal considered that only the Most Favoured Nation (MFN) clause contained in that treaty could authorise to a certain extent adopting a sort of evolutionary interpretation. In the words of the tribunal pursuing its reasoning:

> It is open to serious question, moreover, whether these special kinds of multilateral treaty are at all analogous to bilateral engagements regulating a particular area of the relations between one Party and the other. Here a bargain is a (reciprocal) bargain and the Parties must be held to what they agreed to, but not more, or less. The common thread among the multilateral examples just referred to is that their nature or circumstances provide evidence that the Parties themselves intended or understood that an evolutionary approach was appropriate to the interpretation and application of what they had agreed upon, and exactly the same common thread is to be found in the two bilateral cases the Claimant invokes (the *Gabcikovo/Nagymaros case* in the International Court of Justice and the *Iron Rhine* arbitration). No such evidence is available here; the preambular references mentioned above offer nothing of the kind. The Tribunal inclines to the opposite view, namely that, so far as the treaty parties foresaw and wished to admit an evolutionary development at all, the MFN clause in Article 3 was their chosen vehicle for doing so.

The *RosInvestCo UK Ltd v The Russian Federation* case, therefore, perceives evolutionary interpretation as almost a 'blasphemy' in investment treaty arbitration. This posture is sometimes more of a facade than a reflection of a strong and consistent approach by investment tribunals to the issue of evolutionary interpretation.

Indeed, in practice evolutionary interpretation occurs more often than one might think. In some (rare) cases, investment tribunals have openly and admittedly engaged in evolutionary interpretation. For example, in interpreting one of the most general, broadly formulated standards, that of FET the tribunal in

[16] ibid, para 39.

Mondev explicitly referred to the concept of evolutionary interpretation. Although the NAFTA Free Trade Commission (FTC) had already issued an Interpretative Note (FTC Note) clarifying and circumscribing the meaning of the standard, the tribunal held that 'having regard to its general language and to the evolutionary character of international law, the standard has *evolutionary* potential' (emphasis added).[17]

In an effort to balance this evolutionary interpretation with the requirement of the Contracting Parties to limit the scope of FET to the minimum standard of treatment under customary international law, the tribunal noted that it did not have unfettered discretion to decide on a subjective basis[18] what was 'fair' or 'equitable' in the circumstances of each particular case. However, a 'reasonable evolutionary interpretation'[19] of NAFTA Article 1105(1) is consistent with normal principles of interpretation and the fact that the content of the minimum standard today cannot be limited to the content of customary international law in the 1920s.

Another example of a tribunal endorsing an ever-expanding interpretation of the FET clause notwithstanding the above-mentioned FTC Note is the *Bilcon* case. Instead of adopting an evolutionary interpretation of the FET standard per se, the tribunal interpreted in an evolutionary manner the customary standard of minimum treatment itself, relying to this end on the awards in *ADF Group Inc v United States*,[20] and *Merrill & Ring Forestry LP v Canada*.[21] Notably, arbitrator Donald McRae issued a Dissenting Opinion disagreeing with the majority's reasoning, counter-arguing that 'the tribunal had in effect introduced the potential for getting damages for what is a breach of Canadian law, where Canadian law does not provide damages for such a breach'.[22]

Given the fact that evolutionary interpretation in international investment arbitration is, thus, much more common than often admitted, it is important to identify the drivers behind it and the different reasons for its occurrence. The following section focuses on those different reasons and the specificities that evolutionary interpretation presents in the investment context.

[17] *Mondev International Ltd v United States of America*, ICSID Case No ARB(AF)/99/2, Award, 11 October 2002, para 119.

[18] On dissenting opinions criticising tribunals of such 'subjectivity', see, eg, the Individual Opinion of Henri Alvarez in *Total SA v The Argentine Republic*, ICSID Case No ARB/04/01, Award, 27 November 2013, para 19: 'Importing a subjective standard into the interpretation of "fair and equitable treatment", in my opinion, has the effect of incorporating a margin of appreciation approach that is not appropriate at the first stage of the analysis, which concerns whether a breach of the standard has occurred'.

[19] *Mondev International Ltd v United States of America*, above n 17, para 123.

[20] *ADF Group Inc v United States of America*, ICSID Case No ARB(AF)/00/1, Award, 9 January 2003, para 179.

[21] *Merrill & Ring Forestry LP v The Government of Canada*, ICSID Case No UNCT/07/1, Award, 31 March 2010, paras 190–93.

[22] *Bilcon of Delaware et al v Government of Canada*, PCA Case No 2009-04, Award on Jurisdiction and Liability, 17 March 2015, Dissenting Opinion of Professor Donald McRae, para 43.

III. The Drivers and Types of Evolutionary Interpretation in Investment Arbitration

The majority of investment disputes are based on BITs. There are more than 3000 BITs to date. In the constellation of treaties, BITs are maybe the most minimalist, not just in terms of the number of pages, but also of content and the formulation of the investment standards included therein. Let's take as an example the BIT between Switzerland and Tunisia, which is only three pages long! Yet, this is the prototype of a BIT. Most of those treaties will only limit themselves to stating that each contracting State shall grant 'fair and equitable treatment'[23] or 'shall accord fair and equitable treatment in accordance with customary international law'.[24] Or they will provide that each contracting State shall accord 'full protection and security'.[25] Not many pages are then necessary to incorporate such succinct, broad and general standards/provisions.[26]

At the same time, because of the very vague and general nature of these investment standards, tribunals cannot escape evolutionary interpretation. Those terms and expressions are not frozen in time. Investment standards and provisions are evolutionary *in se* and in nature.

The question that arises, then, is what are the specificities of evolutionary interpretation in the field of international investment arbitration? One could identify two types of specificities: on the one hand, *functional* specificities, and on the other, *consequential* specificities.

A. Functional Specificities

The first category refers, as its name denotes, to the functions that evolutionary interpretation plays in the field of investment arbitration. There are two specific functions under this grouping: the first is gap-filling, and the second is value promotion.

The gap-filling function ensues from the vague and inherently incomplete nature of investment treaty standards like FET, which makes it imperative for

[23] See, eg, the Agreement between the Government of United Kingdom and Northern Ireland and the Government of the Republic of Argentina, Art 2(2): 'Investments of investors of each Contracting Party shall at all times be accorded fair and equitable treatment'.

[24] See, eg, the 2012 US Model BIT, Art 5(1): 'Each Party shall accord to covered investments treatment in accordance with customary international law, including fair and equitable treatment'.

[25] See, eg, the 2006 French Model BIT, Art 5(1): 'The investments made by nationals or companies of one Contracting Party shall enjoy full and complete protection and safety'.

[26] As Magraw observes, even new-generation international investment agreements continue to be based on older models that include broad and vague provisions, and that in any case, 'no matter how detailed an international investment agreement is, many of the standards therein remain broad and ambiguous (or "generic" and "not static"), indicating that the parties may have wanted to permit flexibility of the terms to adapt and evolve over time'. See Magraw, above n 10.

investment arbitral tribunals to resort to evolutionary interpretation to give content to these standards and identify their various elements. This is the reason why different tribunals have turned to different aspects of the FET standard. Some tribunals have interpreted the standard as good faith[27] while others have focused on transparency and predictability,[28] or the stability of the legal and business framework,[29] and so forth. Such gap-filling is essential for the interpretation and application of the FET standard in individual cases.

Some tribunals have indeed acknowledged – without using explicitly the term 'evolutionary interpretation' – that concepts like FET and minimum standard of treatment are in a constant process of development because of their very nature, and thus gap-filling is a necessary function of the adjudicatory process before investment arbitral tribunals.

The second – less normative – function that evolutionary interpretation performs in investment arbitration is value promotion. In such a scenario, arbitral tribunals would get into the realm of evolutionary interpretation to defend certain values in the system. For instance, let's examine how investment tribunals have interpreted the MFN clause in an evolutive manner by looking at the most well-known case in this regard, ie, the *Maffezini v Spain* case. In that dispute, for the first time a tribunal held that the MFN clause was not limited to substantive advantages but would extend to procedural advantages.[30]

What was the reason for such an evolutionary interpretation of the MFN clause in the Decision on Objections to Jurisdiction rendered by the *Maffezini* tribunal? The tribunal's reasoning for extending the clause to procedural matters was that 'there are *good reasons* to conclude that *today* dispute settlement arrangements are inextricably related to the protection of foreign investors' (emphasis added).[31] This is a clear example of value promotion through evolutionary interpretation, whereby a tribunal departed from a textual interpretative approach and extended the scope of MFN, 'notwithstanding the fact that the basic treaty containing the clause does not refer expressly to dispute settlement as covered by the most favored nation clause'.[32]

A more recent case where the tribunal engaged in evolutionary interpretation for purposes of value promotion was the dispute between the French investors UP and CD Holding Internationale (formerly 'Chèque Dejeuner') and the

[27] See, eg, *Técnicas Medioambientales Tecmed SA v The United Mexican States*, ICSID Case No ARB(AF)/00/2, Award, 29 May 2003; and *MTD Equity Sdn Bhd and MTD Chile SA v Republic of Chile*, ICSID Case No ARB/01/7, Award, 25 May 2004.

[28] See, eg, *Metalclad Corporation v The United Mexican States*, ICSID Case No ARB(AF)/97/1, Award, 30 August 2000.

[29] See, eg, *Occidental Exploration and Production Company v The Republic of Ecuador*, UNCITRAL Arbitration, Case No UN3467, Final Award, 1 July 2004.

[30] *Maffezini v Kingdom of Spain*, ICSID Case No ARB/97/7, Decision on Objections to Jurisdiction, 25 January 2000.

[31] ibid, para 54.

[32] ibid.

Republic of Hungary.[33] In construing the MFN clause, the tribunal interpreted the provision in an 'evolutionary' manner, relying in particular on the 2015 Report of the International Law Commission (ILC) on MFN.[34]

In this intra-EU investment dispute, the respondent objected to the extension of the BIT's MFN clause determining the jurisdiction of the tribunal. Relying on a series of decisions on jurisdiction, including the awards in *Plama Consortium Limited v Republic of Bulgaria*,[35] *Telenor v Hungary*,[36] and the *Salini* case,[37] Hungary argued that the MFN clause could not extend to dispute resolution provisions, as the claimant was seeking, and that the tribunal could consequently not expand its mandate to decide claims expressly excluded by the BIT. Rejecting the *Maffezini* doctrine as inconsistent with the principle of the disputing parties' procedural equality, the respondent noted that to ignore the distinction between jurisdiction and substantive claims would 'impermissibly privilege the rights of investors over those of host states'.[38]

Hungary also recalled the award in *Sanum v Laos*, where the tribunal held that

> to read into a treaty a dispute settlement provision to cover all protections under the treaty by virtue of an MFN clause when the treaty itself provides for very limited access to international arbitration, would result in a substantial re-write of the treaty and an extension of the State parties' consent to arbitration beyond what may be assumed to have been their intention.[39]

However, such a 'substantial r-write' is what the tribunal in the *UP & CD* case did, by engaging in a value-promotion exercise through an evolutionary interpretation of the MFN clause. Holding that the object and purpose of the MFN obligation is to 'ensure that there will be no discrimination between foreign investors',[40] the tribunal examined the three factors of evolutionary interpretation identified in the 2015 ILC report. In contrast to the *Costa Rica v Nicaragua* case before the ICJ, the tribunal did not have recourse to the 'intent' of the parties nor their interpretation and application of the treaty, but to the respondent's 'subsequent practice'.[41]

[33] *UP (formerly Le Chèque Déjeuner) and CD Holding Internationale v Hungary*, ICSID Case No ARB/13/35, Decision on Preliminary Issues of Jurisdiction, 3 March 2016.

[34] ILC 'Report of the International Law Commission on the work of its 67th session (4 May–5 June and 7 July–7 August 2015) UN Doc A/70/10.

[35] *Plama Consortium Limited v Bulgaria*, ICSID Case No ARB/03/24, Decision on Jurisdiction, 8 February 2005.

[36] *Telenor Mobile Communications AS v Hungary*, ICSID Case No ARB/04/15, Award, 13 September 2006.

[37] *Salini Costruttori SpA and Italstrade SpA v Morocco*, above n 11.

[38] *UP (formerly Le Chèque Déjeuner) and CD Holding Internationale v Hungary*, above n 33, para 77.

[39] *Sanum Investments Limited v Lao People's Democratic Republic*, UNCITRAL, Award on Jurisdiction, 13 December 2013, para 358.

[40] *UP (formerly Le Chèque Déjeuner) and CD Holding Internationale v Hungary*, above n 33, para 163.

[41] On the focus of the ICJ's evolutionary interpretation on uncovering the parties' intention in accordance with the rules of the Vienna Convention on the Law of Treaties, see E Bjorge, 'Time Present and Time Past: The Intention of the Parties and the Evolutionary Interpretation of Treaties', ch 5 in this book.

Despite the clear limitation set by the Contracting Parties, of recourse to arbitration only for disputes relating to expropriation, the tribunal decided that the MFN clause should be interpreted in a prospective manner in light of Hungary's subsequent practice of incorporating MFN and FET clauses in all its BITs together with increasingly open arbitration clauses.[42]

Such an evolutionary interpretation of the MFN clause constitutes value promotion as the tribunal based its reasoning for extending the scope of MFN to establish its jurisdiction on the alleged more liberal investment policies that Hungary had adopted in its subsequent treaty practice. Despite the clear wording of the disputed treaty limiting recourse to arbitration only to one category of disputes, the tribunal took the liberty to import and extend arbitration into that treaty assuming that the respondent would have wished to deploy a similar liberalism in its previous treaties.

It becomes evident from the above that evolutionary interpretation in investment arbitration is not based on the intent, or the object and purpose of treaties. The best example of evolutionary interpretation based on intent is the aforementioned *Costa Rica v Nicaragua* dispute, while the most characteristic case of evolutionary interpretation based on the treaty's object and purpose is the WTO Appellate Body report in *US – Shrimp*. In deciding whether the terms 'exhaustible natural resources' in Article XX(g) of the General Agreement on Tariffs and Trade also included non-living resources, the Appellate Body held that the phrase must be interpreted in light of the 'contemporary concerns of the international community regarding the protection and conservation of the environment'.[43] To corroborate this evolutionary interpretation, the Appellate Body made explicit reference to the preamble of the 1994 WTO Agreement and particularly its reference to the 'objective of sustainable development'. Consequently, it held that the generic term 'natural resources' is not static but is rather 'by definition evolutionary'.[44]

Having noted that in investment arbitration evolutionary interpretation is not based on those aspects, but is either gap-filling or value promotion, it is pertinent to examine the consequential specificities, ie, the impacts or effects of such an interpretation in the investment context.

B. The (Outer-) Effects of Evolutionary Interpretation in Investment Arbitration

There are two particular effects of evolutionary interpretation in investment arbitration. The first is the creation of inconsistencies in the investment regime.

[42] *UP (formerly Le Chèque Déjeuner) and CD Holding Internationale v Hungary*, above n 33, paras 165, 174.

[43] WTO Appellate Body Report, *United States – Import Prohibition of Certain Shrimp and Shrimp Products (US – Shrimp)* adopted 6 November 1998, WT/DS58/AB/R, para 129.

[44] ibid, paras 12, 130.

Despite the lack of formal precedent, investment arbitration performs a governance function as tribunals like to refer to their role. There are, thus, two possible impacts resulting from this practice. Either some arbitrators will follow their predecessors, or they will reject the positions of previous tribunals. As a consequence, evolutionary interpretation does not have an ordering effect; that is to say, it does not bring more order in the interpretation and application of IIAs.

An example of inconsistent arbitral awards on the same issue is the *ICS v Argentina*[45] case, compared with the aforementioned decisions in the *Maffezini* and *UP & CD* cases. As opposed to the latter, the *ICS* tribunal declined to interpret the MFN clause in the UK–Argentina BIT prospectively (ie, in an evolutionary manner), and thus did not extend its reach to dispute resolution to enable investors to import dispute resolution clauses from Argentina's other BITs.[46] Notably, the tribunal, thus, took issue not only with the *Maffezini* tribunal but also with two former tribunals that had rendered awards against the same State judging the same issue in the *Impregilo v Argentina*[47] and *Hochtief v Argentina* cases.[48] These inconsistencies are sometimes noted in practice.

The second impact is that evolutionary interpretation leads quasi-automatically to reactions from States. This is something peculiar to the investment regime. It leads in particular to two types of reaction: ex post facto reactions, and ex ante reactions as discussed below.

If States do not subscribe to an evolutionary interpretation adopted by an investment tribunal, they might react in an ex post manner by adopting, for instance a new model of BIT. For example, the United States reacted to the fourth prong of the definition of 'investment', ie, the significant contribution to the economic development of the host State, as established by the *Salini* test. It changed its model BIT in 2004 and made sure that this *Salini* criterion was excluded from the definition of investment.[49]

Sometimes a State's ex post facto reactions show that it has difficulty in grasping the normative content of investment standards. This is demonstrated, for example, by the South African Development Community (SADC) 2012 Model Bilateral Investment Treaty, which includes different options for possible provisions and standards instead of clarifying them in an exclusive and definitive manner. For instance, as regards the definition of 'investment' the model provides three options: one based on the Canadian model BIT; the second following the

[45] *ICS Inspection and Control Services Limited (United Kingdom) v The Republic of Argentina*, UNCITRAL PCA Case No 2010/09, Award on Jurisdiction, 10 February 2012.

[46] ibid, para 317.

[47] *Salini Impregilo SpA v Argentine Republic*, ICSID Case No ARB/15/39, Decision on Jurisdiction and Admissibility, 23 February 2018.

[48] *Hochtief AG v The Argentine Republic*, ICSID Case No ARB/07/31, Decision on Jurisdiction, 24 October 2011.

[49] See the 2004 US Model BIT, Art 1, which provides that: '"Investment" means every asset that an investor owns or controls, directly or indirectly, that has the characteristics of an investment, including such characteristics as the commitment of capital or other resources, the expectation of gain or profit, or the assumption of risk'.

US model text; and the third being an 'entreprise-based definition' closer to the Chinese model.[50] Similarly, in addition to the more traditional FET clause (albeit significantly limited) the SADC model also offers the alternative of a 'fair administrative treatment' clause.[51]

Another instance of an ex post facto State reaction is the interpretative declaration that Argentina and Panama issued following the *Siemens* case,[52] declaring that the MFN clause included in their 1996 investment treaty did not extend to procedural advantages. States have also reacted as regards other treaty standards, especially the FET standard. For example, the European Union and Canada have been trying to incorporate into their Comprehensive Economic and Trade Agreement a provision that brings the FET standard back to its traditional 1927 meaning as established in the *Neer* case.[53] Another approach is for a State to assert some continuous control over the interpretation of a term by arbitral tribunals. For instance, in addition to joint interpretations, the new Indian model BIT provides that a party can issue an individual interpretation that would be notified to the disputing parties and the tribunal, which may take into account such interpretation.[54]

Apart from these *ex post facto* reactions, States can also react *ex ante*, although this is more rare in practice. The best example of such a reaction is the *Pope & Talbot* case,[55] where the NAFTA Commission in the middle of the case – in fact, after the tribunal had already issued a partial award – adopted an interpretative note defining the FET standard in order to pre-empt an evolutionary interpretation by the arbitral tribunal. To this end, the Commission clarified that the standard would be understood as a guarantee of treatment under customary international law not going beyond the minimum standard.[56] The Interpretative Note can also be perceived *in se* as an ex post facto reaction to the awards of previous tribunals that had adopted an expansive reading of the FET clause, in particular in the *Metalclad*[57] and *SD Myers* cases.[58]

[50] See the 2012 SADC Model Bilateral Investment Treaty Template with Commentary, Art 2.

[51] ibid, Art 5.

[52] *Siemens AG v The Argentine Republic*, ICSID Case No ARB/02/8, Decision on Jurisdiction, 3 August 2004.

[53] *LFH Neer and Pauline Neer (USA) v United Mexican States*, Decision on the Merits, 15 October 1926.

[54] See 2016 Indian Model BIT, Art 24.3.

[55] *Pope & Talbot Inc v The Government of Canada*, UNCITRAL, Award on the Merits of Phase 2, 10 April 2001.

[56] See North American Free Trade Agreement, 'Notes of Interpretation of Certain Chapter 11 Provisions' NAFTA Free Trade Commission, 31 July 2001, point B.2: 'The concepts of "fair and equitable treatment" and "full protection and security" do not require treatment in addition to or beyond that which is required by the customary international law minimum standard of treatment of aliens.'

[57] *Metalclad Corporation v The United Mexican States*, above n 28.

[58] *SD Myers, Inc v Government of Canada*, UNCITRAL, First Partial Award, 13 November 2000.

IV. Conclusion

There is definitely a sociological clash of perception when it comes to evolutionary interpretation in the investment arbitration field. Investors usually encourage and call for evolutionary interpretation since such an interpretation usually goes in their favour. States, on the contrary, consider it quite often to be more 'regressive' than evolutionary. One thing that is certain in this context is that one of the reasons for what is called today the crisis of the investment regime, and especially of investment arbitration, is a result of rather abusive and disguised evolutionary interpretation by investment arbitral tribunals. Consequently, one of the challenges in the reform of investor–State dispute settlement will be to re-balance the use of evolutionary interpretation.

One path is to use evolutionary interpretation in investment arbitration as a tool for systemic integration. Evolutionary interpretation should be more about a sustainable development approach, whereby the interpretation of investment standards takes into account developments in other fields of international law, including international environment law, international health law, and international human rights law.[59] The work of UNCTAD on the systemic integration of international investment law with these other legal fields is very relevant in this context. The 'new generation' of international investment policies has to align with other public policies and promote sustainable development.[60] To this end, UNCTAD has identified some main areas of investment reform to enhance systemic consistency such as safeguarding the right to regulate while providing protection and ensuring responsible investment.[61]

In this increasingly complex landscape of investment treaties, evolutionary interpretation by investment arbitral tribunals could play an active role in gap-filling and value promotion to achieve such systemic integration and promote sustainable development. But then one question remains: are investment tribunals the right fora to do so? That remains an open question …

[59] Such an integration approach to evolutionary interpretation is also relevant in other fields, such as the WTO context. See G Cook, 'The Illusion of 'Evolutionary Interpretation' in WTO Dispute Settlement', ch 17 in this book, where the author notes that 'Furthermore, the Appellate Body invoked the notion of an 'evolutionary' interpretation merely as a legal hook for justifying its consideration of non-WTO conventions and instruments post-dating the conclusion of the GATT 1947'.

[60] UNCTAD, *Investment Policy Framework for Sustainable Development* (2015) UNCTAD/DIAE/PCB/2015/5.

[61] UNCTAD, Reform Package for the International Investment Regime (2018), available at: investmentpolicyhub.unctad.org/Upload/Documents/UNCTAD_Reform_Package_2018.pdf.

24

The Role of State Party Pleadings in the Evolutionary Interpretation of International Investment Agreements

KENDRA MAGRAW

I. Introduction

Most international investment disputes involve the interpretation of an international legal instrument, whether a bilateral investment treaty (BIT), another international investment agreement (IIA) such as a free trade agreement (FTA), or a constitutional-type treaty, such as the Convention on the Settlement of Investment Disputes between States and Nationals of Other States (ICSID Convention).[1] Such instruments are subject to the interpretation of tribunals and parties, and may be the basis of the dispute. That the parties to a treaty may interpret its provisions is settled in international law.[2] How they may do so, and which interpretive methods and materials should – or must – be taken into account by tribunals, are more controversial.

In several investor–State disputes, the disputing parties have argued that their interpretive statements contained in their oral or written pleadings (hereinafter referred to as State party pleadings (SPPs)) are significant for the interpretation of IIA. Although such arguments have not been raised exclusively in the context of investor–State dispute settlement (ISDS), they are particularly prevalent therein because of the nature of such disputes, in which treaty parties do not appear against each other in an adversarial setting; rather, their arguments are typically presented independently in separate disputes.[3]

[1] Convention on the Settlement of Investment Disputes between States, and Nationals of Other States (adopted 18 March 1965), 575 *United Nations Treaty Series* 159 (ICSID Convention).

[2] See, eg, *Question of Jaworzina (Polish-Czechoslovakian Frontier)* (Advisory Opinion) [1923] PCIJ Rep Series B no 8, 37; I Sinclair, *The Vienna Convention on the Law of Treaties*, 2nd edn (Manchester, Manchester University Press 1984) 136.

[3] There are notable exceptions to this, such as discretionary treaty mechanisms providing for non-disputing party interventions. See, eg, North American Free Trade Agreement (adopted 17 December 1992) (1993) 32 *International Legal Materials* 612 (NAFTA) Art 1128.

Whether the statements contained in SPPs have interpretive weight, and, if so, their effect on the interpreter, have been addressed with respect to several rules of interpretation under the Vienna Convention on the Law of Treaties (VCLT),[4] notably subsequent agreement (Article 31(3)(a)),[5] subsequent practice (Article 31(3)(b))[6] and supplementary interpretation (Article 32).[7] However, scant, if any, attention has been given to the role of SPPs in the interpretive process in conjunction with other aspects of treaty interpretation, including evolutionary interpretation.

Evolutionary interpretation has been the subject of much scholarship and debate: its status and role in the treaty interpretation process are disputed, and its utilisation sometimes contested.[8] The value of, and recourse to, SPPs are likewise subject to criticism and the parties' views contained therein are often regarded with suspicion.[9] In practice, tribunals have appeared hesitant to heed the interpretations advanced by parties in their pleadings, although some tribunals have

[4] Vienna Convention on the Law of Treaties (adopted 23 May 1969) 1155 *United Nations Treaty Series* 331.

[5] *Telefónica SA v The Argentine Republic*, ICSID Case No ARB/03/20, Decision of the Tribunal on Objections to Jurisdiction, 25 May 2006, para 109; *Aguas del Tunari v Bolivia*, ICSID Case No ARB/02/3, Decision on Respondent's Objections to Jurisdiction, 21 October 2005; *HICEE v The Slovak Republic*, PCA Case No 2009–11, Partial Award, 23 May 2011; *El Paso Energy International Company v Argentine Republic*, ICSID Case No ARB/03/15, Award, 31 October 2011, para 603; *Pope & Talbot Inc v The Government of Canada*, NAFTA, Award on the Merits of Phase 2, 10 April 2001, para 114; *Canadian Cattlemen for Fair Trade v United States of America*, UNCITRAL, Award on Jurisdiction, 28 January 2008; *Methanex Corporation v United States of America*, UNCITRAL, Final Award of the Tribunal on Jurisdiction and Merits, 3 August 2005, (2005) 44 *International Legal Materials* 1345; *Marvin Roy Feldman Karpa v United Mexican States*, ICSID Case No ARB(AF)/99/1, Counter-Memorial of Mexico, 24 May 2001, para 319; *Marvin Roy Feldman Karpa v United Mexican States*, ICSID Case No ARB(AF)/99/1, Award, 16 December 2002.

[6] *Aguas del Tunari*, above n 5; *Gas Natural SDG SA v Argentina*, ICSID Case No ARB/03/10, Decision of the Tribunal on Preliminary Questions of Jurisdiction, 17 June 2005; *Telefónica*, above n 5, para 109; *Urbaser SA and Consorcio de Aguas Bilbao Biskaia, Bilbao Biskaia Ur Partzuergoa v The Argentine Republic*, ICSID Case No ARB/07/26, Decision on Jurisdiction, 19 December 2012, para 51: *El Paso*, above n 5, para 603; *Enron Creditors Recovery Corporation (formerly Enron Corporation) and Ponderosa Assets, LP v Argentina*, ICSID Case No ARB/01/3, Decision on the Argentine Republic's Request for a Continued Stay of Enforcement of the Award (Rule 54 of the ICSID Arbitration Rules), 7 October 2008, para 71; *Mondev International Ltd v United States of America*, ICSID Case No ARB(AF)/99/2, Counter-Memorial on Competence and Liability of Respondent United States, 1 June 2001, 34; *Loewen Group, Inc and Raymond L Loewen v United States of America*, ICSID Case No ARB(AF)/98/3, Counter-Memorial, 3 March 2001, 175–76; *Canadian Cattlemen*, above n 5.

[7] *HICEE*, Partial Award, above n 5; *CME Czech Republic BV v Czech Republic*, UNCITRAL, Final Award, 14 March 2003.

[8] See, eg, PM Dupuy, 'Evolutionary Interpretation of Treaties: Between Memory and Prophecy' in E Cannizzaro (ed), *The Law of Treaties Beyond the Vienna Convention* (Oxford, Oxford University Press, 2011); D French, 'Treaty Interpretation and the Incorporation of Extraneous Legal Rules' (2006) 55 *International & Comparative Law Quarterly* 279, 300.

[9] See, eg, *HICEE v The Slovak Republic*, PCA Case No 2009–11, Dissent of Judge Charles N Brower to the Supplementary and Final Award, 17 October 2011, para 36; R Dolzer and C Schreuer, *Principles of International Investment Law* (Oxford, Oxford University Press, 2008) 35.

done so;[10] however, the role of parties' interpretations in their SPPs in relation to evolutionary interpretation has not been explicitly examined in any known ISDS case.

Therefore, this chapter examines the possible use of SPPs in the evolutionary interpretation of IIAs. Part II briefly introduces the recent trend of reliance on SPPs for the interpretation of IIAs in ISDS; part III examines evolutionary interpretation generally, as well as in relation to IIAs and ISDS; part IV analyses the potential value of SPPs for and via evolutionary interpretation; and part V draws brief conclusions.

II. SPPs and ISDS

In several investor–State disputes, the disputing State party has argued that the parties to an IIA presented interpretations of that IIA in their SPPs that had interpretive effect under the VCLT; for example, that the interpretations made by treaty parties in their SPPs established the subsequent agreement of the parties under Article 31(3)(a) of the VCLT.[11] According to such arguments, the interpretations expressed by the parties in their SPPs must be taken into account by tribunals in the interpretation of the IIA.

Most investor–State disputes involve the interpretation of a BIT or another IIA that contains an investment chapter similar to BITs,[12] such as the North American Free Trade Agreement (NAFTA).[13] Investor–State arbitration is unusual because it is one of the only types of international dispute that is not State-to-State.[14] The fact that States, and treaty parties, do not face one another in the same proceeding may account for why these arguments have been primarily raised in the context of investment disputes. In ISDS, States appear almost exclusively as respondents, unlike traditional State-to-State international adjudicative proceedings where States appear as claimants and as respondents, and typically go head-to-head as opponents in a proceeding.[15] Thus, ISDS respondent States

[10] For an examination of SPPs in relation to subsequent agreement and subsequent practice, in ISDS see K Magraw, 'Investor–State Disputes and the Rise of Recourse to State Party Pleadings as Subsequent Agreements or Subsequent Practice Under the Vienna Convention on the Law of Treaties' (2015) 30 *ICSID Review – Foreign Investment Law Journal* 142.

[11] See, eg, *Aguas del Tunari*, above n 5; *Gas Natural*, above n 6; *Urbaser*, above n 6, para 51; *Telefónica*, above n 5, para 109.

[12] Some ISDS disputes are based on a contract or the domestic investment law of a host State, however. See, eg, ICSID Caseload – Statistics (Issue 2018–2), available at www.icsid.worldbank.org/en/Documents/resources/ICSID%20Web%20Stats%202018-2%20(English).pdf.

[13] NAFTA, above n 3.

[14] Although most BITs with an ISDS provision also provide for State-to-State arbitration.

[15] This same debate is extended to human rights treaties, in which States grant rights to individuals. For further reading, see A Roberts, 'Power and Persuasion in Investment Treaty Interpretation: The Dual Role of States' (2010) 104 *American Journal of International Law* 179, 202–07.

are more likely to adopt concordant (defensive) interpretive stances,[16] while in State-to-State proceedings it is more likely that the opposing State parties will have the opportunity to present their interpretations (which may be disputed) and receive directed responses thereto.[17] These reasons may also explain why the argument that common stances in SPPs can be used in the interpretive process is especially controversial in ISDS.

In addition, certain IIAs allow treaty parties to express their interpretive views even in cases to which they are not a party: for example, NAFTA Article 1128 permits the non-disputing treaty parties to file submissions in ongoing cases of their interpretations of the NAFTA[18] (several subsequent treaties have also adopted this approach).[19] While this does not mean that treaty parties will necessarily have the same interpretations, it enables them to contribute to ongoing interpretive discussions and, as potential respondents, may align their interpretive interests.

There are a few common scenarios in ISDS where the argument has been advanced that the interpretive positions offered by parties in their SPPs have interpretive weight. First, the disputing State party might argue that the interpretation of an IIA that it advances in its pleadings is in agreement with the arguments of the other IIA party as contained in the latter's pleadings from a different proceeding.[20] Second, the State party may argue that its interpretation in its pleadings is in agreement with a statement of the other IIA party that was made extrinsic to any adjudicative proceeding, such as a press release or a statement from a governmental authority.[21] Third, a non-disputing treaty party might intervene to present its interpretive stances in an ongoing dispute in which the disputing treaty party has advanced interpretive positions in its SPPs, either on its own initiative,[22] or at the request of a disputing party[23] or the tribunal.[24]

[16] This is because State parties to this type of treaty view the interpretation of a treaty from the perspective of a respondent, rather than as a claimant, and may seek to limit their liability by adopting conservative interpretations. Of course, States may still have divergent interpretive stances. See Roberts, ibid, 196, 218.

[17] A Roberts, 'Subsequent Agreements and Practice: The Battle over Interpretive Power' in G Nolte (ed), *Treaties and Subsequent Practice* (Oxford, Oxford University Press, 2013) 97.

[18] NAFTA, above n 3, art 1128.

[19] See, eg, Australia–China FTA (2015) art 9.16; Canada–European Union Comprehensive Economic and Trade Agreement (CETA) (2016) art 8.38.

[20] See, eg, *Telefónica*, above n 5; *Gas Natural*, above n 6; *Urbaser*, above n 6, para 51; *El Paso*, above n 5, para 603.

[21] See, eg, *HICEE*, Partial Award, above n 5; *Aguas del Tunari*, above n 5.

[22] See, eg, *Methanex*, Final Award of the Tribunal on Jurisdiction and Merits, above n 5; *Mondev*, above n 6, 34; *Siemens v The Argentine Republic*, ICSID Case No ARB/02/8, United States' Letter to the Annulment Proceeding Tribunal, 1 May 2008.

[23] *Enron*, above n 6, para 71; *Empresas Lucchetti, SA v Republic of Peru*, ICSID Case No ARB/03/4, Award, 7 February 2005, para 7. See also *Ecuador v United States*, PCA Case No 2012-5, Request for Arbitration, 28 June 2011.

[24] See, eg, *Mesa Power Group LLC v Government of Canada*, PCA Case No 2012–17, Notification to Non-disputing Parties and Potential Amicus Curiae, 28 May 2014; see also *Pope & Talbot Inc*, Award on the Merits of Phase 2, above n 5, para 114, fn 110.

While there are many cases in which parties have argued that their SPPs have interpretive weight, this chapter focuses (non-exhaustively) on NAFTA examples, particularly the interpretation of NAFTA's fair and equitable treatment (FET) provision, Article 1105.

In several early NAFTA disputes, FET's meaning was at issue, ie, whether it was subsumed by the customary international law (CIL) minimum standard of treatment (MST) or whether it was a stand-alone obligation.[25] The three NAFTA parties argued in several cases that their SPPs established an agreement on the interpretation of Article 1105 under the VCLT,[26] for example, in *Mondev v United States*,[27] *Loewen v United States*,[28] *Methanex v United States*[29] and *Pope & Talbot v Canada*.

Pope & Talbot played a starring role in this debate; therein, the respondent and disputing State party, Canada, argued that all three NAFTA parties agreed in their SPPs – Canada in its memorials, and Mexico and the United States in their NAFTA Article 1128 submissions – that NAFTA Article 1105 reflected the CIL FET standard.[30] In an April 2001 Partial Award, the tribunal noted the parties' agreement on the interpretation of NAFTA Article 1105 but ultimately dismissed it because of, inter alia, concerns that the interpretation did not reflect the parties' true intentions at the time of drafting.[31] Approximately three months later, while several cases on the matter remained pending, the NAFTA parties exercised their rights under the NAFTA and issued a binding joint interpretive statement, the 31 July 2001 Free Trade Commission (FTC) 'Notes of Interpretation of Certain Chapter 11 Provisions' (FTC Notes), linking FET to CIL. As a result, the *Loewen*, *Mondev* and *Methanex* tribunals did not have to determine

[25] For a historical discussion of the interpretation of NAFTA's FET provision, see, eg, C Giannakopoulos and M Monga, 'History as Interpretative Context in the Evolutionary Interpretation of FET in International Investment Law', ch 26 in this book.

[26] Specifically, Art 31(3)(a) of the VCLT – subsequent agreement – and Art 31(3)(b) – subsequent practice.

[27] The United States argued that the SPPs of the parties – that is 'formal, public submissions to various Chapter Eleven tribunals' – amounted to subsequent practice establishing an agreement under Art 31(3)(b) of the VCLT that was binding on the tribunal. *Mondev*, above n 6, 33–34.

[28] The United States argued that its SPPs in *Loewen* and Mexico and Canada's SPPs from domestic proceedings amounted to subsequent practice establishing an agreement under Art 31(3)(b) of the VCLT, and that this should be given considerable weight. *Loewen*, above n 6, 175–76.

[29] All three parties argued that they were in agreement: the United States in its pleadings as the respondent in *Methanex*, and Canada and Mexico via the NAFTA Art 1128 mechanism in *Methanex*. See *Methanex v United States*, UNCITRAL, Post-Hearing Submission of Respondent United States of America (20 July 2001) 2–4. See also *Methanex v United States*, UNCITRAL, Response of Respondent United States of America to Methanex's Post-Hearing Submission (27 July 2001) 2–6.

[30] Canada also argued the same with regard to the NAFTA's expropriation provision, Article 1110. *Pope & Talbot v Canada*, Canada's Submission respecting Post-Hearing Article 1128 Submissions filed by Mexico and the US, 1 June 2000.

[31] *Pope & Talbot Inc*, Award on the Merits of Phase 2, above n 5, paras 79, 112–14.

the status of the parties' interpretive agreements in their SPPs, rather applying the FTC Notes.[32]

Despite concerns similar to those mentioned by the *Pope & Talbot* tribunal,[33] some ISDS tribunals[34] have accepted that SPPs have a role in the interpretive process under the VCLT, namely as subsequent practice (Article 31(3)(b))[35] or supplementary material (Article 32).[36] In addition, SPPs may also have significant roles to play in the evolutionary interpretation of IIAs, both regarding whether it is appropriate to make an evolutionary interpretation of the IIA provision or term in question, as well as to what the substantive content of such evolutionary interpretation might be.

III. Evolutionary Interpretation

Before examining the potential role of SPPs in the evolutionary interpretation of IIAs, it is necessary to briefly address evolutionary interpretation, which is itself a controversial tool in the treaty interpretation toolkit. This section: (A) provides a brief introduction to evolutionary interpretation; (B) examines the evolutionary interpretation of IIAs; and (C) discusses the evolutionary interpretation of IIAs in ISDS, again looking to the NAFTA experience.

A. Introduction

Evolutionary interpretation is the notion that, in certain circumstances, a treaty should be interpreted in a manner that allows its terms to evolve over time to account for changes and developments. The International Court of Justice (ICJ) defined evolutionary interpretation as:

> [S]ituations in which the parties' intent upon conclusion of the treaty was, or may be presumed to have been, to give the terms used – or some of them – a meaning or

[32] See, eg, *Methanex*, Final Award of the Tribunal on Jurisdiction and Merits, above n 5, part II, ch B, para 21. However, the *Pope & Talbot* tribunal defiantly refused to apply the FTC Notes in its subsequent award. See *Pope & Talbot Inc v The Government of Canada*, NAFTA, Decision in Respect to Damages, 31 May 2002; 41 *International Legal Materials* 347, paras 11–16.

[33] Other concerns include: (1) inequality of the parties since the investor is not a treaty party; (2) non-attribution of SPPs to the disputing State party (because of, eg, retention of external counsel); and (3) States could instead conclude formal agreements or amend the IIA.

[34] Those that have not have cited formal grounds concerning the agreement of the parties (an element of both VCLT Art 31(3)(a) and (b)), such as the lack of acceptance or intent to enter an agreement. See, *Telefónica*, above n 5, para 113; *Aguas del Tunari*, above n 5, para 251; *HICEE*, Partial Award, above n 5, paras 130–31, 134.

[35] *Canadian Cattlemen*, above n 5, para 189.

[36] *HICEE*, Partial Award, above n 5, para 136.

> content capable of evolving, not one fixed once and for all, so as to make allowance for, among other things, developments in international law.[37]

Such situations can include when treaty terms are 'generic' or 'not static,' in which case the parties 'must be deemed to have accepted them as such'.[38] If a term is considered generic, 'the presumption necessarily arises that its meaning was intended to follow the evolution of the law in force at a given time'.[39]

There are different theories justifying the evolutionary interpretation of treaties. The theory used by the ICJ is that evolutionary interpretation gives effect to the treaty parties' express or implied intent. According to this approach, evolutionary interpretation is considered an outcome of the proper application of the means of interpretation to establish the intentions of the parties;[40] such 'means of interpretation' include VCLT Articles 31 and 32.[41] As a result, it has been argued that evolutionary interpretation is not necessarily considered a principle of treaty interpretation *stricto sensu*.[42]

On the other hand, some authors opine that evolutionary interpretation is a departure from the parties' intentions,[43] while others lament attempts to find the parties' subjective intent as being precisely what the VCLT meant to avoid.[44] The different approaches notwithstanding, the ICJ has endorsed the party intentions approach.

If it is accepted that evolutionary interpretation is not a separate means of interpretation, it is then intertwined with the application of VCLT Articles 31 and 32.[45] The will of the parties is thus discerned objectively vis-a-vis 'the text of

[37] *Dispute Regarding Navigational and Related Rights (Costa Rica v Nicaragua)* (Judgment) [2009] ICJ Rep 213, 242, para 64.

[38] *Legal Consequences for States of the Continued Presence of South Africa in Namibia (South West Africa) notwithstanding Security Council Resolution 276 (1970)* (Advisory Opinion) [1971] ICJ Rep 16, 31.

[39] *Aegean Sea Continental Shelf (Greece v Turkey)* (Judgment) [1978] ICJ Rep 3, 32, para 77.

[40] *Navigational and Related Rights*, above n 37, para 64.

[41] See ILC, *Draft Conclusions on Subsequent Agreements and Subsequent Practice in Relation to the Interpretation of Treaties, with commentaries* (2018) Doc A/73/10, 51, item 8.

[42] R Gardiner, *Treaty Interpretation*, 2nd edn (Oxford, Oxford University Press, 2015) 467. On the other hand, tribunals have applied evolutionary interpretation as a 'relevant rule of international law applicable between the parties' under Art 31(3)(c) of the VCLT. *Award in the Arbitration regarding the Iron Rhine ('Ijzeren Rijn') (Belgium v Netherlands)* (2005) 27 *Reports of International Arbitral Awards* 35, 73, paras 79–80; *Philip Morris Brand Sàrl (Switzerland), Philip Morris Products SA (Switzerland) and Abal Hermanos SA (Uruguay) v Oriental Republic of Uruguay*, ICSID Case No ARB/10/7, Award, 8 July 2016, para 290. Evolutionary interpretation is linked to the concept of systemic integration, which is reflected in Art 31(3)(c) of the VCLT. See T Gazzini, *Interpretation of International Investment Treaties* (Oxford, Hart Publishing, 2016) 107.

[43] J Crawford, *State Responsibility: The General Part* (Cambridge, Cambridge University Press, 2011) 315–18.

[44] AK Bjorklund, 'The Enduring but Unwelcome Role of Party Intent in Treaty Interpretation' (2018) 112 *American Journal of International Law* 44.

[45] ILC, *Draft Conclusions on Subsequent Agreements and Subsequent Practice in Relation to the Interpretation of Treaties*, above n 41, 51, item 8.

the treaty and other relevant factors in terms of interpretation'.[46] In certain circumstances, '*not* to make an evolutionary interpretation would be that which would run counter to the intentions of the parties'.[47]

Several categories have been identified that may indicate when undertaking an evolutionary interpretation could be appropriate, including: (i) the treaty's terms embrace change of meaning; (ii) the treaty forms part of a regime 'inherently adapted to development', for example, treaties 'stating broad propositions of principle which necessarily involve elaboration to have precise effect'; and (iii) developments in the legal system impact a treaty, for example, 'emerging fields of law'.[48] All of the categories identified above are applicable to IIAs, as discussed below.

B. Evolutionary Interpretation of IIAs

It has been suggested that evolutionary interpretation might be particularly appropriate for certain types of treaties, including IIAs.[49] The nature of certain treaties, especially those intended to govern the relations of parties over an extended period of time, often give rise to situations where technology, law or other factors have changed significantly from when the treaty was concluded to the time of its application, necessitating that the treaty be interpreted in light of such developments in order for it to remain effective. With respect to IIAs, there are several generalised factors that make evolutionary interpretation particularly relevant, including in relation to SPPs, namely: (i) their characteristics; (ii) the circumstances of their conclusion; and (iii) their historical context.

First, some common characteristics of IIAs make them prime candidates for evolutionary interpretation, namely their substantive content and their duration. While it is impossible to accurately summarise such characteristics since there are currently over 3300 IIAs, the 'typical' 1990s BIT (which remains the bulk of IIAs concluded to date) consists of between approximately eight to 15 articles, of which perhaps three to five are broad and ambiguous substantive obligations on host States, such as FET or MST.[50] This has begun to change in recent years as parties have learned from ISDS cases, with some States concluding more

[46] *Navigational and Related Rights*, above n 37, 237, para 48. See also E Bjorge, 'Time Present and Time Past: The Intention of the Parties and the Evolutionary Interpretation of Treaties', ch 5 in this book.

[47] E Bjorge, *The Evolutionary Interpretation of Treaties* (Oxford, Oxford University Press, 2014) 9 (emphasis in original).

[48] Gardiner, above n 42, 468. Marceau has also identified similar categories. See G Marceau, 'Evolutive Interpretation by the WTO Adjudicator' (2018) 21 *Journal of International Economic Law* 791, 793.

[49] ILC *Draft Conclusions on Subsequent Agreements and Subsequent Practice in Relation to the Interpretation of Treaties 2013*, ILC Report 2013 UN Doc A/68/10, 19.

[50] For a further discussion of the use of evolutionary interpretation for IIAs, see MM Mbengue and A Florou, 'Evolutionary Interpretation in Investment Arbitration: About a Judicial Taboo', ch 23 in this book.

detailed IIAs, containing, for example, exhaustive lists, exceptions and explanatory annexes.[51] Nonetheless, the vast majority of the IIAs in force today are 'older generation' IIAs whose provisions are broad and vague, and some newer treaties are still based on these models.[52] Even if an IIA is detailed, however, many of the standards therein remain broad and ambiguous (or 'generic' and 'not static') indicating that the parties may have wanted to permit flexibility of the terms to adapt and evolve over time.

With regard to duration, parties typically enter into IIAs for an initial period of (varying) years, which are then automatically extended.[53] Such treaties also typically contain 'survival clauses' providing that even after an IIA party gives notice of termination, the IIA remains in force for an additional period of time, during which the parties can still be subject to disputes thereunder. The length of survival clauses varies, ranging from five to 30 years. Thus, IIAs may govern investment promotion and protection regimes between treaty parties for significant periods of time, even after termination.[54]

Second, another peculiarity of IIAs are the circumstances and context of the conclusion of the vast majority of IIAs, which occurred in the 1990s. Investment arbitration was relatively unknown at that time, and BITs, the most popular IIA to conclude then, were typically entered into with very limited negotiation of their terms, sometimes at mass-signature sessions held by international organisations where ministers would sign multiple BITs in a day with little or no discussion thereon, usually without consulting a legal team.[55] Capital-importing States often accepted the model BIT of a capital-exporting State, without any modification of the terms or possibly substantive knowledge thereof. As a result, the overwhelming majority of IIAs, especially BITs, do not have *travaux préparatoires* or any other material or State practice that explains a State's understanding of a given treaty's terms, aside from possible domestic ratification processes.

Third, from a historical and geopolitical perspective, the 1990s was a period of rapid trade liberalisation and globalisation, during which BITs, FTAs and regional trade agreements proliferated. Stemming from the signature of nearly 2000 IIAs in less than 10 years,[56] international investment law quickly catapulted into a specialised area of law as disputes began to arise. Further, international investment law was largely developed by ad hoc arbitral tribunals in a system without mandatory

[51] See, eg, CETA, above n 19.

[52] See, eg, UNCTAD, *Investment and New Industrial Policies*, World Investment Report (2018) 98.

[53] For a description of different types of IIA extensions, see UNCTAD, 'International Investment Policymaking in Transition: Challenges and Opportunities of Treaty Renewal' (June 2013) 4 IIA Issues Note 3–5.

[54] UNCTAD, *Global Value Chains: Investment and Trade for Development, World Investment Report* (2013) 108–10.

[55] LNS Poulsen and E Aisbett, 'Diplomats Want Treaties: Diplomatic Agendas and Perks in the Investment Regime' (2016) 7 *Journal of International Dispute Settlement* 72.

[56] See 'Bilateral Investment Treaties' UNCTAD, UNCTAD/ITE/IIA/2, 1, available at: www.unctad.org/en/Docs/poiteiiad2.en.pdf.

stare decisis, with respect to vague and ambiguous norms and obligations. Thus, the resulting arbitral awards and the substantive standards of international investment law that emerged therefrom may have deviated from what IIA signatories understood their obligations to mean at signature.

In addition, ISDS exploded during the digital revolution, in which, for example, SPPs and arbitral awards became readily available on the internet. Thus, it could be argued that development during this time period makes the evolutionary interpretation of IIAs particularly appropriate, and the recourse to SPPs logical. As stated by the *Hesham Talaat v Indonesia* ISDS tribunal:

> [I]n respect of the interpretation of a treaty relating to a subject matter such as the settlement of investment disputes which has undergone a rapid transformation between the date of the Treaty and the date of the interpretation, then the Tribunal must consider in this context the rule of inter-temporal interpretation.[57]

C. Evolutionary Interpretation in ISDS

Despite the potential utility of the evolutionary interpretation of IIAs, ISDS tribunals have not frequently relied on it,[58] which is not entirely surprising given that evolutionary interpretation is not uniformly embraced. However, this could also be explained by the still relatively short time period that has passed since the entry into force of most of these agreements in the 1990s/2000s and the subsequent boom in investment arbitration – ie, interpreters may not perceive that enough time has passed to explicitly utilise evolutionary interpretation with respect to treaties that are only approximately 20 years old. However, a few ISDS tribunals have done so;[59] further to this chapter's focus, only the NAFTA case of *Merrill & Ring Forestry v Canada* will be discussed herein.

Merrill & Ring was initiated in 2006; like the NAFTA cases discussed above, the issue arose concerning the meaning of the FET standard with relation to CIL. While the tribunal accepted that the 2001 FTC Notes were binding according to the NAFTA's provisions, the tribunal noted that the interpretations in the FTC Notes may not reflect the current state of CIL, the 'evolutionary nature' of which the tribunal was 'mindful of' and 'which provides scope for the interpretation of [NAFTA's FET article], even in the light of the FTC's 2001 interpretation'.[60]

[57] *Hesham Talaat v Republic of Indonesia*, UNCITRAL, Award on Respondent's Preliminary Objections to Jurisdiction and Admissibility of the Claims, 12 June 2012, para 72.3. The inter-temporal rule is comprised of two concepts, one of which is evolutionary interpretation. See M Dawidowicz, 'The Effect of the Passage of Time on the Interpretation of Treaties: Some Reflections on *Costa Rica v Nicaragua*' (2011) 24 *Leiden Journal of International Law* 201.

[58] For a discussion of the reluctance of ISDS tribunals to explicitly refer to evolutionary interpretation, see Mbengue and Florou, above n 50.

[59] See, eg, *Philip Morris v Uruguay* above n 42, para 290; *RosInvestCo UK Ltd v The Russian Federation*, SCC Case No V079/2005, Award on Jurisdiction, October 2007, para 121.

[60] *Merrill & Ring Forestry LP v The Government of Canada*, ICSID Case No UNCT/07/1, Award, 31 March 2010, paras 190, 192.

Canada argued that if an evolutionary interpretation of FET was appropriate at all, such evolution must have occurred subsequent to the issuance of the FTC Notes, and that no such evolution of the standard had taken place. The tribunal disagreed, effectively sidestepping the FTC Notes,[61] and proceeded to re-analyse the CIL standard that the FTC Notes tied FET to[62] (which the tribunal even noted that Canada had adhered to as the relevant standard in its SPPs in other NAFTA disputes)[63] to conclude that there was a specialised standard in business, trade and investment.[64]

Further, the tribunal noted that:

> [I]f the FTC Interpretation was construed so as to narrow the protection against unfair and inequitable treatment to an international minimum standard requiring outrageous conduct of some kind, then consistency would demand that the same standard be followed in respect of claims made by the NAFTA States in respect of the conduct of other countries affecting business, trade or investment interests of their citizens abroad. Yet this is not the case under current international practice.[65]

While the tribunal failed to provide explicit examples of the 'current international practice' on which it relied, it had previously mentioned the claims brought by governments on behalf of their nationals before the Iran–US Claims tribunal.[66] Thus, the tribunal ascribes weight to the interpretive legal arguments made in the form of claims brought by States as claimants, which comprise part of the SPPs of a given dispute. All the more interesting is that, in arriving at its conclusions, the tribunal looked to the SPPs/State practice not of the disputing State party (ie, Canada), but rather one of its treaty partners (ie, the United States) with respect to the latter's SPPs made in respect of a treaty (ie, the Algiers Accords) that was not the treaty in dispute (ie, the NAFTA) and to which Canada was not a party.

Merrill & Ring thus illuminates possible roles that States' interpretations in SPPs may play in ISDS and particularly with relation to evolutionary interpretation, as addressed further below.

IV. SPPs and Evolutionary Interpretation

Given the circumstances of the conclusion of most existing IIAs and the unusual characteristics of IIAs and ISDS, SPPs may be the medium through which States

[61] The tribunal said that the FTC Note 'does not refer to the specific content of [CIL] at a given moment and it is not an interpretative note of such content. Accordingly, the matter needs to be examined in the light of the evolution of customary law over time', ibid, para 194.

[62] The Neer standard. See *LFH Neer and Pauline Neer (USA) v United Mexican States*, Decision on the Merits, 15 October 1926 (1951) 4 *Reports of International Arbitral Awards* 60.

[63] *Merrill & Ring v Canada*, above n 60, para 195.

[64] ibid, para 200.

[65] ibid, para 212.

[66] ibid, para 207.

most consistently, frequently and sometimes publicly address the interpretation of the IIAs that they are party to, which may further have a role to play with regard to the evolutionary interpretation of IIAs, as evident from *Merrill & Ring* above.

SPPs are a form of State practice.[67] Courts and tribunals have had recourse to a wealth of State practice to illuminate parties' interpretations with respect to the evolutionary interpretation of treaties.[68] Further, SPPs have been specifically linked to the evolutionary interpretation of bilateral treaties outside ISDS, notably in the *Pulp Mills* ICJ case. In *Pulp Mills*, Argentina and Uruguay agreed in their SPPs that certain principles of international environmental law were applicable to the dispute, although they disagreed on their content and consequences.[69]

The ICJ noted the parties' agreement that general principles of international law applied to the proceeding, but only applied some of the rules of international environmental law that the parties agreed applied.[70]

Judge Cançado Trindade dissented on this point, noting that the treaty must be interpreted in light of the development of international law at the time of interpretation, and that the parties agreed that the excluded principles applied.[71] In other words, Judge Trindade found it persuasive that the parties agreed in their SPPs that certain principles applied to the treaty's interpretation and felt that this implicated evolutionary interpretation.

Judge Trindade's reasoning can be extended to SPPs interpretations in ISDS, especially in relation to the evolutionary interpretation of IIAs. The interpretations of an IIA made in parties' SPPs may provide illuminative information that could lead an interpreter to determine that the parties' intent was to give evolutionary interpretation to certain terms of an IIA, or conversely, that such was not their intention.

For example, SPPs could be used to illustrate that the meaning – or even the parties' understanding – of a term has changed over time, ie, that it evolved, which would demonstrate the parties' intent that the treaty term in question be given an evolutionary meaning. In other words, if in their SPPs, the parties have offered evolutionary interpretations of a treaty to account for developments in law or circumstance, an interpreter could take that into consideration. Similarly, since

[67] ILC, *Draft Conclusions on Subsequent Agreements and Subsequent Practice in Relation to the Interpretation of Treaties*, above n 41, 17, item 18; Roberts, 'Power and Persuasion', above n 15, 217–20.

[68] Such as, eg, States' explanatory statements at ratification (*Iron Rhine* above n 42, para 82) and protocols (*EC-Measures Affecting the Approval and Marketing of Biotech Products*, 7 February 2006, WT/DS291-293/INTERIM, 299, para 7.67.

[69] See *Pulp Mills on the River Uruguay (Argentina v Uruguay)*, Argentina Memorial, 15 January 2007, paras 3.158–3.160; *Pulp Mills on the River Uruguay (Argentina v Uruguay)*, Uruguay Rejoinder, 29 July 2008, paras 5.6, 5.23.

[70] *Pulp Mills on the River Uruguay (Argentina v Uruguay)* (Judgment) [2010] ICJ Rep 14, 43, para 57.

[71] *Pulp Mills on the River Uruguay (Argentina v Uruguay)*, Dissent of Jude Cançado Trindade [2010] ICJ Rep 135, 161–76, paras 97–113.

treaty parties may appear in numerous proceedings, if their interpretations of an IIA term in their SPPs has changed over time or if SPPs provide evidence of how a concept has evolved, this could be further support for an evolutionary interpretation of an IIA.[72] Similarly, the *Merrill & Ring* tribunal relied on the claims advanced in the NAFTA parties' SPPs to indicate that a standard should be given an evolutionary, investment-law specific, meaning (albeit this interpretation was contrary to the NAFTA parties' SPPs in other disputes, including from that proceeding).

On the other hand, SPPs could reveal that the treaty parties' interpretation of an IIA concept remained static, thus indicating that an evolutionary interpretation is not appropriate. An example is the discussion surrounding the meaning of the NAFTA FET standard, which the treaty parties believed to have one meaning (ie, that the standard was tied to the CIL standard) while ISDS tribunals determined it had another meaning (ie, that FET had acquired an investment-law specific meaning).[73] When tribunals did not accept the NAFTA parties' agreed interpretations presented in their SPPs over the course of several disputes,[74] the parties took the next step and issued the binding FTC Notes in order to force recognition and application of their interpretations (arguably unsuccessfully),[75] a phenomenon characterised by Mbengue and Florou as 'ex post facto reactions' to evolutionary interpretations by ISDS tribunals.[76] Along this vein, at least one arbitrator in an ISDS case has relied on the FTC Notes as an indication of why the majority's 'disguised recourse to evolutionary interpretation' was inappropriate (specifically that the FET provision in a BIT should not be read to encompass legitimate expectations), since the NAFTA parties issued the FTC Notes precisely in response to ISDS tribunals' interpretations that the NAFTA parties considered to be incorrect.[77] Later in his argument, the arbitrator referred to the interpretations presented in the SPPs of the disputing party in that case, Argentina, to illustrate its agreement with the standard laid out in the FTC Notes.[78]

[72] eg, Mexico's SPPs from NAFTA disputes (its pleadings and Art 1128 submissions) reveal its evolving interpretations of some of NAFTA's provisions. See, eg, LP Coulombe et al, 'Standards under the North American Free Trade Agreement' (2011) 10 CTEI Working Paper.

[73] Similar discussions have arisen with regard to, eg, Most Favoured Nation clauses in IIAs. See, eg, *Telefónica*, above n 5; *Gas Natural*, above n 6.

[74] See, eg, *Methanex Corporation v United States of America*, UNCITRAL, Post-Hearing Submission of Respondent United States of America, n 2920 July 2001, 2–4 (arguing this was a subsequent agreement under Art 31(3)(a)); *Grand River Enterprises Six Nations Ltd et al v United States of America*, UNCITRAL, Counter-Memorial of the Respondent the United States of America, 22 December 2008, 63 (referencing Canada and Mexico's Art 1128 submissions in *Methanex*; the United States' Art 1128 submissions in *Pope & Talbot*; and Canada's Counter-Memorial in *Merrill & Ring Forestry v Canada*).

[75] See, eg, *Pope & Talbot Inc*, Award on the Merits of Phase 2, above n 5, para 79.

[76] See Mbengue and Florou above n 50 (giving as an example, in addition to the FTC Notes, the interpretive declaration issued by Argentina and Panama following the *Siemens* case (*Siemens AG v The Argentine Republic*, ICSID Case No ARB/02/8, Decision on Jurisdiction, 3 August 2004).

[77] See *Suez, Sociedad General de Aguas de Barcelona SA and Vivendi Universal SA v The Argentine Republic*, ICSID Case No ARB/03/19, Decision on Liability, 30 July 2010, Separate Opinion of Pedro Nikken, para 6.

[78] ibid, para 9.

Indeed, the NAFTA MST/FET saga illustrates that SPPs can play a role in both respects, given that the *Merrill & Ring* tribunal relied on two occasions on separate examples of SPPs in reaching a contrary interpretation than that put forward by the disputing NAFTA party in its SPPs (submitted in that case and in other cases). Furthermore, the tribunal used SPPs as one justification to sidestep the NAFTA parties' attempt to bind tribunals' interpretations via the FTC Notes.

In this regard, the potential role of SPPs in the evolutionary interpretation of IIAs is twofold: (i) as evidence of the treaty parties' intent of whether the treaty or term should be given an evolutionary interpretation; and (ii) as substantive guidance to what that interpretation should be. Under this rubric, the tribunal may still arrive at the interpretation it determines is correct since such interpretations are not binding;[79] however, the tribunal should address the treaty parties' SPP interpretations in arriving at its conclusions and should convincingly justify any departure therefrom. The weight of SPPs could vary depending on, for example, their frequency – such as when several similar submissions have been made before multiple tribunals over a period of time. Non-disputing party SPPs, such as those under NAFTA Article 1128, could also provide stronger evidence of evolving (or static) interpretive understandings.

The use of SPPs for the purposes of evolutionary interpretation is all the more appropriate if one accepts the view that evolutionary interpretation is an attempt to find the parties' intent. Parties' SPPs that very clearly state the parties' interpretation of a treaty term are clear examples of what the parties intend that treaty to mean; all the more so considering their SPPs contain interpretive statements directed to an arbitrator who is empowered to issue a binding ruling on that matter.[80] An interpreter attempting to identify the parties' intention must do so 'on the basis of the means of interpretation that are available at the time of the act of interpretation,'[81] which for many IIAs may only be the parties' SPPs. If SPPs either explicitly state that the parties intended that a concept be ascribed an evolutionary interpretation, or on the other hand, that the parties did not intend for that type of interpretation to be applied, such statements may provide additional material to a tribunal that is trying to ascertain whether the evolutionary interpretation of a treaty is appropriate.

Furthermore, some ISDS tribunals have already relied on SPPs as subsequent practice and supplementary means of interpretation under VCLT Articles 31(3)(b) and 32, respectively.[82] Therefore, if it is accepted that evolutionary interpretation

[79] See, eg, ILC, *Draft Conclusions on Subsequent Agreements and Subsequent Practice in Relation to the Interpretation of Treaties*, above n 41, 10, item 4.

[80] Of course, such statements are not made at the time of the treaty's conclusion but rather during a proceeding, which could pose a temporal problem if proper intent is considered solely to be the original intent of the parties at the conclusion of the IIA. Thus, the temporal aspect of what the parties intended the treaty to mean at the time of conclusion may provide some limitation on the extent of the role that SPPs play, if this factor is considered dispositive.

[81] ILC, 'Interpretations of Treaty Terms as Capable of Evolving Over Time' (2018) A/73/10, 97, para 9.

[82] *Canadian Cattlemen*, above n 5; *HICEE*, Partial Award, above n 5.

is the proper application of the means of interpretation, for example, VCLT Articles 31 and 32,[83] then the agreed interpretive positions of the parties in their SPPs could play a very important, and perhaps mandatory, role in the evolutionary interpretation of IIAs.

Indeed, in practice, SPPs have already been tied to evolutionary interpretation.[84] It is not a leap to extend this to party interpretations of IIAs in SPPs, as has already been recognised to an extent by, for example, the *Merrill & Ring* NAFTA tribunal; doing so may fulfil the will of the parties, render the treaty effective or provide convincing evidence for whether evolutionary interpretation of an IIA is appropriate.

V. Conclusion

The above reveals that SPPs could have an informative role to play in the evolutionary interpretations of IIAs in ISDS disputes, as a primary means by which treaty parties can present their interpretations of the often broad and ambiguous IIA provisions that govern the investment promotion and protection regimes between parties for potentially significant periods of time. Indeed, some adjudicators have looked to State practice, including SPPs and interpretive statements, when undertaking evolutionary interpretations of treaties, demonstrating that the parties' arguments presented in their SPPs may assist the evolutionary interpretation of IIAs in ISDS.

SPPs are only one of many sources that may possibly illuminate the evolutionary meaning of an IIA. In other words, SPPs may not necessarily be binding or authoritative, nor overrule a term's ordinary meaning or the discernable intent of the parties at the IIA's conclusion, but could be used as a piece of the interpretive puzzle. For example, SPPs would be more persuasive for purposes of an IIA's evolutionary interpretation in situations: (i) where the parties have presented the same interpretations in multiple SPPs in different proceedings – like in the NAFTA FET/MST cases; or (ii) when SPP practice indicates that the parties have interpreted a treaty in an evolutionary manner, or on the contrary, when States assert in their SPPs – explicitly or implicitly – that evolutionary interpretation is not appropriate. Either way, SPPs could provide pertinent information to tribunals, as 'it may be difficult for the interpreter to establish the willingness of the contracting parties to use a term whose meaning could evolve'.[85]

If tribunals ignore the parties' interpretations of IIAs put forward in their SPPs, however, this could contribute to the current 'backlash' against ISDS. In the NAFTA context, this is reflected in the draft text of the renegotiated NAFTA

[83] ILC, *Draft Conclusions on Subsequent Agreements and Subsequent Practice in Relation to the Interpretation of Treaties*, above n 41, 51, item 8.

[84] By Judge Trindade in his dissent in *Pulp Mills*, see above n 71.

[85] Gazzini, above n 42, 106.

(renamed the United States–Mexico–Canada Agreement (USMCA)),[86] which has vastly reduced ISDS provisions.[87] Giving interpretive weight to the parties' interpretations in their SPPs, especially in relation to evolutionary interpretation, may not only satisfy States that their interpretations are not being ignored, but may also allow tribunals to give effect to the over 3300 IIAs currently in existence, many of whose terms are unlikely to be renegotiated in the near future, while international investment law continues its rapid evolution.

[86] eg, ISDS is eliminated entirely between Canada and Mexico. United States–Mexico–Canada Agreement, available at: ustr.gov/trade-agreements/free-trade-agreements/united-states-mexico-canada-agreement/united-states-mexico.

[87] N Bernasconi-Osterwalder, 'USMCA Curbs How Much Investors Can Sue Countries – Sort Of', *IISD*, available at: www.iisd.org/library/usmca-investors. Notwithstanding reduced ISDS access, the USMCA gives the non-disputing treaty parties (USMCA adopts the nomenclature 'Non-Disputing Annex Parties') the right to make a submission on a matter of interpretation, indicating the value that the parties assign to the availability of such submissions. United States–Mexico–Canada Agreement,availableat:ustr.gov/trade-agreements/free-trade-agreements/united-states-mexico-canada-agreement/united-states-mexico, art 14.D.7.

25

Investment Treaty Signatories' Joint Interpretation and the Case of the NAFTA Free Trade Commission: Evolutionary Interpretation or Modification?

JENNIFER RADFORD, GREGORY TEREPOSKY AND KUN HUI

I. Introduction

The definition of 'evolutionary interpretation' is unsettled.[1] In general, evolutionary interpretation connotes that the meaning of a treaty term may change over time.[2] In his seminal work on evolutionary treaty interpretation, Eirik Bjorge demystifies the concept of evolutionary interpretation through the lens of the treaty parties' intention. He argues that evolutionary interpretation revolves around one fundamental question: what is the treaty parties' intention?[3] Bjorge argues that evolutionary interpretation is not a separate method of interpretation. Instead, it is the result of a proper application of Article 31 of the Vienna Convention on the Law of Treaties (VCLT) so as to establish the parties' intention in international adjudication.[4]

This chapter builds on Bjorge's argument and applies it to disputes arising in the investor–State dispute settlement (ISDS) context. We argue that in investment treaty regimes, State parties are well positioned to provide joint interpretations to clarify their collective intention so as to lead to evolutionary treaty interpretation.

[1] R Gardiner, *Treaty Interpretation*, 2nd edn (Oxford, Oxford University Press, 2015) 467.

[2] C Djeffal, *Static and Evolutive Treaty Interpretation: A Functional Reconstruction* (Cambridge, Cambridge University Press, 2016) 18–19; ST Helmersen, 'Evolutive Treaty Interpretation: Legality, Semantics and Distinctions' (2013) 6 *European Journal of Legal Studies* 127, 128.

[3] E Bjorge, *The Evolutionary Interpretation of Treaties* (Oxford, Oxford University Press, 2014) 2; see also E Bjorge, 'Time Present and Time Past: The Intention of the Parties and the Evolutionary Interpretation of Treaties', ch 5 in this book.

[4] Bjorge, *The Evolutionary Interpretation of Treaties*, ibid, 9–10, 63.

In other words, not only can international courts and tribunals undertake evolutionary treaty interpretation in adjudication, but States can also steer evolutionary interpretation by issuing joint interpretations when an interpretative dispute arises. The rationale of our argument is that State parties to international treaties are best suited to speak for their collective intention for treaties to which they are a party. A pre-established joint interpretative mechanism provides the treaty parties with the means of doing so. A joint interpretation mechanism embedded in a treaty informs investors and tribunals alike that in addition to tribunals' interpretations of parties' intention in adjudication, State parties will provide interpretation of a treaty provision when they see fit. Such State-initiated interpretation ensures rather than hinders due process of dispute resolution. In sum, State parties' joint interpretation is State-led evolutionary interpretation which is a highly beneficial mechanism.

The joint interpretation issued by the Free Trade Commission (FTC) – composed of trade ministers – of the North American Free Trade Agreement (NAFTA) is the first one of its kind. On 31 July 2001, the FTC issued Notes of Interpretation of Certain Chapter 11 Provisions (FTC Interpretation). The FTC Interpretation provides that the extent of protection provided by the fair and equitable treatment provision set out in Article 1105 does not go beyond the customary international law minimum standard of treatment to aliens.

Immediately following its issuance, the FTC Interpretation received criticisms from disputing parties in ongoing cases,[5] practitioners and scholars.[6] They contended that the FTC Interpretation is a disguised treaty modification 'plotted' by the NAFTA parties. Moreover, they asserted that the FTC Interpretation jeopardises the integrity and the due process of the NAFTA arbitration process. Others considered this was the NAFTA parties' reassertion of their control over regulatory and interpretation authorities.[7] However, some scholars argued that the FTC Interpretation is not treaty modification but rather the FTC's legitimate exercise of its interpretative rights.[8]

In this chapter, we reassess the above debate from the perspective of evolutionary interpretation. Unlike the critics, we argue that the FTC Interpretation is

[5] *Pope & Talbot Inc v The Government of Canada*, UNCITRAL, Investor's Reply re Implications of the Interpretation of NAFTA Article 1105 by the NAFTA Commission, 10 September 2001, 3–5.

[6] CH Brower, II, 'Why the FTC Notes of Interpretation Constitute a Partial Amendment of NAFTA Article 1105' (2006) 46 *Virginia Journal of International Law* 347; G Kaufmann-Kohler, 'Interpretative Powers of the Free Trade Commission and the Rule of Law' in F Bachand (ed), *Fifteen Years of NAFTA Chapter 11 Arbitration* (New York, JurisNet, LLC 2011).

[7] E Methymaki and A Tzanakopoulos, 'Masters or Puppets? Reassertion of Control through Joint Investment Treaty Interpretation' in A Kulick (ed), *Reassertion of Control over the Investment Treaty Regime* (Cambridge, Cambridge University Press, 2017); S Schill, *The Multilateralization of International Investment Law* (Cambridge, Cambridge University Press, 2009) 271.

[8] A Roberts, 'Power and Persuasion in Investment Treaty Interpretation: The Dual Role of States' (2010) 104 *American Journal of International Law* 179; W Alschner, 'The Return of the Home State and the Rise of "Embedded" Investor–State Arbitration' in S Lalani and R Polanco Lazo (eds), *The Role of State in Investor–State Arbitration* (Leiden, Brill Nijhoff, 2015).

not treaty modification. It is State-led evolutionary treaty interpretation which is entirely appropriate. This is because State parties are the best positioned to speak for their drafting and negotiation intentions. To determine the meaning of a treaty term, the treaty parties' collective interpretation speaks with greater weight than arbitral tribunals' interpretation of the parties' purported intention. As NAFTA's Article 2001 authorises the FTC to do so *when* an interpretative dispute arises, the FTC Interpretation ensures the due process and the predictability of the Chapter 11 arbitration process for its participants. This is contrary to the allegations that the FTC Interpretation disrupts the due process of NAFTA Chapter 11 arbitration. As State-led evolutionary interpretation, State parties' joint interpretative efforts allow for State intent to be translated into reality. As such, the FTC Interpretation serves as a model for future investment treaty regimes to adopt.

This chapter includes the following parts. Part II introduces the NAFTA FTC and its mandate. Part III illustrates the debate revolving around the nature of the FTC Interpretation in NAFTA cases. While doing so, we demonstrate that the FTC Interpretation is neither treaty modification nor the NAFTA States' reassertion of their sovereignty. Instead, issuing the FTC Interpretation is the NAFTA parties' exercise of their rights of treaty interpretation embedded in the NAFTA. Part IV reinforces our position through the perspective of evolutionary treaty interpretation. Part V concludes that the FTC Interpretation is the NAFTA parties' contribution to evolutionary interpretation. Thus, the FTC Interpretation tool serves as an example for future treaty negotiators and investment tribunals.

II. The FTC and its Mandate

The FTC was established according to Article 2001 of the NAFTA. One of its mandates is to 'resolve disputes that may arise regarding [the NAFTA's] interpretation and application'.[9] Article 1131(2) provides that '[a]n interpretation by the [Free Trade] Commission of a provision of this Agreement shall be binding on a Tribunal established under this Section'.[10] Together, Articles 2001 and 1131 empower the FTC to issue binding interpretation when interpretative disputes arise regarding NAFTA Chapter 11 provisions.

On 31 July 2001, the FTC, for the first time, exercised its interpretative power and issued the FTC Interpretation.[11] The FTC Interpretation covers two issues. First, transparency. Second, the understanding of the relationship between the minimum standard of treatment and the fair and equitable treatment in

[9] North American Free Trade Agreement (adopted 17 December 1992); (1993) 32 *International Legal Materials* 612 (NAFTA) Art 2001(2)(c).

[10] ibid, Art 1131(2).

[11] NAFTA Free Trade Commission, 'Notes of Interpretation of Certain Chapter 11 Provision', 31 July 2001.

Article 1105. This chapter focuses on the second aspect – the interpretation of NAFTA's Article 1105.

NAFTA's Article 1105 is titled 'minimum standard of treatment' and its subsection one provides that:

> 1. Each Party shall accord to investments of investors of another Party treatment in accordance with international law, including fair and equitable treatment and full protection and security.

The decisions of three cases – *Metalclad*, *SD Myers*, and *Pope & Talbot* prompted the FTC to issue the FTC Interpretation. Those three tribunals found that the respondent States violated Article 1105's fair and equitable treatment (FET) standard.[12] The NAFTA parties were concerned that such a broad interpretation of Article 1105 made by the three tribunals would lead to future tribunals reaching similar interpretations.[13] To check this unintended broad interpretation on a going forward basis, the three NAFTA parties issued the interpretation of Article 1105.[14] Thus, some commentators state that the FTC issued the Interpretation to correct the mistakes made by prior tribunals.[15] This appears clear from the FTC Interpretation's opening statement, which provides that '[h]aving reviewed the operation of proceedings conducted under Chapter Eleven', the FTC adopted the following interpretation of Article 1105. It provides that:

> 2. Minimum Standard of Treatment in Accordance with International Law
>
> 1. Article 1105(1) prescribes the customary international law minimum standard of treatment of aliens as the minimum standard of treatment to be afforded to investments of investors of another Party.
> 2. The concepts of 'fair and equitable treatment' and 'full protection and security' do not require treatment in addition to or beyond that which is required by the customary international law minimum standard of treatment of aliens.
> 3. A determination that there has been a breach of another provision of the NAFTA, or of a separate international agreement, does not establish that there has been a breach of Article 1105(1).[16]

The FTC Interpretation emphasises that its aim is to 'clarify and reaffirm the meaning of certain of its provisions'. The FTC Interpretation connects the minimum standard of treatment with customary international law. It then specifies

[12] *Metalclad Corporation v The United Mexican States*, ICSID Case No ARB(AF)/97/1, Award, 30 August 2000; *SD Myers, Inc v Government of Canada*, UNCITRAL, First Partial Award, 13 November 2000; *Pope & Talbot Inc v The Government of Canada*, UNCITRAL, Award on the Merits of Phase 2, 10 April 2001.

[13] T Weiler, 'NAFTA Investment Arbitration and the Growth of International Economic Law' (2002) 36 *Canadian Business Law Journal* 405, 422.

[14] P Dumberry, *The Fair and Equitable Treatment Standard: A Guide to NAFTA Case Law on NAFTA 1105* (The Netherlands, Wolters Kluwer, 2013) 66; Brower, above n 6, 352.

[15] Dumberry, ibid, 68, 70; Weiler, 'NAFTA Investment Arbitration and the Growth of International Economic Law', above n 13, 426.

[16] NAFTA Free Trade Commission, 'Notes of Interpretation'.

that the FET standard provided in Article 1105 does not go beyond the customary international law minimum standard of treatment.

Immediately following its issuance, the FTC Interpretation received criticisms. One allegation was that the FTC Interpretation was a disguised treaty modification 'plotted' by the NAFTA parties to 'influence the outcome of pending disputes'.[17] Commentators also alleged that the FTC Interpretation was an opportunistic move made by the NAFTA parties to avoid liability in ongoing cases and pre-empt further losses.[18] Others were concerned that the retroactive application of the FTC Interpretation jeopardised the due process of the NAFTA arbitration process as many Chapter 11 cases were pending at the time.[19] Meanwhile, some considered that the FTC Interpretation represented the NAFTA parties' reassertion of their control over regulatory and interpretative authorities.[20] Many authors contended that the FTC Interpretation was not treaty modification but the FTC's legitimate exercise of its interpretative rights.[21]

Investors launched challenges against the FTC Interpretation in cases following its issuance.[22] In the following section, we will illustrate the debate over the FTC Interpretation in NAFTA cases.

III. The Debate of the FTC Interpretation in NAFTA Case Law

The debate over the FTC Interpretation is vividly illustrated by two cases: *Pope & Talbot* and *ADF*. In the former proceeding, the tribunal challenged the nature of the FTC Interpretation. The tribunal declared that it had the power to decide the nature of the FTC Interpretation and decided that the Interpretation amounted to a disguised treaty amendment to be applied retroactively to influence ongoing cases.[23] In contrast, the *ADF* tribunal endorsed the FTC's interpretative power and declared that when all of the treaty parties have submitted to a tribunal their understanding of a NAFTA provision which they negotiated and agreed upon,

[17] Weiler, 'NAFTA Investment Arbitration and the Growth of International Economic Law', above n 13, 422; see also T Weiler, *The Interpretation of International Investment Law: Equity, Discrimination and Minimum Standards of Treatment in Historical Context* (Leiden, Brill Nijhoff, 2013) 250–59.

[18] Brower, above n 6, 352–53.

[19] Kaufmann-Kohler, above n 6, 181–85.

[20] Methymaki and Tzanakopoulos, above n 7, 155, 177–79; Schill, above n 7, 271.

[21] JC Thomas, 'A Reply to Professor Brower' (2002) *Columbia Journal of Transnational Law* 433, 453–55; Roberts, above n 8, 181; Alschner, above n 8, 293–333.

[22] *Pope & Talbot v Canada*, Investor's Reply, above n 5, 3–5; *Mondev International Ltd v United States of America*, ICSID Case No ARB(AF)/99/2, Award, 11 October 2002, para 102; see also *Methanex Corporation v United States of America*, UNCITRAL, Second Opinion of Professor Sir Robert Jennings, QC, 6 September 2001.

[23] *Pope & Talbot Inc v The Government of Canada*, UNCITRAL, Award in Respect of Damages, 31 May 2002, para 47.

there is no more authoritative instruction for a tribunal than the parties' intention crystallised in a joint interpretation.[24] Many NAFTA decisions followed the path of the *ADF* tribunal and declared that the FTC Interpretation is binding.[25] However, in 2008, the *Merrill Ring* tribunal second-guessed the nature of the FTC Interpretation.[26]

In this section, we review the debate of the FTC Interpretation as reflected in NAFTA case law. While doing so, we refute the argument that the FTC Interpretation is an amendment but rather treaty interpretation in the form of subsequent agreement as found in Article 31(3)(a) of the VCLT. We then show that the FTC Interpretation is not the NAFTA parties' reassertion of their sovereign right but the legitimate exercise of their interpretative rights embedded in NAFTA's Article 1331.

A. *Pope & Talbot v Canada*

While the *Pope & Talbot* tribunal was in the process of rendering an award on damages, the FTC issued its Interpretation. In its decision on damages, the *Pope & Talbot* tribunal considered the notion that the FTC Interpretation is a treaty amendment disguised in the form of a treaty interpretation.

During the damages phase, Canada submitted the FTC Interpretation to the tribunal for its consideration in the calculation of the appropriate quantum of damages. Before the tribunal made its decision, it posed the following question to the parties: 'Should the [FTC]'s interpretation be considered to have a retroactive effect on the rulings previously made by NAFTA tribunals?'[27] In response, Pope & Talbot argued that as the FTC Interpretation constituted treaty modification, it cannot have retrospective effect. Thus, the tribunal was not bound by it.[28] Canada disagreed. Canada replied that by its own terms, the FTC Interpretation was not an amendment of the provisions of the treaty. Canada asserted that the FTC Interpretation amounted to 'interpretations of Chapter Eleven in order to clarify and reaffirm the meaning of certain of its provisions'.[29] In its award on damages, the tribunal first claimed that it had 'a duty to consider' whether the FTC

[24] *ADF Group Inc v United States of America*, ICSID Case No ARB(AF)/00/1, Award, 9 January 2003, para 177.

[25] See, eg, *Loewen Group, Inc and Raymond L Loewen v United States of America*, ICSID Case No ARB(AF)/98/3, Award, 26 June 2003, para 126; *Cargill, Incorporated v United Mexican States*, ICSID Case No ARB(AF)/05/2, Award, 18 September 2009, para 268.

[26] *Merrill & Ring Forestry LP v The Government of Canada*, ICSID Case No UNCT/07/1, Award, 31 March 2010, para 191.

[27] *Pope & Talbot Inc v The Government of Canada*, Tribunal's Letter re Implication of the Interpretation of NAFTA Article 1105 by the NAFTA Commission, 14 August 2001.

[28] *Pope & Talbot v Canada*, Investor's Reply, above n 5, 5.

[29] *Pope & Talbot Inc v The Government of Canada*, Canada's Submission re Implications of the Interpretation of NAFTA Article 1105 by the NAFTA Commission, 10 September 2001.

had acted in accordance with Article 2001 and not simply accepted whatever the FTC had stated to be an interpretation for the purpose of Article 1131(2).[30] The tribunal stated that 'were the Tribunal required to make a determination whether the [FTC]'s action is an interpretation or an amendment, it would choose the latter';[31] it nevertheless stated that the FTC Interpretation was binding.[32] In light of the FTC Interpretation, the tribunal did not consider that its previous ruling that Canada had violated Article 1105 should be reversed.[33] Ultimately, the tribunal found Canada's act egregious and rendered an award with damages in favour of the investor.[34]

Merrill & Ring is another arbitration in which the tribunal doubted the FTC Interpretation. In the tribunal's analysis on the scope of Article 1105(1)'s fair and equitable treatment, it considered the FTC Interpretation.[35] The tribunal agreed with the claimant that 'the FTC Interpretation seems in some respect to be closer to an amendment of the treaty, than a strict interpretation'.[36] Further, it found that 'the binding character of the FTC Interpretation' does not mean it 'necessarily reflects the present state of customary and international law'.[37]

B. *ADF v United States*

In *ADF*, one of the questions the investor asked the tribunal to decide was whether the FTC Interpretation was an interpretation or amendment. The tribunal categorically stated that it did not have the power to determine for itself whether the FTC Interpretation was truly an interpretation or an amendment. The tribunal explained that:

> We observe … that the FTC Interpretation of 31 July 2001 expressly purports to be an interpretation of several NAFTA provisions, including Article 1105(1), and not an 'amendment', or anything else. No document purporting to be an amendment has been submitted by either the Respondent or the other NAFTA Parties … But whether a document submitted to a Chapter 11 tribunal purports to be an amendatory agreement in respect of which the Parties' respective internal constitutional procedures necessary for the entry into force of the amending agreement have been taken, or an interpretation rendered by the FTC under Article 1131(2), we have the Parties themselves – all the Parties – speaking to the Tribunal. No more authentic and authoritative source of instruction on what the Parties intended to convey in a particular provision of NAFTA, is possible. Nothing in NAFTA suggests that a Chapter 11 tribunal may determine for

[30] *Pope & Talbot v Canada*, Award in Respect of Damages, above n 23, para 23.
[31] ibid, para 47.
[32] ibid, paras 49–51.
[33] ibid, para 52.
[34] ibid, paras 67, 88.
[35] *Merrill & Ring v Canada*, above n 26, para 191.
[36] ibid, 192.
[37] ibid.

> itself whether a document submitted to it as an interpretation by the Parties acting through the FTC is in fact an 'amendment' which presumably may be disregarded until ratified by all the Parties under their respective internal law.[38]

Many NAFTA tribunals take a similar approach. For example, in *Methanex*, the tribunal found that 'the FTC interpretation would be entirely legal and binding on a tribunal seized with a Chapter 11 case'.[39] In *Mondev*, the tribunal stated that the FTC Interpretation constitutes 'the definitive statement of what the parties intended from the source designated by the Treaty as the ultimate and most authoritative source of its meaning, the Parties themselves', therefore, '[t]here is no difficulty in accepting this as an interpretation of the phrase "in accordance with international law"'.[40]

C. Comments

We submit that the *ADF* tribunal's reasoning is persuasive.[41] As the *Methanex* tribunal has stated, the FTC Interpretation qualifies as a subsequent agreement on interpretation falling within the ambit of Article 31(3)(a) of the VCLT.[42] According to the International Law Commission, 'an agreement as to the interpretation of a provision reached after the conclusion of a treaty represents an authentic interpretation by the parties that must be read into the treaty for the purpose of its interpretation'.[43] As such, even without the authorisation from Articles 2001 and 1131, the NAFTA parties are able to issue a joint interpretation that constitutes 'subsequent agreement between the parties regarding the interpretation of the treaty or the application of its provision' according to Article 31(3)(a) of the VCLT. When treaty parties conclude additional interpretative agreements on the treaties, they speak unanimously regarding their intention to other stakeholders under those treaties.

The NAFTA adds two extra layers of authority upon the FTC's Interpretation. First, the FTC is established and empowered to resolve an interpretative dispute on the proper understanding of a NAFTA Chapter 11 provision *when* the disputes arise according to Article 2001. Thus, the FTC is the authoritative body to issue a binding subsequent agreement that falls within Article 31(3)(a) of the VCLT. Second, the interpretative status of the FTC Interpretation is elevated by the governing law clause of NAFTA – Article 1131 – which provides that the FTC's interpretation has a binding effect on NAFTA Chapter 11 tribunals.

[38] *ADF v United States*, above n 24, para 177.

[39] *Methanex Corporation v United States of America*, UNCITRAL, Final Award of the Tribunal on Jurisdiction and Merits, 3 August 2005 pt IV, ch C, para 20.

[40] *Mondev v United States*, Award, above n 22, paras 103, 121.

[41] Dumberry, above n 14, 79.

[42] *Methanex v United States*, above n 39, pt IV, ch C, para 20.

[43] T Gazzini, *Interpretation of International Investment Treaties* (Oxford, Hart Publishing, 2016) 337.

This leads us to the interpretative nature of the FTC Interpretation. Two authors, JC Thomas and Wolfgang Alschner, refute the allegation against the FTC Interpretation that it is treaty amendment viewed from different angles. Thomas derives his arguments from the NAFTA text itself. In our opinion, he correctly states that Articles 2001 and 1131 enshrine the FTC's interpretative power and its Interpretation as part of the governing law on NAFTA Chapter 11 cases. Accordingly, the FTC Interpretation is not only an interpretation but unquestionably binding on parties in any given dispute at any time. When tribunals ignore this governing law, they are inviting judicial review.[44]

Wolfgang Alschner explains that the establishment of an 'embedded' FTC interpretation mechanism is attributable to NAFTA's hybrid nature of being a treaty that touches upon both trade and investment issues.[45] Thus, the trade law's intergovernmental features found their way into the investment chapter of NAFTA.[46] One example that Alschner points to is Article IX:2 of the WTO Agreement on authoritative interpretation, which provides that '[t]he Ministerial Conference and the General Council shall have the exclusive authority to adopt interpretations of this Agreement and of the Multilateral Trade Agreements'.[47] Further, Alschner argues that because of the United States' experience in Friendship, Commerce and Navigation agreements, the United States negotiators were more willing to insert public international law tools into the arbitration process, such as the FTC Interpretation mechanism.[48] He concludes that the 'embedded' FTC interpretation mechanism in the NAFTA was designed not as a response to the rising numbers of investment arbitrations, but rather a superior mechanism for governing investment dispute resolution.[49] Alschner's argument was confirmed by the United States in the hearing of the *Mondev* case. In that hearing, the United States stated that Article 1131 of the NAFTA is 'a rule designed just so that the parties could assure that what they meant by NAFTA's terms could be made known whenever there were misinterpretations'.[50] As the FTC Interpretation was embedded in the NAFTA long before any Chapter 11 cases emerged, the argument that the FTC Interpretation is 'plotted' by NAFTA parties while disputes were emerging should be rejected. It is NAFTA parties' legitimate exercise of their 'embedded' treaty interpretation rights.

The textual and historical analysis demonstrates that the FTC Interpretation is an interpretation not an amendment. Although both the *Pope & Talbot* and the *Merrill Ring* tribunals second-guessed the nature of the 'embedded' FTC

[44] Thomas, above n 21, 454–56.

[45] Alschner, above n 8, 303–04.

[46] ibid, 304.

[47] Agreement Establishing the World Trade Organization (adopted 15 April 1994) 1867 *United Nations Treaty Series* 3, Art IX: 2.

[48] Alschner, above n 8, 305.

[49] ibid.

[50] *Mondev v United States*, Hearing Transcript, 22 May 2002, 670; see also *Mondev v United States*, Award, above n 22, para 103; Gazzini, above n 43, 337.

Interpretation, they eventually accepted its binding effect. This prevents their decisions from challenge in national courts. However, their rationale hinders the States' collective effort to promote consistent application and interpretation of a treaty through a State-initiated joint interpretation mechanism. In the section that follows, we will argue and explain that the FTC Interpretation constitutes State-led evolutionary interpretation. For State-led evolutionary interpretation, States – the architects of the treaties – are suited to express their intention collectively.

IV. Why is the FTC Interpretation State-led Evolutionary Interpretation?

As we have noted, the definition of evolutionary interpretation is undecided.[51] In general, evolutionary interpretation connotes that the meaning of a treaty term may change over time.[52] In his seminal work on evolutionary interpretation, Eirik Bjorge argues that evolutionary interpretation is an interpretative exercise taken by international adjudicators to properly apply Articles 31 and 32 of the VCLT to address one question: What is the treaty parties' common intention?[53]

In the *Navigational Rights* decision made by the International Court of Justice (ICJ), the ICJ concludes that there are two means to reach evolutionary interpretation. First, the ICJ found that the subsequent practice of parties within the meaning of Article 31(3)(b) of the VCLT can result in evolutionary interpretation due to the parties' tacit agreement.[54] Second, the ICJ found that in some circumstances, the parties' common intention can be presumed to be given to some or all the terms. As a result, the content of these terms is capable of evolving.[55]

In his book, Bjorge briefly addresses the first dimension – the subsequent practice of the parties – in the *Navigational Rights* case and turns to focus his analysis on the second dimension on the role of international adjudicative bodies in evolutionary interpretation.[56] Bjorge argues that the core of evolutionary interpretation is about *international adjudicators*' proper application of the various means of treaty interpretation codified in the VCLT's Articles 31 and 32 to determine the parties' common intention on the meaning of a treaty term.[57]

[51] Gardiner, above n 1, 467.

[52] Djeffal, above n 2, 18–19; Helmersen, above n 2, 128.

[53] Bjorge, *The Evolutionary Interpretation of Treaties*, above n 3, 9–10, 63.

[54] *Dispute Regarding Navigational and Related Rights (Costa Rica v Nicaragua)* (Judgment) [2009] ICJ Rep 213, para 64; see also Bjorge, *The Evolutionary Interpretation of Treaties*, above n 3, 76.

[55] *Navigational and Related Rights*, ibid, para 64; see also Bjorge, *The Evolutionary Interpretation of Treaties* above n 3, 76.

[56] Bjorge, *The Evolutionary Interpretation of Treaties*, above n 3, 59, 76–77.

[57] ibid, 2.

Situating ourselves within the context of the NAFTA, we explore the first dimension of evolutionary treaty interpretation laid out by the ICJ in the *Navigational Rights* case – State parties' subsequent practice.[58] Our interest is this: as the ascertainment of the common intention of the treaty parties is the cornerstone of the evolutionary treaty interpretation in tribunal-led evolutionary interpretation, how can *States* participate and contribute to the evolutionary interpretation? Is there a State-led evolutionary interpretation? To address this question, we look beyond the subsequent State practice regarding the interpretation of the treaty. We examine to what extent the combination of subsequent agreements and subsequent practice of States, as part of the various means of Article 31 of the VCLT, can assist State-led evolutionary treaty interpretation.

We submit that there is State-led evolutionary interpretation and that States themselves are well positioned to contribute to the evolutionary treaty interpretation. The intention-driven rationale of tribunal-led revolutionary treaty interpretation applies to State-led evolutionary interpretation. In other words, State-led evolutionary interpretation is also intention driven. A joint interpretation mechanism is an effective way for States to express their collective intention when an interpretative dispute arises. In fact, to determine the meaning of a treaty term, the treaty parties' collective interpretation speaks with greater weight than arbitral tribunals' interpretation of the parties' purported intention. Further, a joint interpretation puts both investors and tribunals on clear notice of the State parties' interpretative power.[59] In this vein, the joint interpretative effort does not undermine the due process of the arbitration; rather it benefits all stakeholders under the treaties.

The NAFTA FTC Interpretation demonstrates that State-led evolutionary interpretation can be carried out through States' subsequent agreements and reinforced by their subsequent practice. As we have set out above, NAFTA's Articles 2001 and 1131 provide the three State parties with the means to issue binding interpretations. Further, Article 1128 of the NAFTA permits non-disputing parties to submit their opinions on any given ongoing dispute.[60] This is the NAFTA parties' consistent subsequent practice. In practice, the NAFTA parties have consistently reinforced their positions that the fair and equitable treatment does not go beyond the minimum standard of treatment to aliens under the customary international law in NAFTA Chapter 11 arbitration.[61]

[58] For a review of the ISDS tribunals' role in evolutionary treaty interpretation that this chapter does not touch upon, see C Giannakopoulos and M Monga, 'History as Interpretative Context in the Evolutionary Interpretation of FET in International Investment Law', ch 26; and MM Mbengue and A Florou, 'Evolutionary Interpretation in Investment Arbitration: About a Judicial Taboo' ch 23 in this book.

[59] Roberts, above n 8, 216.

[60] On the role of the State pleadings in evolutionary treaty interpretation, see K Magraw, 'Role of State Party Pleadings in the Evolutionary Interpretation of International Investment Agreements', ch 24 in this book.

[61] See, eg, *Loewen v United States*, Second Submission of Government of Canada Pursuant to NAFTA Article 1128, 27 June 2002; *Loewen v United States*, Mexico's Third 1128 Submission, 2 July 2002; see also Alschner, above n 8, 328–30.

We note that Christian Djeffal argues that *specification* is not evolutionary interpretation. He explains that specification only clarifies and defines the meaning of a term for the first time, since it was unclear previously.[62] Under Djeffal's theoretical framework, the FTC Interpretation may not be considered as evolutionary interpretation because it only 'clarif[ies] and reaffirm[s]' the meaning of NAFTA Article 1105. We disagree. In our view, although both the State-led evolutionary interpretation and the tribunal-led evolutionary interpretation are intention driven, they have one critical distinction: the scope of the State intention is different. For the State-led evolutionary treaty interpretation, the scope of the collective intention of State parties encompasses their efforts to interpret the meaning of a treaty term, whether it is to clarify the meaning of a term or to ascertain its evolving nature. In reality, the meaning of a treaty term often becomes clear post signature that the language selected is too vague when being applied. While the mutual clarification of the meaning of a term by State parties may be a specification on the technical level, it is State-led evolutionary treaty interpretation in the form of subsequent agreements on treaty interpretation. Moreover, States' joint interpretation of a term's meaning may lead to tribunals' further evolutionary treaty interpretation when they follow the States' collective intention.[63] Therefore, States' efforts and rights to express their mutual drafting intention on a treaty term's meaning cannot be downsized to technical specification: It is State-led evolutionary interpretation that provides guidance to all stakeholders under the treaty. It even prompts future tribunal-led evolutionary treaty interpretation.

To conclude, in our view the FTC Interpretation is State-led evolutionary treaty interpretation. First, State parties' joint interpretation speaks unanimously for State parties' intention. It qualifies as a subsequent agreement that fall within the purview of Article 31(3)(a) of the VCLT. In the NAFTA context, it is reinforced by NAFTA parties' subsequent practice through Article 1128 submissions. Second, joint interpretation clarifies the law and ensures the consistent application of the given provision in the future.[64] Thus, proactive State involvement in treaty interpretation through a joint interpretative mechanism ensures the evolutive interpretation of the treaties.[65] In this regard, we submit that greater State involvement, in the form of State-led interpretation, is likely to drive investment arbitration towards more moderate and balanced outcomes.[66]

V. Conclusion

The FTC Interpretation is State-led evolutionary treaty interpretation. The virtue of the State-led evolutionary treaty interpretation as represented by the FTC

[62] Djeffal, above n 2, 23.
[63] Magraw, above n 60.
[64] Gazzini, above n 43, 337–39.
[65] ibid, 338–39.
[66] Alschner, above n 8, 297.

Interpretation is that it speaks for the common understanding of a treaty provision among all treaty parties directly to the other stakeholders under the treaty. Similar to tribunal-led evolutionary treaty interpretation, State-led evolutionary treaty interpretation is also intention driven. Unlike the tribunal-led evolutionary treaty interpretation, State-led evolutionary treaty interpretation encompasses States' joint efforts to clarify their initial drafting and negotiation intention that ensures the consistent application and evolving development of a treaty term. The State-initiated interpretation mechanism contributes to the consistent application and evolving development of the treaty as it provides tribunals with interpretative guidance from treaty parties themselves. It may even prompt further tribunal-led evolutionary treaty interpretation if tribunals follow the States' collective intention. Therefore, the FTC Interpretation mechanism, the first one of its kind, serves as a model for future investment treaty regimes to adopt.

26

History as Interpretative Context in the Evolutionary Interpretation of FET in International Investment Law

CHARALAMPOS GIANNAKOPOULOS AND MALVIKA MONGA

I. Introduction: FET as an Evolutive Concept

The most frequently alleged and successfully invoked provision in treaty-based investor–State dispute settlement (ISDS) cases is the fair and equitable treatment (FET) standard.[1] Nearly all international investment agreements (IIAs), whether bilateral investment treaties (BITs) or free trade agreements (FTAs) with investment protection provisions, contain an FET clause.[2] FET clauses are vaguely worded. Some IIAs link the content of FET to customary international law or to the 'minimum standard of treatment (MST) of aliens' under customary international law, while other IIAs leave their FET provisions unqualified and with no such reference. In addition, investment tribunals often treat FET clauses as introducing an adaptive and evolutive standard.[3] FET has for example been described

[1] According to UNCTAD's ISDS Navigator (database), an FET breach is the most frequently alleged IIA breach (alleged in 460 cases out of a total of 553 cases currently listed). It is also the most successfully invoked IIA breach, being successful in 121 out of 189 cases currently recorded by UNCTAD, compared with the second most successfully invoked breach (ie, indirect expropriation, successful in 57 cases only). Data accurate as of 12 April 2019, and available at: www.investmentpolicyhub.unctad.org/ISDS/FilterByBreaches.

[2] According to UNCTAD's IIA Mapping Project (database), the exact number of IIAs containing an FET clause in some shape or form is 2440 out of a total of 2571 IIAs currently analysed. Data accurate as of 12 April 2019, and available at: investmentpolicyhub.unctad.org/IIA/mappedContent#iiaInnerMenu.

[3] eg, *SAUR International SA v Argentina*, ICSID Case No ARB/04/4, Décision sur la Compétence et sur la Responsabilité, 6 June 2012, para 494 (arguing that when a treaty refers to FET 'in conformity with principles of international law', then it refers to such principles as currently understood); *LG&E Energy Corp, LG&E Capital Corp, and LG&E International, Inc v Argentine Republic*, ICSID Case

as 'to some extent a flexible [standard] which must be adapted to the circumstances of each case'.[4]

The present contribution enters the debate of the evolutive nature of FET by using North American Free Trade Agreement (NAFTA) case law as a primary basis. The NAFTA Contracting Parties have argued clearly in favour of the evolutive nature of NAFTA's FET clause in the context of particular disputes.[5] To recall, following the Free Trade Commission's binding interpretation of NAFTA's Article 1105 in 2001, the content of FET in that agreement is linked to the MST under customary international law.[6] Against this backdrop, the present contribution seeks to understand what role historical considerations can play in providing systemic interpretative 'context' to the interpretation of FET, when FET is linked to the MST.[7] We seek to answer the following question in particular. How does an appreciation of the historical context of the treatment of aliens under international law become relevant, from a methodological point of view, in arguing for FET's evolutive character in those situations? This question is moreover relevant not only for NAFTA, but also for all the IIAs that link the content of their FET clauses to the content of the MST under customary international law.[8]

No ARB/02/1, Decision on Liability, 3 October 2006, para 123 (stating that the interpretation of FET varies with the course of time and with the circumstances of each case); *Ronald S Lauder v The Czech Republic*, UNCITRAL Rules, Final Award, 3 September 2001, para 292 (describing FET as 'subjective and depend[ing] heavily on a factual context').

[4] *Waste Management, Inc v United Mexican States*, ICSID Case No ARB(AF)/00/3, Award, 30 April 2004 (*Waste Management II*), para 99.

[5] See *Pope & Talbot Inc v The Government of Canada*, UNCITRAL Rules, Award in Respect of Damages, 31 May 2002, paras 57–62 (stating Canada's position that it is a facet of international law that customary international law evolves through State practice); *Mondev International Ltd v United States of America*, ICSID Case No ARB(AF)/99/2, Award, 11 October 2002, paras 124–25 (stating Canada's and Mexico's position that, like all customary international law, the MST can evolve); *ADF Group Inc v United States of America*, ICSID Case No ARB(AF)/00/1, Award, 9 January 2003, para 179 (stating the United States' position that customary international law is not 'frozen in time' and that the MST does evolve).

[6] Art 1105(1) NAFTA (signed 17 December 1992, entered into force 1 January 1994), including the FTC Notes of Interpretation of 31 July 2001. Art 1105(1) NAFTA, entitled 'Minimum Standard of Treatment', states: 'Each Party shall accord to investments of investors of another Party treatment in accordance with international law, including fair and equitable treatment and full protection and security'. In response to awards that have treated this wording as indicating that FET demanded a higher standard of protection than what 'international law' prescribes, the NAFTA parties issued in 2001 an interpretative note clarifying, among others: first, that 'Article 1105(1) prescribes the customary international law minimum standard of treatment of aliens as the minimum standard of treatment to be afforded to investments of investors of another Party'; and second, that '[t]he concepts of "fair and equitable treatment" and "full protection and security" do not require treatment in addition to or beyond that which is required by the customary international law minimum standard of treatment of aliens'. For further discussion on the FTC Notes of Interpretation, see J Radford, G Tereposky and K Hui, 'Investment Treaty Signatories' Joint Interpretation and the Case of the NAFTA Free Trade Commission: Evolutionary Interpretation or Modification?', ch 25 in this book, arguing that the Notes were not a treaty modification but State-led evolutionary treaty interpretation.

[7] We thus use a broad understanding of 'context', similar to what D McRae, 'Evolutionary Interpretation: The Relevance of Context', ch 7 in this book advocates.

[8] eg, Art 14.6 USMCA (signed 30 November 2018); Art 14.5 Australia–Japan EPA (signed 8 July 2014, entered into force 15 January 2015); Art 7 Benin–Canada BIT (signed 9 January 2013, entered into force 12 May 2014); Art 5 Chile–Uruguay BIT (signed 25 March 2010, entered into force 18 March 2012); Art 2 China–Colombia BIT (signed 22 November 2008, entered into force 2 July 2013).

We proceed as follows. We will examine the reasons offered for the evolutionary interpretation of FET in NAFTA case law where, as mentioned above, FET is linked to the MST under customary international law (section II). We then examine instances where FET clauses are regarded as autonomous. In doing so, we attempt to see whether the historical context of the MST may still have a role to play in the interpretation of those clauses as well (section III). Ultimately, this contribution suggests that any attempt at interpreting any FET clause in an evolutive manner must depend on the understanding of FET's historical context and cannot be based exclusively on a contemporary perspective. In doing so, the historical context may make the manner of interpreting the FET standard evolutively methodologically sounder, even though the historical context cannot tell us what specific meaning is to be given to FET in concrete instances of application.

II. Evolutionary Interpretation of FET, When Linked to the MST Under Customary International Law

The discussion below draws from NAFTA case law and distinguishes between the '*Glamis*' and the '*Bilcon*' approaches of demonstrating the evolutionary nature of FET. These two cases are chosen as typical examples of two different, but often used, ways of arguing for the need to interpret FET in an evolutionary manner in cases where FET is linked to the MST under customary international law. The following examines how each interpretative approach fares methodologically when viewed against history as relevant systemic context.

A. The *Glamis* Approach and the MST Under Customary International Law in Historical Context

The *Glamis* approach may be described as an originalist interpretative approach. It sees the content of the MST encapsulated in the 1926 *Neer* case standard of 'outrage, bad faith and wilful neglect of duty' and at the same time acknowledges that this standard is evolutive (ie, State action that was not regarded as shocking or egregious in the 1920s may be so regarded today).[9] Upon closer inspection, however, the *Glamis* approach suffers from historical inaccuracy. To see why, a brief historical account of the MST is warranted.

The origins of the legal concept of the MST can be traced back to a 1910 speech given by Elihu Root at the American Society of International Law.[10] Root did not

[9] *Glamis Gold, Ltd v The United States of America*, UNCITRAL Rules, Award, 8 June 2009, paras 598–618; similarly, *Cargill, Incorporated v United Mexican States*, ICSID Case No ARB(AF)/05/2, Award, 18 September 2009, para 286 (stating that the current customary international law standard of FET reflects the adaptation of the *Neer* standard to current conditions).

[10] E Root, 'The Basis of Protection to Citizens Residing Abroad' (1910) 4 *American Journal of International Law* 517.

refer to an 'international minimum standard' but to an 'established standard of civilization', which he described as 'a standard of justice, very simple, very fundamental, and of such general acceptance by all civilised countries as to form part of the international law of the world'.[11] Even though foreigners abroad were in principle subject to the same treatment that the host State granted to its own nationals, this national treatment could never fall below the aforementioned standard.[12] Root did not base his minimum standard on customary international law, but rather on what one could describe as the early twentieth century equivalent of general principles of law. Such a view of the ontology of the MST is also confirmed by Edwin Borchard. Referring to Root's exposition of the minimum standard, Borchard noted:

> The international standard is compounded of general principles recognized by the domestic law of practically every civilized country, and it is not to be supposed that any normal [S]tate would repudiate it or, if able, fail to observe it.[13]

In determining the MST's content, modern arbitral practice has often referred to the 1926 decision of the Mexico–United States General Claims Commission in the *Neer* claim as a historical source.[14] In *Neer*, a denial of justice claim arising out of the murder of an American citizen in Mexico and the police investigation that ensued, the Commission set a high standard for finding a violation of international law:

> Without attempting to announce a precise formula, it is in the opinion of the Commission possible to go a little further … and to hold (first) that the propriety of governmental acts should be put to the test of international standards, and (second) that the treatment of an alien, in order to constitute an international delinquency, *should amount to an outrage, to bad faith, to wilful neglect of duty, or to an insufficiency of governmental action so far short of international standards that every reasonable and impartial man would readily recognize its insufficiency* (emphasis added).[15]

However, as can be seen from subsequent decisions of the Commission, it was the Commission's intention that this high-threshold standard would not be generally applicable. It was rather meant to apply, on the one hand, to any conduct of

[11] ibid, 521.

[12] ibid, 522.

[13] E Borchard, 'The "Minimum Standard" of the Treatment of Aliens' (1939–40) 38 *Michigan Law Review* 445, 458. For the same position, more recently, see: AC Blandford, 'The History of Fair and Equitable Treatment before the Second World War' (2017) 32 *ICSID Review – Foreign Investment Law Journal* 287; C McLachlan, L Shore and M Weiniger, *International Investment Arbitration: Substantive Principles*, 2nd edn (Oxford, Oxford University Press, 2017) 271–73 (paras 7.11–7.16).

[14] *LFH Neer and Pauline Neer (USA) v United Mexican States*, Decision on the Merits, 15 October 1926 (1951) IV *Reports of International Arbitral Awards* 60. Tribunals that have considered the *Neer* formula as reflecting the state of the MST under customary international law today include: *Alex Genin, Eastern Credit Limited, Inc and AS Baltoil v The Republic of Estonia*, ICSID Case No ARB/99/2, Award, 25 June 2001, para 367; *Glamis v USA*, Award, above n 9, para 627; *Cargill v Mexico*, Award, above n 9, para 286.

[15] *Neer v Mexico*, above n 14, 61–62.

a country's judiciary and, on the other, to actions by the executive or the legislative branches of a government but only in cases of so-called indirect responsibility (ie, where authorities failed to provide redress for injury suffered by an alien but caused by other private actors).[16] In other words, the Commission envisaged the *Neer* standard would apply only in cases of a denial of justice by the courts or of a failure by other State organs to provide the necessary means to redress wrongs suffered by an alien that were not initially attributable to the State. In contrast, in cases of so-called direct responsibility (ie, involving injury to an alien resulting directly from the actions of the executive or the legislative branches), the lower-threshold standard of 'ordinary standards of civilisation' would apply.[17]

Taking into account the above as systemic interpretative context leads to two remarks about the MST. First, the MST was originally based on general principles of law and not on customary international law. Second, the content of the MST with respect to acts directly attributable to the State is historically not encapsulated in the *Neer* standard of 'outrage, bad faith and wilful neglect of duty' (other than the two exceptions referred to above); but rather on the notion of ordinary standards of civilisation which, again, leads back to an enquiry into general principles.[18] Therefore, even if one concedes that the Mexico–United States General Claims Commission jurisprudence offers a statement of the MST under customary international law,[19] the *Neer* test would still be inapplicable to claims directly challenging administrative or legislative acts of the host State, like those most often brought by foreign investors today.[20] Rather, the less exacting 'ordinary standards of civilisation' would be applicable, which requires a tribunal to enter into a more nuanced analysis of the contemporary principles of political morality that may be applicable to the international treatment of foreign investors.

Despite this historical background, the 2009 decision in *Glamis v USA* held that a violation of the MST under customary international law would require State conduct that is 'sufficiently egregious and shocking – a gross denial of justice, manifest arbitrariness, blatant unfairness, a complete lack of due process, evident discrimination, or a manifest lack of reasons', while acknowledging that 'it is entirely possible that, as an international community, we may be shocked by

[16] *BE Chattin (USA) v United Mexican States*, Decision, 23 July 1927 (1951) 4 *Reports of International Arbitral Awards* 282, 285–88.

[17] See also, *Harry Roberts (USA) v United Mexican States*, Decision, 2 November 1926, (1951) 4 *Reports of International Arbitral Awards* 77, 79–80; *HG Venable (USA) v United Mexican States*, Decision, 8 July 1927 (1951) 4 *Reports of International Arbitral Awards* 219, in particular, *cf* passage at 224 with passage at 226.

[18] Also, J Paulsson and G Petrochilos, '*Neer*-ly Misled?' (2007) 22 *ICSID Review – Foreign Investment Law Journal* 242, 257 (concluding more generally that the *Neer* formula has very limited relevance for the interpretation of the FET standard).

[19] *cf Railroad Development Corporation v Republic of Guatemala*, ICSID Case No ARB/07/23, Award, 29 June 2012, para 216, casting doubt on the widely held view that *Neer* reflected customary international law even at that time.

[20] Also see, *Mondev v USA*, Award, above n 5, para 115 ('[T]here is insufficient cause for assuming that provisions of bilateral investment treaties, and of NAFTA, while incorporating the *Neer* principle in respect of the duty of protection …, are confined to the *Neer* standard of outrageous treatment where the issue is the treatment of foreign investment by the State itself').

State actions now that did not offend us previously'.[21] Nevertheless, there remains the unanswered methodological question of how to determine the content of the MST under customary international law today. There is an attempt to address this question in the treatment of the *Bilcon* approach below.

B. The *Bilcon* Approach and the Paradox of the Evolving MST Under Customary International Law

The *Bilcon* approach is somewhat different from the *Glamis* approach examined above. It accepts that FET must be interpreted by reference to the MST under customary international law. However, it does not consider the content of the MST under customary international law to be found in the *Neer* standard, yet still claims that its content continues to evolve over time.[22] The *Bilcon* approach may thus be described as a type of a 'living instrument' interpretative approach.[23] How is history as interpretative context methodologically relevant here? It can be argued that it is by helping to resolve what seems like a contradiction present in the *Bilcon* approach between, on the one hand, considering the MST as embedded in customary law, and, on the other, regarding the content of the MST under customary international law as constantly evolving.

If one takes the view that the content of the MST is to be found in customary law, as for example the NAFTA Contracting Parties do,[24] then speaking about

[21] *Glamis v USA*, Award, above n 9, para 22.

[22] *William Ralph Clayton, William Richard Clayton, Douglas Clayton, Daniel Clayton and Bilcon of Delaware Inc v Government of Canada*, UNCITRAL Rules, PCA Case No 2009-04, Award on Jurisdiction and Liability, 17 March 2015, para 433 [emphases added]:

> 'NAFTA Article 1105 is, then, identical to the minimum international standard. The crucial question – on which the Parties diverge – is what is the content of the contemporary international minimum standard that the tribunal is bound to apply. NAFTA awards make it clear that the international minimum standard is not limited to conduct by host [S]tates that is outrageous. The contemporary minimum international standard involves a more significant measure of protection'.

Similarly: *Merrill & Ring Forestry LP v The Government of Canada*, UNCITRAL Rules, ICSID Administered Case, Award, 31 March 2010, para 211; *ADF v USA*, Award, above n 5, para 179. For an additional discussion of these cases, see also MM Mbengue and A Florou, 'Evolutionary Interpretation in Investment Arbitration: About a Judicial Taboo', ch 23 in this book.

[23] The term is borrowed from the case law of the European Court of Human Rights and indicates that the object of interpretation must be interpreted in the light of present-day conditions (eg, see, *Tyrer v United Kingdom* Series A no 26 (1978) 2 EHRR 1, para 31).

[24] eg, see, *Mesa Power Group, LLC v Government of Canada*, UNCITRAL Rules, PCA Case No 2012-17, Government of Canada Observations on the Award on Jurisdiction and Merits in *William Ralph Clayton, William Richard Clayton, Douglas Clayton, Daniel Clayton and Bilcon of Delaware, Inc v Canada*, 14 May 2015, para 17, stating that 'the *Bilcon* Tribunal … failed to determine the positive content of Article 1105 by looking to customary international law', and that '[i]n order to establish a breach of Article 1105 the Claimant must prove, using [S]tate practice and *opinio juris*, that the complained of treatment falls below the treatment required by customary international law'. See similar statements in, ibid, Second Submission of the United States of America, 12 June 2015, paras 8–15; ibid, Second Submission of Mexico Pursuant to NAFTA Art 1128, 12 June 2015, paras 8–11.

the *contemporary* meaning of the MST may appear odd. The reason for this is the following. Under the so-called traditional view, customary international law is formed by State practice that is general and sufficiently consistent, and because the practising States believe that they conform to a legal obligation (*opinio juris*). Such a description of customary international law is, at once, a description of the process of formation of a customary norm and a description of that norm's content.[25] This implies that, the moment the existence of a customary norm is ascertained, the content of that norm is simultaneously determined and 'locked-in' in time.

Because of this, customary international law in its 'traditional' sense does not change easily. Any divergent practice following identification of a customary norm does not immediately denote the emergence of a new customary norm, but rather an attempt to go beyond what customary international law provides. This is not to say that the content of customary international law cannot evolve with the passage of time; but such evolution cannot happen as easily, or as frequently, as modern arbitral practice seems to suggest.[26] And in any event, ascertaining whether the content of a new customary norm has emerged requires an extensive examination of State practice that tribunals rarely, if ever, do.

Under these working assumptions, it appears odd that several NAFTA tribunals purporting to apply the MST under customary international law have, for example, still considered the investor's legitimate expectations as relevant to their analysis.[27] For even if we consider legitimate expectations as a binding general principle (a proposition recently rejected by the ICJ in *Bolivia v Chile*),[28] it is certainly not one of a customary law status, nor is there any evidence adduced that the MST has evolved to include it.

This seeming contradiction however dissipates if we consider that ascertaining the existence of a norm of international law, and determining that norm's content

[25] eg, Draft conclusion 2[3] provisionally adopted by the ILC in its work on customary international law states: 'To determine the *existence and content* of a rule of customary international law, it is necessary to ascertain whether there is a general practice that is accepted as law (*opinio juris*)' (International Law Commission, 'Identification of Customary International Law: Text of the Draft Conclusions Provisionally Adopted by the Drafting Committee', 68th Session (2 May–10 June and 4 July–12 August 2016), UN Doc A/CN.4/L.872, 30 May 2016 (emphasis added)).

[26] eg, *Chemtura Corporation (formerly Crompton Corporation) v Government of Canada*, UNCITRAL Rules, Award, 2 August 2010, para 121 ('At the outset, the Tribunal notes that it is not disputed that the scope of Article 1105 of NAFTA must be determined by reference to customary international law. Such determination cannot overlook the evolution of customary international law, nor the impact of BITs on this evolution').

[27] eg, *Mobil Investments Canada Inc and Murphy Oil Corporation v Canada*, ICSID Case No ARB(AF)/07/4, Decision on Liability and on Principles of Quantum, 22 May 2012, paras 135–36, 152–53; *International Thunderbird Gaming Corporation v United Mexican States*, UNCITRAL Rules, Award, 26 January 2006, paras 146–48, 194–96; *Glamis v USA*, Award, above n 9, para 627; *Bilcon v Canada*, Award on Jurisdiction and Liability, above n 22, para 455.

[28] *Obligation to Negotiate Access to the Pacific Ocean (Bolivia v Chile)* (Judgment) [2018], para 162 ('[i]t does not follow from such references that there exists in general international law a principle that would give rise to an obligation on the basis of what could be considered a legitimate expectation').

over time, need not always follow the same reasoning process.[29] Determining content over time is the result of an interpretative process, and customary international law should in principle not be exempted from this.[30] Thus, the obligation of a host State to accord treatment in accordance with the international minimum standard may nowadays be enshrined in customary international law (meaning that it applies as the default rule and is opposable to all States), yet its content need not be determined solely by reference to processes of customary norm-creation.[31]

Indeed, as the brief historical examination above shows, the content of the MST originally was to be determined based on what was at that time known as ordinary standards of civilisation and today is known as general principles of law. Both these descriptions of the MST's content are inherently evolutive. Following this process of reasoning to determine the content of the MST would result in the inclusion of principles or doctrines of customary nature (eg, prohibition of uncompensated expropriation, prohibition of denial of justice), but could also go beyond that. This is not a plea for a low-threshold of MST,[32] but a suggestion for rendering methodologically sounder the arguments for the evolutive nature of the MST when FET is seen as linked to it.

[29] On this, also see, J d'Aspremont, *Formalism and the Sources of International Law: A Theory of the Ascertainment of Legal Rules* (Oxford, Oxford University Press, 2011) 157 ('It is argued here that the criteria on the basis of which international legal rules are ascertained are not necessarily the same as those through which the *content* of law is determined' (emphasis in original)).

[30] For recognition that customary international law norms may be subject to interpretation, see, *Case Concerning Military and Paramilitary Activities in and against Nicaragua (Nicaragua v United States of America)* (Merits) [1986] ICJ Rep 14, para 178 ('Rules which are identical in treaty law and in customary international law are also distinguishable by reference to the methods of interpretation and application'); also, P Merkouris, 'Interpreting the Customary Rules on Interpretation' (2017) 19 *International Community Law Review* 126, 134–35 (arguing that rejecting the possibility that customary international law is subject to interpretation leads to the counterintuitive conclusion that a customary international law norm must be re-identified by State practice/*opinio juris* each and every time it is applied by a court). What the specific methods or rules for interpreting customary international law are, is still unclear. Judge Tanaka has offered a possible reply in saying that '[t]he method of logical and teleological interpretation can be applied in the case of customary law as in the case of written law' (*North Sea Continental Shelf (Federal Republic of Germany v Denmark; Federal Republic of Germany v Netherlands)* (Judgment) [1969] ICJ Rep 3, Dissenting Opinion of Judge Tanaka, 182). Building on Tanaka, P Merkouris, *Article 31(3)(c) VCLT and the Principle of Systemic Integration: Normative Shadows in Plato's Cave* (Leiden, Brill/Nijhoff, 2015) 263–69, describes interpretation of customary international law norms as an exercise in systemic and teleological interpretation.

[31] Also see, G Schwarzenberger, *International Law: Volume 1*, 3rd edn (London, Stevens & Sons Ltd, 1957) 231 ('[I]t is arguable that the law-creating process on which [the minimum] standard now rests is either international customary law or the general principles of law recognised by civilised nations'); cited with approval in *ADF v USA*, Award, above n 5, para 185.

[32] As McLachlan et al, above n 13, 273 (para 7.17), argue, a low threshold for breach is precluded from the very fact that FET and the MST are international standards and cannot be considered as a continuation of domestic politics and litigation by other means. Indeed, tribunals (at least in the context of the NAFTA) have generally adopted rather high thresholds (eg, *Mesa Power v Canada*, Award, 24 March 2016, above n 24, paras 501–05; *Bilcon v Canada*, Award on Jurisdiction and Liability, above n 22, paras 441–45; *Waste Management II*, Award, above n 4, paras 98–99).

III. Evolutionary Interpretation of FET, When Not Linked to the MST Under Customary International Law: Is there a Truly Autonomous FET?

Not all IIAs clearly and explicitly link FET to the MST under customary international law. In fact, most IIAs do not.[33] The question to be addressed in this section, therefore, is how the historical context of the MST can become relevant in the evolutionary interpretation of the FET standard in those IIAs that do not link FET to the MST.

Before continuing, a caveat is in order. The aim here is not to determine whether FET clauses that are not explicitly linked to the MST under customary international law are, in fact, independent clauses or just the MST in another – more neutral and less controversial – name. Views on this issue fall on both sides.[34] The determinative criterion ultimately depends on whether one concludes that the MST, as a concept, managed to survive the legitimacy challenges levelled against it by the newly independent States during the 1960s and 1970s. These States had objected to any duty to provide foreign investors with anything beyond national treatment, as they still regarded the concept of an MST to be an instrument of subjugation and exploitation, and a bar to their economic emancipation.[35] The result was that FET emerged as the key legal norm during the rise of IIAs that occurred in the 1990s. It is still unclear, however, whether the FET standard was

[33] According to UNCTAD's IIA Mapping Project (database), only about 3% of IIAs (out of a total of 2.571 IIAs analysed) clearly equate FET to the MST, whereas the vast majority (approximately 77%) contain a completely unqualified FET provision. It is noteworthy, however, that the trend of qualifying FET provisions with a reference to the MST has increased over time. Data accurate as of 12 April 2019, and available at: www.investmentpolicyhub.unctad.org/IIA/mappedContent#iiaInnerMenu.

[34] For the position that FET is an independent standard, see, P Dumberry, *Fair and Equitable Treatment: Its Interaction with the Minimum Standard and Its Customary Status* (Leiden, Brill/Nijhoff, 2018); H Haeri, 'A Tale of Two Standards: "Fair and Equitable Treatment" and the Minimum Standard in International Law' (2011) 27 *Arbitration International* 27, 34–35; C Schreuer, 'Fair and Equitable Treatment in Arbitral Practice' (2005) 6 *Journal of World Investment and Trade* 357, 360; R Dolzer and M Stevens, *Bilateral Investment Treaties* (The Hague, Martinus Nijhoff, 1995) 60; S Vasciannie, 'The Fair and Equitable Treatment Standard in International Investment Law and Practice' (1999) 70 *The British Year Book of International Law* 99, 104–05; FA Mann, 'British Treaties for the Promotion and Protection of Investments' (1981) 52 *The British Year Book of International Law* 241, 244. For the position that FET is a modern-day shorthand for the MST, see: M Paparinskis, *The International Minimum Standard and Fair and Equitable Treatment* (Oxford, Oxford University Press, 2013) 5–6, 160–66; J Roman Picherack, 'The Expanding Scope of the Fair and Equitable Treatment Standard: Have Recent Tribunals Gone Too Far?' (2008) 9 *Journal of World Investment & Trade* 255, 264; G Sacerdoti, 'Bilateral Treaties and Multilateral Instruments on Investment Protection' (1997) 269 *Recueil des cours de l'académie de droit international* 251, 341; Blandford, above n 13, 289; *Suez, Sociedad General de Aguas de Barcelona SA and Vivendi Universal, SA v The Argentine Republic*, ICSID Case No ARB/03/19, Decision on Liability, 30 July 2010, Separate Opinion of Arbitrator Pedro Nikken, para 15.

[35] Dumberry, above n 34; eg, see, Art 2 of the Charter of Economic Rights and Duties of States, UNGA Res 3281 (XXIX), 12 December 1974, A/RES/29/3281.

meant to be a reference to the MST or to operate independently from it. To clarify, the aim here is not to answer that question, but to articulate a general prescription about how to interpret FET, even if FET is to be regarded as independent and autonomous. Put differently, even if FET is an independent and autonomous standard, can its interpretation be completely detached from an understanding of the MST's historical content?

In this scenario, the answer must be a negative one. Drawing up a completely independent FET standard for purposes of interpretation could risk arbitrariness. Interpretation is a holistic exercise and disregarding the broader context of the reality of international relations applicable to the object of interpretation could lead to questionable results. An examination of the two most common paths of reasoning used in a 'truly autonomous' construction of FET can help demonstrate this point.

Tribunals that treat FET as an autonomous concept commonly put greater emphasis on the plain or ordinary meaning when interpreting the standard evolutively. Taken on its own, this could be problematic because searching for the ordinary meaning of abstract terms like 'fair' and 'equitable' may lead to equally abstract, and thus unhelpful, terms like 'just', 'even-handed', 'unbiased', or 'legitimate'.[36] None of these terms refer to an established body of law as background systemic context. The danger, as Vasciannie puts it, is that decisions as to whether investors have been treated fairly and equitably would be made without reference to any technical understanding of the meaning of FET,[37] which risks turning the interpretation of FET into a tautology.[38] This may cause tribunals to produce decisions with serious methodological lapses in reasoning.[39]

[36] eg, *Azurix Corp v The Argentine Republic*, ICSID Case No ARB/01/12, Award, 14 July 2006, para 360; *MTD Equity Sdn Bhd and MTD Chile SA v Republic of Chile*, ICSID Case No ARB/01/7, Award, 25 May 2004, para 113.

[37] Vasciannie, above n 34, 103–04. More generally, McLachlan et al, above n 13, 271 (para 7.11), argue that the autonomous/non-autonomous FET controversy is misguided and simplistic because '[i]t suggests that the only choice open to a tribunal is between a complete discretion to determine whether particular conduct is "unfair and inequitable" on the one hand, and the application of a conception of customary international law "frozen in amber" at some time in the past'. This strict separation, the authors continue, is also deceptive for the additional reason that it suggests that there exists a clearly identifiable content to the MST under customary international law.

[38] eg, UNCTAD, *Fair and Equitable Treatment*, UNCTAD Series on Issues in International Investment Agreements (UN Publications, 1999), 40 ('the presence of a provision assuring fair and equitable treatment in an investment instrument does not automatically incorporate the international minimum standard for foreign investors. Where the fair and equitable standard is invoked, the central issue remains simply whether the actions in question are in all the circumstances fair and equitable or unfair and inequitable').

[39] eg, see, the *Tecmed* decision, for the tribunal's essential absence of any demonstrable reasoning in coming up with its famous lengthy definition of FET. The principal justification offered by the tribunal was that the meaning assigned resulted 'from an autonomous interpretation, taking into account the text of Article 4(1) of the Agreement according to its ordinary meaning (Article 31(1) of the Vienna Convention), or from international law and the good faith principle'. This is a far cry from a proper justification of the meaning to be given to a legal provision. At best, it is a mere assurance that this is indeed the ordinary meaning of 'fair and equitable' within the context of the FET provision of the

Other tribunals have also used the object and purpose of the applicable IIA, with equally questionable results. In *MTD v Chile*, the tribunal took the plain meaning of FET in combination with preambular references to the goals of investment protection, promotion and stimulation of capital flows, and thus described FET as imposing proactive obligations on States to protect investors' expectations with respect to these goals.[40] The cases of *Enron v Argentina*, *CMS v Argentina*, and *Occidental v Ecuador* are also relevant examples. Failing to find adequate guidance from the plain meaning of each IIA's FET clause, all three tribunals relied instead on preambular references to the desirability of FET for maintaining a stable framework for investment and for the maximum effective use of economic resources. From that, each tribunal then garnered support for the proposition that the expectation of maintaining a stable legal and business environment is an essential element of fair and equitable treatment.[41] Such interpretations appear too broad. For even though a dramatic change in the regulatory environment may be a relevant element to consider in determining an FET violation, transforming expectations of stability and predictability into legal obligations (under FET), based only on non-operative preambular clauses, would appear to be a stretch.

It may not be surprising, therefore, to see that even tribunals that regard FET as an independent standard, have often treated the independent FET and the MST as coterminous in certain situations or have turned to the more developed case law of NAFTA awards (where FET is clearly linked to the MST) for support.[42] Such a move is helped by the historical commonalities between FET and the MST: both standards have the same broad objective (ie, protecting aliens/investors abroad vis-a-vis the regularity of the host State's conduct towards them), and so, both standards may be said to involve an enquiry into general principles of good governance.[43]

applicable BIT (*Técnicas Medioambientales Tecmed, SA v United Mexican States*, ICSID Case No ARB (AF)/00/2, Award, 29 May 2003, paras 153–55).

[40] *MTD v Chile*, Award, above n 36, para 113.

[41] *Enron Corporation and Ponderosa Assets, LP v Argentine Republic*, ICSID Case No ARB/01/3 (also known as: *Enron Creditors Recovery Corp and Ponderosa Assets, LP v The Argentine Republic*), Award, 22 May 2007, paras 259–60; *CMS Gas Transmission Company v The Republic of Argentina*, ICSID Case No ARB/01/8, Award, 12 May 2005, paras 273–74; *Occidental Exploration and Production Company v The Republic of Ecuador*, LCIA Case No UN3467, Final Award, 1 July 2004, para 183.

[42] eg, *Rumeli Telekom AS and Telsim Mobil Telekomunikasyon Hizmetleri AS v Republic of Kazakhstan*, ICSID Case No ARB/05/16, Award, 29 July 2008, para 611; *Biwater Gauff (Tanzania) Ltd v United Republic of Tanzania*, ICSID Case No ARB/05/22, Award, 24 July 2008, para 590 ff; *Siemens AG v The Argentine Republic*, ICSID Case No ARB/02/8, Award, 6 February 2007, para 291 ff; *Saluka Investments BV v The Czech Republic*, UNCITRAL Rules, Partial Award, 17 March 2006, para 291; *Azurix v Argentina*, Award, above n 36, para 361; *CMS v Argentina*, Award, above n 41, paras 282–84; *Occidental v Ecuador (LCIA case)*, Final Award, above n 41, paras, 189–90; *SAUR v Argentina, Jurisdiction and Responsibility*, above n 3, para 494.

[43] For support, see: M Jacob and SW Schill, 'Fair and Equitable Treatment: Content, Practice, Method' in M Bungenberg, J Griebel, S Hobe and A Reinisch (eds), *International Investment Law: A Handbook* (Munich, CH Beck, 2015) 711–13 (paras 24–26); McLachlan et al, above n 13, 268 ff (para 7.01 ff); UNCTAD, *Fair and Equitable Treatment* above n 38, 12; also in: *Enron v Argentina*, Award, above n 41, para 257; *Merrill & Ring v Canada*, Award, above n 22, para 187.

A tentative suggestion now follows. Through what could be described as a feedback loop, the MST and the autonomous FET may gradually converge in practice.[44] On the one hand, tribunals use conceptions of the MST as a baseline to interpret the FET standard. The MST seen in its historical context provides arbitrators with a – however limited or imprecise – idea about the values or principles of political morality behind the international treatment of foreigners abroad,[45] which commentators have narrowed down to three interconnected concepts (ie, legality, the rule of law, good governance),[46] and from which tribunals may draw inferences about the cases presented before them. On the other hand, the more accepted these interpretations become, the more widespread becomes the view that the boundaries of minimum treatment to be afforded to investors are evolving and shifting over time.

IV. Conclusion

History plays an important role in providing relevant systemic context for the evolutionary interpretation of the FET standard. This holds true both in IIAs where FET is linked to the MST under customary international law and in IIAs where FET is seen as a self-standing, autonomous concept. This should come as no surprise since, to speak of something as evolving over time, implies that one moves from point A to another point B, which inevitably requires one to first look back in order to construct the path forward.

This contribution has shown that, in IIAs where FET is linked to the MST under customary international law, the historical context is interpretatively relevant in two important ways. First, it serves as a useful tool providing one with the ability to go back and understand the decisions taken by past tribunals, and in analysing them, to avoid any inaccurate interpretations of governing standards. Second, it provides a way of interpreting FET in a way that is arguably methodologically sounder than the *Glamis* and *Bilcon* approaches mentioned. In particular, taking the historical context into account provides one with a firmer basis upon which to argue that the content of the MST is inherently evolutive. This contribution has also shown that, even in IIAs where FET is not linked to the MST under customary international law but is treated as an autonomous concept, it can still

[44] eg, see: *Sempra Energy International v The Argentine Republic*, ICSID Case No ARB/02/16, Award, 28 September 2007, para 302; UNCTAD, *Fair and Equitable Treatment: A Sequel*, UNCTAD Series on Issues in International Investment Agreements II (UN Publications, 2012) 90; Jacob and Schill, above n 43, 706–09 (paras 8–17).

[45] For a similar position, see, Paparinskis, above n 34, 166–67.

[46] eg, see: KJ Vandevelde, 'A Unified Theory of Fair and Equitable Treatment' (2010–11) 43 *New York University Journal of International Law and Politics* 43; McLachlan et al, above n 13, 268 ff (para 7.01 ff); Jacob and Schill, above n 43, 713 ff (para 27 ff); *Suez v Argentina*, Liability, Separate Opinion of Arbitrator Pedro Nikken, above n 34 para 20.

be methodologically sound to treat the autonomous FET and the MST as having similar scopes or boundaries.

At the same time, it is imperative to note the limits of historical enquiries. The historical context tells us how to approach the interpretation of FET methodologically, and in a way that could minimise arbitrary decisions. But, in and of itself, the historical context cannot tell us what specific meaning is to be given to FET in concrete instances of application. It would appear that considerations of an axiological nature are also necessary.

PART VI

Evolutionary Interpretation in EU Law

27

Articulating Evolutionary Interpretation and the Rule of Law: The EU as a Composite Legal Order Based on Relative Rules of Law

NICOLAS LEVRAT

I. Introduction

Darwin had to find himself on a remote group of Pacific Islands to grasp and later formulate the theory of evolution. There, he realised, that species had not been created as such, but that their peculiar forms were the result of their interactions over generations with a specific environment, *in casu* the Galapagos Islands. He could have concluded that this specific environment had particular consequences on living species; but he went further and theorised that any living species in any given environment would evolve, adapt, in the most relevant manner as regards its environment.[1] It seems to us that evolutionary interpretation in legal theory has not yet gone much further than what could be termed special contextual interpretation. In other words, in the same way that the Galapagos Islands constitute a singular environment that have an impact on the evolution of species, it has been discovered that World Trade Organization (WTO) law constitutes a singular environment that promotes evolutionary interpretation, or the European Convention on Human Rights constitutes a singular environment that promotes evolutionary interpretation, and so on; reflections on evolutionary interpretation did not try, before this book, to generalise the concept beyond each particular legal environment. We would like to explore the conditions of a more general theory of evolutionary interpretation, beyond each legal regime, through the observations of evolutionary norms interpretation in different contexts.

In that respect, the European Union (EU) offers an interesting case study. The singularity of the EU legal order, and its defining multilevel structure may

[1] C Darwin, *On the Origins of Species* (London, John Murray, 1859).

make it a legal *ersatz* of the Galapagos archipelago for the study of evolutionary interpretation. Based on this tentative approximation, our reasoning draws insights from the theory of evolution as well as from fundamental physics, more specifically Einstein's work on the special theory of relativity;[2] and naturally also from a careful reading of EU case law. We shall in the first part reflect on the paradoxical relationship of EU law with evolutionary interpretation (II). Our second part will leads us to formulate a special relative rules of law theory for EU law (III), is a conclusion to this chapter.

II. The Paradoxical Relationship of EU Law with Evolutionary Interpretation

If evolutionary interpretation appears to be a ground-breaking principle in many fields of international law, as the contributions to this book attest, its relevance for EU law may be less salient. Not that EU law is immune from evolutionary interpretation; quite the contrary: the interpretative techniques used for decades by the Luxembourg-based European judges go largely beyond what is termed as evolutionary interpretation. In fact, as we shall show in the first part of this chapter, EU law could most likely do without evolutionary interpretation (A), although the very concept of EU law is a product of evolutionary interpretation (B).

A. EU Law Could Do Without Evolutionary Interpretation

Commentators regularly claim[3] that evolutionary interpretation allows international regimes change at a relatively low cost (Kolb advances the concept of a 'mini-*clausula rebus sic stantibus*').[4] Formal treaty change is a time-consuming and difficult exercise; therefore evolutionary interpretation is a proper and legitimate palliative to treaty change, allowing judges to adapt the rules of a treaty as enunciated at the time of its conclusion to changing circumstances (or environment) over time.[5]

[2] A Einstein, 'Zur Elektrodynamik bewegter Körper' (1905) 17 *Analen der Physik* 891. As we are not erudite physicists, and not being so familiar with Maxwell–Lorentz equations of electromagnetism, we are thankful to Carlo Rovelli for his excellent work of vulgarisation of these theories of physic in his small book, C Rovelli, *L'ordre du Temps* (Milano, Adephi, 2017) (French translation 2018, Paris, Flammarion). As the special theory of relativity is limited to electrodynamics, our theory of relative rules of law is limited to EU law. So far.

[3] See, among others, E Bjorge, *The Eevolutionary Iinterpretation of Treaties* (Oxford, Oxford University Press, 2014); C Brolmann, 'Law-making Treaties: Form and Function in International Law' (2005) 74 *Nordic Journal of International Law* 383; M Waibel, 'Demystifying the Art of Interpretation' (2011) 22 *European Journal of International Law* 571.

[4] R Kolb, 'Evolutionary Interpretation in International Law: Some Short and Less than Trail-Blazing Reflections', ch 3 in this book.

[5] T Gehring, 'Treaty-making and Treaty Evolution' in D Bodansky et al (eds), *The Oxford Handbook of Iinternational Environmental Law* (Oxford, Oxford University Press, 2007).

Although treaty revisions under the EU legal regime require unanimity among Member States, not only for adopting amendments, but also for ratification of treaty changes before they may produce legal effects,[6] treaty revisions in fact have been numerous. About 17 treaty modifications, including major ones – like the Maastricht Treaty (1992) or the Lisbon Treaty (2007) – have taken place since 1957. Accordingly, although the 1957 Rome Treaty establishing the European Economic Community (EEC) is still in force,[7] it has a very different normative[8] and institutional[9] content compared with its original version. The Maastricht Treaty even renamed it 'Treaty establishing the European Community' (that was supposed to translate into words – actually one less word – the spectacular extension of EEC competences beyond the economic realm). And now this same treaty, after significant modifications by the Amsterdam (1997) and Nice (2001) Treaties, was yet again restructured and re-baptised as 'Treaty on the Functioning of the European Union' (TFEU), this time by the Lisbon Treaty.

Due to this practice of treaty revisions, one could easily claim that evolutionary interpretation is not really needed in EU law. When the EU legal regime requires an evolution of the legal effects of the treaties that are at its foundation, the Europeans simply implement a treaty change. Notwithstanding, the concept of EU law itself, is a direct and continuing product of evolutionary interpretation of the 1957 Rome EEC Treaty by the Court of Justice of the European Union (CJEU), as we show below.

[6] Art 48, para 4 of the Treaty on the European Union (TEU) states: 'The amendments shall enter into force after being ratified by all the Member States in accordance with their respective constitutional requirements'. There is a special revision procedure described in Art 48 para 7 of the TEU that does not require ratification by Member States; it has however a very limited scope and has so far never been used.

[7] If one reads carefully the Treaty on the Functioning of the European Union (TFEU), the last sentence reads as such: 'Done at Rome this twenty-fifth day of March in the year one thousand nine hundred and fifty-seven' (OJEU C 202/199, 7 June 2016). This even though the appellation of the current treaty (TFEU) in which this sentence appears only emerged through the Lisbon Treaty (signed on 7 December 2007, entered into force on 1 December 2009).

[8] Many new fields of cooperation have been added, such as environment, research, social and economic cohesion (all three through the single European Act (SAE, Luxembourg 1986). European monetary union, culture, public health, consumer protection, trans-European networks and development aid (Maastricht, 1992). Asylum, immigration and visas, employment and public health (Amsterdam, 1997). Judicial and police cooperation, energy, tourism, civil protection, administrative cooperation and humanitarian aid (Lisbon, 2007).

[9] New institutions have emerged, such as the European Court of Auditors (Brussels Treaty of 22 July 1975 modifying some financial provisions and instituting a European Court of Auditors). The European Central Bank (foreseen by the Maastricht Treaty, but instituted only in 1997 succeeding the European Monetary Institute, formally included in the Treaty through the Nice Treaty (2001) and recognised as a proper institution by the Lisbon Treaty (2007)). The European Council (included in the Rome Treaty by the Lisbon revision (2007), but instituted since the SAE outside the Rome Treaty). The Committee of the Regions (1992 Maastricht revision).

Substantial new procedures were introduced by treaty revisions, such as the powers of the European Parliament to approve EEC/EC/EU budget (Brussels Treaty of 22 November 1970); the designation of MEPs through direct election (Council decision of 20 September 1976); the co-decision procedure for the European Parliament (EP) initiated by the Maastricht Treaty (1992) for certain subject matters; generalised (with remaining exceptions) by the Lisbon Treaty (2007). New principles were introduced, such as the respect for human rights or democracy requirements (Single European Act) or the principle of subsidiarity (Maastricht).

B. The Concept of EU Law as an Autonomous Legal Order is Itself a Product of Evolutionary Interpretation

The CJEU, in its interpretation of the founding the European Communities' founding treaties, has assumed that it is only loosely tied to the letter of the treaties. One rarely finds in the CJEU case law, efforts to ascertain the parties' intention at the time they drafted or revised their treaties.[10] The CJEU very soon affirmed its intention to interpret the provisions of EU law according to the ultimate goal of the European integration process (realisation of the single market first, to today's goal of realisation of 'an ever closer union among the peoples of Europe'), and not the letter of the treaties.[11] Teleological interpretation may be the closest approximate, and certainly it is a useful tool, for evolutionary interpretation. As early as the 1960s, the CJEU openly claimed that it was practising teleological interpretation, not only invoking the EEC's goals or objectives to interpret the founding Rome Treaty, but even relying on 'the spirit' of the Treaty.[12]

In this 1963 leading case, the Court, basing itself on 'the preamble to the Treaty which refers not only to governments but to peoples',[13] and the functions assigned to the EEC institutions, determined that

> the objective of the EEC Treaty, which is to establish a Common Market, the functioning of which is of direct concern to interested parties in the Community, implies that this Treaty is more than an agreement which merely creates mutual obligations between the contracting states.[14]

[10] 'La référence à l'intention des auteurs des textes ne joue qu'un rôle secondaire dans l'interprétation du droit de l'Union européennes, bien que la Cour n'exclue pas par principe de l'utiliser' ('The reference to the intention of the text's authors only play a secondary role in the interpretation of EU law, even though the Court does not exclude its use in principle'); J Rideau, *Droit institutionnel de l'Union européenne*, 6th edn (Paris, LGDJ, 2010) 223. However, interpretation methods of the CJEU seem to evolve and recent case law (Judgment (Full Court) 27 November 2012, *Pringle* C-370/12, EU:C:2012:756, 135 or Judgment (Full Court) 10 December 2018, *Wightman* C-621/18, EU:C:2018:999, 47) have made reference to the condition of the adoption of the Treaty. Also see, K Lenaerts and J Gutiérrez-Fons, 'To Say What the Law of the EU Is: Methods of Interpretation and the European Court of Justice' (2014) 20 *Columbia Law Journal* 3, esp 23–33 on 'The Increasing Importance of the *Travaux Préparatoires*'.

[11] As the CJEU Judgment of 10 December 2018 in *Wightman* clearly shows, historical interpretation in order to ascertain the meaning of a specific provision is secondary to contextual and teleological interpretation: 'In that respect, it should be borne in mind that, according to settled case-law of the Court, the interpretation of a provision of EU law requires that account be taken not only of its wording and the objectives it pursues, but also of its context and the provisions of EU law as a whole. The origins of a provision of EU law may also provide information relevant to its interpretation (see, to that effect, judgment of 27 November 2012, Pringle, C-370/12, EU:C:2012:756, paragraph 135; judgments of 3 October 2013, Inuit Tapiriit Kanatami and Others v Parliament and Council, C-583/11 P, EU:C:2013:625, paragraph 50 and the case-law cited, and of 17 March 2016, Parliament v Commission, C-286/14, EU:C:2016:183, paragraph 43)' (*Wightman*, above n 10, 47).

[12] 'The first question of the *Tariefcommissie* is whether Article 12 of the Treaty has direct application in national law in the sense that nationals of Member States may on the basis of this Article lay claim to rights which the national court must protect. To ascertain whether the provisions of an international treaty extend so far in their effects it is necessary to consider the spirit, the general scheme and the wording of those provisions' (Judgment, 5 February 1963, *Van Gend & Loos* C-26/62, EU:C:1963:1).

[13] ibid.

[14] ibid.

Thus the treaty objective used for the teleological interpretation is not even fully spelled out in the treaty, but is itself a product of CJEU interpretation.

Furthermore, the Court inferred from these interpretative elements that 'the conclusion to be drawn from this is that the Community constitutes a new legal order of international law'.[15] The Court even went one step further the following year, asserting that 'by contrast with ordinary international treaties, the EEC Treaty has created its own legal system',[16] with no reference to its international law origins.

Legal doctrine subsequently concluded, based on these two cases, that Community law (nowadays EU law)[17] constitutes a *sui generis* legal order,[18] autonomous from national and international law, but nevertheless characterised by the integration of Community law within the national legal orders of Member States with an absolute precedence over all norms of the national legal order, including constitutional provisions.[19] Such an assertion of the singularity of an (EEC) EU legal order is not found in any specific treaty provision, but is based on the doctrinal reception of the evolutionary interpretation of the treaty founding the EEC proposed by the CJEU in its 1960s case law.

Despite many subsequent treaty revisions, as mentioned in this section's introduction, these defining characteristics of EU law were never formally embedded in the founding treaties. Eventually however, the EU Member States, gathered in Lisbon on 13 December 2007 to adopt its latest European treaty, felt compelled to adopt a declaration on the primacy of EU law stating:

> The Conference recalls that, in accordance with well settled case law of the Court of Justice of the European Union, the Treaties and the law adopted by the Union on the basis of the Treaties have primacy over the law of Member States, under the conditions laid down by the said case law.[20]

[15] ibid

[16] Judgment of 15 July 1964, *Costa* C-6/64, EU:C:1964:66.

[17] It is accepted that EU law is the successor of Community law, based on the interpretation of Art 13.1 of the TEU which states. 'The Union shall replace and succeed the European Community'. In view of recent EU law developments, we have doubts on the relevance of this assertion and the defining features of EU law seem to be drifting away from those of Community law. See N Levrat, 'Is the EU a Proper Successor to the European Community?' in A Weyembergh and F Ponjaert (eds), *Mélanges en hommage à Mario Telo* (Presses de l'Université de Bruxelles, forthcoming 2019).

[18] P Pescatore, *Le droit de l'intégration: émergence d'un phénomène nouveau dans les relations internationales selon l'expérience des Communautés européennes* (The Hague, AW Sijthoff, 1972) (English translation with the same editor in 1974); WJ Ganshof Van der Meersch, *L'ordre juridique des Communautés européennes et le droit international* (Leiden, Martinus Nijhoff, 1975).

[19] 'It follows from all these observations that the law stemming from the Treaty, an independent source of law, could not, because of its special and original nature, be overridden by domestic legal provisions, however framed, without being deprived of its character as Community law and without the legal basis of the Community itself being called into question' (*Costa*, above n 16).

[20] Declaration concerning primacy, OJEU C 202/344, 7 June 2016. The Declaration also includes an Annex which reads as follows: 'The Conference has also decided to attach as an Annex to this Final Act the Opinion of the Council Legal Service on the primacy of EC law as set out in 11197/07 (JUR 260): "Opinion of the Council Legal Service of 22 June 2007. It results from the case-law of the Court of Justice that primacy of EC law is a cornerstone principle of Community law. According to the Court,

Thus, as confirmed by this declaration, the EU Member States themselves accept that the most defining feature of EU law[21] is not treaty-based, but stems from the CJEU's evolutionary case law!

III. Evolutionary Interpretation in the EU Rule of Law-based Multilevel Legal System: A Route to Relative Rules of Law Paradigm

A rule of law-based legal order is standard for liberal democratic States. The EU, despite not being a State, claims that the rule of law is one of its founding values.[22] Article 19 of the Treaty of the European Union (TEU, defining the role of the CJEU states that 'it shall ensure that in the interpretation and application of the Treaties the law is observed'. This raises the question why, when the CJEU stretches the limits of its evolutionary interpretation paradigm, is it still ensuring that the law is being observed in the interpretation and application of the treaties? In other words, is evolutionary interpretation appropriate in a multilevel legal system based on the rule of law (as is claimed by Article 2 of the TEU)?

Interestingly, we did not find many references to the concept of evolutionary interpretation in domestic law. On reflection, it seems obvious that evolutionary interpretation deals directly with the role and responsibilities of judges in a given legal order. In domestic legal orders, the authority of judges is balanced with effective legislative and executive powers, neither of which really exist at the international level. Judicial implementation of domestic legal norms is guaranteed in a liberal democratic State; however, the ability of judges to interpret statutes

this principle is inherent to the specific nature of the European Community. At the time of the first judgment of this established case law (Costa/ENEL,15 July 1964, Case 6/641 (1)) there was no mention of primacy in the treaty. It is still the case today. The fact that the principle of primacy will not be included in the future treaty shall not in any way change the existence of the principle and the existing case-law of the Court of Justice"'.

[21] 'The essential characteristics of the Community legal order which has thus been established are in particular its primacy over the law of the Member States and the direct effect of a whole series of provisions which are applicable to their nationals and to the Member States themselves' (Opinion of the Court, 14 December 1991, Opinion 1/91, EU:C:1991:490, 21).

[22] Art 2 of the TEU reads: 'The Union is founded on the values of respect for human dignity, freedom, democracy, equality, the rule of law and respect for human rights, including the rights of persons belonging to minorities. These values are common to the Member States in a society in which pluralism, non-discrimination, tolerance, justice, solidarity and equality between women and men prevail'. The CJEU had been reluctant to acknowledge the existence of a rule of law principle, mostly because its deliberations are always held in French, and the concept of rule of law in French is worded 'Etat de droit'. As the EU is not a State (Etat), the Court has since 1986 referred to the concept of 'Communauté de droit' (legal community) as a substitute for 'Etat de droit' (see Judgment of 23 April 1986, *Les Verts v European Parliament*, C-294/83, EU:C:1986:166, 23).

and other legal texts is bound by strict limitations.[23] On the contrary, judicial implementation in international law is rarely guaranteed, due to the principle of State sovereignty, and has remained much less important in international law than in domestic legal systems. Therefore, the development of judicial fora (courts, arbitral tribunals, national jurisdictions implementing international legal norms) in which international law is extensively interpreted by judges or arbitrators – instead of unilateral interpretation by State governments to justify their complying or non-complying behaviour – has been seen as a positive development. It somehow contributes to the development of an international law aiming at a rule of law-based system.[24] Viewed from this position, evolutionary interpretation attracts more sympathy in a 'striving towards a rule of law international legal order' than in domestic rule of law-based legal orders.

Could it therefore be that evolutionary interpretation is fit for legal systems where the rule of law is not clearly guaranteed, whereas tensions arise when it coexists with the principle of legal certainty in a rule of law-based legal system? The EU is an interesting case study for addressing such a question, due to both the multilevel structure of its legal order and its commitment to respect for the rule of law.

The EU has established, through the evolutionary interpretation of the CJEU, as we have shown above, a legal order where the rule of law is implemented.[25] If, as in current international law, evolutionary interpretation appeared as an interesting and useful tool for developing respect for the law in a legal system in which the capacity for judicial control of the proper implementation of legal norms was not acquired (EEC in the 1960s), is such interpretative method still justified in a rule of law-based legal system (EU today)? (A). To avoid a negative answer, we need to make clear that the rule of law governing the EU legal system is not the classical rule of law principle – as understood within national legal orders – but an original type of relative rules of law,[26] leading to a conceptualisation of a relative rules of law based EU legal order (B).

[23] See for the evolution and role of the interpretative power of judges over time and legal systems, B Frydman, *Le sens des Lois* (Brussels, Bruylant, 2005).

[24] Regarding this issue, we shall only refer to the brilliant General Course given by Ian Brownlie at The Hague Academy of International Law in 1995: I Brownlie, *The Rule of Law in International Affairs: International Law at the Fiftieth Anniversary of the United Nations*, Vol 1 (The Hague, Martinus Nijhoff Publishers, 1998). There is however abundant literature on the topic. We have personally strongly taken position against the pre-condition for a rule of law system in international relations (N Levrat, 'D'une exigence de légalité dans les relations internationals contemporaines' in CA Morand (ed), *La crise des Balkans de 1999* (Brussels, Bruylant, 2000).

[25] See K Alter, *Establishing the Supremacy of European Law: The Making of an International Rule of Law in Europe* (Oxford, Oxford University Press, 2010). The CJEU first referred to a rule of law based on European legal order in *Les Verts v European Parliament*, above n 22.

[26] We have expressed our doubts about the promotion of the (classical) rule of law by the EU in N Levrat, 'L'Etat de droit est-il une valeur européenne don't l'UE assure la promotion?' in D Sidjanskiet al (eds), *Union de valeurs? La mise en oeuvre des valeurs et des principes fondamentaux de l'Union européenne* (Geneva, Publications CCDSEE, 2018).

A. Evolutionary Interpretation and the Problem of *Contra Legem* Interpretation

Article 189 of the Treaty Establishing the European Community (currently Article 288 of the TFEU) played a very central role in the development of both the direct effect and precedence principles of EC/EU law in Member States' national legal orders.[27] This Article differentiates among legal acts (regulations, directives, decisions, recommendations and opinions) of EU law, with different legal effects, both in EU and in national legal orders. Contrary to regulations, directives do not appear to have a direct effect on the national legal orders of Member States, as this Article reads, 'a directive shall be binding, as to the result to be achieved, upon each Member State to which it is addressed, but shall leave to the national authorities the choice of form and methods'.[28]

Although well aware of this distinction between regulations and directives, the CJEU, in 'evolutionary case law' developed in the 1970s and early 1980s, recognised that when a Member State has failed to properly transpose a directive into its national legal order, the directive may, under certain conditions, have a 'direct effect'. Therefore, some provisions of a directive, if a Member State has failed to transpose them into its domestic law within the time frame allowed by the directive itself, and provided the provisions are sufficiently precise and unconditional, may be directly implemented for the benefit of private actors in domestic law.[29] Further, due to this potential direct effect of directives, if the national transposition takes place but risks producing inadequate legal effects, the CJEU requires that the national courts interpret the national norms in conformity with the directive,[30] and if need be, discard the national norms if those norms risk making a conforming interpretation impossible.[31]

In the Amsterdam Treaty (1997), the Member States decided to create within the third pillar of the EU (cooperation for justice and home affairs) a new category of legal acts for development of such cooperation, which would have a legal effect equivalent to that of a directive.[32] This new category of acts was termed 'framework

[27] The second paragraph of Art 189 TEC/288 TFEU (the text has remained the same over the years) concerning regulations reads as follow: 'A regulation shall have general application. It shall be binding in its entirety and directly applicable in all Member States'. It has been used in the two cases quoted in section I of this chapter to justify both direct effect (1963, *Van Gend & Loos*) and precedence of EEC law (1964, *Costa*).

[28] Art 288.3 of the TFEU (formerly Art 189 of the TEEC and Article 249 of the TEC).

[29] The issue of the direct effect of a directive was first raised in 1974 (Judgment, 4 December 1974, *Van Duyn* C-41/74, EU:C:1974:133) and the criteria for recognising a direct effect were clearly enunciated in 1982 (Judgment, 19 January 1982, *Becker* C-8/81, EU:C:1982:7).

[30] Judgment of 10 April 1984, *Von Colson & Kamann* C-14/83, EU:C:1984:153.

[31] Judgment of 12 June 1989, *Fratelli Costanzo* C-103/88, EU:C:1989:256, 30, 31.

[32] The Maastricht Treaty, instituting the EU, dramatically increased the fields of cooperation among EEC Member States. However, cooperation in the field of police and justice (as well as a common security and foreign policy (CSFP)) were considered too closely linked to State sovereignty to be included in the EC Treaty. They were embedded in a new treaty on the European Union, in which the

decisions'. Thus Article 34(2)(b) of the TEU (as it was worded at that time) reads as follows:

> The Council may adopt framework decisions for the purpose of approximation of the laws and regulations of the Member States. Framework decisions shall be binding upon the Member States as to the result to be achieved but shall leave to the national authorities the choice of form and methods. They shall not entail direct effect.

The intention of the Member States adopting that text and adding a specific sentence on the absence of direct effect seems quite clear; it even appears to be a deliberate safeguard measure written into the Treaty to prevent evolutionary interpretation of the possible direct legal effects of 'framework decisions'.

Never mind the intention of the parties and the clear text of the Treaty, less than 10 years after the entry into force of the Amsterdam Treaty, on 16 June 2005, the European judges in their *Pupino* judgment held that under certain conditions, framework decisions may entail a conforming interpretation, a principle inferred from the possible direct effect of directives![33] This is a clear *contra legem* interpretation. Interestingly, the French government, which intervened in the proceedings of the *Pupino* case, raised the argument of a *contra legem* interpretation:

> The French Government argues that the national court is seeking to apply certain provisions of the Framework Decision in place of national legislation, whereas, in accordance with the very wording of Article 34(2)(b) EU, Framework Decisions cannot have such a direct effect. It further points out that, as the national court itself acknowledges, an interpretation of national law in accordance with the Framework Decision is impossible. In accordance with the case-law of the Court of Justice, the principle that national law must be given a conforming interpretation cannot lead to an interpretation that is *contra legem*, or to a worsening of the position of an individual in criminal proceedings, on the basis of the Framework Decision alone, which is precisely what would happen in the main proceedings.[34]

Not only was the French government's argument discarded by the Court, but in fact, the CJEU using the same reasoning reached an opposite conclusion, stating that since a *contra legem* interpretation of national law was not possible on the basis of the conforming interpretation doctrine, because it would mean a *contra legem* interpretation of the EU Treaty provision, this might justify the national Court broadening its interpretative methods and substituting conforming interpretation with a form of evolutionary interpretation of national law provisions based 'on the whole national law in order to assess how far it can be *applied in such a way as not*

EC institutions had no competences, and the cooperation would only develop along intergovernmental practices. If CSFP remains to this day an intergovernmental matter, Justice and Home Affairs (JHA) was transferred to the EC Treaty with the Amsterdam Treaty (1997). For an analysis of these evolutions, see N Levrat, 'L'Union européenne au prisme de l'évolution différenciée de la PESC et de la JAI, de Maastricht à nos jours' in G Grin et al (eds), *Formes d'Europe. Union européenne et autres organisations*, Cahiers Rouge de la Fondation Jean Monnet pour l'Europe no 218 (Paris, Economica, 2018).

[33] See above n 29.

[34] Judgment of 16 June 2005, *Pupino* C-105/03, EU:C:2005:386, 24.

to produce a result contrary to that envisaged by the framework decision' (emphasis added).[35] That is to say that, short of a *contra legem* interpretation of EU law by recognising a direct effect of a framework decision in contradiction with the clear wording of the Treaty, creative evolutionary interpretation by a national court may lead to the required result within the national legal order. The CJEU does not require the national judges to discard national law when such law contradicts clear prescriptions of the treaty[36] or a directive,[37] but they shall ensure that they interpret 'the whole of national law' to reach a result equivalent to a *contra legem* interpretation through the wording subtlety of a double negation.

In other words, it is clear that such creative interpretation as suggested by the CJEU raises questions about legal certainty. Can the subjects of EU law refer to the written content of EU norms to ascertain their legal obligations, or are they left with the uncertainty flowing from the self-acquired interpretative leeway of the European judges, further accorded to national judges implementing EU law within their domestic legal order, as stated by the *Pupino* ruling?[38] In the singular EU multilevel legal order, is it possible that, short of a full integration into one single legal order, the issue of evolutionary interpretation in the framework of the preliminary ruling needs to be balanced against the principle of legal certainty in each legal order?[39]

B. Towards a Relative Rules of Law Paradigm: An Approach to Special Relative Legality

What this *contra legem*/evolutionary interpretation trend may mean in the EU legal order, is that the same provision, worded in the same way, may somehow have a different – but coherent[40] – meaning within the EU legal order, depending on its legal environment. Incidentally, this is precisely what Darwin's original theory of evolution postulates; however, and this is where the transposition of evolution theory in the legal discipline may be problematic, such a conclusion would be contrary to the principle of legal certainty, which is closely associated with

[35] ibid, 47.

[36] Judgment of 9 March 1978, *Simmenthal* C-106/77, EU:C:1978:49.

[37] *Fratelli Constanzo*, above n 31.

[38] In practice, EU Member States seem to live quite well with that legal risk, other than making a few political declarations opposing the Court rulings. As an example, following the *Pupino* ruling on the potential legal effect of framework decisions, this category of EU legal acts has been abandoned by the Lisbon Treaty, and harmonisation in the field of judicial cooperation in criminal matters is now being achieved through directive … with potential direct effect (see Art 83.2 of the TFEU).

[39] Expressing the same reserve, see, E Paunio, *Legal Certainty in Multilingual EU Law: Language, Discourse and Reasoning at the European Court of Justice* (London, Routledge, 2016). Also see the similar arguments raised by the Italian government in the *Simmenthal* case, above n 36.

[40] Since the Court states 'in a way as not to produce a result contrary to that envisaged', see above n 35.

the 'classical' rule of law principle.[41] At the same time, it appears an inescapable consequence of implementing the concept of evolutionary interpretation in a multilevel rule of law-based legal system such as the EU legal order. This is why we suggest that the CJEU refers in the EU legal order to the original concept of relative rules of law instead of the classical principle of the rule of law.[42] First, let us take note that the CJEU fully accepts that the exact same provision, worded in the exact same way, may produce different legal effect in different legal contexts.

In the early 1990s, following dramatic geopolitical tremors in Europe (fall of the Berlin Wall, collapse of the Soviet Union), Member States from the EU and the European Free Trade Association (EFTA) agreed to conclude a comprehensive treaty to extend the benefit of the EU internal market to EFTA countries, although they were not members of the EU. So contrary to ordinary treaties that create a legal regime which is extraneous from each party's legal order, the purpose of the Agreement establishing the European Economic Area (EEA) was to extend the EEC single market beyond the EEC. Therefore, the EEA Agreement refers directly to EC treaty provisions.

To guarantee the integrity of the EEC legal order and the principle of homogeneous interpretation, the EEA Agreement also conferred jurisdiction on an EEA court if a legal dispute arose concerning the implementation or interpretation of the EEA Treaty (including the references made to the EC Treaty). At the request of the European Commission[43] the Court examined this dispute settlement mechanism and concluded that it did not sufficiently guarantee the integrity of EEC law. As a consequence, the dispute settlement mechanism instituting an EEA court had to be renegotiated.

Although the envisaged EEA court would have been composed of five judges (out of eight) emanating from the CJEU – thus ensuring that the interpretation of CJEU judges would always prevail in the EEA court – and although 'essentially, the rules [which are to apply] are those laid down in the corresponding provisions of the EEC and ECSC Treaties and in measures adopted pursuant thereto',[44] the CJEU considered such a situation as a threat to the integrity and autonomy of the EC legal order. In its Opinion the Court bluntly states: 'it follows that homogeneity of the rules of law throughout the EEA is not secured by the fact that the provisions

[41] J Maxeiner starts his article 'Some realism about legal certainty in the globalization of the rule of law' (2008) 31 *Houston Journal of International Law* 27, 28 with the following sentence: 'Legal certainty is a central tenet of the rule of law as understood around the world'.

[42] See Levrat, L'Etat de droit est-il une valeur européenne don't l'UE assure la promotion?', above n 26, for more developments on this original concept of EU rules of law.

[43] According to Art 238 of the TEC. The procedure is nowadays spelled out, with the exact same wording, in Art 218.11 of the TFEU: 'A Member State, the European Parliament, the Council or the Commission may obtain the opinion of the Court of Justice as to whether an agreement envisaged is compatible with the Treaties. Where the opinion of the Court is adverse, the agreement envisaged may not enter into force unless it is amended or the Treaties are revised'.

[44] Opinion 1/91, above n 21, 4.

of Community law and those of the corresponding provisions of the agreement are identical in their content or wording'.[45]

The Court's reason for such a strong statement is the following:

> The fact that the provisions of the agreement and the corresponding Community provisions are identically worded does not mean that they must necessarily be interpreted identically. An international treaty is to be interpreted not only on the basis of its wording, but also in the light of its objectives …
>
> With regard to the comparison of the objectives of the provisions of the agreement and those of Community law, it must be observed that the agreement is concerned with the application of rules on free trade and competition in economic and commercial relations between the Contracting Parties. In contrast, … the provisions of the EEC Treaty on free movement and competition, far from being an end in themselves, are only means for attaining those objectives [of European integration].
>
> The context in which the objective of the agreement is situated also differs from that in which the Community aims are pursued. The EEA is to be established on the basis of an international treaty which, essentially, merely creates rights and obligations as between the Contracting Parties and provides for no transfer of sovereign rights to the intergovernmental institutions which it sets up. In contrast, the EEC Treaty, albeit concluded in the form of an international agreement, none the less constitutes the constitutional charter of a Community based on the rule of law …
>
> It follows from those considerations that homogeneity of the rules of law throughout the EEA is not secured by the fact that the provisions of Community law and those of the corresponding provisions of the agreement are identical in their content or wording.[46]

This conclusion is most worrying, because as the Court acknowledges, the very purpose of the EEA Treaty as specified in its Article 1, it to guarantee homogeneity in the application of the treaty provisions between all the parties.[47] This is problematic because such is the aim of most international legal regimes, whereas an inescapable consequence of evolutionary interpretation – more or less as Darwin concluded with regard to living species – is divergence in results, not convergence under a single common regime. Due to teleological or evolutionary interpretation, any international legal regime – short of an international regime whose implementation relies solely on its own international mechanism excluding any implementation in national law – when implemented in different national legal orders, will produce, thanks to evolutionary interpretation, potentially different legal effects, making their very raison d'être unattainable.[48]

Even worse: if the CJEU was consistent with itself, it should also admit that EU law itself cannot – since rules of EU law have to be implemented within national

[45] ibid, 22.

[46] ibid, 14–16, 18–22.

[47] ibid, 5.

[48] We explore this other paradox in a contribution entitled N Levrat, 'The Theoretical Implications of Supranationality and Legitimacy in a legal perspective' in M Telo and A Weyembergh (eds), *The Supranationality at stake?* (Routledge, forthcoming, 2019).

legal orders, and despite CJEU pretence to a monopoly in the area of treaty interpretation – be guaranteed to produce the same legal effect in each national legal order.[49] The inclusion of norms from an international legal order into any other legal order (national or international) cannot guarantee homogeneous interpretation, as a consequence of taking evolutionary interpretation seriously. So, should evolutionary interpretation be banned from EU law because it does not allow for the homogeneous legal effect of EU law, as the principle of certainty – as associated with the rule of law principle – and the prohibition of discrimination as spelled out in Articles 10 and 18 of the TFEU would require?

That apparent contradiction was elegantly solved from the outset of the CJEU's evolutionary EU case law. As the *Costa* judgment tells us in 1964,

> by contrast with ordinary international treaties, the EEC Treaty has created its own legal system which, on the entry into force of the treaty, became an integral part of the legal systems of the Member States and which their courts are bound to apply.[50]

So the EEC (and subsequent EU) Treaty is not distinct from national law; it is 'an integral part of the legal system of Members States'. As a result:

> The integration into the laws of each Member State of provisions which derive from the Community, and more generally the terms and the spirit of the Treaty, make it impossible for the States, as a corollary, to accord precedence to a unilateral and subsequent measure over a legal system accepted by them on a basis of reciprocity. The executive force of Community law cannot vary from one State to another in deference to subsequent domestic laws, without jeopardising the attainment of the objectives of the Treaty set out in Article 5 (2) and giving rise to the discrimination prohibited by Article 7.[51]

The Court does not require that the legal effect of EC rules be the same in each national legal order, but only that 'its executive force does not vary from one State to another'. This requirement does not prevent diverging evolutionary trajectories of EC/EU law in different national legal orders, as long as their executive force is commensurate; in much the same way that time may be different but equally accurate in different electromagnetic systems according to Maxwell equations.[52] In that respect, the EU legal system is not comparable to a national legal system: it is a composite legal system, which exists as an integral part of the legal system of each Member State,[53] and which is based on horizontal reciprocity and mutual trust; and not a unidimensional legal system based on delegation, order and control, as in a pyramidal legal order model.

[49] Contrary to the pretence for homogeneous interpretation on which the Court grounds the interpretative mission assigned to it by Art 19.1 of the TEU.

[50] *Costa*, above n 16.

[51] ibid.

[52] See above n 2.

[53] See for developments on this point, I Raducuand and N Levrat, 'Le métissage des ordres juridiques européens (une "théorie impure" de l'ordre juridique)' (2007) 2007 *Cahiers de droit européen* 111.

When the CJEU pretends to impose the precedence of EU law over national law, and the homogeneous interpretation of EU law in each Member State, it has very few, if any, coercive means to reach this end. Actually, no legal proceeding allows the CJEU to strike down a provision of national law contradicting EU law. It may only ask every single national judge to do so.[54] So this specific nature and consistency of EU law[55] is not based on a hierarchy of judicial authority – as you would find in a domestic legal order so as to be able to maintain its consistency and guarantee the rule of law principle – but on a dialogue between national and European judges,[56] based on shared values and mutual trust.[57] Is that sufficient to guarantee respect for the rule of law, especially acknowledging the relevance of evolutionary interpretation? Certainly, such a system is not viable with a rule of law concept which relies on a monolithic concept of legal certainty.[58] It may only be consistent with a rule of law principle that is a relative rules of law principle.

IV. Conclusion

We must thus conclude that the coherence of the EU legal system can only be achieved in a relative rules of law paradigm. The EU is founded on rules of law as a shared value among its Member States. This is a shared value of national rules of law that are 'common to the Member States',[59] and not a specific EU rule of law, distinct from the shared national rules of law, which constitute together EU rule of law. Thus, the precise concrete legal effect of EU law dispositions may differ in

[54] '[A] national court which is called upon, within the limits of its jurisdiction, to apply provisions of Community law is under a duty to give full effect to those provisions, if necessary refusing of its own motion to apply any conflicting provision of national legislation, even if adopted subsequently, and it is not necessary for the court to request or await the prior setting aside of such provision by legislative or other constitutional means' (*Simmenthal*, above n 36). For the importance and functioning of this 'decentralized constitutinal control mechanism', see N Levrat, 'De la CEE à l'UE: le jeu dangereux d'une progression vers la Fédération par la déconstruction de l'édifice juridique communautaire' (2019) *Le jeu du droit dans le fédéralisme coopératif, no spécial de la Revue Fédéralisme, Régionalisme* (forthcoming).

[55] See Lenaerts and J Gutiérrez-Fons, above n 10, for the importance of consistent interpretation of EU law, esp 33 ff.

[56] 'In particular, the judicial system as thus conceived has as its keystone the preliminary ruling procedure provided for in Article 267 TFEU, which, by setting up a dialogue between one court and another, specifically between the Court of Justice and the courts and tribunals of the Member States, has the object of securing uniform interpretation of EU law (see, to that effect, *Van Gend & Loos*, above n 12), thereby serving to ensure its consistency, its full effect and its autonomy as well as, ultimately, the particular nature of the law established by the Treaties' (Opinion of the Court, 18 December 2014, Opinion 2/13, EU:C:2014:2454, 176).

[57] 'This legal structure is based on the fundamental premise that each Member State shares with all the other Member States, and recognises that they share with it, a set of common values on which the EU is founded, as stated in Article 2 TEU. That premise implies and justifies the existence of mutual trust between the Member States that those values will be recognised and, therefore, that the law of the EU that implements them will be respected' (ibid, 168). Also see K Lenaerts, 'La vie après l'avis: exploring the principle of mutual (yet not blind) trust' (2017) 54 *Common Market Law Review* 805.

[58] Above n 39.

[59] Art 2 of the TEU.

each national legal order, as long as its primacy cannot be contested: 'because of its special and original nature, [it could not] be overridden by domestic legal provisions, however framed, without being deprived of its character as Community law and without the legal basis of the Community itself being called into question'.[60]

So, EU rule of law is not a monolithic rule of law principle, but a composite rule of law based on 28 all equally valid, but not necessarily identical, rule of law principles. This relative rule of law principle allows us to understand the apparently paradoxical assertion of the Karlsruhe judges in their 1993 Maastricht judgment,[61] in which they recognised the absolute precedence of EC law over German law, including the Bundesgrundgesetz, because the *Bundesgrundgesetz* recognises EU law's pre-eminence. This is a strange loop typical of those you might find in Esher's drawings.[62] The precedence of EU law is grounded in German law in the Bundesgrundgesetz, while it is grounded in EU law in 'the spirit of the treaty' and 'the special and original nature' of 'a legal system accepted by them [Member States, *in casu* Germany] on the basis of reciprocity'.[63] Both positions are true and compatible, due to mutual trust,[64] and the preliminary ruling procedure – the keystone of the EU legal order,[65] which allowed its emergence[66] and ensures its consistency.[67] The EU is thus a composite multilevel rules of law-based legal order which incorporates, thanks to the relative nature of its rules of law concept, evolutionary interpretation as its founding, defining and functional principle. Attentive readers may have noted that in its Opinion 1/91 the CJEU refers to 'homogeneity of the *rules* of law throughout the EEA'[68] and not to the homogeneity of the *rule* of law. Indeed, rule of law in EU law is not unique but plural. In that respect, the special relativity principle – acknowledging that they may be several different rules of law simultaneously coexisting and simultaneously valid, even though not identical – allows, in our view, a better grasp of the nature of the EU legal system than the abundant 'pluralistic literature'. Special relativity in EU rules of law allows a combining of coherence and variation, or as was almost proclaimed as the EU motto, 'unity in diversity'[69] in legal terms.

[60] *Costa*, above n 16.

[61] B VerfGE 89, 155 – *Maastricht*.

[62] See for developments on this concept of strange loops, D Hofstadter, *Gödel, Escher, Bach* (New York, Vintage Books, 1980).

[63] All the three quotes from the *Costa* Judgment, above n 16.

[64] The principle was originally identified as 'mutual recognition' and formalised in a 20 February 1979 Judgment, *Cassis de Dijon* C-120/78, EU:C:1979:42.

[65] See above n 56.

[66] See section II.B above in this chapter.

[67] Opinion 2/13, above n 56.

[68] See above n 44.

[69] Envisaged EU motto by the failed 29 October Rome Treaty establishing a Constitution for Europe.

28

Multilingualism and the Dynamic Interpretation of European Union Law

MATTIAS DERLÉN

I. Introduction: The Interpretative Approach of the CJEU

The Court of Justice of the European Union (CJEU) is known for its radical approach to interpretation.[1] It has certainly emphasised the need for an evolutionary interpretation of European Union law,[2] but it has clearly gone far beyond this approach. The CJEU has famously interpreted silences in the founding EU treaties to include seminal constitutional principles, granting European Union (EU) law direct effect and supremacy and including a wide range of fundamental rights not originally enumerated in the treaties.[3] In short, the interpretative approach of the CJEU has gone beyond evolutionary, to revolutionary. The Luxembourg court is famously guided by 'une certaine idée de l'Europe',[4] and it has sought to achieve a uniform and effective EU legal system.[5]

This contribution moves beyond the general discussion of interpretation of EU law and concentrates on the specific aspect of multilingualism. The equal

[1] See, eg, M Lasser, *Judicial Deliberations – A Comparative Analysis of Transparency and Legitimacy* (Oxford, Oxford University Press, 2004).

[2] See, eg, Judgment of 6 October 1982, *CILFIT* 283/81, EU:C:1982:335, para 20. See also N Levrat, 'Articulating Evolutionary Interpretation and the Rule of Law: EU as a Composite Legal Order Based on Relative Rules of Law', ch 27 in this book.

[3] For an overview see M Derlén, 'Multilingualism and Legal Integration in Europe' in R Temmerman and M Van Campenhoudt (eds), *Dynamics and Terminology. An Interdisciplinary Perspective on Monolingual and Multilingual Culture-bound Communication* (Amsterdam, John Benjamins Publishing Company, 2014) 23–24.

[4] P Pescatore, 'The Doctrine of Direct Effect: An Infant Disease of Community Law' (1983) 8 *European Law Review* 155, 157.

[5] Regarding the twin virtues of effectiveness and uniformity see, eg, Derlén, 'Legal Integration', above n 3, 28–30.

authenticity of 24 different languages in the EU legal regime, see further below, has an impact on the interpretation of EU provisions, but the question is what kind of impact. This contribution will challenge the traditional view of multilingualism as little more than an excuse to move from literal to teleological methods of interpretation and present a more positive view of the connection between multilingualism and the dynamic interpretation of EU law.

II. Short Overview of the EU Language Regime

The literature discussing the EU language regime in general is extensive, so only a short introduction will be given here.[6] We will focus on the existence of a plurality of language regimes, in the sense that the treaties and secondary acts adopted by the Union institutions follow one regime, and judgments from the CJEU follow another.[7]

When it comes to treaties and secondary acts, such as regulations and directives, the EU adopts full multilingualism. Thus, these documents are not only available but also equally authentic in all 24 official[8] languages.[9] This follows from Article 55 of the EU Treaty (TEU) and Article 358 of the Treaty on the Functioning of the European Union (TFEU), regarding treaties, and from Regulation 1/58 regarding secondary acts. The EU also employs full multilingualism when it comes to external working languages. It follows, for example, from Article 41.4 of the Charter of Fundamental Rights, as well as Article 2 in Regulation 1/58, that citizens have the right to communicate with the European Union in the official language of their choice, and to receive a reply in the same language. Unsurprisingly, full multilingualism does not mean that the Union institutions work in all

[6] For a more extensive discussion of the EU language regime, including the viability of potential reforms see M Derlén, 'Multilingualism and the European Court of Justice: Challenges, Reforms and the Position of English after Brexit' in E Guinchard and M Granger (eds), *The New EU Judiciary – An Analysis of Current Judicial Reforms* (Alphen aan den Rijn, Kluwer Law International 2018).

[7] The EU also includes other languages regimes, such as that of the Office for the Harmonisation of the Internal Market (OHIM). For a discussion of the language regime of OHIM see, eg, CJW Baaij, *Legal Integration and Language Diversity: Rethinking Translation in EU Lawmaking* (Oxford, Oxford University Press, 2018) 87–88.

[8] The term 'official language' is here used to denote a language listed in Regulation 1/58. The CJEU itself uses the term official languages, see, eg, Judgment of 25 July 2018, *Nestlé* C-84/17 P, C-85/17 P and C-95/17 P, EU:C:2018:596, para 35.

[9] Bulgarian, Czech, Croatian, Danish, Dutch, English, Estonian, Finnish, French, German, Greek, Hungarian, Irish, Italian, Latvian, Lithuanian, Maltese, Polish, Portuguese, Romanian, Slovak, Slovenian, Spanish and Swedish. Full multilingualism does not exclude temporary derogations. Such derogations have been in place for both Maltese and Irish, limiting the categories of documents translated into these languages. See regarding Irish Council Regulation (EC) No 920/2005, [2005] OJ L156/3 and Council Regulation (EU, Euratom) 2015/2264, [2015] OJ L322/1. See regarding Maltese Council Regulation (EC) No 930/2004, [2004] OJ L169/1 and Council Regulation (EC) No 1738/2006, OJ [2006] L329/1.

24 languages internally. Rather, the institutions adopt internal (and unofficial)[10] working languages, often the 'big three': English, French and German.[11]

The political choice of full multilingualism does not tell us what the legal implications of multilingualism are. In the EU, this was left for the CJEU to decide. Theoretically, the Court could have concluded that the equal authenticity of all official languages had the consequence that private actors could rely on the national language version, at least under certain circumstances.[12] However, that is not the route the CJEU opted for. Instead, it adopted what will here be referred to as the 'single meaning' approach. According to this approach the various language versions form the meaning of an EU provision together, necessitating a comparative approach in the interpretation of the provision. Thus, full multilingualism and equal authenticity means interdependence, not independence from the perspective of individual language versions. We will return to the idea of the single meaning below, and its appeal to the CJEU.

CJEU judgments,[13] an increasingly important source of law in their own right,[14] follow a different language regime. The Court operates in all 24 official languages from an external perspective, in that all can serve as the language of a case,[15] but when it comes to the final judgment the language regime is monolingual, as only the version in the language of the case is authentic.[16] Coupled with the well-known existence of an unofficial internal working language (French) at the CJEU,[17] the risk of confusion is clear, when national courts and other actors have to make a choice between the formal, de jure, original and the informal, de facto, original (French).[18]

The interaction between these two different language regimes will be discussed further below.

[10] The internal working languages are unofficial in the sense that they are not regulated. Regulation 1/58 permits the use of working languages in Art 6, but it does not regulate the issue further. The unofficial standing also means that the Union institutions cannot privilege certain languages when employing personnel, as demonstrated by the Judgment of 24 September 2015, *Italy and Spain v Commission*, T-124/13 and T-191/13, EU:T:2015:690, paras 113–17.

[11] See for an overview, eg, W Robinson, 'How the European Commission Drafts Legislation in 20 Languages' (2005) 53 *Clarity* 4.

[12] A right to rely on a single language version could exist as long as the version in question is free from vagueness or ambiguity, a so-called case of doubt-criterion; see further, M Derlén, 'In Defence of (Limited) Multilingualism: Problems and Possibilities of the Multilingual Interpretation of European Union Law in National Courts' in A Kjaer and S Adamo (eds), *Linguistic Diversity and European Democracy* (Farnham, Ashgate, 2011) 144–45.

[13] This discussion only concerns the Court of Justice, but the General Court follows the same language regime, see arts 44–49 of the Rules of Procedure of the General Court.

[14] See, eg, Lasser, above n 1, 107–12.

[15] Rules of Procedure of the Court of Justice, arts 36–37.

[16] ibid, art 41.

[17] M Derlén, 'Multilingual Interpretation of CJEU Case Law: Rule and Reality' (2014) 3 *European Law Review* 295, 299–301.

[18] For discussion see M Derlén, 'A Single Text or a Single Meaning: Multilingual Interpretation of EU Legislation and CJEU Case Law in National Courts' in S Šarčević (ed), *Language and Culture in EU Law – Multidisciplinary Perspectives* (Farnham, Ashgate 2015).

III. Multilingualism and Interpretation: The Interrelationship

Even early in the Union's history, Advocate General Lagrange quipped that 'all … languages are authentic, which means that no single one of them is authentic'.[19] This statement captures the traditional understanding of the relationship between EU multilingualism and the dynamic interpretation of EU provisions. This understanding is negative, in the sense that multilingualism is seen as reducing the importance of language in general. More specifically, the existence of – or simply the potential for – diverging language versions reduces the Court's ability to rely on a literal interpretation. Bluntly speaking, the CJEU can use multilingualism as a handy excuse for disregarding the wording of EU provisions, moving quickly on to contextual and teleological arguments of interpretation.[20]

This view of the relationship between multilingualism and dynamic interpretation of EU law should not be dismissed out of hand. In many ways, it captures important aspects of the CJEU's approach. One of the recurring phrases employed by the Court, the *Regina v Bouchereau* formula, emphasises the need to move on from the literal to teleological interpretation. It states:

> The different language versions of a community text must be given a uniform interpretation and hence in the case of divergence between the versions the provision in question must be interpreted by reference to the purpose and general scheme of the rules of which it forms a part.[21]

In situations of diverging language versions, the Court sometimes employs what I have termed the 'radical teleological' approach, often quoting *Regina v Bouchereau* or later cases.[22] It then tends to abandon discussion of the language versions as soon as it detects a divergence, or sometimes even when a divergence is only hinted at. An example of the latter is the *Commission v Spain* case.[23] Here the CJEU found that it was not necessary to examine whether the other language versions followed the wording of the Spanish version of the directive, as the interpretation indicated by the Spanish version had to be re-evaluated based on the purpose of the directive.

However, this is not the only approach used by the CJEU in situations of diverging language versions, and not the only formula regularly cited on matters

[19] Opinion of Advocate General Lagrange in Case 13/61 *Kledingverkoopbedrijf de Geus en Uitdenbogerd v Robert Bosch GmbH and Maatschappij tot voortzetting van de zaken der Firma Willem van Rijn*, EU:C:1962:11, 70.

[20] For an overview of the literature, see M Derlén, *Multilingual Interpretation of European Union Law* (Alphen aan den Rijn, Kluwer Law International, 2009) 36–43. See regarding the concept dynamic interpretation L Crema, 'The Interpretive Work of Treaty Bodies: How They Look at Evolutionary Interpretation, and How Other Courts Look at Them', ch 9 in this book.

[21] Judgment of 27 October 1977, *Bouchereau* 30/77, EU:C:1977:172, para 14.

[22] Derlén, Multilingual Interpretation of European Union Law, above n 20, 47–48.

[23] Judgment of 16 September 2004, *Commission v Spain* C-227/01, EU:C:2004:528, paras 43–48.

of multilingualism. The Court also uses the '*Stauder* formula', with a rather different message.[24] We will return to the *Stauder* formula in section IV below.

By focusing on only one approach to multilingual interpretation the discussion tends to underestimate the attention given to the language versions. Thus, it could appear that the CJEU does not take language seriously but uses it only as a stepping stone towards contextual and teleological interpretative arguments.

This contribution will discuss the other side of multilingual interpretation at the CJEU, and its relationship to dynamic interpretation. This could be termed the 'positive approach', as compared with the traditional, negative approach. According to this approach the multilingual character of European Union law still facilitates a dynamic interpretation of EU provisions, but not in the sense that language is disregarded in favour of other arguments. Instead, interaction with the various language versions enables the CJEU, as well as national courts and other actors, to adapt the interpretation and to avoid what are seen as unfortunate results.

IV. The Interpretative Contribution of the Single Meaning Approach

By employing the single meaning approach to the interpretation of the treaties and secondary acts the CJEU can create interpretative room to manoeuvre, which includes clarifying vague or ambiguous language versions but also adjusting the interpretation indicated by a specific language version.

In these cases the CJEU sometimes refers to the so-called *Stauder* formula. It originally read as follows:

> When a single decision is addressed to all the member states the necessity for uniform application and accordingly for uniform interpretation makes it impossible to consider one version of the text in isolation but requires that it be interpreted on the basis of both the real intention of its author and the aim he seeks to achieve, in the light in particular of the versions in all four languages.[25]

An example using the single meaning to clarify vague language versions is the *EMU Tabac* case, concerning excise duty.[26] In most of the language versions it was unclear whether individuals had to physically transport the goods themselves for a specific taxation regime to apply, but the Danish and Greek language versions made it clear that this was indeed the case. The CJEU emphasised that the meaning of the provision was established by the language versions together, and that

[24] Judgment of 12 November 1969, *Stauder* 29/69, EU:C:1969:57.

[25] ibid, para 3. Modern versions normally refer to EU law in general and 'all language versions' rather than the specific number of official languages; see, eg, Judgment of 15 March 2018, *Deichmann* C-256/16, EU:C:2018:187, para 49.

[26] Judgment of 2 April 1998, *EMU Tabac* C-296/95, EU:C:1998:152.

this was unaffected by the fact that Danish and Greek are languages of limited diffusion.[27]

This first variant of the single meaning approach is arguably less controversial, as the vagueness or ambiguity of one or more (or, as in *EMU Tabac*, most) language versions necessitates further interpretation. We can find many examples of this kind of approach in national courts. In those situations, it is normally the national language version that is vague or unclear, and the meaning is determined by having regard to other language versions. The main difference between national courts and the CJEU is that national courts will normally consult only one or a few other language versions, and rarely all of them. They will not regularly examine languages of limited diffusion unless they are regionally well-known languages, such as Danish in Sweden.[28] Given that most language versions were equally unclear in the *EMU Tabac* case it is reasonable to assume that many national courts would not have been able to solve the interpretative issue in the same way as the CJEU did. This was reflected in the plaintiffs' protestations in the case. They emphasised the need for legal certainty and argued that vague concepts should be interpreted to their advantage. However, the CJEU concluded that the provision was not vague, as the Danish and Greek language versions could not be considered ambiguous.[29] This is a forceful illustration of the single meaning approach. The meaning of the provision is determined by all the language versions together, and thus the provision cannot be vague or ambiguous if one or more versions indicates a clear meaning. As indicated by the plaintiffs in *EMU Tabac* this is not without problems or challenges for individuals and companies, as a language of limited diffusion might indicate the clear meaning.

However, the Court applies the single meaning in a more controversial way when confronting a language version diverging from the other versions without necessarily being vague or ambiguous. In these situations, the CJEU has favoured following the majority meaning, ie, the meaning indicated by the majority (often an overwhelming majority) of language versions. This is what Solan terms identifying outliers.[30] The *Ferriere* and *Konservenfabrik Lubella* cases are examples of this approach.

In the *Konservenfabrik Lubella* case, regarding Regulation 1932/93, the German version deviated from all other language versions, referring to sweet cherries rather than sour cherries.[31] However, the CJEU found that the content of the regulation could not be regarded as uncertain, as the error of the German version could be remedied by having regard to the other language versions.[32]

[27] ibid, paras 33–40.

[28] See for an overview, eg, Derlén, *Multilingual Interpretation of European Union Law*, above n 20, 303–05; and Derlén, 'In Defence of (Limited) Multilingualism', above n 12, 161–62.

[29] *EMU Tabac*, above n 26, paras 38–40.

[30] LM Solan, 'The Interpretation of Multilingual Statutes by the European Court of Justice' (2009) 34 *Brooklyn Journal of International Law* 277, 293.

[31] Judgment of 17 October 1996, *Konservenfabrik Lubella* C-64/95, EU:C:1996:388, para 16.

[32] ibid, paras 16–18.

The *Ferriere* case is another example of this situation.[33] It concerned what was then Article 85 EC, on agreements limiting competition.[34] All language versions, except the Italian, made it clear that the agreement in question had to have limiting competition as its object or effect for Article 85 to apply. In other words, the requirements were alternative. However, the Italian version indicated that they were cumulative, so that an agreement had to have limiting competition as both its object and effect for the relevant Article to apply. The CJEU concluded that the clarity of the Italian version did not matter, as the interpretation had to be determined by the language versions together. Consequently, the alternative requirement prevailed.[35]

Often, the CJEU does not articulate the reasons for the significance of a majority meaning, but there are exceptions to this rule. The *García* and *Cabrera* joined case is such an exception.[36] Here the Court concluded as follows:

> In the present cases, as the Spanish-language version of Article 11(3) of Regulation No 562/2006 is the only one which diverges from the wording of the other language versions, it must be concluded that the real intention of the legislature was not to impose an obligation on the Member States concerned to expel, from their territory, third-country nationals in the event that they have not succeeded in rebutting the presumption referred to in Article 11(1), but to grant those Member States the option of so doing.[37]

Consequently, the language versions together form the meaning of an EU provision, rather than the individual language versions. This means that a true outlier, a language version standing alone against all other versions, cannot be seen as expressing the legislator's intention.

In all these situations the CJEU employs the single meaning approach. The wording of the provision in question in all the language versions is a crucial part of the interpretation and thus the Court manages to resolve potential ambiguities and circumvent outliers.

V. The Strong Narrative of the Single Meaning

In section IV above we discussed the impact of the single meaning approach to treaty and secondary law interpretation. Formally, an interpreter should not apply this approach when interpreting CJEU case law, as this area is governed by a different language regime. However, the single meaning approach has turned out to be a powerful narrative, breaking out of its confines and expanding into other areas.

[33] Judgment of 17 July 1997, *Ferriere* C-219/95, EU:C:1997:375.
[34] Now Art 101 TFEU.
[35] *Ferriere*, above n 33, paras 14–15.
[36] Judgment of 22 October 2009, *García and Cabrera* C-261/08 and C-348/08, EU:C:2009:648.
[37] ibid, para 56.

The Court's approach adopted for treaties and secondary law has thus also been used for interpreting CJEU judgments.

However, before we discuss the spillover effect from secondary law to case law something should be said about the opposite, ie, the spillover from case law to secondary law. This is a phenomenon mostly found in national courts, not (at least not explicitly) in the CJEU itself. In national courts the idea of an original has proved contagious.[38] We can find examples of national courts falling back on the idea of an original, a single language that is decisive in the interpretation of the provision, when interpreting the secondary law of the Union. However, there is no consensus as to which version is the original. Instead, interpreters have adopted a number of approaches. This includes treating the (presumed) drafting language of the act as the original,[39] all the official languages at the time of adoption of the act (but not official languages added later) as originals,[40] and finally treating the French version as decisive because the internal working language of the Court of Justice is French.[41]

The examples of spillover in the opposite direction are more numerous, including also the Advocates General and the CJEU itself. This development is particularly noticeable when it comes to the interpretation of CJEU judgments.[42] As noted above the language regime of judgments provides for a single, authentic original, but this has not prevented all the above-mentioned actors from taking other languages into account. A certain amount of confusion reigns, evidenced not least by one Advocate General adopting different approaches in different cases.[43] However, among the approaches adopted we can identify the traditional single meaning approach.

For example, Advocate General van Gerven clearly went beyond the formal language regime of judgments in the *BASF* case. When interpreting the judgment of the General Court under appeal he dismissed the interpretation indicated by the English language version of the case, because it diverged from the wording of the Dutch, French, German and Italian versions of the same judgment. As the English version stood alone against the other versions the latter must be regarded as 'most faithfully reproduc[ing] the point of view of the Court of First Instance'.[44]

[38] For discussion and examples see Derlén, 'A Single Text or a Single Meaning', above n 18, 60–63.

[39] *Assange v Swedish Prosecution Authority* [2012] UKSC 22, para 58.

[40] *Rxworks Limited v Hunter* [2008] Chancery Division ECC 15, 255.

[41] *Barkworth v Commissioners of Customs and Excise*, Value Added Tax Tribunal London [1987] 3 CMLR 507.

[42] Another example of spillover of the single meaning idea is the interpretation of the old European Coal and Steel Community Treaty, authentic only in French. See further Derlén, 'Multilingualism and the European Court of Justice', above n 6, 343.

[43] Derlén, 'Multilingual Interpretation of CJEU Case Law', above n 17, 313.

[44] Opinion of Advocate General Van Gerven in Judgment of 15 June 1994, *Commission v BASF* C-137/92, EU:C:1993:268, fn 68.

Setting aside the English language version was hardly surprising, as its wording deviated from the German version, and German was the language of the case. Likewise, the inclusion of the French version is understandable from a practical perspective, if not necessarily a formal one. Being the internal working language of the Court, it made practical sense to consult it. However, the Dutch and Italian versions had no special position, legally or practically, but were simply translations.[45] The fact that van Gerven still thought it to be of interest to examine and use the Dutch and Italian versions indicates a significant influence for the single meaning approach.

The CJEU itself has also indicated support for the single meaning idea when interpreting case law, but it has been more reticent in elaborating the underlying reasons. In cases such as *Bacardi*, *Aalborg*, and *JCB* the CJEU turned to languages other than the language of the case to resolve the interpretative question.[46] More specifically, in all three cases the Court deviated from the wording of the language of the case, as each arguably suffered from errors, by turning to the other language versions. In *Bacardi* the Court even referred to the above-mentioned *Stauder* formula, thus clearly indicating a single approach to the interpretation of secondary law and judgments.[47]

Finally, even national courts appear to have picked up on the single meaning idea as a general approach to the interpretation of EU law, including case law. The *Laval* case from the Swedish Labour Court is perhaps the most striking example of this.[48] When interpreting the preliminary ruling it had requested from the CJEU, the Labour Court found a divergence of meaning regarding one of the interpretative issues. According to the Labour Court it was clear that the action taken by the Swedish trade unions violated EU law. However, it was less clear who was responsible for the breach of EU law – the trade unions or the Swedish legislator. The Swedish, French and German language versions indicated the latter, while the Danish and English versions supported the former interpretation. The Labour Court found the interpretation suggested by the Danish and English versions more persuasive, concluding that the trade unions were responsible for the breach of EU law. This is particularly noteworthy, as both the language of the case (Swedish) and the de facto original (French) were overridden by two languages with no formal status.[49]

[45] The use of the word 'simply' should, naturally, not be taken as in any way diminishing the important and difficult work of the Court translators. It simply refers to the fact that the Dutch and Italian versions were neither de jure nor de facto originals.

[46] Judgment of 27 September 2001, *Bacardi* C-253/99, EU:C:2001:490; Judgment of 7 January 2004, *Aalborg* C-204/00 P, C-205/00 P, C-211/00 P, C-213/00 P, C-217/00 P and C-219/00 P, EU:C:2004:6; and Judgment of 21 September 2006, *JCB* C-167/04 P, EU:C:2006:594. For discussion of the cases see Derlén, 'Multilingual Interpretation of CJEU Case Law', above n 17, 301–05.

[47] *Bacardi*, above n 46, paras 41 and 45.

[48] AD 2009 nr 89.

[49] For further discussion see Derlén, 'A Single Text or a Single Meaning', above n 18, 65–66.

VI. Conclusions: A Dynamic and Uniform Approach to the Interpretation of EU Law

The discussion above demonstrates that a more positive understanding of the connection between multilingualism and dynamic interpretation is possible, supplementing the traditional view. Rather than abandoning the wording of the language versions as soon as a divergence is found, the CJEU can adopt the single meaning approach and hence create a certain interpretative freedom. Furthermore, this approach is so influential at the Court, and beyond it, that it spills over to the interpretation of CJEU judgments, even though this area is regulated by a different language regime.

PART VII

Conclusion

29

Conclusion

KENNETH KEITH

Certainly, the interpretation of treaties is an art rather than a science; though it is part of the art that it should have an appearance of science.[1]

The interpreter, when exercising that art to discover the meaning of a treaty, may have to resolve the balance between stability and change, static and dynamic readings, heritage and heresy. The authors of the chapters of this valuable book have examined the practising of that art by many courts and tribunals and other bodies in several contrasting areas of international law; they have also considered more general issues including those of a theoretical kind. Their work allows the readers, including this one, to draw some conclusions or at least to cast some reflections. I offer some of my own.

I begin with the proposition that there are treaties and treaties. One size does not fit all. The reference in the first footnote in this book is to a work by AD McNair, a one-time judge and president of both the International Court of Justice and the European Court of Human Rights. I return to one of his earlier articles, published almost 90 years ago. Its title captures its essence – the functions and differing legal character of treaties.[2] He anticipates, and indeed goes beyond, the distinctions made in the Vienna Convention on the Law of Treaties 1969, Articles 5, 53, 56(1)(b), 60(5), 62(2)(a) and 64.

First, McNair distinguishes between treaties of a constitutional character, such as the Covenant of the League of Nations; treaties declaratory of international law or of a law-making kind such as the Hague Conventions of 1899 and 1907; treaties comparable to a conveyance, transferring sovereignty over territory or determining a boundary; treaties creating an objective status, benefiting all the nations of the world; and treaties equivalent to contracts in national law, contracts which themselves may vary greatly, for instance from those which capture a discreet transaction to those which govern a long term, even permanent, relationship.

[1] RY Jennings, 'General Course: Principles of International Law' (1967) 121 *Recueil des cours de l'académie de droit international* 323, 544.

[2] AD McNair, 'The Functions and Differing Legal Character of Treaties' (1930) 11 *The British Year Book of International Law* 100.

Second, he distinguishes, convincingly to me at least, between the legal effects of those different categories of treaties. No doubt, with the passage of time, some of his analysis could be updated, for instance by reference to the International Law Commission's work on the effect of armed conflict on treaties,[3] a matter to which McNair gives some attention, but its essence remains.

To begin with a constitutional treaty, we find the International Court of Justice in the *Namibia* Opinion in 1971 being willing to give an extensively updated meaning to, or application of, the principle of the sacred trust of civilisation stated, over 50 years earlier, in the Covenant of the League of Nations. In that case developments external to the original text, particularly the 1960 Declaration on Decolonization, were critical.[4] Subsequent developments, even over a much shorter period, may also play a part, as in the *Pulp Mills* case where general language in a 1975 treaty was interpreted in the light of more recent practice requiring an environmental impact assessment when the proposed industrial action may have a significant transboundary impact.[5]

Boundaries fixed by treaty receive special treatment under customary international law and the Vienna Convention: the boundaries, subject to the forces of nature, remain fixed, not affected by breach of other provisions of the treaty, by fundamental change of circumstance, by the outbreak of war between the parties, by changes in the parties to the treaty or even by the disappearance of the treaty itself. But the treaty may include provisions that are capable of having a changing meaning or application. In the *Navigational Rights* case, for instance, in addition to its finding, discussed in an earlier chapter, about the meaning and application of the expression '*objetos de comercio*', the ICJ ruled that, over the course of the century and a half since the boundary treaty was concluded, the interests that were to be protected through the exercise by Nicaragua, as the territorial sovereign, of its power of regulation of the river in the public interest may well have changed in ways that the parties could never have anticipated: protecting the environment, it said, is a notable example.[6] I might recall that the Stockholm Declaration on the Human Environment was adopted only in 1972, following close on the heels of Rachel Carson's *Silent Spring* (1963).[7] New scientific findings have been influential as well in human rights cases.

The three cases mentioned, along with some of the human rights cases, have in common that broad wording or a general power was in issue, as was also the case with the provisions of the human rights and refugee treaties addressed in

[3] Annexed to GA Resolution 66/99, UN Doc A/RES/66/99 (9 December 2011).

[4] *Legal Consequences for States of the Continued Presence of South Africa in Namibia (South West Africa) notwithstanding Security Court Resolution 276 (1970)* (Advisory Opinion) [1971] ICJ Rep 16, paras 52–54.

[5] *Pulp Mills on the River Uruguay (Argentina v Uruguay)* (Judgment) [2010] ICJ Rep 14, para 204.

[6] *Dispute Regarding Navigational and Related Rights (Costa Rica v Nicaragua)* (Judgment) [2009] ICJ Rep 213, para 89.

[7] R Carson, *Silent Spring* (Boston, MA, Houghton Mifflin, 1963).

earlier chapters. But other provisions of the treaties in those cases have a different character. They are specific, with a stable meaning – South Africa, as mandatory of South West Africa was obliged to make a report each year to the League of Nations on the actions it was taking to meet its obligations under the Mandate; the parties in the *Pulp Mills* case were subject to precise procedural obligations; and the Costa Rica–Nicaragua boundary is for the most part on the 'right bank' of the river. Such mixes of general and specific wording are to be seen in treaties in others of the areas discussed.

To be added to developments in scientific understanding, as recognised in the *Pulp Mills* case, are major changes in social attitudes, as seen in human rights and refugee cases. Such changes in understanding may be clarified and consolidated through various processes associated with certain treaty regimes, processes that enable those involved as national or international judges or administrators to share information and opinion.

A further factor favouring a broader reading or application of a treaty text, although mentioned only occasionally, may be the difficulty of amending some of the treaties. The Whaling Convention appears to provide an exception since the International Whaling Commission has the power to amend, by majority vote, the schedule to the Convention regulating the numbers of whales to be taken and areas and times of catch. However, the State parties may exempt themselves from such amendments and, as well, they have the power to withdraw on six months' notice.

The sense I have given so far may be far too rosy. Several chapters describe strong forces against an evolutionary reading or application of treaties. The State parties, in exercise of their sovereignty, have agreed, often following very hard-fought negotiations, to a particular text, nothing more and nothing less. The Uruguay Round, which led to the current World Trade Organization (WTO) agreements, lasted for more than six years and involved over 120 national delegations. According to one very strongly held view, it is not for unaccountable judges or arbitrators to add to the obligations that States have so carefully formulated; international courts and tribunals are not legislators. The opposition to what is seen as overreach is demonstrated, for instance, in the difficulties the WTO dispute settlement process faces at the moment, in the withdrawals from the International Convention on the Settlement of Investment Disputes and from bilateral investment treaties and in the use by the NAFTA parties, even in the course of a pending case, of their power through the Free Trade Commission in effect to amend the Agreement. Such opposition may also be seen in State attitudes to what they see as overbroad readings of human rights treaties, notably in respect of measures taken by States to respond to terrorist acts, and refugee protection, as indicated by significant opposition to the Global Compact for Safe, Orderly and Regular Migration adopted by the UN General Assembly in December 2018.[8]

[8] GA Res 73/195, UN Doc A/RES/73/195 (11 January 2019).

A distinct reason for opposing an evolutionary reading relates to treaties imposing criminal responsibility on individuals. The principles of the non-retrospectivity of criminal liability and penalty and of legality are long and well established. The criticism, some unfounded, based on those principles, directed at the Nuremberg Tribunal and its Charter must be kept in mind. Were the principles put in jeopardy when, for instance, an international criminal tribunal established as a basis for criminal liability the concept of joint criminal enterprise, a concept which appears to run beyond the specific crimes established in the tribunal's statute?

A final reflection concerns judicial technique. Are courts and tribunals, or some of them, now more and more willing to address contextual material which runs far beyond that identified in Article 31(2) of the Vienna Convention on the Law of Treaties? I have the sense that some are, if with caution. To go back to the *Namibia* case, the ICJ called for the Covenant of the League of Nations, along with the Mandate, to be interpreted within the framework of the entire legal system prevailing at the time of the decision, that is in 1971.[9] Courts and tribunals may also sometimes suggest that they are not giving the treaty terms a wider meaning but rather a wider application as, for instance, technology develops, scientific knowledge increases or social attitudes change – is this a way perhaps of deflecting criticism against judicial overreach?

[9] Above n 4, para 54.

INDEX

www.ingramcontent.com/pod-product-compliance
Ingram Content Group UK Ltd.
Pitfield, Milton Keynes, MK11 3LW, UK
UKHW020232290926
15470UKWH00002B/495

9 781509 929887